POETS
AND
POEMS

BLOOM'S LITERARY CRITICISM 20TH ANNIVERSARY COLLECTION

BLOOM'S LITERARY CRITICISM 20TH ANNIVERSARY COLLECTION

POETS
AND
POEMS

Harold Bloom
Sterling Professor of the Humanities
Yale University

CHELSEA HOUSE
PUBLISHERS
A Haights Cross Communications Company ®

Philadelphia

©2005 by Chelsea House Publishers, a subsidiary of
Haights Cross Communications.

A Haights Cross Communications Company ®

www.chelseahouse.com

Introduction © 2005 by Harold Bloom.

Printed and bound in the United States of America.
10 9 8 7 6 5 4 3 2 1

Library of Congress Cataloging-in-Publication Data

Bloom, Harold.
  Poets and poems / Harold Bloom.
     p. cm. — (Bloom's 20th anniversary collection)
  ISBN 0-7910-8225-3 (hc) — ISBN 0-7910-8364-0 (pb) 1. Poetry, Modern—
History and criticism. I. Title.
  PN1161.B56 2005
  809.1'03—dc22

                              2005008636

Cover designed by Takeshi Takahashi
Cover illustration by David Levine
Layout by EJB Publishing Services

Table of Contents

Preface

Harold Bloom

I BEGAN EDITING ANTHOLOGIES OF LITERARY CRITICISM FOR CHELSEA House in early 1984, but the first volume, *Edgar Allan Poe: Modern Critical Views*, was published in January, 1985, so this is the twentieth anniversary of a somewhat Quixotic venture. If asked how many separate books have been issued in this project, I no longer have a precise answer, since in so long a span many volumes go out of print, and even whole series have been discontinued. A rough guess would be more than a thousand individual anthologies, a perhaps insane panoply to have been collected and introduced by a single critic.

Some of these books have surfaced in unlikely places: hotel rooms in Bologna and Valencia, Coimbra and Oslo; used-book stalls in Frankfurt and Nice; on the shelves of writers wherever I have gone. A batch were sent by me in answer to a request from a university library in Macedonia, and I have donated some of them, also by request, to a number of prisoners serving life sentences in American jails. A thousand books across a score of years can touch many shores and many lives, and at seventy-four I am a little bewildered at the strangeness of the endeavor, particularly now that it has leaped between centuries.

It cannot be said that I have endorsed every critical essay reprinted, as my editor's notes have made clear. Yet the books have to be reasonably reflective of current critical modes and educational fashions, not all of them provoking my own enthusiasm. But then I am a dinosaur, cheerfully naming myself as "Bloom Brontosaurus Bardolator." I accept only three criteria for greatness in imaginative literature: aesthetic splendor, cognitive power, wisdom. What is now called "relevance" will be in the dustbins in less than a generation, as our society (somewhat tardily) reforms prejudices and inequities. The fashionable in literature and criticism always ebbs away into Period Pieces. Old, well-made furniture survives as valuable antiques, which is not the destiny of badly constructed imaginings and ideological exhortings.

Time, which decays and then destroys us, is even more merciless in obliterating weak novels, poems, dramas, and stories, however virtuous these may be. Wander into a library and regard the masterpieces of thirty years ago: a handful of forgotten books have value, but the iniquity of oblivion has rendered most bestsellers instances of time's revenges. The other day a friend and former student told me that the first of the Poets Laureate of twentieth-century America had been Joseph Auslander, concerning whom even my still retentive memory is vacant. These days, Mrs. Felecia Hemans is studied and taught by a number of feminist Romantic scholars. Of the poems of that courageous wisdom, who wrote to support her brood, I remember only the opening line of "Casabianca" but only because Mark Twain added one of his very own to form a couplet:

The boy stood on the burning deck
Eating peanuts by the peck.

Nevertheless, I do not seek to affirm the social inutility of literature, though I admire Oscar Wilde's grand declaration: "All art is perfectly useless." Shakespeare may well stand here for the largest benign effect of the highest literature: properly appreciated, it can heal part of the violence that is built into every society whatsoever. In my own judgment, Walt Whitman is the central writer yet brought forth by the Americas—North, Central, South, Caribbean—whether in English, Spanish, Portuguese, French, Yiddish or other tongues. And Walt Whitman is a healer, a poet-prophet who discovered his pragmatic vocation by serving as a volunteer, unpaid wound-dresser and nurse in the Civil War hospitals of Washington, D.C. To read and properly understand Whitman can be an education in self-reliance and in the cure of your own consciousness.

The function of literary criticism, as I conceive it in my gathering old age, is primarily appreciation, in Walter Pater's sense, which fuses analysis and evaluation. When Pater spoke of "art for art's sake' he included in the undersong of his declaration what D.H. Lawrence meant by "art for life's sake," Lawrence, the most provocative of post-Whitmanian vitalists, has now suffered a total eclipse in the higher education of the English-speaking nations. Feminists have outlawed him with their accusations of misogyny, and they describe him as desiring women to renounce sexual pleasure. On this supposed basis, students lose the experience of reading one of the major authors of the twentieth century, at once an unique novelist, story-teller, poet, critic, and prophet.

An enterprise as vast as Chelsea House Literary Criticism doubtless reflects both the flaws and the virtues of its editor. Comprehensiveness has been a goal throughout, and I have (for the most part) attempted to set aside many of my own literary opinions. I sorrow when the market keeps an important volume out of print, though I am solaced by the example of my idol, Dr. Samuel Johnson, in his *Lives of the Poets*. The booksellers (who were both publishers and retailers) chose the poets, and Johnson was able to say exactly what he thought of each. Who remembers such worthies as Yalden, Sprat, Roscommon, and Stepney? It would be invidious for me to name the contemporary equivalents, but their name is legion.

I have been more fully educated by this quest for comprehensivness, which taught me how to write for a larger audience. Literary criticism is both an individual and communal mode. It has its titans: Johnson, Coleridge, Lessing, Goethe, Hazlitt, Sainte-Beuve, Pater, Curtius, Valèry, Frye, Empson, Kenneth Burke are among them. But most of those I reprint cannot be of that eminence: one makes a heap of all that can be found. Over a lifetime in reading and teaching one learns so much from so many that no one can be certain of her or his intellectual debts. Hundreds of those I have reprinted I never will meet, but they have helped enlighten me, insofar as I have been capable of learning from a host of other minds.

Introduction

Harold Bloom

I FIRST FELL IN LOVE WITH POETRY SEVENTY YEARS AGO, WHEN I WAS four. Though born in the Bronx, I spoke and read only Yiddish at that age, and the poets were the best of those who had come to the United States: Moshe Leib Halpern, Mani Leib, H. Leivick, Jacob Glatstein. Thanks to the Melrose branch of the Bronx Public Library, I soon taught myself to read English by immersing myself in the study of Anglo-American poetry. Only dim memories of such early favorites as Vachel Lindsay still abide in me, but I gradually read my way through vast areas of poetry. By the time somewhere between ten and twelve years old, I had begun to love William Blake and Hart Crane with a particular intensity. Memorizing them, without effort because of incessant rereading, I came to possess them with a kind of implicit understanding, which I certainly could not have externalized until many years later.

Sometimes I am asked, by poets who are close friends, why I never began to write my own poems, but from the beginning the art seemed to me daemonic and magical. To have entered it, except as an appreciative reader, would have involved crossing a sacred threshold. I kept on reading Blake and Crane, and they led me to Shelley, Wallace Stevens, Yeats, Milton, and at last to Shakespeare.

At what age I began to comprehend more fully what I reread, I cannot now mark with any certainty. Self-education has its hazards (my English pronunciation is still eccentric) but it armors against reductiveness: political, religious, philosophical, and mere fashions in criticism. T.S. Eliot fascinated me by his poetry, yet repelled me simultaneously by his dogmatic prose. At fifteen or so I read through *The Sacred Wood* and *After Strange Gods*, disliking the latter, and disheartened by the former. At least, *After*

Strange Gods led me to D.H. Lawrence, attracted to him by Eliot's extraordinarily violent denunciation.

The first critic of poetry I admired was G. Wilson Knight, whom much later I came to know and like personally. As a Cornell freshman barely seventeen, I purchased and read to pieces Northrop Frye's *Fearful Symmetry*, his majestic study of Blake. I was a kind of disciple to Frye for nearly two decades, until in the summer of 1967 I woke up from a nightmare on the morning of my thirty-seventh birthday and began writing a curious prose rhapsody called "The Covering Cherub or Poetic Influence". After many revisions, this was published in January 1973 as *The Anxiety of Influence*, but Frye had condemned it when I sent him a version in September 1967, after which we agreed to disagree forever about the nature of poetry and criticism.

At seventy-four, I continue to possess by memory almost all of the poetry I ever have loved. Perhaps memory (without which reading and thinking are alike impossible) over-determined my critical orientation. If you cannot forget Shakespeare, Milton, Wordsworth, Keats, Tennyson, Walt Whitman, Emily Dickinson, then you are not greatly tempted by resentful pronouncements that certain inadequate poets deserve study because of their gender, sexual orientation, ethnic origin, skin pigmentation and similar criteria.

The astonishing richness of Anglo-American poetic traditions is confined in this volume to mostly lyrical and meditative work, since much of it appears in the volumes on *The Epic* and *Dramatists and Dramas* in this six-book series. I regret the omission of a younger poet like Henri Cole, who will prove to be canonical, and of others who will endure, like John Brooks Wheelwright and Leonie Adams in the generation of Hart Crane.

Wallace Stevens remarked that the function of poetry is to help us lead our lives. I tend to modify that to the specific question that Freud called reality testing, which is learning to endure mortality. At moments of danger and of severe illness I have resorted to the fierce comfort of reciting poems to myself, whether out loud or silently. Not being much of a beach-person, I go there only to chant Walt Whitman, Hart Crane, Stevens, generally in solitude addressing the wind and the waves. Poetry cannot heal the organized violence of society, but it can perform a work of healing for the self. Stevens called poetry a violence from within set against a violence from without. He also reminded us that the mind was the most terrible force in the world, for it only could defend us from itself. Hart Crane beautifully and poignantly hoped that poetry could bring him "an improved infancy". Nothing will give us that, or return the beloved dead to us. Consolation, after the work of mourning is complete, reaches some of us from elegiac poetry. Like William and Henry James, I find a profound measure of enhancement in hearing Whitman's "When Lilacs Last in the Dooryard Bloom'd" chanted aloud, whether by another or by myself. Or I find existence heightened by listening to a tape of John Gielgud reciting Milton's *Lycidas* or Ralph Richardson delivering Coleridge's *The Rime of the Ancient Mariner*. I will finish with this because I want to hear Wallace Stevens himself read out *The Auroras of Autumn* on another tape. In the twilight of existence, such an experience accumulates its own value.

Petrarch

(1304-1374)

Idolatry, however repugnant to an Augustinian moralist, is at the linguistic level the essence of poetic autonomy. Because language and desire are indistinguishable in a literary text, we may say that by accusing his persona of an idolatrous passion Petrarch was affirming his own autonomy as a poetic: creator.

—JOHN FRECCERO

THE ANGUISH OF CONTAMINATION (OR ANXIETY OF INFLUENCE) NO LONGER seems to me a particularly modern (or Romantic) malady. Jeremiah the prophet shadows the poet of the Book of Job, Jesus Ben Sirach in his Ecclesiasticus is haunted by Ecclesiastes (Koheleth), and Aristophanes savagely mauls Euripides for his misprisions of Aeschylus. If we add Plato's agon with Homer, and the Gnostics' sense of belatedness in regard both to Plato and the Hebrew Bible, then we have a considerable catalog of ancient literary sorrows.

Petrarch's relation to Dante is enormously complex and difficult to judge, partly because Petrarch's own influence upon poetry after him was so great that it veils everything that is problematical in Petrarch's over whelming originality. Each strong poet strives to make himself seem more different from his central precursor than he actually is, and Petrarch's strong misreading of Dante, implicit in Petrarch's own poetry, has affected us more than we can know, particularly in helping to present some among us with a Dante wholly given over to the allegory of the theologians, and so apparently altogether free of idolatrous or Petrarchan passion, at least in the *Commedia*. Here Robert M. Durling returns us to the deep affinities between Dante's *rime petrose* and Petrarch's *rime sparse*:

To see one's experience in terms of myth is to see in the myth the possibility of the kind of allegorical meaning that was called tropological. Petrarch knew and used freely the traditional allegorical interpretations of the Ovidian myths. But he dissociated them from clear-cut moral judgments, and in this he was closer to the Dante of the *petrose* than of the *Commedia*. To say that falling in love and becoming a love poet is a transformation into a laurel tree involves the sense that the channeling of the vital energy of frustrated love into the sublimated, eternizing mode of poetry has consequences not fully subject to conscious choice or to moral judgment. For Petrarch the perfection of literary form, which exists polished and unchanging on the page in a kind of eternity, is achieved only at the cost of the poet's natural life. His vitality must be metamorphosed into words, and this process is profoundly ambiguous. If on the one hand Petrarch subscribes to—even in a sense almost single-handedly founds—the humanistic cult of literary immortality and glory, on the other hand he has an acute awareness that writing poetry involves a kind of death. This recognition has something very modern about it; it gives a measure of the distance that separates Petrarch from Dante, who gambled recklessly on the authority his poem would have as a total integration. Petrarch is always calling attention to the psychologically relative, even suspect, origin of individual poems and thus of writing itself. His hope is that ultimately the great theme of praise will redeem even the egotism of the celebrant.

It is fascinating to me that one could substitute Rilke's name for Petrarch's here, and still retain coherence, particularly if one also substituted Goethe for Dante. What Freccero calls an idolatrous passion (for Laura, for poetry, for literary immortality and glory), Durling calls a kind of death. Both critics are true to Petrarch, and to Rilke, or Yeats, or Wallace Stevens, all of them in a profound sense still Petrarchans. Or perhaps we could say that all of them, like Petrarch himself, come out of the strongest of Dante's stony lyrics, the great sestina "To the Dim Light and the Large Circle of Shade." I give it here in Dante Gabriel Rossetti's piercing version, the best poem that Rossetti ever wrote:

To the dim light and the large circle of shade
I have clomb, and to the whitening of the hills,

There where we see no colour in the grass.
Natheless my longing loses not its green,
It has so taken root in the hard stone
Which talks and hears as though it were a lady.

Utterly frozen is this youthful lady,
Even as the snow that lies within the shade;
For she is no more moved than is the stone
By the sweet season which makes warm the hills
And alters diem afresh from white to green,
Covering their sides again with flowers and grass.

When on her hair she sets a crown of grass
The thought has no more room for other lady,
Because she weaves the yellow with the green
So well that Love sits down there in the shade,—
Love who has shut me in among low hills
Faster than between walls of granite-stone.

She is more bright than is a precious stone;
The wound she gives may not be healed with grass:
I therefore have fled far o'er plains and hills
For refuge from so dangerous a lady;
But from her sunshine nothing can give shade,—
Not any hill, nor wall, nor summer-green.

A while ago, I saw her dressed in green,—
So fair, she might have wakened in a stone
This love which I do feel even for her shade;
And therefore, as one woos a graceful lady,
I wooed her in a field that was all grass
Girdled about with very lofty hills.

Yet shall the streams turn back and climb the hills
Before Love's flame in this damp wood and green
Burn, as it burns within a youthful lady,
For my sake, who would sleep away in stone
My life, or feed like beasts upon the grass,
Only to see her garments cast a shade.

How dark soe'er the hills throw out their shade,

Under her summer-green the beautiful lady
Covers it, like a stone covered in grass.

The Lady Pietra degli Scrovigni, sublimely hard-hearted, takes her place with Shakespeare's Dark Lady of the Sonnets as a muse stimulating one of the two greatest Western poets since Homer and the Bible to unprecedented depths of imaginative degradation. Dante, already quester if not yet pilgrim, climbs the high hills, presumably at twilight, or on a winter day, in search of fulfillment, only to find that he is in love with a Medusa. Petrarch's Laura, in one of her aspects, is also a Medusa who transforms her poet into a stone man. Freccero and Durling agree that Petrarch is properly ambivalent about being the object of such a transformation. The ironies of Dante doubtless transcend those of his son Petrarch, but all the ironies of Dante's sestina seem directed against the poet himself, and not against the superbly cruel Pietra, who reduces her lover to the condition of Nebuchadnezzar, feeding like beasts upon the grass. Troubadour love, culminating in the poetry of Arnaut Daniel, emphasized the oxymoronic destructiveness of the obsessive image of the beloved that the poet carried in his head. This is the disaster of a particular moment, the precise time when the poet falls in love, akin to falling in battle. A purely secularized moment so intense is bound to become a confrontation with the Medusa. Here is Poem 30 of the *rime sparse*, a sestina in which Petrarch has the courage to confront Dante's stony sestina:

A youthful lady under a green laurel
I saw, whiter and colder than snow
not touched by the sun many and many years,
and her speech and her lovely face and her locks
pleased me so that I have her before my eyes
and shall always have wherever I am, on slope or shore.

Then my thoughts will have come to shore
when green leaves are not to be found on a laurel;
when I have a quiet heart and dry eyes
we shall see the fire freeze, and burning snow;
I have not so many hairs in these locks
as I would be willing, in order to see that day, to wait years.

But because time flies and the years flee
and one arrives quickly at death
either with dark or with white locks,

I shall follow the shadow of that sweet laurel
in the most ardent sun or through the snow,
until the last day closes these eyes.

There never have been seen such lovely eyes,
either in our age or in the first years;
they melt me as the sun does the snow:
whence there comes forth a river of tears
that Love leads to the foot of the harsh laurel
that has branches of diamond and golden locks.

I fear I shall change my face and my locks
before she with true pity will show me her eyes,
my idol carved in living laurel;
for, if I do not err, today it is seven years
that I go sighing from shore to shore
night and day, in heat and in snow.

Inwardly fire:, though outwardly white snow,
alone with these thoughts, with changed locks,
always weeping I shall go along every shore,
to make pity perhaps come into the eyes
of someone who will be born a thousand years from now—
if a well-tended laurel can live so long.

Gold and topaz in the sun above the snow
are vanquished by the golden locks next to those eyes
that lead my years so quickly to shore.

Durling's translation is prose, and attempts to be literal; Rossetti breaks through his own rhetorical sublimations and repressions in the impassioned verse of his Dante translations. Yet, without prejudice to Petrarch (or to Durling), a contrast of Dante's and Petrarch's Italian texts seems to me productive of results remarkably similar to a juxtaposition of Rossetti and Durling. I cannot conceive of a lyric poet more gifted at what I call "poetic misprision" than Petrarch; his sestina is a beautiful evasion of Dante's, yet an evasion whose gestures depend upon the stony sestina of the great precursor. The unifying element in those gestures is their striking and indeed audaciously deliberate idolatry, cunningly analyzed both by Durling and by Freccero. I wish to add to Durling and Freccero only the speculation that Petrarch's idolatrous gestures, here and elsewhere, are revisionary tropes, figures or ratios intended to widen the distance between Dante and Petrarch. In order to clear a space for his own art, Petrarch overtly takes the spiritual (and aesthetic) risk of substituting idolatry for typology, Laura for Beatrice.

Dante's sestina, if judged by the moral code of the *Commedia*, would condemn its poet to the Inferno, but then that is an overt power of the poem: this is the deep degradation of Dante before his conversion, before his turn (or return) to Beatrice. Still, poetically his degradation is Sublime, and can be said to mark a limit for the erotic Sublime. The obsessive force of his sestina is unmatched and is still productive in our century in poems like the sleepwalker's ballad of Lorca and the laments for barren passion of Yeats. Dante's sestina spares neither the Lady Pietra nor himself. She is stone, not flesh, and utterly frozen, as much a victim of the Medusa as the Medusa herself. You cannot flee from Pietra; her icy sunshine penetrates every covert place, and so allows no shade. She will not take fire for Dante as other ladies do, despite his hyperbolical devotion (or because of it?) and her lovely green is profoundly sinister, because it is the color of Dante's desire, and not nature's green at all. In some dark sense the Lady Pietra is antithetical to Beatrice, so that Dante's passion for her is decidedly idolatrous, anti-Augustinian, and a triumph for the allegory of the poets over the allegory of the theologians.

Petrarch memorializes the seventh anniversary of his falling in love with Laura, which he celebrates as a falling into idolatry, since it is also a falling into poetic strength. Fire indeed will freeze snow, snow burn, before Petrarch gives up poetry, since poetry alone allows him "to make pity perhaps come into the eyes / of someone who will be born a thousand years from now," a prophecy now two-thirds accomplished in time. All that is idolatrous enough, but Petrarch superbly culminates his sestina by giving scandal, by subverting Psalm 119, which in the Vulgate reads, "I have loved Your commandments above gold and topaz," to which Petrarch replies:

> Gold and topaz in the sun above the snow
> are vanquished by the golden locks next to those eyes
> that lead my years so quickly to shore.

The golden locks of Laura have replaced God's commandments, in a remarkable turn upon Dante's Pietra, whose "curling yellow mingles with the green / so beautifully that Love comes to stay in the shade there." Petrarch has won a victory over Dante's trope, but at the high cost of an idolatry beyond nearly all measure. Dante's response to Petrarch's sestina can be heard proleptically throughout the *Commedia*, which teaches us that what we behold must be the truth, since great or small we gaze into that mirror in which, before we think, we behold our thought. What Petrarch beholds is at once poetry, fame, and death; he does not behold a transcendental truth, or for that matter a demonic one. He asserts a limited authority, because after Dante's extraordinary authority no other sort could be persuasive or authentic. Dante, like Milton, casts a shadow of belatedness over those who come after. Petrarch, whose genius had to flourish just one generation later and whose own father had been a friend of Dante's, exiled from Florence with Dante, chose a gorgeous solipsism as his poetic stance. Call that solipsism idolatry or what you will; Petrarch urges you to do so. As a wager with mortality, such a stance invented lyric poetry as we continue to know it today.

William Shakespeare

(1564–1616)

IS THERE AN EQUIVALENT IN SHAKESPEARE'S SONNETS TO HIS MOST ORIGINAL power as a dramatist: to represent changes in his characters as ensuing from their overhearing of what they themselves say, whether to others or to themselves? Does the condensed art of a sonnet allow Shakespeare to become one of his own characters, as it were, caught in the process of changing as a reaction to, or reflection of, his own utterance? I do not mean to ask again how dramatic the Sonnets are or are not. Rather, I wonder if any among the Sonnets fulfill A.D. Nuttall's fine assertion for Shakespearean mimesis, that it makes us see aspects of reality we never could have seen without it.

The aesthetic strength of the Sonnets has little to do with their appearance in a sequence, as more seems to be lost than gained when we read them straight through in order. As a rough series of isolated splendors, the best among them are rightly judged to be the most eminent in the language, superior not only to Spenser, Sidney, and Drayton, but also to Milton, Wordsworth, and Keats. They have a monumental quality difficult to match in any Western language, worthy of the poet of "The Phoenix and the Turtle."

Not many critics have preferred Sonnet 94 to all the other sonnets, but it has intrigued nearly every commentator because of its ambivalences:

> They that have power to hurt, and will do none,
> That do not do the thing they most do show,
> Who moving others, are themselves as stone,
> Unmoved, cold, and to temptation slow,
> They rightly do inherit heaven's graces,
> And husband nature's riches from expense;

They are the lords and owners of their faces,
Others but stewards of their excellence.
The summer's flow'r is to the summer sweet,
Though to itself it only live and die,
But if that flow'r with base infection meet,
The basest weed outbraves his dignity:
    For sweetest things turn sourest by their deeds;
    Lilies that fester smell far worse than weeds.

Stephen Booth sees this as "a stylistic mirror of the speaker's indecision," and observes that "The sentences wander from attribute to attribute in such a way that a reader's response to 'them' who are the subject of lines 1–8 swings repeatedly back and forth between negative and positive." The crucial question then would be: Is the speaker's indecision resolved through the implications of the couplet ending the poem? But that in turn depends upon another question: how undecided truly is the speaker in regard to "them"?

If you choose not to hurt someone else, even as your outward semblance intimates you almost certainly are about to do so, there may be a considerable touch of sadomasochism in you. Or you may be like Hamlet, who most provokes the love of the audience in act 5, where he is beyond the reach of love. An unmoved mover is more a divinity than a magnet, and so rightly inherits heaven's graces. So far at least the poem that I encounter is no mirror of its speaker's supposed indecision.

To "husband nature's riches from expense" may mean to hold one's sexuality in reserve, to abstain from expending it, but I am reluctant, in the context of Sonnet 94, to so restrict the sense of "nature's riches." We think of Hamlet as one of nature's great treasures because we think of him as an adventure of and in the spirit. In act 5, he manifests extraordinary disinterestedness; are we so far from that Hamlet if we speak of him as husbanding nature's riches from expense? In full and final control, the Hamlet of act 5 indeed is the lord and owner of his face, the outward image that he turns to Elsinore and to the audience. That brings us to the puzzling line: "Others but stewards of their excellence," where the emphasis upon "their" clearly gives us not "others" but "lords and owners" as the antecedent. To continue with my *Hamlet* analogue, Horatio is a prime instance of one of those stewards of excellence, who survive to tell the story of the greater figures they admire and love.

On this reading, the hero, Hamlet or another, is "the summer's flower," sweet to Horatio and the audience, but essentially living and dying by and for himself, for ends we can only partly apprehend, let alone accept.

The crisis of meaning turns upon the nature of the base infection that the hero meets. I do not accept a reading that associates the infection with the weed, for the "base" in "base infection" means "debasing" or potentially debasing, whereas "the basest weed" is already debased. Think of poor Othello as summer's flower debased by the infection of jealous madness, and so fallen into the terrible lack of dignity of his madness at its incoherent worst. Hamlet is precisely a being who is not turned sourest by his deeds, not a lily that festers.

I hardly seek to turn the Sonnets (1592 to 1596, or so) into a prophecy of *Hamlet* (1600 to 1601) or rather say of *Othello* (1604), but Sonnet 94 is emblematic of the tragedian who was to come, unless indeed it was written later than most of the other sonnets, which is possible enough. On my reading, it is the negative equivalent of what Wordsworth celebrated when he chanted that feeling comes in aid of feeling, and diversity of strength attends us if but once we have been strong. Strength, in Shakespeare, becomes horror when feeling comes to prey upon feeling, and Othello or Macbeth fall into ruin the more dreadfully because, in their different ways, they were so strong.

I do not find then the ambivalences in Sonnet 94 that so many, including Empson, have found, and so I do not find the speaker changing in the final couplet. I would suppose then that the Sonnets, even at their strongest, are indeed lyric rather than dramatic, marvelously conventional rather than personally expressive. Wordsworth and Keats learn from Shakespeare in their sonnets, but are closer to Milton because they put into their sonnets, as Milton sometimes did, the burden of their prophecy. Shakespeare, who had the power to hurt, nevertheless husbanded nature's riches from expense in his Sonnets and chose rather to live and die not only to himself, in his tragedies.

John Donne and the 17th-Century Metaphysical Poets

(1572-1631)

I

ABRAHAM COWLEY IS A POET REMEMBERED TODAY ONLY BY SCHOLARS, AND I doubt that he has a dozen readers a year among them, whether in America or in Britain. In the later seventeenth century he was regarded as a canonical poet, hugely influential, very much the Ezra Pound of his era. Though faded by Johnson's day, he was still famous enough to lead off the *Lives of the Poets*, where he, rather than Donne, is regarded as the founder and chief ornament (rather dimmed) of the Metaphysical school or line of wit, the bad old way superseded by Dryden and Pope.

Literary history, particularly the history of criticism, has a habit of making ludicrous many of a period's firm judgments. When I was young, Shelley was ignored or deprecated in literary and academic circles, and Donne was considered the paradigm of poetry. In the age of Eliot (or the Pound Era, if you prefer), you were dismissed as barbaric or eccentric if you believed that *Song of Myself* was the central American poem, or that Hart Crane was a permanent poet, and W.H. Auden perhaps something less than that.

Johnson himself thought his *Life of Cowley* the best of the *Lives*, since his discussion of the Metaphysical poets (he took his name for them from Dryden) was a pioneer venture. It may be unfashionable to believe this, but Johnson's discussion of the school of Donne seems to me still the most adequate we possess, despite the perpetual Donne revivals which go on continuously, from Coleridge through Arthur Symons in the nineteenth century, and endlessly in our own.

Johnson, whatever his blindnesses and flaws, remains the most fecund and suggestive literary critic in the language, with only Hazlitt and Ruskin as his near rivals. It could hardly be expected that he should have preferred John Donne to Alexander Pope; I do not, and in any case Johnson's analysis of Metaphysical poetry still seems to me more just than any of the modern defenses, down to the persuasive attempt by Louis Martz to substitute "the meditative poem" for "the metaphysical poem" as a category. Martz gives a very useful account of both terms, and of their complex interaction:

> Meditation points toward poetry, in its use of images, in its technique of arousing the passionate affections of the will ...
>
> For critical and historical purposes we should, I believe, attempt to distinguish between the "metaphysical" and the "meditative" qualities in this poetry ...
>
> ["Metaphysical"] poems tend to begin abruptly, in the midst of an occasion; and the meaning of the occasion is explored and grasped through a peculiar use of metaphor. The old Renaissance "conceit," the ingenious comparison, is developed into a device by which the extremes of abstraction and concreteness, the extremes of unlikeness, may be woven together into a fabric of argument unified by the prevailing force of "wit."

This is responsible and lucid, though a long way from the fierce verve of Johnson on the same matter:

> Wit, like all other things subject by their nature to the choice of man, has its changes and fashions, and at different times takes different forms. About the beginning of the seventeenth century appeared a race of writers that may be termed the metaphysical poets ...
>
> The metaphysical poets were men of learning, and to shew their learning was their whole endeavour ...
>
> If the father of criticism has rightly denominated poetry ... *an imitative art*, these writers will, without great wrong, lose their right to the name of poets; for they cannot be said to have imitated any thing; they neither copied nature nor life; neither painted the forms of matter, nor represented the operations of intellect.
>
> Those however who deny them to be poets, allow them to be wits. Dryden confesses of himself and his contemporaries, that they fall below Donne in wit, but maintains that they surpass him in poetry.

If Wit be well described by Pope, as being "that which has been often thought, but was never before so well expressed," they certainly never attained, nor ever sought it; for they endeavoured to be singular in their thoughts, and were careless of their diction. But Pope's account of wit is undoubtedly erroneous: he depresses it below its natural dignity, and reduces it from strength of thought to happiness of language.

If by a more noble and more adequate conception that be considered as Wit, which is at once natural and new, that which, though not obvious, is, upon its first production, acknowledged to be just; if it be that, which he that never found it, wonders how he missed; to wit of this kind the metaphysical poets have seldom risen. Their thoughts are often new, but seldom natural; they are not obvious, but neither are they just; and the reader, far from wondering that he missed them, wonders more frequently by what perverseness of industry they were ever found.

But Wit, abstracted from its effects upon the hearer, may be more rigorously and philosophically considered as a kind of *discordia concors*; a combination of dissimilar images, or discovery of occult resemblances in things apparently unlike. Of wit, thus defined, they have more than enough. The most heterogeneous ideas are yoked by violence together; nature and art are ransacked for illustrations, comparisons, and allusions; their learning instructs, and their subtilty surprises; but the reader commonly thinks his improvement dearly bought, and though he sometimes admires is seldom pleased.

Wit is, for Johnson, as he says: "strength of thought" and not mere "happiness of language." Though he went on to deny Donne and his followers a share either in "the pathetick" or "the sublime," Johnson gave them what was, for him, a measure of true praise:

Yet great labour, directed by great abilities, is never wholly lost: if they frequently threw away their wit upon false conceits, they likewise sometimes struck out unexpected truth: if their conceits were far-fetched, they were often worth the carriage. To write on their plan, it was at least necessary to read and think. No man cold be born a metaphysical poet, nor assume the dignity of a writer, by descriptions copied from descriptions, by imitations borrowed from imitations, by traditional imagery, and hereditary similies, by readiness of rhyme, and volubility of syllables.

In perusing the works of this race of authours, the mind is exercised either by recollection or inquiry; either something already learned is to be retrieved, or something new is to be examined. If their greatness seldom elevates, their acuteness often surprises; if the imagination is not always gratified, at least the powers of reflection and comparison are employed; and in the mass of materials which ingenious absurdity has thrown together, genuine wit and useful knowledge may be sometimes found, buried perhaps in grossness of expression, but useful to those who know their value; and such as, when they are expanded to perspicuity, and polished to elegance, may give lustre to works which have more propriety, though less copiousness of sentiment.

Reading and thinking are activities Johnson always recommended to poets, particularly at his own moment, yet these paragraphs of praise are qualified by the absence of Johnson's deepest veneration, which is for wisdom and its poetic refinement through elaborate invention. Johnson is careful to deny Cowley (and Donne, his master) invention, the essence of poetry, though his care is uneasily qualified by an implicit realization that is made explicit in *The Rambler* No. 125:

Definitions have been no less difficult or uncertain in criticism than in law. Imagination, a licentious and vagrant faculty, unsusceptible of limitations, and impatient of restraint, has always endeavoured to baffle the logician, to perplex the confines of distinction, and burst the enclosures of regularity. There is therefore scarcely any species of writing, of which we can tell what is its essence, and what are its constituents; every new genius produces some innovation which, when invented and approved, subverts the rules which the practice of foregoing authors had established.

We cannot fault Johnson for not seeing Donne as such a new genius of innovation, and not merely because we would excuse the critic's blindness as a product of the vagaries of taste. Towards Donne, Johnson is both puzzled and respectful. His Donne is "a man of very extensive and various knowledge," "abstruse and profound," "indelicate," whose work, when improper, "is produced by a voluntary deviation from nature in pursuit of something new or strange." But this Donne troubles Johnson, as Cowley does not. What Donne calls into question is Johnson's criteria of the general or the universal, and the natural, and to have provoked the great critic in regard to those criteria is to have manifested indubitable poetic strength.

II

Johnson had a great distrust of devotional verse, which I suspect was a hidden element in his ambivalence towards the Metaphysical poets. Even in the *Life of Cowley*, the distrust is evidenced, when Johnson discusses Cowley's frigid religious epic, the *Davideis*:

> Sacred History has been always read with submissive reverence, and an imagination over-awed and controlled. We have been accustomed to acquiesce in the nakedness and simplicity of the authentick narrative, and to repose on its veracity with such humble confidence, as suppresses curiosity. We go with the historian as he goes, and stop with him when he stops. All amplification is frivolous and vain; all addition to that which is already sufficient for the purposes of religion, seems not only useless, but in some degree profane.
>
> Such events as were produced by the visible interposition of Divine Power are above the power of human genius to dignify. The miracle of Creation, however it may teem with images, is best described with little diffusion of language: *He spake the word, and they were made.*

Two very diverse judgments, moral and aesthetic, uneasily mingle here. "Submissive reverence," with one's imagination "over-awed and controlled," is hardly a proper stance for any critic, let alone the strongest critic in Western literary tradition. This moral position is curiously reinforced by Johnson's keen aesthetic apprehension of the sublime economy of style manifested by the Authorized Version of the Holy Bible, much of it the work of the preternaturally eloquent William Tyndale and of Miles Coverdale. Poor Cowley has little hope of sustaining close comparison to Tyndale, but that is his Johnsonian punishment for daring to provoke a great critic into "submissive reverence." At that, Cowley fared better than the unfortunate Edmund Waller, whose Sacred Poems stimulated Johnson to the most powerful strictures against religious verse ever written:

Contemplative piety, or the intercourse between God and the human soul, cannot be poetical. Man admitted to implore the mercy of his Creator, and plead the merits of his Redeemer, is already in a higher state than poetry can confer.

The essence of poetry is invention; such invention as, by producing something unexpected, surprises and delights. The topicks of devotion are few, and being few are universally known; but few as they are, they can be made no more; they can receive no grace from novelty of sentiment, and very little from novelty of expression.

Poetry pleases by exhibiting an idea more grateful to the mind than things themselves afford. This effect proceeds from the display of those parts of nature which attract, and the concealment of those which repel the imagination: but religion must be shewn as it is; suppression and addition equally corrupt it; and such as it is, it is known already.

From poetry the reader justly expects, and from good poetry always obtains, the enlargement of his comprehension and elevation of his fancy; but this is rarely to be hoped by Christians from metrical devotion. Whatever is great, desireable, or tremendous, is comprised in the name of the Supreme Being. Omnipotence cannot be exalted; Infinity cannot be amplified; Perfection cannot be improved.

The employments of pious meditation are Faith, Thanksgiving, Repentance, and Supplication. Faith, invariably uniform, cannot be invested by fancy with decorations. Thanksgiving, the most joyful of all holy effusions, yet addressed to a Being without passions, is confined to a few modes, and is to be felt rather than expressed. Repentance, trembling in the presence of the Judge, is not at leisure for cadences and epithets. Supplication of man to man may diffuse itself through many topicks of persuasion; but supplication to God can only cry for mercy.

Of sentiments purely religious, it will be found that the most simple expression is the most sublime. Poetry loses its lustre and its power, because it is applied to the decoration of something more excellent than itself. All that verse can do is to help the memory, and delight the ear, and for these purposes it may be very useful; but it supplies nothing to the mind. The ideas of Christian Theology are too simple for eloquence, too sacred for fiction, and too majestick for ornament; to recommend them by tropes and figures, is to magnify by a concave mirror the sidereal hemisphere.

How well do Donne's devotional poems, or Herbert's, or those of Crashaw, Vaughan, Traherne withstand this formidable theoretical assault? Do the meditative poems of the Metaphysical school escape the indictment that their tropes merely "magnify by a concave mirror the sidereal hemisphere"?

Perhaps Johnson could be accused of overstating the aesthetic risk of devotional verse, yet he is refreshingly original and all but unique among critics in addressing himself to this difficult, and for him painful matter. It should be noted that Johnson's exalted praise of Milton, extraordinary in a critic who opposed Milton in politics, religion, and cultural vision, is founded upon the critic's conviction that Milton almost uniquely overcomes the limitations of a religious poetry:

> Pleasure and terrour are indeed the genuine sources of poetry; but poetical pleasure must be such as human imagination can at least conceive, and poetical terrour such as human strength and fortitude may combat. The good and evil of Eternity are too ponderous for the wings of wit; the mind sinks under them in passive helplessness, content with calm belief and humble adoration.
>
> Known truths, however, may take a different appearance, and be conveyed to the mind by a new train of intermediate images. This Milton has undertaken, and performed with pregnancy and vigour of mind peculiar to himself. Whoever considers the few radical positions which the Scriptures afforded him, will wonder by what energetick operation he expanded them to such extent, and ramified them to so much variety, restrained as he was by religious reverence from licentiousness of fiction.

It is by the standard of *Paradise Lost* as a Christian poem that Johnson found the meditative poetry of the school of Donne unpersuasive and uninteresting. As readers of Donne's sublime hymns, or Herbert's *The Temple*, we rightly are convinced that Johnson's sensibility was surprisingly narrow when he read the Metaphysicals. On the basis of his quotations from Donne in the *Life of Cowley*, Johnson seems to have shied away from Donne's divine poems, and he avoids quoting from Herbert. What seems an overwhelming virtue of Metaphysical devotional verse, its detailed imagery and highly individualized figurations, must have offended Johnson's Horatian passion for the universal. Certainly he had little patience for the minute particulars of the Metaphysical trope:

> The fault of Cowley, and perhaps of all the writers of the meta-physical race, is that of pursuing his thoughts to their last ram-ifications, by which he loses the grandeur of generality; for of the greatest things the parts are little; what is little can be but pretty, and by claiming dignity becomes ridiculous. Thus all the power of description is destroyed by a scrupulous enumer-ation; and the force of metaphors is lost, when the mind by the mention of particulars is turned more upon the original than the secondary sense, more upon that from which the illustra-tion is drawn than that to which it is applied.

III

Frank Kermode, a foremost contemporary critic of Donne, accurate-ly remarks: "It remains true that to write of the fortunes of Donne in the past seventy years is, in effect, to write less about him than about the aes-thetic preoccupations of that epoch." I would amplify Kermode's observa-tion, fifteen years later, by suggesting that the years 1915–1955 had very different "aesthetic preoccupations" than the years 1955–1985, or than the years remaining to this century are likely to have. Eliot, as Kermode says, sought to associate his own poetry with the mode of Donne, but Eliot's poetry, as Kermode does not say, in fact derives from Tennyson and Whitman. *The Waste Land* has far more in common with "Maud" and "When Lilacs Last in the Dooryard Bloom'd" than it does with *The Second Anniversarie* or "A Nocturnall upon S. Lucies Day." Kermode associates the restoration of Donne "to his place among the English poets" with the restoration of "wit to its place in poetry." Johnson associated wit with poet-ry and Pope. I myself find more wit in the Shelley of *The Triumph of Life* than in Donne, but then I am of a different critical generation from that of Kermode.

I doubt that future defenses of Donne and of his school will organ-ize themselves as Modernist celebrations of a Metaphysical agility in wit. Donne seems now as archaic as Spenser, and as specialized as Ben Jonson. The Eliotic vogue for him is now over, and with it is gone the New Critical notion that every good short poem must follow the paradigm of a Donne lyric or meditation. Johnson's powerful critique of the Metaphysicals may not be the last word, but it has recovered a good part of its force during the past thirty years. The recent essays reprinted in this volume manifest a serious attempt to appreciate the school of Donne on a basis very different from the one that extends from Eliot to Kermode. Donne and Herbert do not seem to me poets of the eminence of Spenser and Milton, and a critical epoch that preferred them to Spenser and Milton was certain to pass away as an almost grotesque interlude in the history of taste. But they are the principal devotional poets in the language, hardly equalled by Hopkins or by the Eliot of the *Quartets* or the later Auden. Whatever Johnson thought, the sacred Milton was anything but a devotional poet. A sect of one, Milton persuasively redefined Christianity almost as drastically as William Blake did. Curiously enough, it was rather Donne and Herbert, and their fellows, who merited Johnson's praise. For them, the good and evil of Eternity were not "too ponderous for the wings of wit."

Anne Bradstreet

(1612–1672)

IT IS APPROPRIATE THAT THE FIRST CONSIDERABLE AMERICAN POET SHOULD have been a woman, Anne Bradstreet, who addressed her own book with a charming sense of the difference involved in being a woman poet:

> If for thy father asked, say thou hadst none;
> And for thy mother, she alas is poor,
> Which caused her thus to send thee out of door.

A comparison of Bradstreet with Quarles, her indubitable if unexciting precursor, would reveal his greater skill at craft and her far more interesting poetic and human personality. Whether one wishes to believe, with the feminist critic Wendy Martin, that Bradstreet's poetry constitutes a mode of "subversive piety" may depend upon the ideological perspective of the individual reader. But she certainly had more wit, vitality, and humanity, in herself and in her poems, than Quarles possessed.

No American poet, except Walt Whitman, to this day is Emily Dickinson's peer, so that in moving from Bradstreet to Dickinson we enter upon the mystery of what will always remain, beyond all ironies, the American Sublime. Attempts to find women precursors for Dickinson are not likely ever to prove persuasive. Her agon, immense and capable, is with Emerson and with the High Romantic poets, and ultimately with the Bible itself. To undertake such a struggle is beyond the capacity of any American poet except for Dickinson and Whitman, even of Wallace Stevens. Whitman's subtle inventiveness, his uncanny mastery of figuration and nuances of diction, above all his astonishing powers of regenerating multiple selves out of his own abyss of being, more than compensate for his relative lack of cognitive strength. Dickinson is cognitively so endowed, and so original, that her only peers among poets writing in English might be Shakespeare, Milton, and Blake. Like them, she reconceptualizes very nearly every idea she considers, and more in the overt mode of Milton and of Blake than in Shakespeare's extraordinary and deftly misleading manner. Like Milton and the High Romantics, she excels at the difficult art of making herself prior to what genetically precedes her. Consider the remarkable poem 290:

> Of Bronze—and Blaze—
> The North—Tonight—
> So adequate—it forms—
> So preconcerted with itself—
> So distant—to alarms—
> An Unconcern so sovereign
> To Universe, or me—
> Infects my simple spirit
> With Taints of Majesty—
> Till I take vaster attitudes—
> And strut upon my stem—
> Disdaining Men, and Oxygen,
> For Arrogance of them—
>
> My splendors, are Menagerie—
> But their Competeless Show
> Will entertain the Centuries
> When I, am long ago,
> An Island in dishonored Grass—
> Whom none but Beetles—know.

This overtly is "about" the northern lights, but actually is mediated by Emerson's essay, "The Poet" (1843):

> For it is not metres, but a metre-making argument, that makes a poem,—a thought so passionate and alive, that, like the spirit of a plant or an animal, it has an architecture of its own, and adorns nature with a new thing. The thought and the form are equal in order of time, but in the order of genesis the thought is prior to the form. The poet has a new thought: he has a whole new experience to unfold; he will tell us how it was with him, and all men will be the richer in his fortune. For, the experience of each new age requires a new confession, and the

world seems always waiting for its poet. I remember, when I was young, how much I was moved one morning by tidings that genius had appeared in a youth who sat near me at table. He had left his work, and gone rambling none knew whither, and had written hundreds of lines, but could not tell whether that which was in him was therein told: he could tell nothing but that all was changed,—man, beast, heaven, earth, and sea. How gladly we listened! how credulous! Society seemed to be compromised. We sat in the aurora of a sunrise which was to put out all the stars. Boston seemed to be at twice the distance it had the night before, or was much farther than that. Rome, — what was Rome? Plutarch and Shakespeare were in the yellow leaf, and Homer no more should be heard of. It is much to know that poetry has been written this very day, under this very roof, by your side. What! that wonderful spirit has not expired! these stony moments are still sparkling and animated! I had fancied that the oracles were all silent, and nature had spent her fires, and behold! all night, from every pore, these fine auroras have been streaming.

Emerson is frolicking here, and yet his thought is so passionate and alive, his meter-making argument so compelling, that his little fable of the youth has its darker side also. The image of the aurora begins here as dawn, indeed an apocalyptic sunrise that might dim all the stars for good, but by a marvelous crossing is transformed into the aurora borealis proper, streaming from every pore of the night. The northern lights therefore represent, for Emerson, a reversal of belatedness into earliness, executed here with superb irony, since the belatedness belongs to Shakespeare and Homer, and the earliness to "a youth who sat near me at table."

Dickinson, frequently deft at taking hints from Emerson and then swerving away from them (in a process ably studied by Joanne Feit Diehl), seems to have taken the hint with more than usual dialectical agility in "Of Bronze—and Blaze—." I no longer agree with Charles R. Anderson's strong commentary upon this poem, which interprets its teaching as being that "the mortal poet corrupts his true nature if he attempts to be divine" and that "the poet must remain earth-bound." That tends to negate Dickinson's subtler ironies, which dominate the poem. The North, meaning the night sky and the auroras streaming through it, is so adequate as to overwhelm what might seem adequate desire to Dickinson, and infects her "simple spirit" with sublime longings. Her own bronze and blaze becomes the rhetorical stance of her poetry, which rises to the heights ("vaster attitudes") in order to manifest a sovereign unconcern all her own. Certainly the crucial irony is in "And strut upon my stem," which is a negative or downward metamorphosis, but only of the natural woman, as it were, and not of the poet. To say that her Splendors are Menagerie is indeed to admit that she is a performer, but the ancient Pindaric assertion of canonical renown and poetic survival follows with enormous authority. To be a "Competelesss Show," able to entertain the centuries, indeed is to be preconcerted with oneself, to be distant to alarms, even to the prophecy of one's organic fate.

Why do we apprehend, beyond error, that "Of Bronze—and Blaze" was written by a woman? In a way more singular and persuasive than any other woman poet has managed (at least since Sappho), Dickinson in scores of her strongest poems compels us to confront the part that gender plays in her poetic identity:

> The Tint I cannot take—is best—
> The Color too remote
> That I could show it in Bazaar—
> A Guinea at a sight—
>
> The fine—impalpable Array—
> That swaggers on the eye
> Like Cleopatra's Company—
> Repeated—in the sky—
>
> The Moments of Dominion
> That happen on the Soul
> And leave it with a Discontent
> Too exquisite—to tell—
>
> The eager look—on Landscapes—
> As if they just repressed
> Some Secret—that was pushing
> Like Chariots—in the Vest—
>
> The Pleading of the Summer—
> That other Prank—of Snow—
> That Cushions Mystery with Tulle,
> For fear the Squirrels—know.
>
> Their Graspless manners—mock us—
> Until the Cheated Eye

Shuts arrogantly—in the Grave
Another way—to see—

"Of Bronze—and Blaze" does not quite name the auroras, which is a
typical procedure for Dickinson. "The Tint I cannot take—is best" goes
further and avoids naming anything. American male theorists and poets
from Emerson and Whitman through Stevens and W.C. Williams are programmatic in urging an unnaming upon us, and Stevens in particular
achieves some of his greatest effects in that mode:

This is nothing until in a single man contained,
Nothing until this named thing nameless is
And is destroyed. He opens the door of his house

On flames. The scholar of one candle sees
An Arctic effulgence flaring on the frame
Of everything he is. And he feels afraid.

This is the crisis of "The Auroras of Autumn," where "this named
thing" is the aurora borealis, which flames forth to frighten the poet or
scholar of one candle and so undoes his attempt to enact the program of
unnaming. But Dickinson, shrewdly exploiting her identity as woman
poet, chooses another way to see, a way that unnames without defiance or
struggle. The best tint is what she cannot take, too remote for showing,
impalpable, too exquisite to tell, secret, graspless. Such a tint seems
unavailable to the eye of the male poet, even to a Keats or a Shelley, even
to Wordsworth's extraordinary mediation between the visual and the
visionary. No woman poet since Dickinson has had the power to teach us
so urgently and intuifively that women need not see as men see, need not
will as men will, need not appropriate for themselves as men perhaps need
to do. Freud, when he sadly admitted that women were a mystery, echoed
the bafflement of Milton, and might have been echoing Blake. Only three
men who wrote in English—Chaucer, Shakespeare, Samuel Richardson—
seem able to convey the sense of a difference between women and men in
a way comparable to the greatest women writers in the language, Jane
Austen, George Eliot, Dickinson. If Austen is comparable to Chaucer as a
craftsman in irony and George Eliot comparable to Richardson as a moral
psychologist of the Protestant temperament, then Dickinson is quite comparable to some of the subtlest aspects of Shakespearean representation.
Without Shakespeare, our sense of reality would be much diminished.
Without Dickinson, our sense of reality might not be diminished, but we

would know far less than we do about the sufferings and the satisfactions of a really isolated consciousness at its highest powers, particularly if it were the consciousness of a woman.

Andrew Marvell

(1621–1678)

MARVELL IS THE MOST ENIGMATIC, UNCLASSIFIABLE, AND UNAFFILIATED major poet in the language. It is finally unhelpful to call his poetry Metaphysical, Mannerist, Epicurean, Platonist, or Puritan, though all of those terms somehow are applicable. One of the most original poets in Western tradition, Marvell had no strong precursors, though Spenser may be near his hidden root. His poetry has a clear relation to the schools of Donne and Jonson, but is of neither, unlike that of such contemporaries as Randolph, Carew, and Lovelace. The distance from Milton, his greatest contemporary and the subject of one of his most admirable and admiring poems, is remarkable. His authentic affinities were with quite minor French poets who came after the Pléiade, Théophile de Viau (1590–1626) and Antoine–Girard de Saint-Arrant (1594–1661).

Post-Pléiade French pastoralists can be said to have invented Marvell's lyric mode, but there is absolutely nothing Gallic about Marvell's own poetry. Nor are there Marvellian poets after Marvell. T.S. Eliot, though his essay on Marvell has been so influential, is a Tennysonian-Whitmanian elegist of the self, whose actual verse has more in common with that of William Morris than with Marvell.

Eliot's celebrated essay, still being exalted by Frank Kermode and others, is in fact quite bad, being replete with irrelevant assertions as to how much better a poet Marvell is than Shelley, Keats, Wordsworth, Tennyson, Browning, Hardy, and Yeats, all of whom lacked what Eliot "designated tentatively as wit, a tough reasonableness beneath the slight lyric grace." We learn also from Eliot that Marvell surpasses the "L'Allegro" and "Il Penseroso" of Milton, a judgment that might have provoked some amiable skepticism in Marvell himself. Poor William Morris, a poet not very relevant to Marvell's mode, is also dragged in for a drubbing, and Eliot concludes that Browning, whose "A Toccata of Galuppi's" may be the most maturely sophisticated shorter poem in the language, "seems oddly immature, in some way, beside Marvell." Two years after his 1921 essay on Marvell, Eliot changed his mind anyway, in a review of the Nonesuch Press edition of Marvell's *Miscellaneous Poems*, where we learn that Marvell, unlike Chaucer and Pope, is "fantastical," conceit-ridden, and is in any case not as great a poet as Bishop Henry King, author of the "Exequy" but not of much more that engages us now. Though Kermode is Eliot's declared inheritor as a Marvell critic, I find his general emphasis more useful than his precursor's:

> To conclude: Marvell is not a philosophical poet; in his role as poet he engaged his subjects as poetry, bringing to them a mind of great intelligence and intelligently ordered learning. Our knowledge of his religious and political thought helps us only a little more than our knowledge of his personal life (quick temper, preference for solitary drinking) and can be related to the substance of his poetry only very cautiously and generally (the power of a mind engaged but detached, the alertness, leaning on the wind). Negatively, we can learn a lot from other poetry, and from the nature and contemporary use of allegory (habitual intermittency defined by the cult of acuteness or wit, and the resonantly defined detail). Broad categories are misleading; using words such as "puritan," "Platonist," even such as "nature" and "wit," we must constantly discriminate: wit is not seventeenth-century property but an ancient instrument of poetry and of religion, nature an indescribably complex inheritance of assumptions and meanings.

My only dissent here would be to go a bit further; that Marvell was a bad-tempered, hard-drinking lifelong bachelor and controversialist is more helpful knowledge than everything we know of his religion and politics, for the paradoxical reason that such a personality simply does not manifest itself in the poems, except perhaps for the satires. The Mower poems, my subject in this introduction, could have been written by a good-tempered married man who never touched alcohol and had little notion of religious and political quarrels. Yet they are at once absolutely idiosyncratic and personal, and totally universal in scope and emphasis, which is only to say that they are very great, very enigmatic lyric poems rather than philosophical tractates or scholarly investigations.

If Marvell is a poet's poet, then his lyrics and meditations have a particularly refreshing function for us right now, when poetry is studied as everything except poetry, be it politics, societal discontents, gender struggles, historicisms, philosophies, psychologies, semiotics, or what you will. Good critics, when once they still read poems as poems, accurately found in Marvell the culmination of the European pastoral lyric that Theocritus had inaugurated. Thomas G. Rosenmeyer, in his fine book on Theocritus, *The Green Cabinet* (1969), concluded that in the pastoral mode, "the poem as a whole is a trope, rather than any one portion of it." As a principle, this seems truer even of Marvell than of Theocritus and Virgil. Marvell's Mower poems are extended metaphors for a highly individual view of how our fall caused nature's loss of value also, so that the wounding power of sexual love became the wound that sexuality itself ended by being. William Empson interpreted the Mower most grandly:

> In these meadows he feels he has left his mark on a great territory, if not on everything, and as a typical figure he has mown all the meadows of the world; in either case Nature gives him regal and magical honors, and I suppose he is not only the ruler but the executioner of the daffodils—the Clown as Death.

In one aspect the pastoral Mower may be the Clown as Death, but in the enigmatic Mower poems this most original of Marvell's tropes cannot be uncovered once and for all. In "The Mower against Gardens," the Mower ends by insisting that "the gods themselves with us do dwell," presumably because we are not altogether fallen anymore than nature is, since "the sweet fields" still to all dispense / A wild and fragrant innocence." This is very different from the extraordinary triad of "Damon the Mower," "The Mower to the Glowworms," and "The Mower's Song," all of them reliant upon a great text in Isaiah:

> The voice said, Cry. And he said, What shall I cry? All flesh is grass, and all the goodliness thereof is as the flower of the field:
>   The grass withereth, the flower fadeth: because the spirit of the LORD bloweth upon it: surely the people is grass.
>   The grass withereth, the flower fadeth: but the word of our God shall stand for ever.
>   (Isa. 40:6–8)

In Walt Whitman, the grass becomes flesh, a metamorphosis in which Marvell preceded Whitman. Damon the Mower, stung by Juliana's scorching beams, attains involuntarily a congruence of inner qualities and outer emblems:

> Sharp like his scythe his sorrow was,
> And withered like his hopes the grass.

Marvell's Mower, absurdly enough, is both the ridiculous Polyphemus, the Cyclops of Theocritus, and, I suspect, the Adam Kadmon or unfallen God-Man of Kabbalistic and Hermetic tradition. That is, Damon is Adam, Adam both debased beneath and exalted beyond the Adam of Genesis. Damon is the Clown as Death, if you will, but he is (or was) also the Clown as a more abundant, preexistent life, not so much the Cyclops or Virgil's Corydon as the

Platonic dream of a divine human before the crashing downwards of a catastrophic creation. Marvell's more-than-ironic mode conveys mysteries only through an immensely sophisticated humor, edged by the reality principle of mortality. Ruth Nevo adroitly describes "Damon the Mower" as "a pastoral elegy for the quiet mind disturbed radically by desire unsatisfied," which sensibly leaves undefined whose mind that is, and how cosmological the desire may be. Geoffrey Hartman, sinuously seeking to match the subtle Marvell, finds the theme of the Mower poems in "the labor of hope," with "hope in nature frustrated by love or by the very strength of hope." Hartman's Mower is rather like the afflicted heroine of Wordsworth's "The Ruined Cottage"; what had been cultivated in hope is now destroyed in hope, as the end is hastened. The instrument of that hastening is death's scythe, which dominates the final three exquisite stanzas of this eleven-stanza lyric:

> "How happy might I still have mowed,
> Had not Love here his thistles sowed!
> But now I all the day complain,
> Joining my labour to my pain;
> And with my scythe cut down the grass,
> Yet still my grief is where it was:
> But, when the iron blunter grows,
> Sighing, I whet my scythe and woes."
> While thus he threw his elbow round,
> Depopulating all the ground,
> And, with his whistling scythe, does cut
> Each stroke between the earth and root,
> The edged steel by careless chance

Did into his own ankle glance;
And there among the grass fell down,
By his own scythe, the Mower mown.
"Alas!" said he, "these hurts are slight
To those that die by love's despite.
With shepherd's-purse, and clown's-all-heal,
The blood I staunch, and wound I seal.
Only for him no cure is found,
Whom Juliana's eyes do wound.
'Tis death alone that this must do:
For Death thou art a Mower too."

"The Mower mown" might well have been the poem's title, except for its neglect of Damon in his self-apotheosis:

"I am the Mower Damon, known
Through all the meadows I have mown.
On me the morn her dew distills
Before her darling daffodils.
And, if at noon my toil me heat,
The sun himself licks off my sweat.
While, going home, the evening sweet
In cowslip-water bathes my feet."

That does not seem to me the Clown as Death so much as the Clown as Hermetic Adam, living in a place very much his own, and even more his self, being at home all the time. We see Damon Adam fall again in stanzas 9–11, and so lose his home, possibly forever:

The Mower to the Glowworms

Ye living lamps, by whose dear light
The nightingale does sit so late,
And studying all the summer night,
Her matchless songs does meditate;

Ye country comets, that portend
No war, nor prince's funeral,
Shining unto no higher end
Than to presage the grass's fall;

Ye glowworms, whose officious flame
To wandering mowers shows the way,
That in the night have lost their aim,
And after foolish fires do stray;

Your courteous lights in vain you waste,
Since Juliana here is come,
For she my mind hath so displaced
That I shall never find my home.

This extraordinary lyric, addressed by the fallen Mower to the luminaries of his severely shrunken world, is surely one of the most mysterious
and beautiful poems in the language. I cannot reread it or recite it to
myself without evoking the beautiful quatrains that Blake added to *The
Gates of Paradise* when he reengraved that little Prophetic Book, addressing the quatrains "To the Accuser Who is the God of this World." But
"The Mower to the Glowworms" has no Jobean associations, even if it too
is a lost traveller's dream under the hill. "The grass's fall" is the fall of the
flesh, and the third stanza might almost have been written by William
Blake.

The first stanza of "The Mower's Song" recapitulates the last stanza
here, where the Mower's mind is displaced, but the revision is in a finer tone:

My mind was once the true survey
Of all these meadows fresh and gay,
And in the greenness of the grass
Did see its hopes as in a glass;
When Juliana came, and she
What I do to the grass, does to my thoughts and me.

Juliana is the Charmer as Death, and the remainder of the poem centers itself upon the extraordinary revelations of that last line, Marvell's solitary and unique instance of a refrain:

But these, while I with sorrow pine,
Grew more luxuriant still and fine,
That not one blade of grass you spied,
But had a flower on either side;
When Juliana came, and she
What I do to the grass, does to my thoughts and me.

Unthankful meadows, could you so
A fellowship so true forgo,
And in your gaudy May-games meet,
While I lay trodden under feet?
When Juliana came, and she
What I do to the grass, does to my thoughts and me.

But what you in compassion ought,
Shall now by my revenge be wrought:
And flow'rs, and grass, and I and all,
Will in one common ruin fall.
For Juliana comes, and she
What I do to the grass, does to my thoughts and me.

And thus, ye meadows, which have been
Companions of my thoughts more green,
Shall now the heraldry become
With which I will adorn my tomb;
For Juliana comes, and she
What I do to the grass, does to my thoughts and me.

Damon, resenting the flowers, truly resents a green world that will survive his own now irretrievable fall. But his true resentment is also an apocalyptic paradox, since his "revenge" of "one common ruin" is pragmatically a further riot of what Whitman calls the flag of the poet's disposition, out of hopeful green stuff woven. The heraldry of green will make the entire earth the Mower's tomb, but such a heraldry will bury scythe and scyther alike, give death to Death, and perhaps herald the rebirth of Damon as Adam Kadmon, the Primal Man forever not to be mown down.

William Blake

(1757–1827)

WHAT HAPPENS TO A POEM AFTER IT HAS SUCCEEDED IN CLEARING A SPACE for itself? As the poem itself begins to be misread, both by other poems and by criticism, is it distorted in the same way or differently than it has been distorted by itself, through its own activity in misreading others? Clearly its meanings do change drastically between the time that it first wrestles its way into strength, and the later time that follows its canonization. What kinds of misreading does canonization bring about? Or, to start further back, why call the canonization of texts a necessary misreading of texts?

What is canonization, in a purely secular context, and why ought criticism to talk about it? Criticism in fact hardly has talked about canon-formation, at least for quite a while now, and the process is a troublesome one, and so not easy to discuss. Canon-formation, in the West, began in the creation of Scripture, when the rabbis accepted certain texts and rejected others, so as to arrive at last at the library of thirty-nine books now commonly referred to as the Old Testament. The rabbis were no more unanimous than any other body of literary critics, and some of the disputes about canonization were not settled for several generations. The three main divisions of the Hebrew Bible—the Law, the Prophets, the Writings or Wisdom literature—represent three stages of canon-formation. It is likely that the Law was canonized by about 400 B.C., the Prophets by about 100 B.C., the Writings not until A.D. 90.

"Canon" as a word goes back to a Greek word for a measuring rule, which in Latin acquired the additional meaning of "model." In English we use it to mean a church code, a secular law, a standard or criterion, or a part of the Catholic Mass, or as a musical synonym for a kind of fugue, or in printing for a size of type. But we also use it for authoritative lists of works, sacred or secular, by one author or by many. The Greek word *kanon* was of

Semitic origin, and it is difficult to distinguish between its original meanings of "reed" or "pipe," and "measuring rod." Canon-formation or canonization is a richly suggestive word for a process of classic-formation in
poetic tradition, because it associates notions of music and of standards.

But before considering poetic canon-formation, I want to go back to
the biblical process of canonization. Samuel Sandmel makes the useful
observation that before a text was canonized, it could be copied with inat-
tention, as you or I tend to copy. But, he adds: "Once a writing became
canonical, it was copied with such relentless fidelity that even the inherited mistakes and the omissions and the telescoping were retained." The late
Edmund Wilson, perhaps not understanding the indirect descent of academic textual scholars from these pious copyists, complained bitterly at its
modern continuance, but we can attain a critical realization about how a
copying-canonization fosters misreading, of a peculiarly uninteresting,
weak, and unproductive kind. A canonical reading, like a canonical copy-
ing, attempts to stop the mind by making a text redundantly identical with
itself, so as to produce a total presence, an unalterable meaning. So many
texts, so many meanings—might be the motto of weak canonization. But
there is also strong canonization, and it is more dangerous, whether carried on by the Academy of Ezra, the Church, the universities, or most of
all by strong critics from Dr. Samuel Johnson to the present day. Though
my own texts-for-reading in this [essay] will be two famous lyrics by Blake,
London and *The Tyger*, I will try to illustrate the ways in which strong canonization misreads by a religious example, before I turn to Blake. But
before I come to my religious example, I want to say something about the
transition from religious to secular canon-formation.

Whether in religion or in poetry, or (as I suspect) everywhere else as
well, memory is a crucial mode of thought, as Hannah Arendt remarks in
the context of political philosophy. We can make a more drastic assertion;
in poetry memory is always the most important mode of thought, despite
Blake's passionate insistences upon the contrary view. The reason why
most strong post-Enlightenment poems end with schemes of transumption or metaleptic reversals, with defensive patterns of projection and/or
introjection, with imagery of earliness and/or belatedness, in short with
the revisionary ratio I have called the *apophrades* or Return of the Dead, is
that, particularly in poems, the past, like the future, is always a force, and
indeed, in poems, the future's force is directed to driving the poem back
into the past, no matter what the poet is trying to do.

Hannah Arendt tells us that political thought as a tradition goes from
Plato to Marx, and ends there. I suppose we could say that moral psychology as a tradition goes from Plato to Freud and ends there. But poetry as

a tradition has no Marx or Freud (though Wordsworth came closest to that end-stop position) because you cannot break the tradition without ceasing to write poetry, in the sense that the tradition from Homer to Goethe defines poetry, and Wordsworth's best poetry paradoxically breaks the tradition only to extend it, but at the high cost of narrowing and internalizing the tradition, so that all subsequent attempts to get beyond Wordsworth have failed. Blake was a much less original poet than Wordsworth, as I think we are only beginning to understand. Despite his surface innovations, Blake is closer to Spenser and to Milton than he is to Wordsworth, and far closer than Wordsworth is to Spenser and Milton. Wordsworth imposed himself upon the canon; Blake, though a major intellectual revisionist, was more imposed upon *by* the canon than modern Blake scholarship is willing to accept or admit.

I return to the process of canonic imposition. E.R. Curtius sums it up by saying: "Canon formation in literature must always proceed to a selection of classics." But Curtius, so far as I can tell, hardly distinguishes between religious and secular canon-formation. A secular tradition presumably is open to intruders of genius, rather more readily than a religious tradition, and surely this difference is the crucial one between revisionism and heresy. Revisionism alters *stance*; heresy alters *balance*. A secular canon stands differently, after it subsumes a great revisionist, as British poetry manifested a different relation between the poet and the poem, after Wordsworth. But a religious canon is thrown out of balance by a great heretic, and cannot subsume him unless it is willing to be a different religion, as Lutheranism and Calvinism were very different religions from Catholicism. Joachim of Flora or Eckhart could not become canonical texts, but in the secular canon Blake has been legitimatized. What this has done to Blake is now my concern, a concern I want to illuminate first by one large instance of the reading peculiarities brought about through religious canonization. The book *Koheleth* or Ecclesiastes is, rather astonishingly, a canonical work, part of Scripture. The book Ecclesiasticus, or *The Wisdom of Jesus the Son of Sirach*, was not taken into the canon, and is part of the Old Testament Apocrypha.

As literary works, they both are magnificent; in the King James version, it would be difficult to choose between them for rhetorical power, but Ecclesiastes is far stronger in the original. Their peculiar fascination for my purposes is that they exist in a relation of precursor and ephebe, with Koheleth or Ecclesiastes, written about 250 B.C., being the clearly dominant influence upon Ben Sirach or Ecclesiasticus, written about 200 B.C. By a splendid irony, the canonical Koheleth is a highly problematic text in regard to normative Judaism, while the uncanonical Ben Sirach is explicitly and unquestionably orthodox, a monument to normative Judaism.

Koheleth derives from the Hebrew word *kahal*, meaning "the community" or "the congregation." The Greek "Ecclesiastes," meaning a member of the *ecclesia* or assembly of citizens, is not a very exact equivalent. Neither word, Hebrew or Greek, means "the Preacher," which is a famous mistranslation for Koheleth. Tradition identifies Koheleth with Solomon, a beautiful but false idea. Like his imitator Ben Sirach, Koheleth worked in the literary genre of Wisdom Literature, a vast genre in the ancient Near East. "Instruction" is a synonym for "Wisdom" in this sense, and may be a better modern translation for *Hokmah*, which really meant: "How to live, what to do," but was also used as a synonym for poetry and song, which were not distinguished from Instruction.

Robert Gordis, in the most widely accepted modern study of Koheleth, shows that Koheleth was a teacher in one of the Wisdom academies in third-century B.C. Jerusalem, teaching aristocratic youths, in a quasi-secular way. His ambiance was anything but prophetic, and his highly individual vision of life and religion was much closer to what we would call skeptical humanism than it was to the central traditions of Judaism. God, for Koheleth, is the Being who made us and rules over us, but Koheleth has nothing more to say about Him. God is there at our beginning and at our end; in between what matters is our happiness. How did *this* book become canonized?

Not without a struggle, is part of the answer. The two great interpretative schools of the rabbis Hillel and Shammai fought a long spiritual war over Koheleth, and the Hillelites did not win a final victory until A.D. 90 when the Council of Jamnia (Jabneh) closed out Scripture by affirming that Koheleth was part of the canon. The school of Shammai sensibly asserted that the book was self-contradictory, merely literary, not inspired by God, and was marked plainly by skepticism towards the Torah. The Hillelites insisted that the book was by Solomon (though surely even they knew this was a pious fiction), and pointed to certain passages in the book that were traditionally Torah-oriented. What was the motive of the Hillelites? Theologically, they were liberals, and presumably Koheleth helped them to achieve more daring and open interpretations of the Law. Yet the deeper motive, as with the great Rabbi Akiba's passion for the *Song of Songs*, seems to have been what we call literary or aesthetic esteem. Koheleth was, rhetorically and conceptually, too good a book to lose. Though both a belated and an audacious work, it was taken permanently into Scripture. I myself am a mere amateur at biblical scholarship, yet I want to go further in expressing the misreading of this canonization, for as

I read it, Koheleth is a revisionist poem, a strong misprision of Torah, which suffered the happy irony of being absorbed by the precursor against whom it had rebelled, however ambivalently. Koheleth 3:14 echoes Deuteronomy 4:2 and 13:1 in a revisionist way, so as to change the emphasis from the Law's splendor to human powerlessness. It echoes passages in Kings, Samuel, and Leviticus, so as to undo the moral point from a categorical insistence upon righteousness as a divine commandment to the skeptical view that moral error is inevitable and even necessary, but that righteousness is always more humanly sensible if only you can achieve it. Robert Gordis insightfully remarks that Koheleth refers only to Torah and to Wisdom Scripture, and wholly ignores the canonical prophets, as nothing could be more antithetical to his own vision than Isaiah and Ezekiel.

Let us contrast to Koheleth his eloquent and more traditionally pious ephebe Ben Sirach, who about a half-century later seems to have followed much the same profession, teaching pragmatic Wisdom, of a literary kind, at an upper-class academy in Jerusalem. Ben Sirach can be described as the Lionel Trilling of his day, even as his precursor, Koheleth, seems a figure not wholly unlike Walter Pater or even Matthew Arnold, in Arnold's more skeptical moments, though I hasten to add that Arnold was hardly in Koheleth's class as poet or intellect. Ben Sirach, by a charming but not unexpected antithetical irony, echoes or alludes constantly to Koheleth, but always canonically misreading Koheleth into a Shammai-like high Pharisaic orthodoxy. Wherever Koheleth urges the necessity of pleasure, Ben Sirach invokes the principle of echoing Koheleth while urging restraint, but in the vocabulary of his precursor. Robert Gordis observes that wherever Koheleth is literal in his meaning, Ben Sirach interprets him as being figurative. Any close comparison of the texts of Ecclesiastes and Ecclesiasticus will confirm the analysis that Gordis makes.

Let me sum up this rather intricate excursus upon Koheleth and the book of Jesus Ben Sirach. The revisionist work, through canonization, is misread by being overfigurated by the canonically informed reader. The derivative, orthodox work, left uncanonized because of its belatedness, is misread by being overliteralized by those who come after it, ourselves included.

I turn to two texts of Blake, two famous *Songs of Experience: London* and *The Tyger*. How are we to read these two revisionist lyrics that Blake intended us to canonize, that indeed now are part of the canon of British poetry? What kinds of misreadings are these poems now certain to demand? *London* is a revisionist text with regard to the book of the prophet Ezekiel; *The Tyger* is a revisionist text with regard to the Book of Job, and also in relation to *Paradise Lost*.

Here is the precursor-text for Blake's *London*, chapter 9 of the Book of Ezekiel:

He cried also in mine ears with a loud voice, saying, "Cause them that have charge over the city to draw near, even every man with his destroying weapon in his hand."

And, behold, six men came from the way of the higher gate, which lieth toward the north, and every man a slaughter weapon in his hand; and one man among them was clothed with linen, with a writer's inkhorn by his side: and they went in, and stood beside the brasen altar.

And the glory of the God of Israel was gone up from the cherub, whereupon he was, to the threshold of the house. And he called to the man clothed with linen, which had the writer's inkhorn by his side;

And the Lord said unto him, "Go through the midst of the city, through the midst of Jerusalem, and set a mark upon the foreheads of the men that sigh and that cry for all the abominations that be done in the midst thereof."

And to the others he said in mine hearing, "Go ye after him through the city, and smite: let not your eye spare, neither have ye pity: Slay utterly old and young, both maids, and little children, and women: but come not near any man upon whom is the mark; and begin at my sanctuary." Then they began at the ancient men which were before the house.

And he said unto them, "Defile the house, and fill the courts with the slain: go ye forth." And they went forth, and slew in the city.

And it came to pass, while they were slaying them, and I was left, that I fell upon my face, and cried, and said, "Ah Lord God! wilt thou destroy all the residue of Israel in thy pouring out of thy fury upon Jerusalem?"

Then said he unto me, "The iniquity of the house of Israel and Judah is exceeding great, and the land is full of blood, and the city full of perverseness: for they say, 'The Lord hath forsaken the earth, and the Lord seeth not.'

"And as for me also, mine eye shall not spare, neither will I have pity, but I will recompense their way upon their head."

And, behold, the man clothed with linen, which had the inkhorn by his side, reported the matter, saying, "I have done as thou hast commanded me."

Chapter 8 of Ezekiel ends with God's warning that he will punish the people of Jerusalem for their sins. Chapter 9 is Ezekiel's prophetic vision of the punishment being carried out, despite the prophet's attempt at intercession on behalf of a saving remnant. The crucial verse for Blake's *London* is clearly the fourth one, which gives Blake not only the central image of his poem but even the rhyme of "cry" and "sigh":

> ... And he called to the man clothed with linen, which had the writer's inkhorn by his side;
> And the Lord said unto him: "Go through the midst of the city, through the midst of Jerusalem, and set a mark upon the foreheads of the men that sigh and that cry for all the abominations that be done in the midst thereof."

This mark is given to the saving remnant of Jerusalem, who alone are to be spared destruction. The Hebrew word for "mark" used here is *taw*, which is the name also of the letter *t*, the last letter of the Hebrew alphabet, even as zed (*z*) is last in ours, or omega is last in the Greek alphabet. Traditional commentary on Ezekiel interpreted this to mean that the taw set upon the forehead of the righteous would be written in ink and signify *tichyeh*, "you shall live," but the *taw* upon the forehead of the wicked would be written in blood and would signify *tamuth*, "you shall die."

The intertextual relationship between Ezekiel and Blake here is quite unmistakable, even though it also has been quite unnoticed, except by myself, in my role as what Blake denounced as a "Satan's Watch-Fiend." How is Blake revising Ezekiel?

Not, so far as I can tell, by his initial equation of London = Jerusalem, which means that from the start all received readings of this poem, including my own, are wholly mistaken in seeing Blake's poem primarily as a protest against repression, whether societal or individual. That is, all received readings have said or intimated that in the poem *London* Blake presents himself as a prophet or prophetic figure, akin to Ezekiel, with the people of London only roughly akin to those of Ezekiel's Jerusalem, in that they are shown as suffering beneath the counterrevolutionary oppression of the regime of William Pitt. On this view the people, however culpable for weakness or lack of will, are the righteous, and only the State and State Church of Pitt are the wicked. From this, a number of other interpretations necessarily follow throughout the poem, down to the famous lines about the harlot and the new-born infant at the poem's close.

I shall demonstrate, with the aid of what I call "antithetical criticism," that all such interpretations are weak, unproductive, canonical

misreadings, quite alien to the spirit of Blake's strong misreading or misprision of Ezekiel, and alien in any case to the letter of Blake's text, to the
words, images, figurations of the strong poem *London*.

Blake begins: "I wander thro' each charter'd street," and so we begin
also, with that wandering and that chartering, in order to define that "L"
Is it an Ezekiel-like prophet, or someone whose role and function are altogether different? To "wander" is to have no destination and no purpose. A
biblical prophet may wander when he is cast out into the desert, when his
voice becomes a voice in the wilderness, but he does not wander when he
goes through the midst of the city, through the midst of Jerusalem the City
of God. There, his inspired voice always has purpose, and his inspired feet
always have destination. Blake knew all this, and knew it with a knowing
beyond our knowing. When he begins by saying that he *wanders* in
London, his Jerusalem, his City of God, then he begins also by saying "I
am not Ezekiel, I am not a prophet, I am too fearful to be the prophet I
ought to be, *I am hid*."

"Charter'd" is as crucial as "wander." The word is even richer with
multiple significations and rhetorical ironies, in this context, than criticism
so far has noticed. Here are the relevant shades-of-meaning: There is certainly a reference to London having been created originally as a city by a
charter to that effect. As certainly, there is an ironic allusion to the celebrated political slogan: "the chartered rights of Englishmen." More subtly,
as we will see, there is a reference to *writing*, because to be chartered is to
be written, since a charter is a written grant from authority, or a document
outlining a process of incorporation. In addition, there are the commercial
notions of hiring, or leasing, indeed of binding or covenanting, always crucial in a prophetic context. Most important, I think, in this poem that turns
upon a mark of salvation or destruction, is the accepted meaning that to be
chartered is to be awarded a special privilege or a particular immunity,
which is established by a written document. Finally, there is a meaning
opposed to "wandering," which is charting or mapping, so as to preclude
mere wandering. The streets of London are chartered, Blake says, and so
he adds is the Thames, and we can surmise that for Blake, the adjective is
primarily negative in its ironies, since his manuscript drafts show that he
substituted the word "chartered" for the word "dirty" in both instances.

As is often the case with strong, antithetical poems that are highly
condensed in their language, Blake's key-words in *London* are remarkably
interrelated, as criticism again has failed to notice. Walter Pater, in his
great essay on *Style*, urges that the strong poet, or "literary artist" as he
puts it, "will be apt to restore not really obsolete or really worn-out words,
but the finer edge of words still in use." Pater meant the restoration of

etymological or original meaning, "the finer edge," and in this Pater was again a prophet of modern or belated poetry. But here Blake, who deeply influenced Pater, was already a pioneer. Let us return to "wander" which goes back to the root *wendh*, from which come also "turn," "weave," and "wind." I quote from Blake's *Auguries of Innocence*, notebook jottings clearly related to his *London*:

> The Whore & Gambler by the State
> Licencd build that Nations Fate
> The Harlots cry from Street to Street
> Shall weave Old Englands winding Sheet
> The Winners Shout the Losers Curse
> Dance before dead Englands Hearse
> Every Night & every Morn
> Some to Misery are Born

Contrast this to the final stanza of *London*:

> But most thro' midnight streets I hear
> How the youthful Harlots curse
> Blasts the new-born Infants tear
> And blights with plagues the Marriage hearse.

The harlot's cry or curse, a loser's curse, weaves a winding sheet for England and every marriage in England by blasting the infant's tear and by blighting with plagues. To weave is to wind is to wander is to turn is to blight and blast. Blight and blast what and how? The surprising answer is: voice, which of course is the prophet's one gift. Blake *wendhs* as the harlot *wendhs*, and both to the same result: the loss of human voice. For what is an "infant"? "Infant," "ban," and "prophet" all come from the same root, the Indo-European *Bha*, which is a root meaning "to speak." And "infant" means one incapable of speech; all the infant can do is weep. The Latin *fari* and the Greek *phanai* both mean "to speak," and "prophet" derives from them. A ban is a stated or spoken interdiction, which means that a ban is a curse, while to curse is to put something or someone under a ban. Ban and voice, in Blake's *London*, are natural synonyms and indeed we can say that the poem offers the following equation: every voice = a ban = a curse = weeping or a blasted tear. But the verbal network is even more intricate. The harlot's curse is not, as various interpreters have said, venereal disease, but is indeed what "curse" came to mean in the vernacular after Blake and still means now: menstruation, the natural cycle in the human female. Let us note the complexity of two more key words in the text: "mark" and "forg'd" in "mind-forg'd manacles." A "mark" is a boundary (or, as Blake said, a "Devourer" as opposed to a "Prolific"); it is also a visible trace, a sign in lieu of writing, and a grade of merit or demerit. To "forge" means to "fabricate" in both senses of "fabricate": to make, as a smith or poet makes, but also to counterfeit. The Indo-European root is *dhabh*, meaning "to fit together" and is related to the Hebrew *dabhar* for "word." "Mind-forg'd manacles" is a phrase deliberately evoking the Western metaphysical problem of dualism, since "manacles" for "hand-cuffs" involves *manus* or hand, and hence bodily act, which is at once made and yet feigned or counterfeited by the opposing principle of mind.

I have involved us in all of this verbal interrelation in order to suggest that Blake's *London* centers itself upon an opposition between *voice* and *writing*, by which I don't mean that somehow Jacques Derrida wrote the poem. No—the poem is precisely anti-Nietzschean, anti-Derridaean, and offers us a terrifying nostalgia for a lost prophetic *voice*, the voice of Ezekiel and religious logocentrism, which has been replaced by a demonic *visible trace*, by a mark, by the writing of the apocalyptic letter *taw*. With this as background, I am at last prepared to offer my own, antithetical, strong misreading of Blake's *London*, of which I will assert only that it is more adequate to the text than the weak misreadings now available to us.

I will commence by offering a very plain summary or paraphrase of what I judge to be the difference in meanings when we juxtapose Blake's *London* with its precursor-text in Ezekiel, chapter 9. Then I will proceed to an antithetical account of Blake's *London*, through a charting of its revisionary ratios, tropes, psychic defenses, and images.

In chapter 8 of Ezekiel, the prophet sits in his house of exile in Babylon, surrounded by the elders of Judah. The Spirit of God raises him, and carries him "in the visions of God to Jerusalem," to the outraged Temple, where graven, idolatrous images of Asherah have been placed as substitutes for the Living God. A further and final vision of the *Merkabah*, God's triumphal chariot, is granted Ezekiel, after which four scenes of idolatry *within* the Temple are revealed to him. Chapter 8 concludes with a fierce warning from God:

> Therefore will I also deal in fury; Mine eye shall not spare, neither will I have pity; and though they cry in Mine ears with a loud voice, yet will I not hear them.

Chapter 9, which I have quoted already, mitigates this only for a small remnant. There are six angels of destruction, with only Gabriel (according to the Talmud) armed with the inkhorn that will spare the righteous. Unlike Gabriel, Blake does not necessarily set a mark, since his "mark in every face I meet," primarily is intransitive, meaning "remark" or "observe."

Blake begins *London* with a curious irony, more a scheme than a figure, or if a figure, then more a figure of thought than of speech. For he adopts the outcast role he called Rintrah, the John-the-Baptist or unheeded forerunner, in place of the prophetic vocation, but in the context of Ezekiel's Jerusalem as well as his own London. In the opening dialectic of presence and absence, precisely what is absent is prophetic direction and prophetic purpose; what is present are chartering and marks. So voice is absent, and only demonic writing is present. Blake's defensive reaction-formation to the call he cannot answer is to be a wanderer, and to mark passively rather than mark actively with the *taws* of righteousness and wickedness, life and death. But righteousness and wickedness are alike absent; present only are weakness and woe, neither of which merits a *taw*, whether of ink or of blood. The synecdoche of the universal human face represents Blake's turning against his own self, for he also is weak and woeful, and not the Ezekiel-like prophet he should be.

The litany of "every" becomes a weird metonymic reification, a regression in moving all men back to a state of infancy, but also an isolation, as this is an "every" that separates out rather than unifies people:

> In every cry of every Man,
> In every Infants cry of fear
> In every voice: in every ban
> The mind-forg'd manacles I hear.

"Every Man" includes the Londoner William Blake, whose voice also must betray the clanking sound of "mind-forg'd manacles," where the mind belongs to every man, again including William Blake. An infant's cry of fear is all-too-natural, for the infant is voiceless but for his fear and hunger, which for him is a kind of fear. When the crucial word "voice" enters the poem, it is put into a metonymic, reductive series with "cry of fear" and "ban," with terror and curse, fear and the threat of fear.

When Blake answers this reduction with a Sublime repressive hyperbole, it is governed by the same "I hear," as spoken by a Jonah, a renegade prophet who never does speak in his own poem, but only hears:

> I hear
> How the Chimney-sweepers cry
> Every blackning Church appalls,

And the hapless Soldiers sigh,
Runs in blood down Palace walls.

The chimney-sweepers' cry, as in the two Blakean songs of the sweeps, is "Weep, weep," due to the cockney lisp of the children, as they attempt to advertise their labor with a voiced "sweep, sweep." The cry of weep helps blacken further the perpetually blackening Church, possibly draping it in a pall through the mark of *taw* in a black ink, giving it an edge over the royal palace, which receives the bloody *taw* of destruction. The soldier's hapless sigh prefigures the curse of the harlot, as both are losers, in the term from *Auguries of Innocence*. But what about Blake's synaesthesia? How, even in Sublime representation, can you *hear* a Church being draped in a pall, and how can you *hear* a sigh running in blood down palace walls. The answer, I think, is given by our map of misreading. What Blake is repressing into this hyperbolical hearing-seeing is the visionary power of the *nabi*, the Hebrew prophet, and the running of the repressed voice down the repressive walls represents not only the soldier's hapless sigh, but the more powerful hapless sigh of the prophet who has repressed the voice that is great within us.

We come then to the final stanza, the most weakly misread of all. Here is the characteristic Romantic ending that follows a limiting metaphor by a representing transumption:

But most thro' midnight streets I hear
How the youthful Harlots curse
Blasts the new-born Infants tear
And blights with plagues the Marriage hearse.

I want to reject altogether the customary interpretation that makes "curse" here a variety of venereal infection, and that makes the infant's condition a prenatal blindness. Instead, I want to reaffirm my own earlier interpretation of the Harlot here as Blake's perpetually youthful Harlot, Nature, not the human female, but the natural element in the human, male or female.

The inside/outside perspectivism here gives us Blake as pent-up voice wandering still at midnight *through* the streets, and through that labyrinth he achieves another synaesthetic hearing-seeing, how another curse or ban or natural fact (menstruation) blasts or scatters another natural fact, the tearlessness of the new-born *infant*. For Blake every natural fact equals every other natural fact. The metalepsis that introjects the future here is one that sees enormous plagues riding along in every marriage coach, blighting life into death, as though every marriage carries the *taw* of destruction. Remember again the doggerel of *Auguries of Innocence*:

> The Harlots cry from street to street
> Shall weave Old Englands winding sheet
> The Winners Shout the Losers Curse
> Dance before dead Englands Hearse

If Old England is dead, then all her marriages are funerals. A cry that weaves a shroud is like a mark of *taw* or a ban chartering weakness and woe. Blake's poem is not a protest, not a prophetic outcry, not a vision of judgment. It is a revisionist's self-condemnation, a Jonah's desperation at *knowing* he is not an Ezekiel. We misread Blake's poem when we regard it as prophecy, and see it as primarily sympathy with the wretched of London, because we have canonized the poem, and because we cannot bear to read a canonical poem as being truly so altogether negative and self-destructive a text.

Even as a revisionist strong poem, Blake's *London* is more a deliberate parody of misprision than it is a revisionist text. Blake's tonal complexities are uncanny, *unheimlich*, here and elsewhere, and like Nietzsche Blake is something of a parodist of world history. There is a grotesque element in *London*, and what we take as Sublime hyperbole is actually more the underthrow of litotes, the characteristic rhetorical figure in grotesque representation. This parody is a clearer strain in Blake's *The Tyger*, which I want to introduce more by way of Nietzsche than by way of its origins in Job and Milton.

Like Nietzsche, and like every other revisionist, Blake desired always to keep origin and aim, source and purpose, as far apart as possible. Nietzsche, if I understand him, believed only in comic or preposterous schemes of transumption, in which a future laughter is introjected and a past tragedy is projected. An aphorism in *Beyond Good and Evil* says that we are

> prepared as was no previous age for a Carnival in the grand style, for laughter and a high-spirited revelry, for transcendental flights of Sublime nonsense and an Aristophanes-like mockery of the universe. Perhaps this is where we shall yet discover the realm of our invention, that realm in which we also still can be original, say as parodists of world history and the clowns of God—perhaps, even if nothing else today has a future, our laughter may yet have a future.

We can observe here that a poem, in this view, must be a parody of a parody, just as a man is a parody of God. But Nietzschean repetition is even more bewildering, for any copy is both a parody of its original, yet also a self-parody. In terms of poetic misprision, this means that any poem is both a misreading of a precursor poem and, more crucially, a misreading of itself. Whether Nietzschean parody is universally applicable I do not know, but it illuminates poems of deliberately cyclic repetition like Blake's *The Tyger* or *The Mental Traveller* or *The Crystal Cabinet*.

Blake's Tyger has a pretty exact analogue in a Nietzschean tiger, a grand deconstructive tiger, in the curious text called *Truth and Falsehood in an Extra-Moral Sense*:

> What indeed does man know about himself? Oh! that he could but once see himself complete, placed as it were in an illumi-nated glass case! Does not nature keep secret from him most things, even about his body ...? Nature threw away the key; and woe to the fateful curiosity which might be able for a moment to look out and down through a crevice in the chamber of con-sciousness and discover that man, indifferent to his own igno-rance, is resting on the pitiless, the greedy, and insatiable, the murderous, and as it were, hanging in dreams on the back of a tiger. Whence, in the wide world, with this state of affairs, aris-es the impulse to truth?

Nietzsche's tiger is human mortality; our illusive day-to-day exis-tence rests us, in dreams, as we ride the tiger who will be, who is our own death, a metaphorical embodiment of the unbearable truth that the pleas-ure-principle and the reality-principle are finally one.

Nietzsche's precursors were Goethe, Schopenhauer, Heine, and Wagner; Blake's were Milton and the Bible. Of all the thirty-nine books of the Old Testament, Job obsessed Blake most. The forerunners of Blake's Tyger are the Leviathan and Behemoth of Job, two horrible beasts who represent the God-ordained tyranny of nature over man, two beasts whose final name is human death, for to Blake nature is death.

God taunts Job by asking him if these great beasts will make a covenant with man? Rashi comments on Behemoth by saying: "prepared for the future," and the apocryphal apocalypses, Enoch and IV Ezra and Baruch, all say that Leviathan and Behemoth are parted only to come together one day, in the judgment, when they will be the food of the Righteous. As God says of Leviathan, if none dare face him, then "Who is able to stand before Me?" Milton brings in the Leviathan (evidently a crocodile in Job) as a whale, but Melville's Moby-Dick is closer to the beasts of Job, and to Blake's Tyger.

At this advanced date, I assert an exemption from having to argue against the usual run of merely trivial misreadings of *The Tyger*. I will oppose my antithetical reading to the received misreading of the earlier Bloom, in books like *The Visionary Company* and *Blake's Apocalypse*, or in the notes to *Romantic Poetry and Prose* in the Oxford Anthology. The fundamental principle for reading *The Tyger* is to realize that this is a dramatic lyric in which William Blake is not, cannot be, the speaker. *The Tyger* is a Sublime or hyperbolical monologue, with little movement in its tropes or images. It is dominated by the single trope of repression, by an unconsciously purposeful forgetting, but this is not Blake's repression. The psychic area in which the whole poem centers is hysteria. What does it mean for a major lyric never to deviate from its own hysterical intensity?

The answer is that Blake, more even than Nietzsche, is a master of creative parody, and he is parodying a kind of greatness that he loves and admires, but vehemently does not wish to join. It is the greatness of William Cowper, and the other poets of the Burkean or Miltonic Sublime in the later eighteenth century. The two dominant images of the poem are both fearful-the burning or fire and the symmetry. Fire is the prime perspectivizing trope in all of Romanticism, as we will see again and again. It stands, most often, for discontinuity or for the possibility of, or desire towards discontinuity. Its opposite, the emblem of repetition or continuity, tends to be the inland sound of moving waters. These identifications may seem purely arbitrary now; I will vindicate them in later chapters.

What are we to make of "symmetry"? Symmetry is a one-to-one ratio, whether on opposite sides of a dividing line, or in relation to a center. A one-to-one ratio means that no revisionism has taken place; there has been no *clinamen*, no catastrophe-creation or breaking-of-the-vessels in the making of the Tyger. Like Leviathan and Behemoth, the Tyger is exactly what his creator meant him to be. But who is his creator? Does this poem set itself, for interpretation, in a relatively orthodox Genesis-Milton context, or in the context of some Gnosis? How fearful is the Tyger's maker? Or is it a canonical misreading that we allow this poem to set itself a genetic context for interpretation, at all?

By common consent of interpreters, *The Tyger* is made up of a series of increasingly rhetorical questions. The model for this series certainly is to be found in the Book of Job, where God confronts Job with crushingly rhetorical questions, all of them reducing to the cruelty of: Where were you, anyway, when I made everything? After all, Job's plea had been "Call Thou, and I will answer" (13:22), and God therefore relies upon a continuous irony as figure-of-thought. But the speaker of *The Tyger* is incapable of deliberate irony; every one of his tropes is, as I have noted already, a hyperbole. What is this profound repression defending against? What furnace is coming up, at last, against the will of this daemonizing speaker?

No speaker could be more determined to insist that origin and aim were the same impulse and the same event. We can surmise that the unconsciously purposeful forgetting of this poem's speaker is precisely that he himself, as an aim or purpose, has been separated irreparably from his point of origin. Confronting the Tyger, who represents his own *daemonic* intensity, the form that is his own force, what Blake would have called Vision or his own Imagination, the dramatic speaker is desperately determined to identify completely the Tyger's aim and purpose with the Tyger's supposedly divine origins.

Yet it is not the speaker's text, but Blake's, and the meaning of the text rises parodistically and even with a wild comedy out of the intertextual juxtapositions between the text itself and texts by Cowper, by Milton, and the text cited from Job.

First Cowper, from Book VI of *The Task*:

The Lord of all, himself through all diffused,
Sustains, and is the life of all that lives.
Nature is but a name for an effect
Whose cause is God. He feeds the secret fire
By which the mighty process is maintained,
Who sleeps not, is not weary; in whose sight
Slow circling ages are as transient days,
Whose work is without labour; whose designs
No flaw deforms, no difficulty thwarts;

Here origin and purpose are one, without strain, anxiety, or repression, or so it seems. Next Milton, from Book VII of *Paradise Lost*, part of the most Sublime creation-scene in the language:

The grassy Clods now Calv'd, now half appear'd
The Tawny Lion, pawing to get free
His hinder parts, then springs as broke from Bonds,
And Rampant shakes his Brinded mane; the Ounce,
The Libbard, and the Tiger, as the Mole
Rising, the crumbl'd Earth above them threw
In Hillocks ...

Milton shows rather less creative anxiety than the poet of Job, even allowing himself a transumption of a Lucretian allusion as if to indicate his own corrective confidence that God's origins and Milton's purposes are one and the same. Blake's speaker is not Blake, nor is he Milton, not even Blake's own Milton. He is Cowper or Job, or rather Cowper assimilated to Job, and both assimilated not to the strong poet or revisionist in Blake, but to Blake's own Spectre of Urthona, that is, the time-bound work-a-day ego, and not what Blake liked to call "the Real Man the Imagination."

I approach an antithetical formula. Blake's revisionism in *London* was to measure the ratios by which he fell short of Ezekiel. Blake's revisionism in *The Tyger* is to measure the ratio by which he surpasses Cowper and Job. Cowper's fearful ratio does not frighten Blake, whose entire dialectic depends upon separating origins, natural or natural religion's, from imaginative aims or revisionist purposes. Yet, in *London*, Blake shows himself knowingly incapable of separating prophetic voice as aim or purpose from the cry, curse, ban of natural voice as origin. We have underestimated Blake's complexities, and his own capacity for self-recognition. He is in no danger of falling into the repetition of the Bard confronting the Jobean Tyger. Yet, in the societal context in which a prophet must vindicate himself, Blake falls silent, and falls into the repetition of the wanderer who flees the burden of prophecy. There can no more be a mute prophet than there can be a mute, inglorious Milton. The prophet or *nabi* is precisely a *public orator*, and not a private mutterer or marker. The *nabi* never moans, as Blake did, "I am hid." Blake, who might have been more, by his own account was human—all too human—and gave in to natural fear. His belatedness, in the spiritual more than in the poetic sense, was a shadow that overcame him.

The Blake of *London* has become a canonical writer, unlike the Ben Sirach of Ecclesiasticus, but like Ecclesiasticus Blake gives us in *London* a text he lacks the authority to sustain. The Blake of *The Tyger*, like the Koheleth of Ecclesiastes, gives us a canonical text that tradition necessarily has misread and goes on misreading. Revisionism or belated creations is a hard task, and exacts a very high price, a price that meaning itself must pay for, by being emptied out from a plenitude to a dearth.

I conclude with a final juxtaposition between the skeptical Koheleth and the passionately certain Blake. Both Ecclesiastes and *The Tyger* are texts of conscious belatedness, though *The Tyger* parodies and mocks its own condition of belatedness. For the Tyger itself, as a Sublime representation, is a self-imposed blocking agent, what Blake called a Spectre, and what Ezekiel and Blake called a Covering Cherub. The guilt suffered by the speaker of Blake's *Tyger* is also Cowper's guilt, and the guilt of a very un-Cowperian figure, Milton's Satan. This is the guilt that Nietzsche, in his *Genealogy of Morals*, called the "guilt of indebtedness." I think that Blake meant something like this when he said in *Jerusalem* that it was easier to forgive an enemy than it was to forgive a friend. The speaker of *The Tyger* confronts a burning, fearful symmetry that exists in a one-to-one ratio with its Creator. Like Job confronting Leviathan and Behemoth, the Cowper-like bard confronts an unacceptable surrogate for the divine Precursor, a surrogate who grants him no priority, and who has authority over him insofar as he is natural. Blake, in mocking a canonical kind of poem, nevertheless is subsumed by the canonical traditions of misreading, as any student of *The Tyger*'s interpretative history could testify.

Where Blake's dramatic speaker is trapped in repetition, Koheleth is a theorist of repetition, not far in spirit from the Stoic Marcus Aurelius. "All words toil to weariness," Koheleth says early on in his book, and so he thinks that fundamentally all the books have been written already. Though he praises wisdom, Koheleth is weary of it. He too might have said: "The flesh is sad alas, and I have read all the books." But he adds: "For wisdom is a defense, even as money is a defense," and the Hebrew translated here in the King James version as "defense" is a word literally meaning "shadow." I end on that identification of the defense against influence with the metonymic trope of shade for wisdom or money, and for the forests of the night that frame the menace of the fire that meant a discontinuity from origins.

William Wordsworth

(1770-1850)

There is a human loneliness,
A part of space and solitude,
In which knowledge cannot be denied.
In which nothing of knowledge fails,
The luminous companion, the hand,
The fortifying arm, the profound
Response, the completely answering voice....

—WALLACE STEVENS

THE PRELUDE WAS TO BE ONLY THE ANTECHAPEL TO THE GOTHIC CHURCH of *The Recluse*, but the poet Wordsworth knew better than the man, and *The Prelude* is a complete and climactic work. The key to *The Prelude* as an internalized epic written in creative competition to Milton is to be found in those lines (754–860) of the *Recluse* fragment that Wordsworth prefaced to *The Excursion* (1814). Wordsworth's invocation, like Blake's to the Daughters of Beulah in his epic *Milton*, is a deliberate address to powers higher than those that inspired *Paradise Lost*:

Urania, I shall need
Thy guidance, or a greater Muse, if such
Descend to earth or dwell in highest heaven!
For I must tread on shadowy ground, must sink
Deep—and, aloft ascending, breathe in worlds
To which the heaven of heavens is but a veil.

The shadowy ground, the depths beneath, and the heights aloft are all in the mind of man, and Milton's heaven is only a veil, separating an allegorical unreality from the human paradise of the happiest and best regions of a poet's mind. Awe of the personal Godhead fades before the poet's reverence for his own imaginative powers:

> All strength—all terror, single or in bands,
> That ever was put forth in personal form—
> Jehovah—with his thunder, and the choir
> Of shouting Angels, and the empyreal thrones—
> I pass them unalarmed.

Blake, more ultimately unorthodox than Wordsworth as he was, had yet too strong a sense of the Bible's power to accept this dismissal of Jehovah. After reading this passage, he remarked sardonically:

> Solomon, when he Married Pharaoh's daughter & became a Convert to the Heathen Mythology, talked exactly in this way of Jehovah as a Very inferior object of Man's Contemplations; he also passed him by unalarm'd & was permitted. Jehovah dropped a tear & follow'd him by his Spirit into the Abstract Void; it is called the Divine Mercy.

To marry Pharaoh's daughter is to marry Nature, the Goddess of the Heathen Mythology, and indeed Wordsworth will go on to speak of a marriage between the Mind of Man and the goodly universe of Nature. Wordsworth is permitted his effrontery, as Solomon the Wise was before him, and, like Solomon, Wordsworth wanders into the Ulro or Abstract Void of general reasoning from Nature, pursued by the ambiguous pity of the Divine Mercy. But this (though powerful) is a dark view to take of Wordsworth's reciprocal dealings with Nature. Courageously but calmly Wordsworth puts himself forward as a renovated spirit, a new Adam upon whom fear and awe fall as he looks into his own Mind, the Mind of Man. As befits a new Adam, a new world with a greater beauty waits upon his steps. The most defiant humanism in Wordsworth salutes the immediate possibility of this earthly paradise naturalizing itself in the here and now:

> Paradise, and groves
> Elysian, Fortunate Fields—like those of old
> Sought in the Atlantic Main—why should they be
> A history only of departed things,
> Or a mere fiction of what never was?
> For the discerning intellect of Man,

When wedded to this goodly universe
In love and holy passion, shall find these
A simple produce of the common day.

No words are more honorific for Wordsworth than "simple" and "common." The marriage metaphor here has the same Hebraic sources as Blake had for his Beulah, or "married land." The true Eden is the child of the common day, when that day dawns upon the great consummation of the reciprocal passion of Man and Nature. What Wordsworth desires to write is "the spousal verse" in celebration of this fulfillment:

and, by words
Which speak of nothing more than what we are,
Would I arouse the sensual from their sleep
Of Death, and win the vacant and the vain
To noble raptures.

This parallels Blake's singing in *Jerusalem*:

Of the sleep of Ulro! and of the passage through
Eternal Death! and of the awaking to Eternal Life.

But Wordsworth would arouse us by speaking of nothing more than what we already are; a more naturalistic humanism than Blake could endure. Wordsworth celebrates the *given*—what we already possess, and for him it is as for Wallace Stevens

As if the air, the mid-day air, was swarming
With the metaphysical changes that occur,
Merely in living as and where we live.

For Wordsworth, as for Stevens, the earth is enough; for Blake it was less than that all without which man cannot be satisfied. We need to distinguish this argument between the two greatest of the Romantics from the simplistic dissension with which too many readers have confounded it, that between the doctrines of innate goodness and original sin. Wordsworth is not Rousseau, and Blake is not St. Paul; they have more in common with one another than they have with either the natural religionist or the orthodox Christian.

Wordsworth's Imagination is like Wallace Stevens's *Angel Surrounded by Paysans*: not an angel of heaven, but the necessary angel of earth, as, in its sight, we see the earth again, but cleared; and in its hearing we hear the still sad music of humanity, its tragic drone, rise liquidly, not harsh or grating, but like watery words awash, to chasten and subdue us. But the Imagination of Wordsworth and of Stevens is "a figure half seen, or seen for a moment." It rises with the sudden mountain mists, and as suddenly departs. Blake, a literalist of the Imagination, wished for its more habitual sway. To marry Mind and Nature is to enter Beulah; there Wordsworth and Blake are at one. Blake insisted that a man more fully redeemed by Imagination would not need Nature, would regard the external world as hindrance. The split between Wordsworth and Blake is not theological at all, though Blake expresses it in his deliberately displaced Protestant vocabulary by using the metaphor of the Fall where Wordsworth rejects it. For Wordsworth the individual Mind and the external World are exquisitely fitted, each to the other, even as man and wife, and with blended might they accomplish a creation the meaning of which is fully dependent upon the sexual analogy; they give to us a new heaven and a new earth blended into an apocalyptic unity that is simply the matter of common perception and common sexuality raised to the freedom of its natural power. Wordsworthian Man is Freudian Man, but Blake's Human Form Divine is not. "You shall not bring me down to believe such a fitting & fitted" is his reaction to Wordsworth's exquisite adjustings of the Universe and Mind. To accept Nature as man's equal is for Blake the ineradicable error. Blake's doctrine is that either the Imagination totally destroys Nature and puts a thoroughly Human form in its place, or else Nature destroys the Imagination. Wordsworth says of his task that he is forced to hear "Humanity in fields and groves / Pipe solitary anguish" and Blake reacts with ferocity:

> Does not this Fit, & is not Fitting most Exquisitely too, but to what?—not to Mind, but to the Vile Body only & to its Laws of Good & Evil & its Enmities against Mind.

This is not the comment of an embittered Gnostic. Blake constructs his poetry as a commentary upon Scripture; Wordsworth writes his poetry as a commentary upon Nature. Wordsworth, while not so Bible-haunted as Blake, is himself a poet in the Hebraic prophetic line. The visible body of Nature is more than an outer testimony of the Spirit of God to him; it is our only way to God. For Blake it is the barrier between us and the God within ourselves. Ordinary perception is then a mode of salvation for Wordsworth, provided that we are awake fully to what we see. The common earth is to be hallowed by the human heart's and mind's holy union with it, and by that union the heart and mind in concert are to receive their bride's gift of phenomenal beauty, a glory in the grass, a splendor in the flower. Until at last the Great Consummation will be achieved, and renovated Man will stand in Eden once again. The human glory of Wordsworth, which he bequeathed to Keats, is in this naturalistic celebration of the possibilities inherent in our condition, here and now. That Wordsworth himself, in the second half of his long life, could not sustain this vision is a criticism of neither the vision nor the man, but merely his loss—and ours.

The Old Cumberland Beggar (1797) is Wordsworth's finest vision of the irreducible natural man, the human stripped to the nakedness of primordial condition and exposed as still powerful in dignity, still infinite in value. The Beggar reminds us of the beggars, solitaries, wanderers throughout Wordsworth's poetry, particularly in *The Prelude* and *Resolution and Independence*. He differs from them in that he is not the agency of a revelation; he is not responsible for a sudden release of Wordsworth's imagination. He is not even of visionary utility; he is something finer, beyond use, a vision of reality in himself. I am not suggesting that *The Old Cumberland Beggar* is the best of Wordsworth's poems outside *The Prelude*; it is not in the sublime mode, as are *Tintern Abbey*, the Great Ode, *Resolution and Independence*. But it is the most Wordsworthian of poems, and profoundly moving.

Nothing could be simpler than the poem's opening: "I saw an aged Beggar in my walk." The Old Man (the capitalization is the poet's) has put down his staff, and takes his scraps and fragments out of a flour bag, one by one. He scans them, fixedly and seriously. The plain beginning yields to a music of love, the beauty of the real:

> In the sun,
> Upon the second step of that small pile,
> Surrounded by those wild unpeopled hills,
> He sat, and ate his food in solitude:
> And ever, scattered from his palsied hand,
> That, still attempting to prevent the waste,
> Was baffled still, the crumbs in little showers
> Fell on the ground; and the small mountain birds,
> Not venturing yet to peck their destined meal,
> Approached within the length of half his staff.

It is difficult to describe *how* this is beautiful, but we can make a start by observing that it is beautiful both because it is so matter of fact, and because the fact is itself a transfiguration. The Old Man is in his own state, and he is radically innocent. The "wild unpeopled hills" complement his own solitude; he is a phenomenon of their kind. And he is no more sentimentalized than they are. His lot is not even miserable; he is too absorbed into Nature for that, as absorbed as he can be and still retain human identity.

He is even past further aging. The poet has known him since his childhood, and even then "he was so old, he seems not older now." The Old Man is so helpless in appearance that everyone—sauntering horseman or toll-gate keeper or post boy—makes way for him, taking special care to keep him from harm. For he cannot be diverted, but moves on like a natural process. "He travels on, a solitary Man," Wordsworth says, and then repeats it, making a refrain for that incessant movement whose only meaning is that it remains human though at the edge of our condition:

> He travels on, a solitary Man;
> His age has no companion. On the ground
> His eyes are turned, and, as he moves along,
> *They* move along the ground; and, evermore,
> Instead of common and habitual sight
> Of fields with rural works, of hill and dale,
> And the blue sky, one little span of earth
> Is all his prospect.

He is bent double, like the Leech Gatherer, and his vision of one little span of earth recalls the wandering old man of Chaucer's *Pardoner's Tale*. But Chaucer's solitary longed for death, and on the ground he called his mother's gate he knocked often with his staff, crying, "Dear mother, let me in." Wordsworth's Old Man sees only the ground, but he is tenaciously alive, and is beyond desire, even that of death. He sees, and yet hardly sees. He moves constantly, but is so still in look and motion that he can hardly be seen to move. He is all process, hardly character, and yet almost stasis.

It is so extreme a picture that we can be tempted to ask, "Is this life? Where is its use?" The temptation dehumanizes us, Wordsworth would have it, and the two questions are radically dissimilar, but his answer to the first is vehemently affirmative and to the second an absolute moral passion. There is

> a spirit and pulse of good,
> A life and soul, to every mode of being
> Inseparably linked.

The Old Man performs many functions. The most important is that of a binding agent for the memories of good impulses in all around him. Wherever he goes,

> The mild necessity of use compels
> To acts of love.

These acts of love, added one to another, at last insensibly dispose their performers to virtue and true goodness. We need to be careful in our reaction to this. Wordsworth is not preaching the vicious and mad doctrine that beggary is good because it makes charity possible. That would properly invoke Blake's blistering reply in *The Human Abstract*:

> Pity would be no more
> If we did not make somebody Poor;
> And Mercy no more could be
> If all were as happy as we.

Wordsworth has no reaction to the Old Man which we can categorize. He does not think of him in social or economic terms, but only as a human life, which necessarily has affected other lives, and always for the better. In particular, the Old Man has given occasions for kindness to the very poorest, who give to him from their scant store, and are the kinder for it. Again, you must read this in its own context. Wordsworth's best poetry has nothing directly to do with social justice, as Blake's or Shelley's frequently does. The old beggar is a free man, at home in the heart of the solitudes he wanders, and he does not intend the humanizing good he passively causes. Nor is his social aspect at the poem's vital center; only his freedom is:

> —Then let him pass, a blessing on his head!
> And, long as he can wander, let him breathe
> The freshness of the valleys; let his blood
> Struggle with frosty air and winter snows;
> And let the chartered wind that sweeps the heath
> Beat his grey locks against his withered face.

Pity for him is inappropriate; he is pathetic only if shut up. He is a "figure of capable imagination," in Stevens's phrase, a Man perfectly complete in Nature, reciprocating its gifts by being himself, a being at one with it:

Let him be free of mountain solitudes;
And have around him, whether heard or not,
The pleasant melody of woodland birds.

Mountain solitudes and sudden winds are what suit him, whether he
reacts to them or not. The failure of his senses does not cut him off from
Nature; it does not matter whether he can hear the birds, but it is fitting
that he have them around him. He has become utterly passive toward
Nature. Let it be free, then, to come in upon him:

              if his eyes have now
Been doomed so long to settle upon earth
That not without some effort they behold
The countenance of the horizontal sun,
Rising or setting, let the light at least
Find a free entrance to their languid orbs.

The Old Man is approaching that identity with Nature that the
infant at first knows, when an organic continuity seems to exist between
Nature and consciousness. Being so naturalized, he must die in the eye of
Nature, that he may be absorbed again:

And let him, *where* and *when* he will, sit down
Beneath the trees, or on a grassy bank
Of highway side, and with the little birds
Share his chance-gathered meal; and, finally,
As in the eye of Nature he has lived,
So in the eye of Nature let him die!

The poem abounds in a temper of spirit that Wordsworth shares
with Tolstoy, a reverence for the simplicities of *caritas*, the Christian love
that is so allied to and yet is not pity. But Tolstoy might have shown the
Old Cumberland Beggar as a sufferer; in Wordsworth he bears the mark
of "animal tranquillity and decay," the title given by Wordsworth to a fragment closely connected to the longer poem. In the fragment the Old Man
travels on and moves not with pain, but with thought:

          He is insensibly subdued
   To settled quiet ...
          He is by nature led

To peace so perfect that the young behold
With envy, what the Old Man hardly feels.

We know today, better than his contemporaries could, what led
Wordsworth to the subject of human decay, to depictions of idiocy, deser-
tion, beggars, homeless wanderers. He sought images of alienated life, as
we might judge them, which he could see and present as images of natural
communion. The natural man, free of consciousness in any of our senses,
yet demonstrates a mode of consciousness which both intends Nature for
its object and at length blends into that object. The hiding places of man's
power are in his past, in childhood. Only memory can take him there, but
even memory fades, and at length fades away. The poet of naturalism, separated by organic growth from his own past, looks around him and sees the
moving emblems of a childlike consciousness in the mad, the outcast, and
the dreadfully old. From them he takes his most desperate consolation,
intimations of a mortality that almost ceases to afflict.

Samuel Taylor Coleridge

(1772–1834)

COLERIDGE, THE YOUNGEST OF FOURTEEN CHILDREN OF A COUNTRY clergyman, was a precocious and lonely child, a kind of changeling in his own family. Early a dreamer and (as he said) a "character," he suffered the loss of his father (who had loved him best of all the children) when he was only nine. At Christ's Hospital in London, soon after his father's death, he found an excellent school that gave him the intellectual nurture he needed, as well as a lifelong friend in the future essayist Charles Lamb. Early a poet, he fell deeply in love with Mary Evans, a schoolfellow's sister, but sorrowfully nothing came of it.

At Jesus College, Cambridge, Coleridge started well, but temperamentally he was not suited to academic discipline and failed of distinction. Fleeing Cambridge, and much in debt, he enlisted in the cavalry under the immortal name of Silas Tomkyn Comberback but kept falling off his horse. Though he proved useful to his fellow dragoons at writing love letters, he was good for little else but stable-cleaning, and the cavalry allowed his brothers to buy him out. He returned to Cambridge, but his characteristic guilt impeded academic labor and when he abandoned Cambridge in 1794 he had no degree.

A penniless young poet, radical in politics, original in religion, he fell in with the then equally radical bard Robert Southey, remembered today as the Conservative Laureate constantly savaged in Byron's satirical verse. Like our contemporary communards, the two poetical youths projected what they named a "pantisocracy." With the right young ladies and, hopefully, other choice spirits, they would found a communistic agrarian-literary settlement on the banks of the Susquehanna in exotic Pennsylvania. At Southey's urging, Coleridge made a pantisocratic engagement to the not very brilliant Miss Sara Fricker, whose sister Southey was to marry.

Pantisocracy died aborning, and Coleridge in time woke up miserably to find himself unsuitably married, the greatest misfortune of his life.

He turned to Wordsworth, whom he had met early in 1795. His poetry influenced Wordsworth's and helped the latter attain his characteristic mode. It is not too much to say that Coleridge's poetry disappeared into Wordsworth's. We remember *Lyrical Ballads* (1798) as Wordsworth's book, yet about a third of it (in length) was Coleridge's, and "Tintern Abbey," the crown of the volume except for "The Rime of the Ancient Mariner," is immensely indebted to Coleridge's "Frost at Midnight." Nor is there much evidence of Wordsworth admiring or encouraging his friend's poetry; toward "The Ancient Mariner" he was always very grudging, and he was discomfited (but inevitably so) by both "Dejection: An Ode" and "To William Wordsworth." Selfless where Wordsworth's poetry was concerned, Coleridge had to suffer his closest friend's neglect of his own poetic ambitions.

This is not an easy matter to be fair about, since literature necessarily is as much a matter of personality as it is of character. Coleridge, like Keats (and to certain readers, Shelley), is lovable. Byron is at least always fascinating, and Blake in his lonely magnificence is a hero of the imagination. But Wordsworth's personality, like Milton's or Dante's, does not stimulate affection for the poet in the common reader. Coleridge has, as Walter Pater observed, a "peculiar charm"; he seems to lend himself to myths of failure, which is astonishing when the totality of his work is contemplated.

Yet it is his life, and his self-abandonment of his poetic ambitions, that continue to convince us that we ought to find in him parables of the failure of genius. His best poetry was all written in the year and half in which he saw Wordsworth daily (1797–8), yet even his best poetry, with the single exception of "The Ancient Mariner," is fragmentary. The pattern of his life is fragmentary also. When he received an annuity from the Wedgwoods, he left Wordsworth and Dorothy to study language and philosophy in Germany (1798–9). Soon after returning, his miserable middle years began, though he was only twenty-seven. He moved near the Wordsworths again and fell in love, permanently and unhappily, with Sara Hutchinson, whose sister Mary was to become Wordsworth's wife in 1802. His own marriage was hopeless, and his health rapidly deteriorated, perhaps for psychological reasons. To help endure the pain he began to drink laudanum, liquid opium, and thus contracted an addiction he never entirely cast off. In 1804, seeking better health, he went to Malta but returned two years later in the worst condition of his life. Separating from Mrs. Coleridge, he moved to London and began another career as lecturer, general man-of-letters, and periodical editor, while his miseries augmented.

The inevitable quarrel with Wordsworth in 1810 was ostensibly reconciled in 1812, but real friendship was not reestablished until 1828.

From 1816 on, Coleridge lived in the household of a physician, James Gillman, so as to be able to keep working and thus avoid total breakdown. Prematurely aged, his poetry period over, Coleridge entered into a major last phase as critic and philosopher, upon which his historical importance depends; but this, like his earlier prose achievements, is beyond the scope of an introduction to his poetry. It remains to ask, What was his achievement as a poet, and extraordinary as that was, why did his poetry effectively cease after about 1807? Wordsworth went on with poetry after 1807 but mostly very badly. The few poems Coleridge wrote, from the age of thirty-five on, are powerful but occasional. Did the poetic will not fail in him, since his imaginative powers did not?

Coleridge's large poetic ambitions included the writing of a philosophic epic on the origin of evil and a sequence of hymns to the sun, moon, and elements. These high plans died, slowly but definitively, and were replaced by the dream of a philosophic *Opus Maximum*, a huge work of synthesis that would reconcile German idealist philosophy with the orthodox truths of Christianity. Though only fragments of this work were ever written, much was done in its place—speculations on theology, political theory, and criticism that were to influence profoundly conservative British thought in the Victorian period and, in quite another way, the American transcendentalism led by Emerson and Theodore Parker.

Coleridge's actual achievement as poet divides into two remarkably diverse groupings—remarkable because they are almost simultaneous. The daemonic group, necessarily more famous, is the triad of "The Ancient Mariner," "Christabel," and "Kubla Khan." The "conversational" group includes the conversation poem proper, of which "The Eolian Harp" and "Frost at Midnight" are the most important, as well as the irregular ode, such as "Dejection" and "To William Wordsworth." The late fragments, "Limbo" and "Ne Plus Ultra," are a kind of return to the daemonic mode. For a poet of Coleridge's gifts to have written only nine poems that really matter is a sorrow, but the uniqueness of the two groups partly compensates for the slenderness of the canon.

The daemonic poems break through the orthodox censor set up by Coleridge's moral fears of his own imaginative impulses. Unifying the group is a magical quest-pattern which intends as its goal a reconciliation between the poet's self-consciousness and a higher order of being, associated with Divine forgiveness; but this reconciliation fortunately lies beyond the border of all these poems. The Mariner attains a state of purgation but cannot get beyond that process. Christabel is violated by

Geraldine, but this too is a purgation rather than a damnation, as her utter innocence is her only flaw. Coleridge himself, in the most piercing moment in his poetry, is tempted to assume the state of an Apollo-rebirth—the youth with flashing eyes and floating hair—but he withdraws from his vision of a poet's paradise, judging it to be only another purgatory.

The conversational group, though so immensely different in mode, speaks more directly of an allied theme: the desire to go home, not to the past but to what Hart Crane beautifully called "an improved infancy." Each of these poems, like the daemonic group, verges upon a kind of vicarious and purgatorial atonement in which Coleridge must fail or suffer so that someone he loves may succeed or experience joy. There is a subdued implication that somehow the poet will yet be accepted into a true home this side of the grave if he can achieve an atonement.

Where Wordsworth, in his primordial power, masters the subjective world and aids his readers in the difficult art of feeling, Coleridge deliberately courts defeat by subjectivity and is content to be confessional. But though he cannot help us to feel, as Wordsworth does, he gives us to understand how deeply felt his own sense of reality is. Though in a way his poetry is a testament of defeat, a yielding to the anxiety of influence and to the fear of self-glorification, it is one of the most enduringly poignant of such testaments that literature affords us.

II

"Psychologically," Coleridge observed, "consciousness is the problem"; and he added somberly: "Almost all is yet to be achieved." How much he achieved Kathleen Coburn and others are showing us. My concern here is the sadder one of speculating yet again about why he did not achieve more as a poet. Walter Jackson Bate has meditated, persuasively and recently, upon Coleridge's human and literary anxieties, particularly in regard to the burden of the past and its inhibiting poetic splendors. I swerve away from Bate to center the critical meditation upon what might be called the poetics of anxiety, the process of misprision by which any latecomer strong poet attempts to clear an imaginative space for himself.

Coleridge could have been a strong poet, as strong as Blake or Wordsworth. He could have been another mighty antagonist for the Great Spectre Milton to engage and, yes, to overcome, but not without contests as titanic as those provided by Blake's *The Four Zoas* and Wordsworth's *The Excursion*, and parental victories as equivocal as those achieved with Blake's *Jerusalem* and Wordsworth's *The Prelude*. But we have no such poems by

Coleridge. When my path winds home at the end of this Introduction, I will speculate as to what these poems should have been. As critical fathers for my quest I invoke first Oscar Wilde, with his glorious principle that the highest criticism sees the object as in itself it really is not, and second, Wilde's critical father, Walter Pater, whose essay of 1866 on "Coleridge's Writings" seems to me still the best short treatment of Coleridge, and this after a century of commentary. Pater, who knew his debt to Coleridge, knew also the anxiety Coleridge caused him, and Pater therefore came to a further and subtler knowing. In the Organic analogue, against which the entire soul of the great Epicurean critic rebelled, Pater recognized the product of Coleridge's profound anxieties as a creator. I begin therefore with Pater on Coleridge, and then will move immediately deep into the Coleridgean interior, to look upon Coleridge's fierce refusal to take on the ferocity of the strong poet.

This ferocity, as both Coleridge and Pater well knew, expresses itself as a near-solipsism, and Egotistical Sublime, or Miltonic godlike stance. From 1795 on, Coleridge knew, loved, envied, was both cheered and darkened by the largest instance of that Sublime since Milton himself. He studied constantly, almost involuntarily, the glories of the truly modern strong poet, Wordsworth. Whether he gave Wordsworth rather more than he received, we cannot be certain; we know only that he wanted more from Wordsworth than he received, but then it was his endearing though exasperating weakness that he always needed more love than he could get, no matter how much he got: "To be beloved is all I need, / And whom I love, I love indeed."

Pater understood what he called Coleridge's "peculiar charm," but he resisted it in the "sacred name of what he called the "relative" spirit against Coleridge's archaizing "absolute" spirit. In gracious but equivocal tribute to Coleridge he observed:

> The literary life of Coleridge was a disinterested struggle against the application of the relative spirit to moral and religious questions. Everywhere he is restlessly scheming to apprehend the absolute; to affirm it effectively; to get it acknowledged. Coleridge failed in that attempt, happily even for him, for it was a struggle against the increasing life of the mind itself.... How did his choice of a controversial interest, his determination to affirm the absolute, weaken or modify his poetic gift.

To affirm the absolute, Pater says—or, as we might say, to reject all dualisms except those sanctioned by orthodox Christian thought—is not *materia poetica* for the start of the nineteenth century, and if we think of a poem like the "Hymn before Sun-Rise, in the Vale of Chamouni," we are likely to agree with Pater. We will agree also when he contrasts Wordsworth favorably with Coleridge, and even with Goethe, commending Wordsworth for "that flawless temperament ... which keeps his conviction of a latent intelligence in nature within the limits of sentiment or instinct, and confines it to those delicate and subdued shades of expression which perfect art allows." Pater goes on to say that Coleridge's version of Wordsworth's instinct is a philosophical idea, which means that Coleridge's poetry had to be "more dramatic, more self-conscious" than Wordsworth's. But this in turn, Pater insists, means that for aesthetic success ideas must be held loosely, in the relative spirit. One idea that Coleridge did not hold loosely was the Organic analogue, and it becomes clearer as we proceed in Pater's essay that the aesthetic critic is building toward a passionate assault upon the Organic principle. He quotes Coleridge's description of Shakespeare as "a nature humanized, a genial understanding, directing self-consciously a power and an implicit wisdom deeper even than our consciousness." "There," Pater comments, with bitter eloquence, "'the absolute' has been affirmed in the sphere of art; and thought begins to congeal." With great dignity Pater adds that Coleridge has "obscured the true interest of art." By likening the work of art to a living organism, Coleridge does justice to the impression the work may give us, but he "does not express the process by which that work was produced."

M.H. Abrams, in his *The Mirror and the Lamp*, defends Coleridge against Pater by insisting that Coleridge knew his central problem "was to use analogy with organic growth to account for the spontaneous, the inspired, and the self-evolving in the psychology of invention, yet not to commit himself as far to the elected figure as to minimize the supervention of the antithetic qualities of foresight and choice." Though Abrams calls Pater "short-sighted," I am afraid the critical palms remain with the relative spirit, for Pater's point was not that Coleridge had no awareness of the dangers of using the Organic analogue but rather that awareness, here as elsewhere, was no salvation for Coleridge. The issue is whether Coleridge, not Shakespeare, was able to direct "self-consciously a power and an implicit wisdom deeper than consciousness." Pater's complaint is valid because Coleridge, in describing Shakespeare, Dante, Milton, keeps repeating his absolute formula that poems grow from within themselves, that their "wholeness is not in vision or conception, but in an inner feeling of totality and absolute being." As Pater says, "that exaggerated inwardness is barren" because it "withdraws us too far from what we can see, hear, and feel," because it cheats the senses and emotions of their triumph. I urge Pater's wisdom here not only against Coleridge, though I share Pacer's love for Coleridge, but against the formalist criticism that continued in Coleridge's absolute spirit.

What is the imaginative source of Coleridge's disabling hunger for the Absolute? On August 9, 1831, about three years before he died, he wrote in his Notebook: "From my earliest recollection I have had a consciousness of Power without Strength—a perception, an experience, of more than ordinary power with an inward sense of Weakness.... More than ever do I feel this now, when all my fancies still in their integrity are, as it were, drawn *inward* and by their suppression and compression rendered a mock substitute for Strength—" Here again is Pater's barren and exaggerated inwardness, but in a darker context than the Organic principle provided.

This context is Milton's "universe of death," where Coleridge apprehended death-in-life as being "the wretchedness of *division.*" If we stand in that universe, then "we think of ourselves as separated beings, and place nature in antithesis to the mind, as object to subject, thing to thought, death to life." To be so separated is to become, Coleridge says, "a soul-less fixed star, receiving no rays nor influences into my Being, *a Solitude which I so tremble at, that I cannot attribute it even to the Divine Nature.* "This, we can say, is Coleridge's Counter-Sublime, his answer to the anxiety of influence, in strong poets. The fear of solipsism is greater in him than the fear of not individuating his own imagination.

As with every other major Romantic, the prime precursor poet for Coleridge was Milton. There is a proviso to be entered here; for all these poets—Blake, Wordsworth, Shelley, Coleridge (only Keats is an exception)—there is a greater Sublime poetry behind Milton, but as its author is a people and not a single poet, and as it is far removed in time, its greatness does not inhibit a new imagination—not unless it is taken as the work of the Prime Precursor Himself, to whom all creation belongs. Only Coleridge, among these poets, acquired a double Sublime anxiety of influence. Beyond the beauty that has terror in it of Milton, was beauty more terrible. In a letter to Thelwall, December 17, 1796, Coleridge wrote: "Is not Milton a *sublimer* poet than Homer or Virgil? Are not his Personages more sublimely cloathed? And do you not know, that there is not perhaps *one* page in Milton's *Paradise Lost,* in which he has not borrowed his imagery from the Scriptures?—I allow, and rejoice that *Christ* appealed only to the understanding & the affections; but I affirm that, after reading Isaiah, or St. Paul's Epistle to the Hebrews, Homer & Virgil are disgustingly *tame* to me, & Milton himself barely tolerable." Yet these statements are rare in Coleridge. Frequently, Milton seems to blend with the ultimate influence, which I think is a normal enough procedure. In 1796, Coleridge also says, in his review of Burke's *Letter to a Noble Lord*: "It is lucky for poetry, that Milton did not live in our days...." Here Coleridge moves toward the center of his concern, and we should remember his formula: "Shakespeare was all men, potentially, except Milton." This leads to a more ambiguous formula, reported to us of a lecture that Coleridge gave on November 28, 1811: "Shakespeare became all things well into which he infused himself, while all forms, all things became Milton—the poet ever present to our minds and more than gratifying us for the loss of the distinct individuality of what he represents." Though Coleridge truly professes himself more than gratified, he admits loss. Milton's greatness is purchased at the cost of something dear to Coleridge, a principle of difference he knows may be flooded out by his monistic yearnings. For Milton, to Coleridge, is a mythic monad in himself. Commenting upon the apostrophe to light at the commencement of the third book of *Paradise Lost*, Coleridge notes: "In all modern poetry in Christendom there is an under consciousness of a sinful nature, a fleeting away of external things, the mind or subject greater than the object, the reflective character predominant. In the *Paradise Lost* the sublimest parts are the revelations of Milton's own mind, producing itself and evolving its own greatness; and this is truly so, that when that which is merely entertaining for its objective beauty is introduced, it at first seems a discord." This might be summarized as: where Milton is not, nature is barren, and its significance is that Milton is permitted just such a solitude as Coleridge trembles to imagine for the Divine Being.

Humphry House observed that "Coleridge was quite unbelievably modest about his own poems; and the modesty was of a curious kind, sometimes rather humble and over-elaborate." As House adds, Coleridge "dreaded publication" of his poetry, and until 1828, when he was fifty-six, there was nothing like an adequate gathering of his verse. Wordsworth's attitude was no help, of course, and the Hutchinson girls and Dorothy no doubt followed Wordsworth in his judgments. There was Wordsworth, and before him there had been Milton. Coleridge presumably knew what "Tintern Abbey" owed to "Frost at Midnight," but this knowledge nowhere found expression. Must we resort to psychological speculation in order to see what inhibited Coleridge, or are there more reliable aids available?

In the *Biographia Literaria* Coleridge is not very kind to his pre-Wordsworthian poetry, particularly to the "Religious Musings." Yet this is where we must seek what went wrong with Coleridge's ambitions—here, and if there were space, in "The Destiny of Nations" fragments (not its arbitrarily yoked-together form of 1817), and in the "Ode to the Departing Year," and in the "Monody on the Death of Chatterton" in its earlier versions. After Wordsworth had descended upon Coleridge, supposedly as a "know-thyself" admonition from heaven but really rather more like a new form of the Miltonic blight, then Coleridge's poetic ambitions sustained another kind of inhibition. The Miltonic shadow on early Coleridge needs to be studied first, before a view can be obtained of his maturer struggles with influence.

With characteristic self-destructiveness; Coleridge gave "Religious Musings" the definitive subtitle: "A Desultory Poem, Written on the Christmas Eve of 1794." The root-meaning of "desultory" is "vaulting," and though Coleridge consciously meant that his poem skipped about and wavered, his imagination meant "vaulting," for "Religious Musings" is a wildly ambitious poem. "This is the time ..." it begins, in direct recall of Milton's "Nativity" Hymn, yet it follows not the Hymn but the most sublime moments of *Paradise Lost*, particularly the invocation to Book III. As with the 1802 "Hymn before Sun-Rise," its great fault as a poem is that it never stops whooping; in its final version I count well over one hundred exclamation points in just over four hundred lines. Whether one finds this habit in Coleridge distressing or endearing hardly matters; he just never could stop doing it. He whoops because he vaults; he is a high jumper of the Sublime, and psychologically he could not avoid this. I quote the poem's final passage with relish and with puzzlement, for I am uncertain as to how good it may be, though it seems awful. Yet its awfulness is at least Sublime; it is not the drab, flat awfulness of Wordsworth at *his* common worst in *The Excursion* or even (heresy to admit this!) in so many passages of *The Prelude*—passages that we hastily skip by, feeling zeal and relief in getting at the great moments. Having just shouted out his odd version of Berkeley—that "life is a vision shadowy of truth"—Coleridge sees "the veiling clouds retire" and God appears in a blaze upon His Throne. Raised to a pitch of delirium by this vision, Coleridge soars aloft to join it:

> Contemplant Spirits! ye that hover o'er
> With untired gaze the immeasurable fount
> Ebullient with Creative Deity!
> And ye of plastic power, that interfused
> Roll through the grosser and material mass
> In organizing surge! Holies of God!
> (And what if Monads of the infinite mind?)
> I haply journeying my immortal course

Shall sometime join your mystic choir! Till then
I discipline my young and novice thought
In ministeries of heart-stirring song,
And aye on Meditation's heaven-ward wing
Soaring aloft I breathe the empyreal air
Of Love, omnific, omnipresent Love,
Whose day-spring rises glorious in my soul
As the great Sun, when he his influence
Sheds on the frost-bound waters—The glad stream
Flows to the ray and warbles as it flows.

Scholars agree that this not terribly pellucid passage somehow combines an early Unitarianism with a later orthodox overlay, as well as quantities of Berkeley, Hartley, Newton, Neoplatonism, and possibly more esoteric matter. A mere reader will primarily be reminded of Milton and will be in the right, for Milton counts here and the rest do not. The Spirits Coleridge invokes are Miltonic angels, though their functions seem to be more complicated. Coleridge confidently assures himself and us that his course is immortal, that he may end up as a Miltonic angel and so perhaps also as a monad of the infinite mind. In the meantime, he will study Milton's "heart-stirring song." Otherwise, all he needs is love, which is literally the air he breathes, the sunrise radiating out of his soul in a stream of song, and the natural sun toward which he flows, a sun that is not distinct from God. If we reflect on how palpably sincere this is, how wholehearted, and consider what was to be Coleridge's actual poetic course, we will be moved. Moved to what? Well, perhaps to remember a remark of Coleridge's: "There are many men, especially at the outset of life, who, in their too eager desire for the end, overlook the difficulties in the way; there is another class, who see nothing else. The first class may sometimes fail; the latter rarely succeed." Whatever the truth of this for other men, no poet becomes a strong poet unless he starts out with a certain obliviousness of the difficulties in the way. He will soon enough meet those difficulties, however, and one of them will be that his precursor and inspirer threatens to subsume him, as Coleridge is subsumed by Milton in "Religious Musings" and in his other pre-Wordsworthian poems. And here I shall digress massively before returning to Coleridge's poetry, for my discourse enters now upon the enchanted and baleful ground of poetic influence, through which I am learning to find my way by a singular light—one that will bear a little explanation.

I do not believe that poetic influence is simply something that happens, that it is just the process by which ideas and images are transmitted from earlier to later poets. In that view, whether or not influence causes anxiety in the later poet is a matter of temperament and circumstance. Poetic influence thus reduces to source-study, of the kind performed upon Coleridge by Lowes and later scholars. Coleridge was properly scornful of such study, and I think most critics learn how barren an enterprise it turns out to be. I myself have no use for it as such, and what I mean by the study of poetic influence turns source-study inside out. The first principle of the proper study of poetic influence, as I conceive it, is that no strong poem has sources and no strong poem merely alludes to another poem. The meaning of a strong poem is another strong poem, a precursor's poem which is being misinterpreted, revised, corrected, evaded, twisted askew, made to suffer an inclination or bias which is the property of the later and not the earlier poet. Poetic influence, in this sense, is actually misprision, a poet's taking or doing amiss of a parent-poem that keeps *finding* him, to use a Coleridgean turn of phrase. Yet even this misprision is only the first step that a new poet takes when he advances from the early phase where his precursor floods him to a more Promethean phase where he quests for his own fire—which must nevertheless be stolen from his precursor.

I count some half-dozen steps in the life cycle of the strong poet as he attempts to convert his inheritance into what will aid him without inhibiting him by the anxiety of a failure in priority, a failure to have begotten himself. These steps are revisionary ratios, and for the convenience of a shorthand, I find myself giving them arbitrary names that are proving useful to me and perhaps can be of use to others. I list them herewith, with descriptions but not examples, as this can only be a brief sketch; I must get back to Coleridge's poetry, with this list helpfully in hand, to find my examples in Coleridge.

1. *Clinamen*, which is poetic misprision proper. I take the word from Lucretius, where it means a "swerve" of the atoms so as to make change possible in the universe. The later poet swerves away from the precursor by so reading the parent-poem as to execute a *clinamen* in relation to it. This appears as the corrective movement of his own poem, which implies that the precursor poem went accurately up to a certain point but then should have swerved, precisely in the direction that the new poem moves.

2. *Tessera*, which is completion and antithesis. I take the word not from mosaic-making, where it is still used, but from the ancient Mystery cults, where it meant a token of recognition—the fragment, say, of a small pot which with

the other fragments would reconstitute the vessel. The later poet antithetically "completes" the precursor by so reading the parent-poem as to retain its teens but to mean them in an opposite sense, as though the precursor had failed to go far enough.

3. *Kenosis*, which is a breaking device similar to the defense mechanisms our psyches employ against repetition-compulsions; *kenosis* then is a movement toward discontinuity with the precursor. I take the word from St. Paul, where it means the humbling or emptying out of Jesus by himself when he accepts reduction from Divine to human status. The later poet, apparently emptying himself of his own afflatus, his imaginative godhood, seems to humble himself as though he ceased to be a poet, but this ebbing is so performed in relation to a precursor's poem-of-ebbing that the precursor is emptied out also, and so the later poem of deflation is not as absolute as it seems.

4. *Daemonization*, or a movement toward a personalized Counter-Sublime in reaction to the precursor's Sublime. I take the term from general Neoplatonic usage, where an intermediary being, neither Divine nor human, enters into the adept to aid him. The later poet opens himself to what he believes to be a power in the parent-poem that does not belong to the parent proper but to a range of being just beyond that precursor. He does this, in his poem, by so stationing its relation to the parent-poem as to generalize away the uniqueness of the earlier work.

5. *Askesis*, or a movement of self-purgation which intends the attainment of a state of solitude. I take the term, general as it is, particularly from the practice of pre-Socratic shamans like Empedocles. The later poet does not, as in *kenosis*, undergo a revisionary movement of emptying but of curtailing: he yields up part of his own human and imaginative endowment so as to separate himself from others, including the precursor, and he does this in his poem by so stationing it in regard to the parent-poem as to make that poem undergo an *askesis* also; the precursor's endowment is also truncated.

6. *Apophrades*, or the return of the dead. I take the word from the Athenian dismal or unlucky days upon which the dead returned to reinhabit the houses in which they

had lived. The later poet, in his own final phase, already burdened by an imaginative solitude that is almost a solipsism, holds his own poem so open again to the precursor's work that at first we might believe the wheel has come full circle and we are back in the later poet's flooded apprenticeship, before his strength began to assert itself in the revisionary ratios of *clinamen* and the others. But the poem is now held open to the precursor, where once it was open, and the uncanny effect is that the new poem's achievement makes it seem to us not as though the precursor were writing it, but as though the later poet himself had written the precursor's characteristic work.

These then are six revisionary ratios, and I think they can be observed, usually in cyclic appearance, in the life's work of every post-Enlightenment strong poet—which in English means, for practical purposes, every post-Miltonic strong poet. Coleridge, to return now to where I began, had the potential of the strong poet but—unlike Blake, Wordsworth, and the major poets after them down to Yeats and Stevens in our time—declined the full process of developing into one. Yet his work, even in its fragmentary state, demonstrates this revisionary cycle in spite of himself. My ulterior purpose in this discussion is to use Coleridge as an instance because he is apparently so poor an example of the cycle I have sketched. But that makes him a sterner test for my theory of influence than any other poet I could have chosen.

I return to Coleridge's first mature poetry and to its *clinamen* away from Milton, the Cowperizing turn that gave Coleridge the Conversation Poems, particularly "Frost at Midnight." Hazlitt quotes Coleridge as having said to him in the spring of 1798 that Cowper was the best modern poet, meaning the best since Milton, which was also Blake's judgment. Humphry House demonstrated the relation between "Frost at Midnight" and *The Task*—a happy one, causing no anxieties, where a stronger poet appropriates from a weaker one. Coleridge used Cowper as he used Bowles, Akenside, and Collins, finding in all of them hints that could help him escape the Miltonic influx that had drowned out "Religious Musings." "Frost at Midnight," like *The Task*, swerves away from Milton by softening him, by domesticating his style in a context that excludes all Sublime terrors. When Coleridge rises to his blessing of his infant son at the poem's conclusion he is in some sense poetically "misinterpreting" the beautiful declaration of Adam to Eve: "With thee conversing I forget all time," gentling the darker overtones of the infatuated Adam's declaration of love. Or, more simply, like Cowper he is not so much humanizing Milton—that will take the strenuous, head-on struggles of Blake, Wordsworth, Shelley, Keats—as he is making Milton more childlike, or perhaps better, reading Milton as though Milton loved in a more childlike way.

The revisionary step beyond this, an antithetical completion or *tessera*, is ventured by Coleridge only in a few pantheistic passages that sneaked past his orthodox censor, like the later additions to "The Eolian Harp" or the veiled vision at the end of the second verse paragraph of "This Lime-Tree Bower My Prison." With his horror of division, his endless quest for unity, Coleridge could not sustain any revisionary impulse which involved his reversing Milton or daring to complete that sacred father.

But the next revisionary ratio, the *kenosis* or self-emptying, seems to me almost obsessive in Coleridge's poetry, for what is the total situation of the Ancient Mariner but a repetition-compulsion, which his poet breaks for himself only by the writing of the poem and then only momentarily? Coleridge had contemplated an Epic on the Origin of Evil, but we may ask, Where would Coleridge, if pressed, have located the origin of evil in himself? His Mariner is neither depraved in will nor even disobedient, but merely ignorant, and the spiritual machinery his crime sets into motion is so ambiguously presented as to be finally beyond analysis. I would ask the question, What was Coleridge trying (not necessarily consciously) to do for himself by writing the poem? And by this question I do not mean Kenneth Burke's notion of trying to do something for oneself as a person. Rather, what was Coleridge the poet trying to do for himself as poet? To which I would answer: trying to free himself from the inhibitions of Miltonic influence by humbling his poetic self and so humbling the Miltonic in the process. The Mariner does not empty himself out; he starts empty and acquires a Primary Imagination through his suffering. But for Coleridge the poem is a *kenosis*, and what is being humbled is the Miltonic Sublime's account of the origin of evil. There is a reduction from disobedience to ignorance, from the self-aggrandizing consciousness of Eve to the painful awakening of a minimal consciousness in the Mariner.

The next revisionary step in clearing an imaginative space for a maturing strong poet is the Counter-Sublime, the attaining of which I have termed *daemonization*, and this I take to be the relation of "Kubla Khan" and "Christabel" to *Paradise Lost*. Far more than "The Rime of the Ancient Mariner," these poems demonstrate a tracking by Coleridge with powers that are *daemonic*, even though the "Rime" explicitly invokes Neoplatonic daemons in its marginal glosses. Opium was the avenging *daemon* or *alastor* of Coleridge's life, his Dark or Fallen Angel, his experiential acquaintance with Milton's Satan. Opium was for him what wandering and moral tale-telling became for the Mariner—the personal shape of repetition-compulsion. The lust for paradise in "Kubla Khan," Geraldine's lust for Christabel—these are manifestations of Coleridge's revisionary daemonization of Milton, these are Coleridge's Counter-Sublime. Poetic Genius, the genial spirit itself, Coleridge must see as daemonic when it is his own rather than when it is Milton's.

It is at this point in the revisionary cycle that Coleridge begins to back away decisively from the ferocity necessary for the strong poet. He does not sustain his *daemonization*; he closes his eyes in holy dread, stands outside the circumference of the *daemonic* agent, and is startled by his own sexual daring out of finishing "Christabel." He moved on to the revisionary ratio I have called *askesis*, or the purgation into solitude, the curtailing of some imaginative powers in the name of others. In doing so, he prophesied the pattern for Keats in "The Fall of Hyperion," since in his *askesis* he struggles against the influence of a composite poetic father, Milton-Wordsworth. The great poems of this *askesis* are "Dejection: An Ode" and "To William Wordsworth," where criticism has demonstrated to us how acute the revision of Wordsworth's stance is, and how much of himself Coleridge purges away to make this revision justified. I would add only that both poems misread Milton as sensitively and desperately as they do Wordsworth; the meaning of "Dejection" is in its relation to "Lycidas" as much as in its relation to the "Intimations" ode, even as the poem "To William Wordsworth" assimilates *The Prelude* to *Paradise Lost*. Trapped in his own involuntary dualisms, longing for a monistic wholeness such as he believes is found in Milton and Wordsworth, Coleridge in his *askesis* declines to see how much of his composite parent-poet he has purged away also.

After that, sadly enough, we have only a very few occasional poems of any quality by Coleridge, and they are mostly not the poems of a strong poet—that is, of a man vaulting into the Sublime. Having refused the full exercise of a strong poet's misprisions, Coleridge ceased to have poetic ambitions. But there are significant exceptions—the late manuscript fragment "Limbo" and the evidently still-later fragment "Ne Plus Ultra." Here, and I think here only, Coleridge experiences the particular reward of the strong poet in his last phase—what I have called the *apophrades* or return of the dead: not a Counter-Sublime but a negative Sublime, like the *Last Poems* of Yeats or *The Rock* of Stevens. Indeed negative sublimity is the mode of these Coleridgean fragments and indicates to us what Coleridge might have become had he permitted himself enough of the perverse zeal that the great poet must exhibit in malforming his great precursor.

"Limbo" and "Ne Plus Ultra" show that Coleridge could have become, at last, the poet of the Miltonic abyss, the bard of Demogorgon. Even as they stand, these fragments make us read Book II of *Paradise Lost* a little differently; they enable Coleridge to claim a corner of Milton's Chaos as his own.

Pater thought that Coleridge had succumbed to the Organic analogue because he hungered too intensively for eternity, as Lamb had said of his old school-friend. Pater also quoted De Quincey's summary of Coleridge: "He wanted better bread than can be made with wheat." I would add that Coleridge hungered also for an eternity of generosity between poets, as between people—a generosity that is not allowed in a world where each poet must struggle to individuate his own breath and this at the expense of his forebears as much as of his contemporaries. Perhaps also, to modify De Quincey, Coleridge wanted better poems than can be made without misprision.

I suggest then that the Organic analogue, with all its pragmatic neglect of the processes by which poems have to be produced, appealed so overwhelmingly to Coleridge because it seemed to preclude the anxiety of influence and to obviate the poet's necessity not just to unfold like a natural growth but to develop at the expense of others. Whatever the values of the Organic analogue for literary criticism—and I believe, with Pater, that it does more harm than good—it provided Coleridge with a rationale for a dangerous evasion of the inner steps he had to take for his own poetic development. As Blake might have said, Coleridge's imagination insisted upon slaying itself on the stems of generation—or, to invoke another Blakean image, Coleridge lay down to sleep upon the Organic analogue as though it were a Beulah-couch of soft, moony repose.

What was our loss in this? What poems might a stronger Coleridge have composed? The *Notebooks* list *The Origin of Evil, an Epic Poem*; *Hymns to the Sun, the Moon, and the Elements—six hymns*; and, more fascinating even than these, a scheme for an epic on "the destruction of Jerusalem" by the Romans. Still more compelling is a March 1802 entry in the *Notebooks*: "Milton, a Monody in the metres of Samson's Choruses—only with more rhymes/—poetical influences—political-moral-Dr. Johnson/." Consider the date of this entry—only a month before the first draft of "Dejection"—and some sense of what *Milton, a Monody* might have been begins to be generated. In March 1802, William Blake, in the midst of his sojourn at Hayley's Felpham, was deep in the composition of *Milton: a Poem in 2 Books, To Justify the Ways of God to Men*. In the brief, enigmatic notes for *Milton, a Monody* Coleridge sets down "—poetical influences—political-moral-Dr. Johnson," the last being, we can assume, a refutation of

Johnson's vision of Milton in *The Lives of the Poets*, a refutation that Cowper and Blake would have endorsed. "Poetical influences," Coleridge says, and we may recall that this is one of the themes of Blake's *Milton*, where the Shadow of the Poet Milton is one with the Covering Cherub, the great blocking agent who inhibits fresh human creativity by embodying in himself all the sinister beauty of tradition. Blake's *Milton* is a kind of monody in places, not as a mourning for Milton, but as Milton's own, solitary utterance as he goes down from a premature Eternity (where he is unhappy) to struggle again in fallen time and space. I take it though that *Milton, a Monody* would have been modeled upon Coleridge's early "Monody on the Death of Chatterton" and so would have been Coleridge's lamentation for his Great Original. Whether, as Blake was doing at precisely the same time, Coleridge would have dared to identify Milton as the Covering Cherub, as the angel or *daemon* blocking Coleridge himself out from the poet's paradise, I cannot surmise. I wish deeply that Coleridge had written the poem.

It is ungrateful, I suppose, as the best of Coleridge's recent scholars keep telling us, to feel that Coleridge did not give us the poems he had it in him to write. Yet we have, all apology aside, only a double handful of marvelous poems by him. I close therefore by attempting a description of the kind of poem I believe Coleridge's genius owed us and which we badly need, and always will need. I would maintain that the finest achievement of the High Romantic poets of England was their humanization of the Miltonic Sublime. But when we attend deeply to the works where this humanization is most strenuously accomplished—Blake's *Milton* and *Jerusalem*, Wordsworth's *Prelude*, Shelley's *Prometheus Unbound*, Keats's two *Hyperions*, even in a way Byron's *Don Juan*—we sense at last a quality lacking, a quality in which Milton abounds for all his severity. This quality, though not in itself a tenderness, made Milton's Eve possible, and we miss such a figure in all her Romanic descendants. More than the other five great Romantic poets, Coleridge was able, by temperament and by subtly shaded intellect, to have given us a High Romantic Eve, a total humanization of the tenderest and most appealing element in the Miltonic Sublime. Many anxieties blocked Coleridge from that rare accomplishment, and of these the anxiety of influence was not the least.

Lord Byron

(1788-1824)

> but man's life it thought,
> And he, despite his terror, cannot cease
> Ravening through century after century,
> Ravening, raging, and uprooting that he may come
> Into the desolation of reality.
>
> —W.B. YEATS

PROMETHEAN MAN

Childe Harold's Pilgrimage

BYRON'S PILGRIMAGE AS POET WILL BE INTRODUCED HERE BY A STUDY OF this series of poems, as we might regard them. Cantos I and II (1812) are merely a descriptive medley, mixing travel and history. Canto III (1816) is a poem in the confessional mode of Rousseau and Wordsworth, and marks Byron's first imaginative maturity. Canto IV (1818) attempts a synthesis of the two previous poems. In it, Byron and Italy are alternatively obsessive themes, and fail to balance, so that Canto III remains probably the best poem of the sequence.

The entire series Byron called *A Romaunt*, and both the title and the verse form (the Spenserian stanza) derive from the romance tradition. The quest-theme of romance previously internalized by Blake and Wordsworth appears again in Shelley's *Alastor* and Keats's *Endymion* under Wordsworth's influence. Canto III of *Childe Harold* manifests a more superficial Wordsworthian influence, probably owing both to Byron's relationship with Shelley in 1816 and to his own reading of *The Excursion*. The theme of a quest away from alienation and toward an unknown good is recurrent in the Romantics, and Byron would have come to it without Wordsworth and Shelley, though perhaps then only in the less interesting way of Cantos I and II.

The alienation of Harold in Canto I is hardly profound, though peculiarly relevant both to Byron's time and to ours:

> Worse than adversity the Childe befell;
> He felt the fulness of satiety.

He has run through Sin's long labyrinth, is sick at heart, and more than a little weary. So are we as we read Cantos I and II, though this is more the fault of his imitators than it is of Byron. Too many Byronic heroes have moved across too many screens, and Byron's rhetoric in Cantos I and II is not yet supple enough to keep us from making the association between the master and his disciples:

> Yet oft-times in his maddest mirthful mood
> Strange pangs would flash along Childe Harold's brow,
> As if the memory of some deadly feud
> Or disappointed passion lurk'd below:
> But this none knew, nor haply cared to know;
> For his was not that open, artless soul
> That feels relief by bidding sorrow flow,
> Nor sought he friend to counsel or condole,
> Whate'er this grief more be, which he could not control.

Most of what follows, in these first two cantos, has been described, quite aptly, as "the rhymed diary of two years' travel." What counts in these cantos is the first emergence of Byron's Romantic hero, Promethean Man, who will reach his culmination as Manfred and Cain, and then be replaced by Don Juan. Manfred and Cain are ravaged humanists, though they acquire some diabolical coloring. Childe Harold is scarcely even a vitalist until Canto III, and ends his quest in Canto IV by implying that the posture of pilgrimage is itself a value worth the affirming. We can agree, provided this pilgrimage has an imaginative element, an energy of vision and creation powerful enough to convert its spiritual emptiness into a deliberate theme. This is in fact Byron's great achievement in the third and fourth cantos; his faltering Prometheanism becomes the vehicle for myth. The myth concerns the condition of European man in the Age of Metternich, and is presented in and by the person of the Pilgrim, a complex wanderer who shares only a name with the Childe Harold of the Romantic guidebook that is Cantos I and II.

Canto III opens with Byron's departure into voluntary exile, as he regrets the loss of his child, left behind with the estranged Lady Byron. The poet gives himself to the ocean's guidance, and is content to go "wher'er the surge may sweep." As he is borne on by wind and water, he states the nature of his alienation. No wonder awaits him; his deeds have pierced the depth of life. His heart has grown hard, having endured too much love, sorrow, fame, ambition, strife. Most important, his thought is now turned away from ordinary reality and towards the refuge of "lone caves, yet rife with airy images," and the visionary shapes of "the soul's haunted cell." Fleeing England, he escapes into his poem, and affirms a therapeutic aesthetic idealism:

> 'Tis to create, and in creating live
> A being more intense, that we endow
> With form our fancy, gaining as we give
> The life we image, even as I do now.
> What am I? Nothing: but not so art thou,
> Soul of my thought! with whom I traverse earth,
> Invisible but gazing, as I glow
> Mix'd with thy spirit, blended with thy birth,
> And feeling still with thee in my crush'd feeling's dearth.

Thought seeks refuge in the creation of poetry, for by it we gain more life, even as Byron gains in the life he images. His own limitations are transcended as he blends himself with the birth of what he creates. Rousseau, in Shelley's *Triumph of Life*, returns from this transcendental illusion to the reality of natural limitation. Byron is so wavering in his own aspiration that he turns from it in his very next stanza:

> Yet must I think less wildly:—I *have* thought
> Too long and darkly, till my brain became,
> In its own eddy boiling and o'erwrought,
> A whirling gulf of phantasy and flame.

Yet to cease in this wild thinking is to submit one's thoughts to others, and Byron says of his Childe Harold *persona*:

> He would not yield dominion of his mind
> To spirits against whom his own rebell'd.

This might be Manfred speaking. And again like Manfred, Harold turns to the mountains for companionship, for "they spake a mutual language." But between the Pilgrim and the Alps lies "an Empire's dust," the legacy of the fallen Titan, Napoleon. The poem pauses to brood on the fate of Prometheanism, and to read in Napoleon the same spirit, "antithetically mixt," that reigns in the Pilgrim. Napoleon is either "more or less than man," yet falls through an aspiration beyond man's hope:

> But quiet to quick bosoms is a hell,
> And *there* hath been thy bane; there is a fire
> And motion of the soul which will not dwell
> In its own narrow being, but aspire
> Beyond the fitting medium of desire;
> And, but once kindled, quenchless evermore,
> Preys upon high adventure, nor can tire
> Of aught but rest; a fever at the core,
> Fatal to him who bears, to all who ever bore.

Blake or Shelley would not have acknowledged that desire had a fitting medium, though Shelley frequently emphasizes its fatality to him who bears it. Byron is already caught between admiration and disapproval of those whose "breath is agitation," of "all that expands the spirit, yet appals." Unlike Wordsworth but like Shelley, he seeks the summits of nature not for their own sake but because they show "how Earth may pierce to Heaven, yet leave vain man below." Nor does Byronic solitude much resemble the Wordsworthian kind. Wordsworth goes apart the better to hear humanity's still sad music emanate from nature. Byron desires to be alone that he may "love Earth only for its earthly sake." If he lives not in himself, it is only to become a portion of the nature around him, and so to evade the burden of being a man, "a link reluctant in a fleshly chain."

Rather unfairly, Byron attributes the same desire to Rousseau, a greater Promethean than Napoleon or Byron:

> His love was passion's essence:—as a tree
> On fire by lightning, with ethereal flame
> Kindled he was, and blasted; for to be
> Thus, and enamour'd, were in him the same.

The fire stolen from Heaven both kindles and blasts, and in Rousseau, human love is one with the stolen flame and in turn becomes existence itself. Byron praises Rousseau as inspired, but dismisses him as "phrensied by disease or woe," an anticipation of modern Babbitry toward

Rousseau's genius. Byron's ambivalence is a necessary consequence of the extraordinary view of the natural world that *Childe Harold's Pilgrimage* develops. Every element given to man is simultaneously a way to moral greatness and divine blessing, and also a quicker way to self-deception and damnation. Every human act that widens consciousness increases both exaltation and despair. No other poet has insisted on maintaining both views with equal vigor, and one can wonder if Byron ever justifies his deliberate moral confusion by fully converting its aesthetic consequences into personal myth.

In Canto IV Byron reaches Rome, the goal of his Pilgrimage, and is moved by its aesthetic greatness to intensify his statement of negations. The mind is diseased by its own beauty, and this auto-intoxication fevers into false creation. So much for the Romantic Imagination. Disease, death, bondage become an obsessive litany:

> Our life is a false nature—'tis not in
> The harmony of things,—this hard decree,
> This uneradicable taint of sin,
> This boundless upas, this all-blasting tree
> Whose root is earth, whose leaves and branches be
> The skies which rain their plagues on men like dew—
> Disease, death, bondage—all the woes we see,
> And worse, the woes we see not—which throb through
> The immedicable soul, with heart-aches ever new.

As Mr. Flosky says in Peacock's *Nightmare Abbey*, after hearing Mr. Cypress (Byron) paraphrase this stanza, we have here "a most delightful speech, Mr. Cypress. A most amiable and instructive philosophy. You have only to impress its truth on the minds of all living men, and life will then, indeed, be the desert and the solitude." But this is to miss, however wittily, the direction of Byron's rhetoric, which does not seek to persuade, but to expose. Mr. Cypress is a marvelous creation, and we are sad to see him depart "to rake seas and rivers, lakes and canals, for the moon of ideal beauty," but he is a better satire upon Childe Harold than he is on Byron the Pilgrim. Mr. Cypress sings a song that ends as Childe Harold might be pleased to end, knowing that "the soul is its own monument." Byron as the Pilgrim of Eternity refuses to yield the human value of his life to his own vision of all-consuming sin:

> But I have lived, and have not lived in vain:
> My mind may lose its force, my blood its fire,

And my frame perish even in conquering pain;
But there is that within me which shall tire
Torture and Time, and breathe when I expire;
Something unearthly, which they deem not of,
Like the remember d tone of a mute lyre,
Shall on their soften'd spirits sink, and move
In hearts all rocky now the late remorse of love.

What survives, as in Shelley, is "like the remember'd tone of a mute lyre." In this case, that means the continued reverberation of this stanza, which accurately predicts its own survival. Seeking an image for such aesthetic immortality, Byron turns to the plastic art around him in Rome. Gazing at the Apollo Belvedere, he sees the statue with the approving eye of neoclassic aesthetics, a doctrine of stoic and firm control, of the selected moment or incident that shall be both representative and exemplary:

Or view the Lord of the unerring bow,
The God of life, and poesy, and light
The Sun in human limbs array'd, and brow
All radiant from his triumph in the fight;
The shaft hath just been shot—the arrow bright
With an immortal's vengeance; in his eye
And nostril beautiful disdain, and might
And majesty, flash their full lightnings by,
Developing in that one glance the Deity.

In the next stanza this statue's informing conception is called "a ray of immortality." Just as Byron, in this poem, makes no attempt to reconcile his conviction of the value of human aspiration with his conviction of sin, so he does not try to bring into harmony this neoclassic aesthetic and Rousseau's vision of art as expressive therapy or Wordsworth's more active theory of a poet's creation. A subsequent stanza demonstrates Byron's awareness of the conflict within his own views:

And if it be Prometheus stole from Heaven
The fire which we endure, it was repaid
By him to whom the energy was given
Which this poetic marble hath array'd
With an eternal glory—which, if made
By human hands, is not of human thought;
And Time himself hath hallow'd it, nor laid

One ringlet in the dust—nor hath it caught
A tinge of years, but breathes the flame with which 'twas
wrought.

The Promethean fire we "endure" rather than enjoy, for its origin is illicit; it was stolen. We repay the Titan for the gift of creative energy by a work like this statue, but though the work is of human hands, it is not of human thought. Byron is enough of a Romantic to credit the artist with Promethean energy, but is also too uneasy about the autonomy of Imagination to credit timelessness to a merely human conception. The statue breathes the stolen flame that wrought it, but the aid of more than human inspiration vivifies it.

The timelessness of art ends the wanderings of Byron's Pilgrim, for he comes to rest before the beauty of Rome, his search accomplished. Byron concludes the poem by offering his Pilgrim to the reader as a means of aesthetic grace of the kind the statue of Apollo has supplied to the Pilgrim himself:

Ye! who have traced the Pilgrim to the scene
Which is his last, if in your memories dwell
A thought which once was his, if on ye swell
A single recollection, not in vain
He wore his sandal-shoon and scallop-shell;
Farewell! with *him* alone may rest the pain,
If such there were—with *you*, the moral of his strain.

The Pilgrim has been a catharsis for his creator, who has sought by his creation to transvalue exile and wandering into an essential good appropriate for a generation whose Titanic force is spent. In an age of reaction and repression the heroic spirit must roam, must indulge the residue of a Promethean endowment, but without yielding to it utterly. Somewhere in the endurance of human art an ultimate value must lie, but Byron cannot give a final assent to any view of human nature or art available to him. In this powerful skepticism that refuses to be a skepticism, but throws itself intensely at rival modes of feeling and thought, the peculiar moral and aesthetic value of Byron's poetry comes into initial being. *Childe Harold's Pilgrimage* has passion and conflict without balance. We turn elsewhere in Byron to find both a clearer exaltation of the Promethean and a firmer control of the critical attitude that seeks to chasten and correct this immense energy.

"Prometheus"

In July 1816, in Switzerland, Byron wrote a short ode in three strophes, "Prometheus." Composed at the same time as the third canto of *Childe Harold's Pilgrimage*, this ode gathers together the diffused Titanism of the romance, and emphasizes the heroic rather than the sinful aspect of Prometheus' achievement and fate. Yet even here there is a troubled undersong, and a refusal to neglect the darker implications of the fire stolen from Heaven. The overt celebration of human aspiration is properly dominant, but is all the more impressive for the juxtaposition of Byron's darker intimations. The gift of fire is the basis of Byron's art and theme, but the gift is unsanctioned by the withdrawn but responsible Power that has lawful possession of energy. Byron's entire poetic career at its most serious—here, in *Manfred, Cain, Don Juan, The Vision of Judgment*—can be understood as an attempt to justify the theft of fire by creating with its aid, while never forgetting that precisely such creation intensifies the original Promethean "Godlike crime." Byron, in this, writes in the line of Milton's prophetic fears, as do Blake in *The Marriage of Heaven and Hell* and Shelley in *Prometheus Unbound*. The fallen Angels in *Paradise Lost* compose poetic laments and celebrations for their Fall and of their deeds respectively, while Satan journeys through Chaos. Milton rises with immense relief from the abyss he so powerfully creates, and the temptations of Prometheanism constitute the dangers he has escaped. The invocations in *Paradise Lost* exist to establish Milton's hope that his inspiration is Divine, and not Promethean and hence Satanic. Byron has no such hope; his inspiration is both glorious and sinful, and his creation glorifies human aspiration (and his own) and increases human culpability.

The ode "Prometheus" defies the sufferings consequent upon such guilt, though it recognizes their reality:

> Titan! to whose immortal eyes
>   The sufferings of mortality,
>   Seen in their sad reality,
> Were not as things that gods despise;
> What was thy pity's recompense?
> A silent suffering, and intense;
> The rock, the vulture, and the chain,
> All that the proud can feel of pain,
> The agony they do not show,
> The suffocating sense of woe,
>   Which speaks but in its loneliness,

And then is jealous lest the sky
Should have a listener, nor will sigh
   Until its voice is echoless.

This begins as the Prometheus of Aeschylus, but the emphasis on the pride of silent suffering starts to blend the Titan into the figure of Byron the Pilgrim of Eternity, who does not show his agony, but whose sense of radical sin is suffocating, and who speaks to the mountains in the glory of mutual solitude. This first strophe commends Prometheus as an accurate as well as compassionate observer of human reality, the function Byron tries to fulfill in his poetry. The start of the second strophe dares to attribute directly to the Titan the Byronic conflict of negations:

Titan! to thee the strife was given
   Between the suffering and the will,
   Which torture where they cannot kill.

Prometheus suffers most, like Byron, in the conflict between his sympathy for and participation in human suffering, and the impious drive of his will in gloriously but sinfully bringing relief to humanity. Byron's will cannot bring fire to us, but can create an art that returns the Titanic gift with the human offering of a poem, itself a mark of creative grace but also an agency of further suffering, as it increases our guilt. This rather vicious circularity, a distinctive feature of Byron's view of existence, is very evident in *Childe Harold's Pilgrimage* and enters into the final strophe of "Prometheus." Byron rises to his theme's power with a firmness of diction and mastery of rhythm that his lyrical verse does not often manifest:

Thy Godlike crime was to be kind,
   To render with thy precepts less
   The sum of human wretchedness,
And strengthen Man with his own mind;
But baffled as thou Overt from high,
Still in thy patient energy,
In the endurance, and repulse
   Of thine impenetrable Spirit,
Which Earth and Heaven could not convulse,
   A mighty lesson we inherit.

The Titan's kindness was "Godlike," yet remains a crime. The Promethean gift would have strengthened Man by making the human mind immortal, but the gift's full efficacy was baffled by God. The stolen fire, thus imperfectly received, is itself a torture to us. What survives unmixed in our Titanic inheritance is the emblem of "patient energy," the endurance that will make Manfred's Spirit impenetrable. Prometheus and Man alike fall short of perfection, and so share one tragic fate, but they share also in a triumphant force:

> Thou art a symbol and a sign
>   To mortals of their fate and force;
> Like thee, Man is in part divine,
>   A troubled stream from a pure source;
> And Man in portions can foresee
> His own funereal destiny;
> His wretchedness, and his resistance,
> And his sad unallied existence:
> To which his Spirit may oppose
> Itself—and equal to all woes,
>   And a firm will, and a deep sense,
> Which even in torture can descry
>   Its own concenter'd recompense,
>   Triumphant where it dares defy,
>   And making Death a Victory.

What is confused, here and throughout Byron, is the attitude toward divinity. The "inexorable Heaven" of the second strophe, which creates for its own pleasure "the things it may annihilate," is nevertheless to be identified with the "pure source" from which Prometheus and Man are only troubled streams. Byron insists upon having it both ways, and he cannot overcome the imaginative difficulties created by his spiritual shuffling. Man's destiny is "funereal," for his "sad unallied existence" is detached from God; such are the consequences of Man's Promethean fall. Byron is like Blake's Rintrah, a voice presaging a new revelation but too passionate and confused to speak its own clear truth. The concentrated requital for Man's tortured striving is merely the glory of a defiant defeat. It is only by making Heaven altogether remote that Byron goes further in *Manfred*, where a defiant Titanism at last attains to its imaginative limits.

Manfred

Manfred, Byron thought, was "of a very wild, metaphysical, and inexplicable kind." The kind is that of Goethe's *Faust* and Shelley's *Prometheus*, the

Romantic drama of alienation and renewal, of the self purged by the self. *Faust* strives for the universal, and *Prometheus* is apocalyptic; *Manfred* is overtly personal, and is meant as a despairing triumph of self, and a denial of the efficacy of even a Titanic purgation. The crime of Manfred is that of Byron, incest deliberately and knowingly undertaken. Oedipus gropes in the dark, the light bursts upon him, and outwardly he allows the light to pass judgment upon him. Manfred, like Byron, claims the right of judging himself.

The Manfred we first encounter in the drama has elements in him of Faust and of Hamlet. The setting is in the Higher Alps, where he has his castle. The opening scene is as it must be: Manfred alone, in a Gothic gallery, and midnight the time. By his deep art he summons a condemned star, his own, and attendant spirits. He asks forgetfulness of self; they offer him only power, and suggest he seek his oblivion in death, but refuse to vouchsafe he will find it there. They serve him only with scorn for his mortality; he replies with Promethean pride. His star manifests itself as Astarte, his sister and mistress, but she vanishes when he attempts to embrace her, and he falls senseless. A spirit song is sung over him, which marks him of the brotherhood of Cain.

The second scene is the next morning out on the cliffs. Manfred, alone, soliloquizes like Milton's Satan on Mount Niphates. But Byron's reference here is a deliberate and critical parody. Satan on Nephates has his crisis of conscience and realizes the depth of his predicament, but refuses to believe that he can escape the self he has chosen, and so is driven at last to the frightening inversion "Evil, be thou my good." Manfred, like Satan, sees the beauty of the universe, but avers that he cannot feel it and declines therefore to love it. But he then proceeds to declare its felt beauty. Like Hamlet, and curiously like Satan, he proclaims his weariness of the human condition:

> Half dust, half deity, alike unfit
> To sink or soar.

He desires to sink to destruction, or soar to a still greater destruction, but either way to cease being human. His attempted suicide is frustrated by a kindly peasant, but the wine offered to revive him has blood upon the brim, and his incestuous act is made directly equivalent to murder:

> I say 'tis blood—my blood! the pure warm stream
> Which ran in the veins of my fathers, and in ours
> When we were in our youth, and had one heart,
> And loved each other as we should not love,

And this was shed: but still it rises up,
Colouring the clouds, that shut me out from heaven.

With his crime established, Manfred descends to a lower valley in the Alps, where he confronts a cataract that he identifies with the steed of Death in the Apocalypse. In a marvelous invention, he calls up the Witch of the Alps, a Shelleyan spirit of amoral natural beauty. To her he speaks an idealized history of the outcast Romantic poet, the figure of the youth as natural quester for what nature has not to give, akin to the idealized portraits of self in Shelley's *Alastor* and Keats's *Endymion*. But the incest motif transforms the quester myth into the main theme of *Manfred*, the denial of immortality if it means yielding up the human glory of our condition, yet accompanied by a longing to transcend that condition. The Witch stands for everything in *Manfred* that is at once magical and preternatural. She scorns the Mage for not accepting immortality, and offers him oblivion if he will serve her. With the fine contempt that he displays throughout for all spirits that are not human, Manfred dismisses her. At no time in the play is Manfred anything but grave and courteous to his servants, the poor hunter, and the meddling Abbot who comes to save his soul. To the machinery of the poem, which he himself continually evokes, he is hostile always. This is most striking when he glides arrogantly into the Hall of Arimanes, the chief of dark spirits, and a veil for the Christian devil.

Arimanes is a Gnostic Satan; like Blake's Satan, he is the god of the natural world, worshiped by the three Fates and by Nemesis, who is a very rough version of the dialectical entity Shelley was to call Demogorgon. Manfred refuses to worship Arimanes, but the dark god nevertheless yields to the poet's request and the Phantom of Astarte appears. Manfred asks her to forgive or condemn him, but she declines, and cannot be compelled by Arimanes, as she belongs "to the other powers," the infinitely remote hidden god of light. But at an appeal from Manfred which is both very human in its pathos and essentially Calvinistic in its temper, she yields just enough to speak her brother's name, to tell him "tomorrow ends thy earthly ills," and to give a last farewell. She leaves a momentarily convulsed Manfred, who is first scorned and then grimly valued in a fine dialogue of demonic spirits:

> *A Spirit*. He is convulsed—This is to be a mortal
> And seek the things beyond mortality.
> *Another Spirit*. Yet, see, he mastereth himself, and makes
> His torture tributary to his will.

Had he been one of us, he would have made
An awful spirit.

The final act rejects Christian comfort with an intensity that comes
from a ferocious quasi-Calvinism. The Abbot seeks to reconcile Manfred
"with the true church, and through the church to Heaven," but Manfred
has no use for mediators. The last scene is in the mountains again, within
a lonely tower where Manfred awaits his end. The Spirits of Arimanes
come to claim him, as the Abbot utters ineffectual exorcisms. In two
remarkable speeches, Manfred's Prometheanism manifests its glory. By
power of will he thrusts the demons back, in repudiation of the Faust legend, and dies his own human death, yielding only to himself:

> The mind which is immortal makes itself
> Requital for its good or evil thoughts,—
> Is its own origin of ill and end—
> And its own place and time: its innate sense,
> When stripp'd of this mortality, derives
> No colour from the fleeting things without,
> But is absorb'd in sufferance or in joy,
> Born from the knowledge of its own desert.

The ultimate model here is again Milton's Satan, who hails his infernal world and urges it to receive its new possessor:

> One who brings
> A mind not to be chang'd by Place or Time.
> The mind is its own place, and in itself
> Can make a Heav'n of Hell, a Hell of Heav'n.

Marlowe's Mephistopheles tells his Faustus that "where we are is
hell." The Devil is an inverted Stoic; we have an idea of ill, and from it we
taste an ill savor. Iago with his blend of the Stoic and the Calvinist is closer to Manfred; both beings, like Webster's Lodovico, could say of their
work that they had limned their night pieces and took pride in the result.
Manfred is a Gothic poet who has written his own tragedy with himself as
protagonist. The Machiavellian villain plots the destruction of others,
whether he himself be man like Iago or demon like Mephistopheles. But,
as Northrop Frye remarks in his theory of myths, "the sense of awfulness
belonging to an agent of catastrophe can also make him something more
like the high priest of a sacrifice." Frye points to Webster's Bosola in *The*

Duchess of Malfi as an example. In the Romantic period this figure becomes a high priest who sacrifices himself, like Manfred or Prometheus. The analogue to Christ hovers in the Romantic background. But to what god does Manfred give himself?

Manfred's last words are a proud, naturalistic farewell to the Abbot:

Old man! 'tis not so difficult to die.

Yet even the defiance here is gracious, for the dying Manfred has previously said to the Abbot, "Give me thy hand." Byron insisted that Manfred's last words contained "the whole effect and moral of the poem." The death of Manfred is clearly a release, not a damnation, for his burden of consciousness has long been his punishment. He drives off the demons, who are not so much seeking to drag him down to an inferno of punishment as trying to compel a human will to abandon itself as being inadequate. Manfred has no assurance of oblivion as he dies, but he has the Promethean satisfaction of having asserted the supremacy of the human will over everything natural or preternatural that would oppose it. The supernatural or spiritual world does not enter into the poem; Manfred's relations, if any, with heavenly grace are necessarily a mystery. His rejection of the Abbot is merely to deny a mediator's relevance.

Cain

Byron went further, into mystery itself, in his dramatic piece *Cain* (1821). Manfred's crime of incest is paralleled by Cain's crime of murder, for Manfred's complete knowing of his sister destroyed her, and Cain's destruction of his brother completes an act of knowledge. Byron's radical conception makes Cain the direct ancestor of a tradition that has not yet exhausted itself, that of the artist not just as passive outcast but as deliberate criminal seeking the conditions for his art by violating the moral sanctions of his society.

For Byron, Cain is the first Romantic. Hazlitt best typifies the Romantic in his portrait of Rousseau: "He had the most intense consciousness of his own existence. No object that had once made an impression on him was ever effaced. Every feeling in his mind became a passion."

This is true of Byron also, and of Cain. The tragedy of Cain is that he cannot accomplish his spiritual awakening without developing an intensity of consciousness which he is ill-prepared to sustain. His imaginativeness flowers into murderousness, as it will later in the terrible protagonists of Dostoevsky. The dialectic that entraps Byron's Cain is simplistic and inexorable. Cain suspects that Jehovah is malicious, and identifies his own exclusion from Paradise with the ultimate punishment of death, which he does not feel he deserves. Lucifer presents him with evidence that an age of innocence existed even before Adam. Cain fears death, but Lucifer hints that death leads to the highest knowledge. As Northrop Frye points out, this "links itself at once with Cain's own feeling that the understanding of death is his own ultimate victory—in other words, with the converse principle that the highest knowledge leads to death." Cain is mistaken because he does not go far enough imaginatively; he moves to a mere negation of the moral law, a simple inversion of Jehovah's repressive ethic. And yet Byron gives him a capacity to have accomplished more than this. At the climactic moment, when Abel has offered up a lamb in sacrifice to Jehovah, and urges his brother to emulate him, Cain offers instead the first fruits of the earth. Abel prays, abasing himself. Cain speaks his defiance directly to Jehovah:

> If a shrine without victim,
> And altar without gore, may win thy favour,
> Look on it! and for him who dresseth it,
> He is—such as thou mad'st him; and seeks nothing
> Which must be won by kneeling: if he's evil,
> Strike him! thou art omnipotent, and may'st—
> For what can he oppose? If he be good,
> Strike him, or spare him, as thou wilt! since all
> Rests upon thee; and good and evil seem
> To have no power themselves, save in thy will;
> And whether that be good or ill I know not,
> Not being omnipotent, nor fit to judge
> Omnipotence, but merely to endure
> Its mandate; which thus far I have endured.

This powerfully ironic speech acquires, in context, the further irony of the demonic, for it precedes the sacrifice of Abel to his brother's inadequately awakened consciousness of man's freedom. God accepts Abel's lamb, and rejects the fruits of the earth. Cain overthrows his brother's altar, in the name of the creation. When Abel interposes himself and cries that he loves God far more than life, he provokes his brother to murder in the name of life and the earth. The act done, the terrible irony of having brought death into the world by his very quest for life destroys Cain's spirit:

> Oh, earth!
> For all the fruits thou hast render'd to me, I
> Give thee back this.

This is the self-imposed culmination of Byron's Prometheanism. We can leave Blake to make the apt answer, before we pass to the satiric poems in which Byron found a less arbitrary balance for his divided universe. Blake replied to *Cain* with the dramatic scene he called *The Ghost of Abel* (1822), addressed "to Lord Byron in the wilderness." Byron is in the state that precedes prophecy, an Elijah or John the Baptist prefiguring a coming of the truth, and his *Cain* prepares Blake's way before him for *The Ghost of Abel*. Byron's error, in Blake's judgment, is to have insisted that the Imagination necessarily participates in the diabolical, so that the poet must be exile, outcast, and finally criminal. This is the pattern of Byron's obsession with incest, an element present in *Cain* in the beautiful relationship between Adah and Cain, who are both sister and brother, and husband and wife. The murder of Abel, in Byron, is a crime of Imagination; not of passion or society. In Blake, as Frye says, "murder cannot be part of genius but is always part of morality," for genius breaks not only with conventional virtue but with conventional vice as well. Byron could not free himself from societal conventions, and so his Promethean poems do not show us the real man, the Imagination, fully at work within him. The digressive, satirical poems and the handful of late lyrics of personal reappraisal come closer to a full expressiveness. The values of the sequence from *Childe Harold* to *Cain* still exist, but Byron's achievement in them is dwarfed by the great Romantic poems of Titanic aspiration, the Ninth Night of *The Four Zoas* and *Prometheus Unbound*.

THE DIGRESSIVE BALANCE

Beppo

Writing to his publisher, John Murray, in October 1817, Byron expressed his admiration for a poem by John Hookham Frere published earlier in the same year. This work, under the pseudonym "Whistlecraft," is an imitation of the Italian "medley-poem," written in *ottava rima*, and inaugurated by the fifteenth-century poet Pulci in his *Morgante Maggiore*. The form is mock-heroic or satirical romance, and the style digressive, colloquial, realistic. Byron, in imitating Frere, had at first no notion that he had stumbled on what was to be his true mode of writing:

I have written a story in eighty-nine stanzas in imitation of him, called *Beppo* (the short name for Giuseppe, that is, the *Joe* of the Italian Joseph), which I shall throw you into the balance of the fourth canto to help you round to your money; but you had perhaps better publish it anonymously.

Beppo, thus offered to Murray as a throw-in with the last canto of *Childe Harold*, is a permanent and delightful poem, and hardly one to need anonymous publication, which it received in 1818. Byron's caution and respect for convention were characteristic, but he had embarked neverthe-less on the great venture of his career, for out of *Beppo* came the greater poems, *Don Juan* and *The Vision of Judgment*, in which the poet at last found aesthetic balance and an individual ethos.

The story of *Beppo*, based on an anecdote of Venetian life told to Byron by the husband of one of his Venetian mistresses, is so slight as to need only a few stanzas of narration. The final version of the poem con-tains ninety-nine stanzas, and could as effectively go on for ninety-nine more, for the poem's point is in its charming digressiveness. The Venice of Byron's prose (and life) suddenly flowers in his verse, and the man himself is before us, all but unconcealed.

Venice and the Carnival before Lent set the place and time:

> This feast is named the Carnival, which being
> Interpreted, implies "farewell to flesh."

As the Venetians "bid farewell to carnal dishes," to "guitars and every other sort of strumming," and to "other things which may be had for asking," Byron moves among them with an eye of kindly irony. *Beppo*, like the Carnival, is an escape into freedom. For a little while, as he thinks, Byron puts aside the world of *Childe Harold*, and the Pilgrim becomes a man who can live in the present. After the introduction, *Beppo* digresses on the happy and parallel themes of Venetian women and gondolas, until Byron introduces his heroine, Laura, whose husband, Beppo, has sailed east on business and failed to return. After a long wait, and a little weeping, she takes a Count as protector:

> He was a lover of the good old school,
> Who still become more constant as they cool.

This leads to a digression on the amiable institution of the "Cavalier Servente," and so to Byron in Italy, who was to play that role for the Countess Teresa Guiccioli, the great love of the poet's life after his half-sister Augusta.

Praises of the Italian climate, landscape, and way of life are followed by Byron's appreciation for Italy's chief adornments, the language and the women:

> I love the language, that soft bastard Latin,
>> Which melts like kisses from a female mouth.

This provides a contrast for a backward glance at England, with its "harsh northern whistling, grunting guttural," its "cloudy climate" and "chilly women." Remembering the circumstances of his exile, Byron shrugs himself off as "a broken Dandy lately on my travels" and takes Laura and the Count, after a six-year relationship, off to a Carnival ball, where Laura encounters a Turk who is the returned Beppo. A digression on Moslem sexual ways flows into another upon authors, which includes an oblique glance at Byron's central theme of lost innocence. The ball ends; Beppo as Turk follows Laura and the Count to the stairs of their palace, and reveals the inconvenient truth. The three go within, drink coffee, and accept a return to the earlier arrangement, Beppo and the Count becoming friends. Byron's pen reaches the bottom of a page:

> Which being finish'd, here the story ends;
> 'Tis to be wish'd it had been sooner done,
> But stories somehow lengthen when begun.

Don Juan

On the back of his manuscript of Canto I of *Don Juan*, Byron scribbled an exemplary stanza:

> I would to heaven that I were so much clay,
>> As I am blood, bone, marrow, passion, feeling—
> Because at least the past were pass'd away—
>> And for the future—(but I write this reeling,
> Having got drunk exceedingly to-day,
>> So that I seem to stand upon the ceiling)
> I say—the future is a serious matter—
>> And so—for God's sake—hock and soda-water!

The empirical world of *Don Juan* is typified in this stanza. The poem is identifiable with Byron's mature life, and excludes nothing vital in that life, and so could not be finished until Byron was. *Don Juan's* extraordinary range of tone is unique in poetry, but Byron's was a unique individuality, pre-eminent even in an age of ferocious selfhood.

Don Juan began (September 1818) as what Byron called simply "a poem in the style and manner of *Beppo*, encouraged by the success of the same." But as it developed, the poem became something more ambitious, a satire of European Man and Society which attempts epic dimensions. In the end the poem became Byron's equivalent to Wordsworth's projected *Recluse*, Blake's *Milton*, Shelley's *Prometheus*, and Keats's *Hyperion*. As each of these attempts to surpass and, in Blake's and Shelley's poems, correct Milton, so Byron also creates his vision of the loss of Paradise and the tribulations of a fallen world of experience. There is no exact precedent for an epic satire of this kind. Byron's poetic idol was Pope, who kept his finest satiric strain for *The Dunciad* and wrote his theodicy, without overt satire, in the *Essay on Man*. Had Pope tried to combine the two works in the form of an Italianate medley or mock-heroic romance, something like *Don Juan* might have resulted. Byron's major work is his *Essay on Man, Dunciad, Rape of the Lock*, and a good deal more besides. Where Byron falls below his Augustan Master in aesthetic genius, he compensates by the range of his worldly knowledge, and the added complexity of bearing the burden of a Romantic Imagination he could neither trust nor eradicate. Much as he wished to emulate Pope, his epic moves in the poetic world of Wordsworth and Shelley, very nearly as much as *Childe Harold* did.

Yet he wills otherwise. The poem's most acute critic, George Ridenour, emphasizes that Byron has chosen "to introduce his longest and most ambitious work with an elaborately traditional satire in the Augustan manner." The seventeen-stanza "Dedication" savages Southey, Wordsworth, and Coleridge, and suggests that Byron is a very different kind of poet and man, whose faults "are at least those of passion and indiscretion, not of calculation, venality, self-conceit, or an impotence which manifests itself in tyranny," to quote Ridenour again. Byron is establishing his *persona* or dramatized self, the satirical mask in which he will present himself as narrator of *Don Juan*. Southey, Wordsworth, and Coleridge are renegades, revolutionary zealots who have become Tories. Southey indeed is an "Epic Renegade," both more venal than his friends (he is poet laureate) and an offender against the epic form, which he so frequently and poorly attempts. As laureate, he is "representative of all the race" of poets, and his dubious moral status is therefore an emblem of the low estate to which Byron believes poetry has fallen:

> And Coleridge, too, has lately taken wing,
> But like a hawk encumber'd with his hood,—

Explaining metaphysics to the nation—
I wish he would explain his Explanation.

Coleridge's flight is genuine but blind. Southey's poetic soarings end in a "tumble downward like the flying fish gasping on deck." As for Wordsworth, his "rather long *Excursion*" gives a "new system to perplex the sages." Byron does not make the mistake of mounting so high, not will he fall so low:

For me, who, wandering with pedestrian Muses,
　　Contend not with you on the winged steed,
I wish your fate may yield ye, when she chooses,
　　The fame you envy, and the skill you need.

He will not attempt the sublime, and thus he need not fall into the bathetic. From Southey he passes to the Master Tory, "the intellectual eunuch Castlereagh," a pillar of the Age of Reaction that followed Napoleon, and the master of Southey's hired song:

Europe has slaves, allies, kings, armies still
And Southey lives to sing them very ill.

The mock dedication concluded, the epic begins by announcing its hero:

I want a hero: an uncommon want,
　　When every year and month sends forth a new one,
Till, after cloying the gazettes with cant,
　　The age discovers he is not the true one:
Of such as these I should not care to vaunt,
　　I'll therefore take our ancient friend Don Juan—
We all have seen him, in the pantomime,
　　Sent to the devil somewhat ere his time.

This last may be a reference to Mozart's *Don Giovanni*. Byron's Don Juan shares only a name with the hero of the legend or of Mozart. At the root of the poem's irony is the extraordinary passivity and innocence of its protagonist. This fits the age, Byron insists, because its overt heroes are all military butchers. The gentle Juan, acted upon and pursued, sets off the aggressiveness of society.

　　The plot of *Don Juan* is too extensive for summary, and the poem's digressive technique would defeat such an attempt in any case. The poem organizes itself by interlocking themes and cyclic patterns, rather than by clear narrative structure. "A deliberate rambling digressiveness," Northrop Frye observes, "is endemic in the narrative technique of satire, and so is a calculated bathos or art of sinking in its suspense." *Don Juan* parodies epic form and even its own digressiveness. Its organization centers, as Ridenour shows, on two thematic metaphors: the Fall of Man, in terms of art, nature, and the passions; and the narrator's style of presentation, in terms of his rhetoric and his *persona*. Juan's experiences tend toward a cyclic repetition of the Fall, and Byron's style as poet and man undergoes the same pattern of aspiration and descent.

Canto I deals with Juan's initial fall from sexual innocence. The tone of this canto is urbanely resigned to the necessity of such a fall, and the description of young love and of Donna Julia's beauty clearly ascribes positive qualities to them. Yet Julia is rather unpleasantly changed by her illicit love affair, and her parting letter to Juan betrays a dubious sophistication when we contrast it to her behavior earlier in the canto. As Byron says, speaking mockingly of his own digressiveness:

> The regularity of my design
> Forbids all wandering as the worst of sinning.

His quite conventional moral design condemns Julia, without assigning more than a merely technical lapse to the seduced sixteen-year-old, Juan. The self-baffled Prometheanism of *Childe Harold* manifests itself again here in *Don Juan*, but now the emphasis is rather more firmly set against it. "Perfection is insipid in this naughty world of ours," and Byron is not prepared to be even momentarily insipid, but the price of passion, with its attendant imperfections, may be damnation. And so Byron writes of "first and passionate love":

> —it stands alone,
> Like Adam's recollection of his fall;
> The tree of knowledge has been pluck'd
> —all's known—
> And life yields nothing further to recall
> Worthy of this ambrosial sin, so shown,
> No doubt in fable, as the unforgiven
> Fire which Prometheus filch'd for us from heaven.

Imaginatively this is an unfortunate passage, as it reduces both Man's crime and the Promethean theft from the level of disobedience, which is voluntaristic, to that of sexuality itself, a natural endowment. Byron's paradoxes concerning sexual love are shallow, and finally irksome. It is not enlightening to be told that "pleasure's a sin, and sometimes sin's a pleasure."

Byron does better when he finds Prometheanism dubiously at work in human inventiveness:

> One makes new noses, one a guillotine,
>> One breaks your bones, one sets them in their sockets.

In an age full of new inventions, "for killing bodies, and for saving souls," both alike made with great good will, the satirist finds a true function in exploring the ambiguities of human aspiration. When Byron merely condemns all aspiration as sinful, he repels us. Fortunately, he does not play Urizen for very long at a time. What is most moving in Canto I is the final personal focus. After extensive ridicule of Coleridge and Wordsworth, Byron nevertheless comes closest to his own deep preoccupations in two stanzas that are no more than a weaker version of the "Intimations" and "Dejection" odes:

> No more—no more—Oh! never more on me
>> The freshness of the heart can fall like dew,
> Which out of all the lovely things we see
>> Extracts emotions beautiful and new;
> Hived in our bosoms like the bag o' the bee.
>> Think'st thou the honey with those objects grew?
> Alas! 'twas not in them, but in thy power
> To double even the sweetness of a flower.

This is a very naive version of the "Dejection" ode. What we receive is what we ourselves give. Byron's scorn of "metaphysics" and "system" in Coleridge and Wordsworth, which is actually a rather silly scorn of deep thought in poetry, betrays him into a very weak though moving performance in the mode of Romantic nostalgia for the innocent vision both of external and of human nature:

> No more—no more—Oh! never more, my heart,
>> Canst thou be my sole world, my universe!
> Once all in all, but now a thing apart,
>> Thou canst not be my blessing or my curse:
> The illusion's gone for ever, and thou art

Insensible, I trust, but none the worse,
And in thy stead I've got a deal of judgment,
Though heaven knows how it ever found a lodgment.

The last couplet helps the stanza, as an ironic equivalent to Wordsworth's "sober coloring" of mature vision, but the preceding lines are weak in that they recall *Peele Castle*, and fall far short of it. Not that Byron is thinking of either Coleridge or Wordsworth in these two stanzas; it is more to the point to note that he might have done better to think of them, and so avoid the bathos of unconsciously, and awkwardly, suggesting their major poetic concerns.

In Canto II Juan is sent on his travels, and suffers seasickness, shipwreck, and the second and greatest of his loves. The shipwreck affords Byron a gruesome opportunity to demonstrate fallen nature at its helpless worst, as the survivors turn to a cannibalism that is rather nastily portrayed. From the flood of judgment only Juan is saved, for only he refrains from tasting human flesh. He reaches shore, a new Adam, freshly baptized from the waves, to find before him a new Eve, Haidée, daughter of an absent pirate. She seems innocence personified, but for Byron no person is innocent. Though it is an "enlargement of existence" for Haidée "to partake Nature" with Juan, the enlargement carries with it the burden of man's fall. Byron himself keenly feels the lack of human justice in this association. First love, "nature's oracle," is all "which Eve has left her daughters since her fall." Yet these moments will be paid for "in an endless shower of hell-fire":

Oh, Love! thou art the very god of evil,
For, after all, we cannot call thee devil.

Canto III is mostly a celebration of ideal love, but its very first stanza pictures Juan as being

loved by a young heart, too deeply blest
To feel the poison through her spirit creeping,
   Or know who rested there, a foe to rest,
Had soil'd the current of her sinless years,
And turn'd her pure heart's purest blood to tears!

This seems an equivocal deep blessing for Haidée, "Nature's bride" as she is. Yet, Byron goes on to say, they were happy, "happy in the illicit indulgence of their innocent desires." This phrasing takes away with one hand what it gives with the other. When, in the fourth canto, all is over,

with Juan wounded and sold into slavery, and Haidée dead of a romanti-
cally broken heart, Byron gives us his most deliberate stanza of moral confusion. Haidée has just died, and her unborn child with her:

> She died, but not alone; she held within
>   A second principle of life, which might
> Have dawn'd a fair and sinless child of sin;
>   But closed its little being without light,
> And went down to the grave unborn, wherein
>   Blossom and bough lie wither'd with one blight;
> In vain the dews of Heaven descend above
> The bleeding flower and blasted fruit of love.

This is a pathetic kind of sentimental neo-Calvinism until its concluding couplet, when it becomes a statement of the inefficacy of heavenly grace in the affairs of human passion. At the start of the fourth canto
Byron has modulated his tone so as to fit his style to the saddest section of
his epic. If a fall is to be portrayed, then the verse too must descend:

> Nothing so difficult as a beginning
>   In poesy, unless perhaps the end;
> For oftentimes when Pegasus seems winning
>   The race, he sprains a wing, and down we tend,
> Like Lucifer when hurl'd from heaven for sinning;
>   Our sin the same, and hard as his to mend,
> Being pride, which leads the mind to soar too far,
> Till our own weakness shows us what we are.

Few stanzas in *Don Juan* or elsewhere are as calmly masterful as that.
The poet attempting the high style is likely to suffer the fate of Lucifer.
Pride goes before the fall of intellect, and the sudden plunge into bathos
restores us to the reality we are. The movement from *Childe Harold* into
Don Juan is caught with fine self-knowledge:

> Imagination droops her pinion,
> And the sad truth which hovers o'er my desk
> Turns what was once romantic to burlesque.

Self-recognition leads to a gentler statement of mature awareness
than Byron usually makes:

And if I laugh at any mortal thing,
   'Tis that I may not weep; and if I weep,
'Tis that our nature cannot always bring
   Itself to apathy, for we must steep
Our hearts first in the depths of Lethe's spring
   Ere what we least wish to behold will sleep:
Thetis baptized her mortal son in Styx;
A mortal mother would on Lethe fix.

This is noble and restrained, and reveals the fundamental desperation that pervades the world of the poem, which is our world. After the
death of Haidée most of the tenderness of Byron passes out of the poem,
to be replaced by fiercer ironies and a reckless gaiety that can swerve into
controlled hysteria. It becomes clearer that Byron's universe is neither
Christian not Romantic, nor yet the eighteenth-century cosmos he would
have liked to repossess. Neither grace nor the displaced grace of the
Secondary Imagination can move with freedom in this universe, and a
standard of reasonableness is merely a nostalgia to be studied. What haunts
Byron is the specter of meaninglessness, of pointless absurdity. He is an
unwilling prophet of our sensibility. The apocalyptic desires of Blake and
Shelley, the natural sacramentalism of Coleridge and Wordsworth, the
humanistic naturalism of Keats, all find some parallels in Byron, but what
is central in him stands apart from the other great Romantics. He lacks
their confidence, as he lacks also the persuasiveness of their individual
rhetorics. Too traditional to be one of them, too restless and driven to be
traditional, impatient of personal myth if only because he incarnates his
own too fully, he creates a poem without faith in Nature, Art, Society, or
the very Imagination he so capably employs. Yet his obsessions betray his
uncertainties of rejection. *Don Juan* cannot let Wordsworth alone, and
cannot bring itself to mention Shelley, Byron's companion during much of
the poem's composition. Until Shelley's death, Byron could not decide
what to make of either the man or the poet, both of whom impressed him
more than he cared to acknowledge. After Shelley's death, Byron seems to
have preferred to forget him, except for one stanza of *Don Juan* where the
puzzle of Shelley continues as a troubling presence:

And that's enough, for love is vanity,
   Selfish in its beginning as its end,
Except where 'tis a mere insanity,
   A maddening spirit which would strive to blend
Itself with beauty's frail inanity,

On which the passion's self seems to depend;
And hence some heathenish philosophers
Make love the main-spring of the universe.

The italics are mine, and indicate the probable Shelley reference. The stanza's first two lines express the mature judgment of Byron on love, a vanity that begins and ends in selfishness, except in the case of the rare spirits who madden themselves and others by questing as though the world could contain the object of their fierce desire. The tone here is uneasy, as it is in Byron's continuous digressions on Wordsworth's *Excursion*. The *Excursion* contains just enough of Wordsworth's greatness both to influence and to repel Byron, and its emphasis on the correction of a misanthropic Solitary may have offended him directly. We cannot know, but a surmise is possible. There are moments in *Don Juan* when Byron longs to make nature his altar, and moments when he is drawn toward a desperate religion of love. His rejection of Wordsworth and evasion of Shelley have deep and mysterious roots within *Don Juan*'s underlying assumptions concerning reality.

After the love-death of Haidée, Byron moves Juan into the world of two rapacious empresses, Gulbeyaz of Turkey and the historical Catherine the Great of Russia. Between these tigresses the poem progresses by an account of a battle between Turks and Russians. After Catherine's court, *Don Juan* starts its last, most interesting and unfinished movement, a view of the English society that Byron had known before his exile. A fierce love, a faithless war, another fierce love, and a social satire of what was closest to Byron's heart form a suggestive sequence. Seduced by a young matron, shipwrecked into an idyll of natural and ideal love, wounded and sold into bondage—the passive Juan has encountered all these adventures without developing under their impact. As he falls further into experience, he does not gain in wisdom, but he does maintain a stubborn Spanish aristocratic pride and a basic disinterestedness. Turkish passion and the horror of battle do not seem to affect him directly, but the embraces of Catherine finally convert his disinterestedness into the sickness of uninterestedness. Probably, like Childe Harold and Byron, the Don begins to feel the "fulness of satiety." His diplomatic rest trip to England is a quest for a renewal of interest, and the quest's goal, Lady Adeline, becomes Byron's last vision of a possible and therefore ultimately dangerous woman. In thus patterning the course of the poem, I have moved ahead of my commentary, and return now to Juan in slavery.

The memorable elements in that episode are the digressions. With Juan pausing, involuntarily, between women, Byron is free to meditate upon the impermanence of all worldly vanities, including poetry. He is back in the mood of *Childe Harold*, from which only the therapy of his own epic can rescue him:

> Yet there will still be bards: though fame is smoke,
>   Its fumes are frankincense to human thought;
> And the unquiet feelings, which first woke
>   Song in the world, will seek what then they sought:
> As on the beach the waves at last are broke,
>   Thus to their extreme verge the passions brought
> Dash into poetry, which is but passion,
> Or at least was so ere it grew a fashion.

Poetry here is expression and catharsis, and nothing more. At most it can help keep the poet (and his readers) sane. Elsewhere in *Don Juan* Byron rates poetry as simultaneously higher and lower, when he sees it as a dangerous mode of evading the consequences of Man's Fall, an evasion that must resolve at last in the consciousness of delusion. The impermanence of poetry is related to human mortality and what lies beyond its limits. Before introducing Juan into a Turkish harem, Byron perplexes himself with the mystery of death, drawing upon "a fact, and no poetic fable." His acquaintance, the local military commandant, has been slain in the street "for some reason, surely bad." As Byron stares at the corpse, he cannot believe that this is death:

>   I gazed (as oft I have gazed the same)
> To try if I could wrench aught out of death
> Which should confirm, or shake, or make a faith;
> But it was all a mystery. Here we are,
>   And there we go:—but *where?* five bits of lead,
> Or three, or two, or one, send very far!
>   And is this blood, then, form'd but to be shed?
> Can every element our element mar?
>   And air—earth—water—fire live—and we dead?
> *We*, whose minds comprehend all things. No more;
> But let us to the story as before.

What is effective here is the human attitude conveyed, but Byron's own turbulence weakens the expression. Few great poets have written quite so badly about death. The Muse of Byron was too lively to accommodate the grosser of his private apprehensions. The paradox of an all-comprehensive mind inhabiting a form vulnerable to every element is the basis of Byron's dualism, his own saddened version of "the ghost in the machine." The inevitable corruption of the body obsesses Byron, and this obsession determines his dismissal of passionate love as a value. Julia was self-corrupted, and Haidée the most natural and innocent of sinners, too harshly judged by her father, himself a great cutthroat but perfectly conventional in questions of his own family's morality. Gulbeyaz is further down in the scale of female culpability. Her features have "all the sweetness of the devil" when he played the cherub. She has the charm of her passion's intensity, but her love is a form of imperial, or imperious, bondage, her embrace a chain thrown about her lover's neck. Her love is a variation of war and preludes Byron's ferocious and very funny satire on the siege, capture, and sack of the Turkish town Ismail by the ostensibly Christian imperial Russian army of Catherine the Great, Juan's next and most consuming mistress. Byron introduces Canto VII and its slaughter by parodying Spenser, whose *Faerie Queene* sang of "fierce warres and faithful loves." For Byron, it is altogether too late in the day to sing so innocently, especially when "the fact's about the same," so his themes are "fierce loves and faithless wars":

> "Let there be light!" said God, "and there was light!"
>   "Let there be blood!" says man, and there's a sea!
> The fiat of this spoil'd child of the Night
>   (For Day ne'er saw his merits) could decree
> More evil in an hour, than thirty bright
>   Summers could renovate, though they should be
> Lovely as those which ripen'd Eden's fruit;
> For war cuts up not only branch, but root.

War completes the Fall of Man, costing us our surviving root in Eden and nullifying the renovating power of nature. This does not prevent Byron from an immense and sadistic joy in recording the butchery and rapine, but his persona as Promethean poet, whose every stanza heightens aspiration and deepens guilt, justifies the seeming inconsistency.

Juan has butchered freely, but refrained from ravishing, and next appears as hero at the court of Catherine the Great, where he falls, not into love, but into "that no less imperious passion," self-love. Flattered by Catherine's preference, Juan grows "a little dissipated" and becomes very much a royal favorite. As this is morally something of a further fall, Byron is inspired to reflect again upon his favorite theme:

Man fell with apples, and with apples rose,
　If this be true; for we must deem the mode
In which Sir Isaac Newton could disclose
　Through the then unpaved stars the turnpike road,
A thing to counterbalance human woes:
　For ever since immortal man hath glow'd
With all kinds of mechanics, and full soon
Steam-engines will conduct him to the moon.

The triumphs of reason are now also identified as sinfully and gloriously Promethean, and Sir Isaac observing the apple's fall is responsible for the paradox that Man's initial fall with apples was a fortunate one. The glowing of human intellect is "a thing to counterbalance human woes," and soon enough will take us to the moon. Byron quickly goes on to qualify his counterbalance as "a glorious glow," due only to his internal spirit suddenly cutting a caper. Cheerfulness thus keeps breaking in, but does not alter the fundamental vision of our world as "a waste and icy clime." That clime surrounds us, and we are "chill, and chain'd to cold earth," as our hero Prometheus was upon his icy rock. But we look up, and see the meteors of love and glory, lovely lights that flash and then die away, leaving us "on our freezing way." *Don Juan* is not only, its poet tells us, "a nondescript and ever-varying rhyme," but it is also "a versified Aurora Borealis," a northern light flashing over us.

Love and glory have flashed too often for Juan, and he begins to waste into a clime of decay just as his creator laments that Dante's "obscure wood," the mid-point of life, draws close. In "royalty's vast arms," Juan sighs for beauty, and sickens for travel. The now motherly Catherine sends her wasting lover on his last quest, a mission to England, and Byron returns in spirit to the Age of Elegance of his triumphant youth, the London of the Regency.

This, *Don Juan*'s last and unfinished movement, is its most nostalgic and chastened. Byron, once "the grand Napoleon of the realms of rhyme," revisits in vision his lost kingdom, the Babylon that sent him into exile and pilgrimage. "But I will fall at least as fell my hero," Byron cries, completing his lifelong comparison to the other Titan of the age. The poem of Juan, Byron says, is his Moscow, and he seeks in its final cantos his Waterloo. Juan has met his Moscow in Catherine, and evidently would have found a Waterloo in the Lady Adeline Amundeville, cold heroine of the final cantos and "the fair most fatal Juan ever met."

The English cantos are a litany for an eighteenth-century world, forever lost, and by Byron forever lamented. The age of reason and love is over, the poet insists, and the age of Cash has begun. The poem has seen sex displaced into war, and now sees both as displaced into money. Money and coldness dominate England, hypocritically masked as the morality that exiled Byron and now condemns his epic. There are other and deeper wounds to be revenged. The Greek and Italian women of the poet's life have given fully of their passion and spirits, and Byron has returned what he could. But England stands behind him as a sexual battlefield where he conquered all yet won nothing, and where at last he defeated himself and fled. Incest, separation, mutual betrayal of spirit are his English sexual legacy. In his sunset of poetry he returns to brood upon English womankind, products of "the English winter—ending in July, to recommence in August." Beneath the Lady Adeline's snowy surface is the proverbial *et cetera*, as Byron says, but he refuses to hunt down the tired metaphor. He throws out another figure: a bottle of champagne "frozen into a very vinous ice."

> Yet in the very centre, past all price,
>   About a liquid glassful will remain;
> And this is stronger than the strongest grape
> Could e'er express in its expanded shape.

Severity and courtliness fuse here into definitive judgment, and bring the spirit of this female archetype to a quintessence:

> And thus the chilliest aspects may concentre
> A hidden nectar under a cold presence.

Adeline is mostly a cold potential in this unfinished poem; her fatality is only barely felt when Byron breaks off, in his preparation for his final and genuinely heroic pilgrimage, to battle for the Greeks. She is Byron's "Dian of the Ephesians," but there is more flesh and activity to "her frolic Grace," the amorous Duchess of Fitz-Fulke. No personage, but an atmosphere, dominates these English cantos, with their diffused autumnal tone and their perfectly bred but desperately bored aristocrats, with whose breeding and boredom alike Byron is more than half in sympathy.

Don Juan, begun as satiric epic, ends as a remembrance of things past, with Byron's last glance at home, and the poet's last tone one of weary but loving irony. The last word in a discussion of *Don Juan* ought not to be "irony," but "mobility," one of Byron's favorite terms. Oliver Elton called Byron's two central traits his mobility and self-consciousness, and the former is emphasized in *Don Juan*. Adeline is so graceful a social performer that Juan begins to feel some doubt as to how much of her is *real*:

> So well she acted all and every part
>> By turns—with that vivacious versatility,
> Which many people take for want of heart.
>> They err—'tis merely what is call'd mobility,
> A thing of temperament and not of art,
>> Though seeming so, from its supposed facility;
> And false—though true; for surely they're sincerest
> Who are strongly acted on by what is nearest.

This is Byron's own defense against our charge that he postures, our feeling doubts as to how much of *him* is real. An abyss lies beneath mobility, but Adeline and Byron alike are too nimble to fall into it, and their deftness is more than rhetorical. The world of *Don Juan*, Byron's world, demands mobility; there is indeed no other way to meet it. Byron defines mobility in a note that has a wry quality, too sophisticated to acknowledge the tragic dimension being suggested: "It may be defined as an excessive susceptibility of immediate impressions—at the same time without *losing* the past: and is, though sometimes apparently useful to the possessor, a most painful and unhappy attribute."

This is Byron's social version of the Romantic term "Imagination," for mobility also reveals itself "in the balance or reconciliation of opposite or discordant qualities: of sameness, with difference; the individual, with the representative; the sense of novelty and freshness, with old and familiar objects." The great Romantic contraries—emotion and order, judgment and enthusiasm, steady self-possession and profound or vehement feeling—all find their social balance in the quality of mobility. Viewed thus, Byron's achievement in *Don Juan* is to have suggested the pragmatic social realization of Romantic idealism in a mode of reasonableness that no other Romantic aspired to attain.

Byron lived in the world as no other Romantic attempted to live, except Shelley, and Shelley at the last despaired more fully. *Don Juan* is, to my taste, not a poem of the eminence of *Milton* and *Jerusalem*, of *The Prelude* or *Prometheus Unbound* or the two *Hyperions*. But it is not a poem of their kind, nor ought it to be judged against them. Shelley said of *Don Juan* that "every word of it is pregnant with immortality," and again: "Nothing has ever been written like it in English, nor, if I may venture to prophesy, will there be; without carrying upon it the mark of a secondary and borrowed light." Byron despaired of apocalypse, and yet could not be content with Man or nature as given. He wrote therefore with the strategy of meeting this life with awareness, humor, and an intensity of creative aspiration, flawed necessarily at its origins. Mobility is a curious and sophisticated ideal; it attempts to meet experience with experience's own ironies of apprehension. It may be that, as Byron's best critic says, *Don Juan* offers us "a sophistication which (in a highly debased form, to be sure) we have already too much of." We have, however, so little besides that a higher kind of sophistication can only improve us. Whatever its utility, *Don Juan* is exuberant enough to be beautiful in a Blakean sense, little as Blake himself would have cared for Byron's hard-won digressive balance.

THE BYRONIC ETHOS

The Vision of Judgment

The parody poem *The Vision of Judgment* contains Byron's best work outside of *Don Juan*. It is, as Byron said, "in the Pulci style," like *Beppo* and *Juan*, but its high good nature reveals a firmer balance than Byron maintains else where in his Italian mock-heroic vein. Southey, the battered poet laureate, is the scapegoat again, as he was in the "Dedication" to *Don Juan*. Byron's treatment of his victim is both more humane and more effective in the *Vision*, once the reader gets past the angry prose preface.

George III died in 1820, and poor Southey performed the laureate's task of eulogizing his late monarch in *A Vision of Judgment* (1821), a poem no better than it needed to be, and not much worse than most of Southey. The laureate's misfortune was to write a preface in which he denounced lascivious literature and attacked the "Satanic school" (Byron and Shelley) for producing it: "for though their productions breathe the spirit of Belial in their lascivious parts, and the spirit of Moloch in those loathsome images of atrocities and horrors which they delight to represent, they are more especially characterized by a satanic spirit of pride and audacious impiety, which still betrays the wretched feeling of hopelessness wherewith it is allied."

Byron was not the man to pass this by. His *Vision of Judgment* takes its occasion from Southey's and permanently fixates the laureate as a dunce. But it does something rather more vital besides. *Don Juan* has its Miltonic side, as we have seen, yet the *Vision* as it develops is even closer to *Paradise Lost* in material, though hardly in spirit or tone. Milton's anthropomorphic Heaven is sublime and also sometimes wearisome, too much like an earthly court in its servile aspects. Byron's burlesque Heaven is sublimely funny. St. Peter sits by the celestial gate and can happily drowse, for very little goes in. The Angels are singing out of tune and are by now hoarse, having little else to do. Down below, George III dies, which does not disturb the yawning Peter, who has not heard of him. But the mad old blind king arrives in the angelic caravan, and with him comes a very great being, the patron of the "Satanic school":

> But bringing up the rear of this bright host
> A Spirit of a different aspect waved
> His wings, like thunder-clouds above some coast
> Whose barren beach with frequent wrecks is paved;
> His brow was like the deep when tempest-toss'd;
> Fierce and unfathomable thoughts engraved
> Eternal wrath on his immortal face,
> And *where* he gazed a gloom pervaded space.

Those "fierce and unfathomable thoughts" remind us of Manfred, but this is great Lucifer himself, come to claim George as his own. The gate of heaven opens, and the archangel Michael comes forth to meet his former friend and future foe. There is "a high immortal, proud regret" in the eyes of each immortal being, as if destiny rather than will governs their enmity:

> Yet still between his Darkness and his Brightness
> There pass'd a mutual glance of great politeness.

Michael is a gentleman, but the Prince of Darkness has the superior hauteur of "an old Castilian poor noble." He is not particularly proud of owning our earth, but he does own it, in this quietly Gnostic poem. But, as befits a poor noble with hauteur, he thinks few earthlings worth damnation save their kings, and these he takes merely as a kind of quitrent, to assert his right as lord. Indeed, he shares Byron's theory of the Fall as being perpetually renewed by Man:

> they are grown so bad,
> That hell has nothing better left to do
> Than leave them to themselves: so much more mad
> And evil by their own internal curse,
> Heaven cannot make them better, nor I worse.

Lucifer's charges against George and his calling of witnesses are nimbly handled. Life comes exuberantly into the poem with the intrusion of Southey upon the heavenly scene. The devil Asmodeus stumbles in, under the heavy load of the laureate, and the poor devil is moved to lament that he has sprained his left wing in the carry. Southey has been writing his *Vision of Judgment*, thus daring to anticipate the eternal decision upon George. The laureate, glad to get an audience, begins to recite, throwing everyone into a horror and even rousing the deceased King from his stupor in the horrible thought that his former laureate, the abominable Pye, has come again to plague him. After a general tumult, St. Peter

> upraised his keys,
> And at the fifth line knock'd the poet down;
> Who felt like Phaeton.

Phaeton (or Phaethon) attempted to drive the chariot of the sun across the sky, but could not control the horses, who bolted, and so Phaethon fell to his death. Southey attempts to ride in the chariot of Apollo, god of poetry, and suffers a fall into the depths, a bathetic plunge. The same imagery of falling is associated with Southey in the "Dedication" to *Don Juan*, but there it is more direct:

> He first sank to the bottom—like his works,
> But soon rose to the surface—like himself.

In the confusion, King George slips into heaven, and as Byron ends his *Vision*, the late monarch is practicing the hundredth psalm, which is only fitting, as it adjures the Lord's people to "enter into his gates with thanksgiving." The ethos of *The Vision of Judgment* is remarkably refreshing. Byron is so delighted by his fable that his good will extends even to Southey, who does not drown like Phaethon but lurks in his own den, still composing. George is in heaven, and the very dignified and high-minded Lucifer back in hell. In this one poem at least, Byron writes as a whole man, whose inner conflicts have been mastered. If the earth is the Devil's, the Devil is yet disinterested, and damnation a subject for urbane bantering. Peculiar as Byron's variety of Prometheanism was, *The Vision of Judgment* makes it clear that we err in calling the poet any genuine sort of a Calvinist:

> for not one am I
> Of those who think damnation better still:
> I hardly know too if not quite alone am I
> In this small hope of bettering future ill
> By circumscribing, with some slight restriction,
> The eternity of hell's hot jurisdiction.

If there is any mockery in the poem which is not altogether good-humored, it is in Byron's conscious "blasphemy":

> I know one may be damn'd
> For hoping no one else may e'er be so;
>   I know my catechism; I know we're cramm'd
> With the best doctrines till we quite o'erflow;
>   I know that all save England's church have shamm'd,
> And that the other twice two hundred churches
> And synagogues.have made a *damn'd* bad purchase.

Religious cant was no more acceptable to Byron than the social or political varieties, however darkly and deeply his own orthodox currents ran. *The Vision of Judgment* is perhaps only a good parody of aspects of *Paradise Lost*, but few of us would prefer Milton's heaven to Byron's as a place in which to live.

"Stanzas to the Po"

Byron's lyrics are an index to his poetic development, though only a few of them are altogether adequate in the expression of his complex sensibility. The best of them include the "Stanzas to the Po" (1819), the undated "Ode to a Lady," which applies the poet's negative Prometheanism to the theme of lost human passion, and the last poems written under the shadow of death at Missolonghi. Byron's personal ethos, the dignity of disillusioned intensity and disinterested heroism, despairing of love and its human limitations but still longing for them, continued to shine out of this handful of lyrics.

The last poems have the poignancy of their occasion, but the "Stanzas to the Po" constitute Byron's finest short poem, and one perfectly revelatory of his mature spirit.

In April 1819 Byron, aged thirty-one, fell in love with the Countess Teresa Guiccioli, aged nineteen, who had been married only a little over a year to the fifty-eight-year-old Count. Byron had already lamented in *Don Juan* the cooling of his heart, now that he was past thirty, but he proved no prophet in this matter. Momentarily separated from Teresa, he wrote the first draft of his "Stanzas to the Po." The firm diction of this beautiful poem shows an Italian influence, probably that of Dante's *Canzioniere*:

> River, that rollest by the ancient walls,
>   Where dwells the Lady of my love, when she

Walks by thy brink, and there perchance recalls
   A faint and fleeting memory of me;

What if thy deep and ample stream should be
   A mirror of my heart, where she may read
The thousand thoughts I now betray to thee,
   Wild as thy wave, and headlong as thy speed!

The movement of this is large and stately, but there is a curious and deliberate reluctance in the rhythm, as if the poet wished to resist the river's swift propulsion of his thoughts toward his absent mistress. As he stares at the river he sees suddenly that it is more than a mirror of his heart. He finds not similitude but identity between the Po and his heart:

Thou tendest wildly onwards to the main.
And I—to loving *one* I should not love.

He should not love only because he had said his farewell to love, and is reluctant to welcome it again. But it has come; he longs desperately for his beloved, yet he still resists the longing:

The wave that bears my tears returns no more:
   Will she return by whom that wave shall sweep?—
Both tread thy banks, both wander on thy shore,
   I by thy source, she by the dark-blue deep.

As the Po is one with the passion of Byron's heart, a love that Teresa reciprocates, the geographical position of the lovers symbolizes the extent to which they have given themselves to their love. Teresa is "by the dark-blue deep," but Byron still lingers by the source, struggling with the past:

But that which keepeth us apart is not
   Distance, nor depth of wave, nor space of earth,
But the distraction of a various lot,
   As various as the climates of our birth.

A stranger loves the Lady of the land,
   Born far beyond the mountains, but his blood
Is all meridian, as if never fann'd
   By the black wind that chills the polar flood.

His hesitation keeps them apart, and he traces it to the division within his own nature. But his blood triumphs, though in his own despite:

> My blood is all meridian; were it not;
> > I had not left my clime, nor should I be,
> In spite of tortures, ne'er to be forgot,
> > A slave again of love,—at least of thee.

> 'Tis vain to struggle—let me perish young—
> > Live as I lived, and love as I have loved;
> To dust if I return, from dust I sprung,
> > And then, at least, my heart can ne'er be moved.

Complex in attitude as these two final stanzas of the poem are, they did not satisfy Byron. As he gives himself again to love, he senses that he also gives himself to self-destruction and welcomes this as a consummation to be wished. By loving again, he is true to both his own past and his own nature, but to a past he had rejected and a nature he had sought to negate. His heart is moved again, and to have its torpor stirred is pain, but this is the pain of life.

Less than two months later, as he made his final decision and moved to join Teresa, he redrafted his poem. Characteristically, the poem is now more indecisive than the man, for he alters the final lines to a lament:

> My heart is all meridian, were it not
> > I had not suffered now, nor should I be
> Despite old tortures ne'er to be forgot
> > The slave again—Oh! Love! at least of thee!

> 'Tis vain to struggle, I have struggled long
> > To love again no more as once I loved,
> Oh! Time! why leave this worst of earliest
> > > Passions strong?
> > To tear a heart which pants to be unmoved?

Byron was too courtly to leave the penultimate line as above, and modified it to "why leave this earliest Passion strong?" With either reading, this makes for a weaker and less controlled climax to the poem than the first version, as it denies the strength of the poet's own will. The first set of "Stanzas to the Po" makes a permanent imaginative gesture, and deserves to be read repeatedly as the universal human legacy it comes so close to being. The heart divided against itself has found few more eloquent emblems.

Last Poems

On the morning of his thirty-sixth birthday, at Missolonghi, where he was to die three months later, Byron finished the poem that is his epitaph:

> 'Tis time this heart should be unmoved,
>   Since others it hath ceased to move:
> Yet, though I cannot be beloved,
>   Still let me love!

He begins with an echo of the final line of the "Stanzas to the Po," but the emphasis is different. He now fears not that he will love again but that he cannot:

> My days are in the yellow leaf;
>   The flowers and fruits of love are gone;
> The worm, the canker, and the grief
>   Are mine alone!

The Macbeth comparison is perhaps rather too melodramatic, but the next stanza modulates to the more appropriate Promethean image of fire:

> The fire that on my bosom preys
>   Is lone as some volcanic isle;
> No torch is kindled at its blaze—
>   A funeral pile.

The fire is not yet out, the volcano not extinct, but the volcano is isolated and the fire will be consumed with the poet. He wears the chain of love (for the abandoned Teresa?) but he cannot share in its pain and power. In a recovery of great rhetorical power he turns upon his grief and delivers himself up to his destiny:

> Tread those reviving passions down,
>   Unworthy manhood!—unto thee
> Indifferent should the smile or frown
>   Of beauty be.

If thou regrett'st thy youth, *why live?*
    The land of honourable death
Is here:—up to the field, and give
    Away thy breath!

Seek out—less often sought than found—
    A soldier's grave, for thee the best;
Then look around, and choose thy ground,
    And take thy rest.

Byron seems to have intended this as his last poem, but his Muses had it otherwise, and ended him with an intense love poem for his page-boy Loukas. The suffering conveyed by this poem clearly has its sexual element, so that the complex puzzle of Byron is not exactly simplified for us, but this is a problem for his biographers, who have reached no agreement upon it. Certainly Byron had homosexual as well as incestuous experience; his questing and experimental psyche, and his conviction of necessary damnation, could have led him to no less. In his final lines he liberates himself from his last verbal inhibition and writes a very powerful homosexual love poem:

I watched thee when the foe was at our side,
    Ready to strike at him—or thee and me.
Were safety hopeless—rather than divide
    Aught with one loved save love and liberty.

I watched thee on the breakers, when the rock
    Received our prow and all was storm and fear,
And bade thee cling to me through every shock;
    This arm would be thy bark, or breast thy bier.

Love and death come dangerously close together in these tense stanzas, so much so that one can understand why Loukas was wary enough to cause Byron to lament:

And when convulsive throes denied my breath
    The faintest utterance to my fading thought,
To thee—to thee—e'en in the gasp of death
    My spirit turned, oh! oftener than it ought.

Thus much and more; and yet thou lov'st me not,
    And never wilt! Love dwells not in our will.

Nor can I blame thee, though it be my lot
  To strongly, wrongly, vainly love thee still.

It is very moving that this agonized hymn to hopeless love should be Byron's last poem. Had he been more of a Promethean he would still not have achieved a better either sexual or rhetorical balance, when one remembers the English and European society through which he had to take his way. But he might have had more faith in his own imaginings, more confidence in his own inventive power, and so have given us something larger and more relevant than *Manfred* in the Romantic mode, good as *Manfred* is. We have *Don Juan*, and the record, still incomplete, of Byron's life. Byron did not seem to regret his not having given us more, and was himself realistic enough to believe that there was no more to give.

Percy Bysshe Shelley

(1792–1822)

Mesdames, one might believe that Shelley lies
Less in the stars than in their earthy wake,
Since the radiant disclosures that you make
Are of an eternal vista, manqué and gold
And brown, an Italy of the mind, a place
Of fear before the disorder of the strange,
A time in which the poet's politics
Will rule in a poets' world.

—WALLACE STEVENS

PERCY BYSSHE SHELLEY, ONE OF THE GREATEST LYRICAL POETS IN WESTERN tradition, has been dead for more than a hundred and forty years, and critics have abounded, from his own day to ours, to insist that his poetry died with him. Until recently, it was fashionable to apologize for Shelley's poetry, if one liked it at all. Each reader of poetry, however vain, can speak only for himself, and there will be only description and praise in this introduction, for after many years of reading Shelley's poems, I find nothing in them that needs apology. Shelley is a unique poet, one of the most original in the language, and he is in many ways *the* poet proper, as much so as any in the language. His poetry is autonomous, finely wrought, in the highest degree imaginative, and has the spiritual form of vision stripped of all veils and ideological coverings, the vision many readers justly seek in poetry, despite the admonitions of a multitude of churchwardenly critics.

The essential Shelley is so fine a poet that one can feel absurd in urging his claims upon a reader:

> I am the eye with which the Universe
>   Beholds itself and knows itself divine;
> All harmony of instrument or verse,
>   All prophecy, all medicine is mine,
>   All light of art or nature—to my song
>   Victory and praise in its own right belong.

That is Apollo singing, in the "Hymn" that Shelley had the sublime audacity to write for him, with the realization that, like Keats, he was a rebirth of Apollo. When, in *The Triumph of Life*, Rousseau serves as Virgil to Shelley's Dante, he is made to speak lines as brilliantly and bitterly condensed as poetry in English affords:

> And if the spark with which Heaven lit my spirit
> Had been with purer nutriment supplied,
>
> Corruption would not now thus much inherit
> Of what was once Rousseau—nor this disguise
> Stain that which ought to have disdained to wear it.

The urbane lyricism of the "Hymn of Apollo," and the harshly self-conscious, internalized dramatic quality of *The Triumph of Life* are both central to Shelley. Most central is the prophetic intensity; as much a result of displaced Protestantism as it is in Blake or in Wordsworth, but seeming more an Orphic than Hebraic phenomenon when it appears in Shelley. Religious poet as he primarily was, what Shelley prophesied was one restored Man who transcended men, gods, the natural world, and even the poetic faculty. Shelley chants the apotheosis, not of the poet, but of desire itself.

> Man, oh, not men! a chain of linked thought,
> Of love and might to be divided not,
> Compelling the elements with adamantine stress;
>   As the sun rules, even with a tyrant's gaze,
>   The unquiet republic of the maze
> Of planets, struggling fierce towards heaven's free wilderness.
>
>   Man, one harmonious soul of many a soul,
>   Whose nature is its own divine control,
> Where all things flow to all, as rivers to the sea ...

The rhapsodic intensity, the cumulative drive and yet firm control of those last three lines in particular, as the high song of humanistic celebration approaches its goal—that seems to me what is crucial in Shelley, and its presence throughout much of his work constitutes his special excellence as a poet.

Lyrical poetry at its most intense frequently moves toward direct address between one human consciousness and another, in which the "I" of the poet directly invokes the personal "Thou" of the reader. Shelley is an intense lyricist as Alexander Pope is an intense satirist; even as Pope assimilates every literary form he touches to satire, so Shelley converts forms as diverse as drama, prose essay, romance, satire, epyllion, into lyric. To an extent he himself scarcely realized, Shelley's genius desired a transformation of all experience, natural and literary, into the condition of lyric. More than all other poets, Shelley's compulsion is to present life as a direct confrontation of equal realities. This compulsion seeks absolute intensity, and courts straining and breaking in consequence. When expressed as love, it must manifest itself as mutual destruction:

> In one another's substance finding food,
> Like flames too pure and light and unimbued
> To nourish their bright lives with baser prey,
> Which point to Heaven and cannot pass away:
> One Heaven, one Hell, one immortality,
> And one annihilation.

Shelley is the poet of these flames, and he is equally the poet of a particular shadow, which falls perpetually between all such flames, a shadow of ruin that tracks every imaginative flight of fire:

> O, Thou, who plumed with strong desire
>   Wouldst float above the earth, beware!
> A Shadow tracks thy flight of fire—
>   Night is coming!

By the time Shelley had reached his final phase, of which the great monuments are *Adonais* and *The Triumph of Life*, he had become altogether the poet of this shadow of ruin, and had ceased to celebrate the possibilities of imaginative relationship. In giving himself, at last, over to the dark side of his own vision, he resolved (or perhaps merely evaded, judgment being so difficult here) a conflict within his self and poetry that had been present from the start. Though it has become a commonplace of recent criticism and scholarship to affirm otherwise, I do not think that Shelley changed very much, as a poet, during the last (and most important) six years of his life, from the summer of 1816 until the summer of 1822. The two poems of self-discovery, of mature poetic incarnation, written in 1816, "Mont Blanc" and the "Hymn to Intellectual Beauty," reveal the two contrary aspects of Shelley's vision that his entire sequence of major poems reveals. The head and the heart, each totally honest in encountering reality, yield rival reports as to the name and nature of reality. The head, in "Mont Blanc," learns, like Blake, that there is no natural religion. There is a Power, a secret strength of things, but it hides its true shape or its shapelessness behind or beneath a dread mountain, and it shows itself only as an indifference, or even pragmatically a malevolence, towards the well-being of men. But the Power speaks forth, through a poet's act of confrontation with it which is the very act of writing his poem, and the Power, rightly interpreted, can be used to repeal the large code of fraud, institutional and historical Christianity, and the equally massive code of woe, the laws of the nation-states of Europe in the age of Castlereagh and Metternich. In the "Hymn to Intellectual Beauty" a very different Power is invoked, but with a deliberate and even austere tenuousness. A shadow, itself invisible, of an unseen Power, sweeps through our dull dense world, momentarily awakening both nature and man to a sense of love and beauty, a sense just beyond the normal range of apprehension. But the shadow departs, for all its benevolence, and despite the poet's prayers for its more habitual sway. The heart's responses have not failed, but the shadow that is antithetically a radiance will not come to stay. The mind, searching for what would suffice, encountered an icy remoteness, but dared to affirm the triumph of its imaginings over the solitude and vacancy of an inadvertent nature. The emotions, visited by delight, felt the desolation of powerlessness, but dared to hope for a fuller visitation. Both odes suffer from the evident straining of their creator to reach a finality, but both survive in their creator's tough honesty and gathering sense of form.

"Mont Blanc" is a poem of the age of Shelley's father-in-law, William Godwin, while the "Hymn to Intellectual Beauty" belongs to the age of Wordsworth, Shelley's lost leader in the realms of emotion. Godwin became a kind of lost leader for Shelley also, but less on the intellectual than on the personal level. The scholarly criticism of Shelley is full of sand traps, and one of the deepest is the prevalent notion that Shelley underwent an intellectual metamorphosis from being the disciple of Godwin and the French philosophical materialists to being a Platonist or Neoplatonist, an all but mystical idealist. The man Shelley may have undergone such a transformation, though the evidence for it is equivocal; the poet Shelley did not. He started as a split being, and ended as one, but his awareness of the division in his consciousness grew deeper, and produced finally the infernal vision of *The Triumph of Life*.

II

> But even supposing that a man should raise a dead body to life before our eyes, and on this fact rest his claim to being considered the son of God; the Humane Society restores drowned persons, and because it makes no mystery of the method it employs, its members are not mistaken for the sons of God. All that we have a right to infer from our ignorance of the cause of any event is that we do not know it ...
>
> (Shelley, Notes On Queen Mab)

The deepest characteristic of Shelley's poetic mind is its skepticism. Shelley's intellectual agnosticism was more fundamental than either his troubled materialism or his desperate idealism. Had the poet turned his doubt against all entities but his own poetry, while sparing that, he would have anticipated certain later developments in the history of literature, but his own work would have lost one of its most precious qualities, a unique sensitivity to its own limitations. This sensitivity can be traced from the very beginnings of Shelley's mature style, and may indeed have made possible the achievement of that style.

Shelley was anything but a born poet, as even a brief glance at his apprentice work will demonstrate. Blake at fourteen was a great lyric poet; Shelley at twenty-two was still a bad one. He found himself, as a stylist, in the autumn of 1815, when he composed the astonishing *Alastor*, a blank verse rhapsodic narrative of a destructive and subjective quest. *Alastor*, though it has been out of fashion for a long time, is nevertheless a great and appalling work, at once a dead end and a prophecy that Shelley finally could not evade.

Shelley's starting point as a serious poet was Wordsworth, and *Alastor* is a stepchild of *The Excursion*, a poem frigid in itself, but profoundly influential, if only antithetically, on Shelley, Byron, Keats, and many later poets. The figure of the Solitary, in *The Excursion*, is the central instance of the most fundamental of Romantic archetypes, the man alienated from others and himself by excessive self-consciousness. Whatever its poetic lapses, *The Excursion* is our most extensive statement of the Romantic mythology of the Self, and the young Shelley quarried in it for imaginatively inescapable reasons, as Byron and Keats did also. Though the poet-hero of *Alastor* is not precisely an innocent sufferer, he shares the torment of Wordsworth's Solitary, and like him:

> sees
> Too clearly; feels too vividly; and longs
> To realize the vision, with intense
> And over-constant yearning—there—there lies
> The excess, by which the balance is destroyed.

Alastor, whatever Shelley's intentions, is primarily a poem about the destructive power of the imagination. For Shelley, every increase in imagination ought to have been an increase in hope, but generally the strength of imagination in Shelley fosters an answering strength of despair. In the spring of 1815 Shelley, on mistaken medical advice, confidently expected a rapid death of consumption. By autumn this expectation was put by, but the recent imagining of his own death lingers on in *Alastor*, which on one level is the poet's elegy for himself.

Most critical accounts of *Alastor* concern themselves with the apparent problem of disparities between the poem's eloquent Preface and the poem itself, but I cannot see that such disparities exist. The poem is an extremely subtle internalization of the quest-theme of romance, and the price demanded for the internalization is first, the death-in-life of what Yeats called "enforced self-realization," and at last, death itself. The *Alastor* or avenging daemon of the title is the dark double of the poet-hero, the spirit of solitude that shadows him even as he quests after his emanative portion, the soul out of his soul that Shelley later called the epipsyche. Shelley's poet longs to realize a vision, and this intense and overconstant yearning destroys natural existence, for nature cannot contain the infinite energy demanded by the vision. Wordsworthian nature, and not the poet-hero, is the equivocal element in *Alastor*, the problem the reader needs to, but cannot, resolve. For this nature is a mirror-world, like that in Blake's "The Crystal Cabinet," or in much of Keats's *Endymion*. Its pyramids and domes are sepulchers for the imagination, and all its appearances are illusive, phantasmagoric, and serve only to thwart the poet's vision, and drive him on more fearfully upon his doomed and self-destructive quest. *Alastor* prophesies *The Triumph of Life*, and in the mocking light of the later poem the earlier work appears also to have been a dance of death.

The summer of 1816, with its wonderful products, "Mont Blanc" and the "Hymn to Intellectual Beauty," was for Shelley, as I have indicated, a rediscovery of the poetic self, a way out of the impasse of *Alastor*. The revolutionary epic, first called *Laon and Cyntha*, and then *The Revolt of Islam*, was Shelley's first major attempt to give his newly directed energies adequate scope, but the attempt proved abortive, and the poem's main distinction is that it is Shelley's longest. Shelley's gifts were neither for narrative nor for straightforward allegory, and the *terza rima* fragment, *Prince Athanase*, written late in 1817, a few months after *The Revolt of Islam* was finished, shows the poet back upon his true way, the study of the isolated imagination. Whatever the dangers of the subjective mode of *Alastor*, it remained always Shelley's genuine center, and his finest poems were to emerge from it. *Prince Athanase* is only a fragment, or fragments, but its first part at least retains something of the power for us that it held for the young Browning and the young Yeats. Athanase, from a Peacockian perspective, is quite like the delightfully absurd Scythrop of *Nightmare Abbey*, but if we will grant him his mask's validity we do find in him one of the archetypes of the imagination, the introspective, prematurely old poet, turning his vision outward to the world from his lonely tower of meditation:

> His soul had wedded Wisdom, and her dower
> Is love and justice, clothed in which he sate
> Apart from men, as in a lonely tower,
>
> Pitying the tumult of their dark estate.

There is a touch of Byron's Manfred, and of Byron himself, in Athanase, and Byron is the dominant element in Shelley's next enduring poem, the conversational *Julian and Maddalo*, composed in Italy in the autumn of 1818, after the poets had been reunited. The middle portion of *Julian and Maddalo*, probably based upon legends of Tasso's madness, is an excrescence, but the earlier part of the poem, and its closing lines, introduce another Shelley, a master of the urbane, middle style, the poet of the "Letter to Maria Gisborne," the "Hymn to Mercury," of parts of *The Witch of Atlas* and *The Sensitive Plant*, and of such beautifully controlled love lyrics as "To Jane: The Invitation" and "Lines Written in the Bay of Lerici." Donald Davie, who as a critic is essentially an anti-Shelleyan of the school of Dr. Leavis, and is himself a poet in a mode antithetical to Shelley's, has written an impressive tribute to Shelley's achievement as a master of the urbane style. What I find most remarkable in this mastery is that Shelley carried it over into his major achievement, the great lyrical drama, *Prometheus Unbound*, a work written almost entirely in the high style, on the precarious level of the sublime, where urbanity traditionally has no place. The astonishingly original tone of *Prometheus Unbound* is not always successfully maintained, but for the most part it is, and one aspect of its triumph is that critics should find it so difficult a tone to characterize. The urbane conversationalist, the relentlessly direct and emotionally uninhibited lyricist, and the elevated prophet of a great age to come join together in the poet of *Prometheus Unbound*, a climactic work which is at once celebratory and ironic, profoundly idealistic and as profoundly skeptical, passionately knowing its truths and as passionately agnostic towards all truth. More than any other of Shelley's poems, *Prometheus Unbound* has been viewed as self-contradictory or at least as containing unresolved mental conflicts, so that a consideration of Shelley's ideology may be appropriate prior to a discussion of the poem.

The clue to the apparent contradictions in Shelley's thought is his profound skepticism, which has been ably expounded by C.E. Pulos in his study, *The Deep Truth*. There the poet's eclecticism is seen as centering on the point "where his empiricism terminates and his idealism begins." This point is the skeptic's position, and is where Shelley judged Montaigne, Hume, and his own older contemporary, the metaphysician Sir William Drummond, to have stood. From this position, Shelley was able to reject both the French materialistic philosophy he had embraced in his youth and the Christianity that he had never ceased to call a despotism. Yet the skeptic's position, though it powerfully organized Shelley's revolutionary polemicism, gave no personal comfort, but took the poet to what he himself called "the verge where words abandon us, and what wonder if we grow dizzy to look down the dark abyss of how little we know." That abyss is Demogorgon's, in *Prometheus Unbound*, and its secrets are not revealed by him, for "a voice is wanting, the deep truth is imageless," and Demogorgon is a shapeless darkness. Yeats, sensing the imminence of his apocalypse, sees a vast image, a beast advancing before the gathering darkness. Shelley senses the great change that the Revolution has heralded, but confronts as apocalyptic harbinger only a fabulous and formless darkness, the only honest vision available to even the most apocalyptic of skeptics. Shelley is the most Humean poet in the language, oddly as his temperament accords with Hume's, and it is Hume, not Berkeley or Plato, whose view of reality informs *Prometheus Unbound* and the poems that came after it. Even Necessity, the dread and supposedly Godwinian governing demon of Shelley's early *Queen Mab*, is more of a Humean than a Holbachian notion, for Shelley's Necessity is "conditional, tentative and philosophically ironical," as Pulos points out. It is also a Necessity highly advantageous to a poet, for a power both sightless and unseen is a power removed from dogma and from philosophy, a power that only the poet's imagination can find the means to approach. Shelley is the unacknowledged ancestor of

Wallace Stevens' conception of poetry as the Supreme Fiction, and *Prometheus Unbound* is the most capable imagining, outside of Blake and Wordsworth, that the Romantic quest for a Supreme Fiction has achieved.

The fatal aesthetic error, in reading *Prometheus Unbound* or any other substantial work by Shelley, is to start with the assumption that one is about to read Platonic poetry. I mean this in either sense, that is, either poetry deeply influenced by or expressing Platonic doctrine, or in John Crowe Ransom's special sense, a poetry discoursing in things that are at any point legitimately to be translated into ideas. Shelley's skeptical and provisional idealism is *not* Plato's, and Shelley's major poems are mythopoeic, and not translatable into any terms but their own highly original ones. Shelley has been much victimized in our time by two rival and equally pernicious critical fashions, one that seeks to "rescue" visionary poetry by reading it as versified Plotinus and Porphyry, and another that condemns visionary poetry from Spenser through Hart Crane as being a will-driven allegorization of an idealistic scientism vainly seeking to rival the whole of experimental science from Bacon to the present day. The first kind of criticism, from which Blake and Yeats have suffered as much as Shelley, simply misreads the entire argument against nature that visionary poetry complexly conducts. The second kind, as pervasively American as the first is British, merely underestimates the considerable powers of mind that Shelley and other poets of his tradition possessed.

Shelley admired Plato as a poet, a view he derived from Montaigne, as Pulos surmises, and he appears also to have followed Montaigne in considering Plato to be a kind of skeptic. Nothing is further from Shelley's mind and art than the Platonic view of knowledge, and nothing is further from Shelley's tentative myths than the dogmatic myths of Plato. It is one of the genuine oddities of critical history that a tough-minded Humean poet, though plagued also by an idealistic and psuedo-Platonic heart, should have acquired the reputation of having sought beauty or truth in any Platonic way or sense whatsoever. No Platonist would have doubted immortality as darkly as Shelley did, or indeed would have so recurrently doubted the very existence of anything transcendent.

The most obvious and absolute difference between Plato and Shelley is in their rival attitudes toward aesthetic experience. Shelley resembles Wordsworth or Ruskin in valuing so highly certain ecstatic moments of aesthetic contemplation precisely because the moments are fleeting, because they occupy, as Blake said, the pulsation of an artery. For Shelley these are not moments to be put aside when the enduring light of the Ideas is found; Shelley never encounters such a light, not even in *Adonais*, where Keats appears to have found a kindred light in death. There is no ladder to climb in Shelley's poetry, any more than there is in Blake's. There are more imaginative states-of-being and less imaginative ones, but no hierarchy to bridge the abyss between them.

III

> It is no longer sufficient to say, like all poets, that minors resemble the water. Neither is it sufficient to consider that hypothesis as absolute and to suppose ... that mirrors exhale a fresh wind or that thirsty birds drink them, leaving empty frames. We must go beyond such things. That capricious desire of a mind which becomes compulsory reality must be manifested—an individual must be shown who inserts himself into the glass and remains in its illusory land (where there are figurations and colors but these are impaired by immobile silence) and feels the shame of being nothing more than an image obliterated by nights and permitted existence by glimmers of light.
>
> (Jorge Luis Borges)

It has been my experience, as a teacher of Shelley, that few recent students enjoy *Prometheus Unbound* at a first reading, and few fail to admire it greatly at a second or later reading. *Prometheus Unbound* is a remarkably subtle and difficult poem. That a work of such length needs to be read with all the care and concentration a trained reader brings to a difficult and condensed lyric is perhaps unfortunate, yet Shelley himself affirmed that his major poem had been written only for highly adept readers, and that he hoped for only a few of these. *Prometheus Unbound* is not as obviously difficult as Blake's *The Four Zoas*, but it presents problems comparable to that work. Blake has the advantage of having made a commonplace understanding of his major poems impossible, while Shelley retains familiar (and largely misleading) mythological names like Prometheus and Jupiter. The problems of interpretation in Shelley's lyrical drama are as formidable as English poetry affords, and are perhaps finally quite unresolvable.

It seems clear that Shelley intended his poem to be a millennial rather than an apocalyptic work. The vision in Act III is of a redeemed nature, but not of an ultimate reality, whereas the vision in the great afterthought of Act IV does concern an uncovered universe. In Act IV the imagination of Shelley breaks away from the poet's apparent intention, and visualizes a world in which the veil of phenomenal reality has been rent, a world like that of the Revelation of St. John, or Night the Ninth of *The Four Zoas*. The audacity of Shelley gives us a vision of the last things without the sanction of religious or mythological tradition. Blake does the same, but Blake is systematic where Shelley risks everything on one sustained imagining.

I think that a fresh reader of *Prometheus Unbound* is best prepared if he starts with Milton in mind. This holds true also for *The Prelude*, for Blake's epics, for Keats's *Hyperion* fragments, and even for Byron's *Don Juan*, since Milton is both the Romantic starting point and the Romantic adversary. Shelley is as conscious of this as Blake or any of the others; the Preface to *Prometheus Unbound* refers to that demigod, "the sacred Milton," and commends him for having been "a bold inquirer into morals and religion." Searching out an archetype for his Prometheus, Shelley finds him in Milton's Satan, "the Hero of Paradise Lost," but a flawed, an imperfect hero, of whom Prometheus will be a more nearly perfect descendant. Shelley's poem is almost an echo chamber for *Paradise Lost*, but all the echoes are deliberate, and all of them are so stationed as to "correct" the imaginative errors of *Paradise Lost*. Almost as much as Blake's "brief epic," *Milton*, Shelley's *Prometheus Unbound* is a courageous attempt to save Milton from himself, and for the later poet. Most modern scholarly critics of Milton sneer at the Blakean or Shelleyan temerity, but no modern critic of Milton is as illuminating as Blake and Shelley are, and none knows better than they did how omnipotent an opponent they lovingly faced, or how ultimately hopeless the contest was.

Paraphrase is an ignoble mode of criticism, but it can be a surprisingly revealing one (of the critic as well as the work of course) and it is particularly appropriate to *Prometheus Unbound*, since the pattern of action in the lyrical drama is a puzzling one. A rapid survey of character and plot is hardly possible, since the poem in a strict (and maddening) sense has neither, but a few points can be risked as introduction. Shelley's source is Aeschylus, insofar as he has a source, but his genuine analogues are in his older contemporary Blake, whom he had never read, and of whom indeed he never seems to have heard. Prometheus has a resemblance both to Blake's Orc and to his Los; Jupiter is almost a double for Urizen, Asia approximates Blake's Jerusalem, while Demogorgon has nothing in common with any of Blake's "Giant Forms." But, despite this last, the shape of Shelley's myth is very like Blake's. A unitary Man fell, and split into torturing and tortured components, and into separated male and female forms as well. The torturer is not in himself a representative of comprehensive evil, because he is quite limited; indeed, he has been invented by his victim, and falls soon after his victim ceases to hate his own invention. Shelley's Jupiter, like Urizen in one of his aspects, is pretty clearly the Jehovah of institutional and historical Christianity. George Bernard Shaw, one of the most enthusiastic of Shelleyans, had some illuminating remarks on *Prometheus Unbound* in *The Perfect Wagnerite*. Jupiter, he said, "is the almighty fiend into whom the Englishman's God had degenerated during two centuries of ignorant Bible worship and shameless commercialism." Shaw rather understated the matter, since it seems indubitable that the Jupiter of Shelley's lyrical drama is one with the cheerfully abominable Jehovah of *Queen Mab*, and so had been degenerating for rather more than two centuries.

Prometheus in Shelley is both the archetypal imagination (Blake's Los) and the primordial energies of man (Blake's Orc). Jupiter, like Urizen again, is a limiter of imagination and of energy. He may masquerade as reason, but he is nothing of the kind, being a mere circumscriber and binder, like the God of *Paradise Lost*, Book III (as opposed to the very different, creative God of Milton's Book VII). Asia is certainly not the Universal Love that Shaw and most subsequent Shelleyans have taken her to be. Though she partly transcends nature she is still subject to it, and she is essentially a passive being, even though the apparently central dramatic action of the poem is assigned to her. Like the emanations in Blake, she may be taken as the total spiritual form or achieved aesthetic form quested after by her lover, Prometheus. She is less than the absolute vainly sought by the poet-hero of *Alastor*, though she is more presumably than the mortal Emilia of *Epipsychidion* can hope to represent. Her function is to hold the suffering natural world open to the transcendent love or Intellectual Beauty that hovers beyond it, but except in the brief and magnificent moment-of-moments of her transfiguration (end of Act II) she is certainly not one with the Intellectual Beauty.

That leaves us Demogorgon, the poem's finest and most frustrating invention, who has been disliked by the poem's greatest admirers, Shaw and Yeats. Had Shaw written the poem, Demogorgon would have been Creative Evolution, and had Yeats been the author, Demogorgon would have been the Thirteenth Cone of *A Vision*. But Shelley was a subtler dialectician than Shaw or Yeats; as a skeptic, he had to be. Shaw testily observed that "flatly, there is no such person as Demogorgon, and if Prometheus does not pull down Jupiter himself, no one else will." Demogorgon, Yeats insisted, was a ruinous invention for Shelley: "Demogorgon made his plot incoherent, its interpretation impossible; it was thrust there by that something which again and again forced him to balance the object of desire conceived as miraculous and superhuman, with nightmare."

Yet Demogorgon, in all his darkness, is a vital necessity in Shelley's mythopoeic quest for a humanized or displaced theodicy. The Demogorgon of Spenser and of Milton was the evil god of chaos, dread father of all the gentile divinities. Shelley's Demogorgon, like the unknown Power of *Mont Blanc*, is morally unallied; he is the god of skepticism, and thus the preceptor of our appalling freedom to imagine well or badly. His only clear attributes are dialectical; he is the god of all those at the turning, at the reversing of the cycles. Like the dialectic of the Marxists, Demogorgon is a necessitarian and materialistic entity, part of the nature of things as they are. But he resembles also the shadowy descent of the Holy Spirit in most Christian dialectics of history, though it would be more accurate to call him a demonic parody of the Spirit, just as the whole of *Prometheus Unbound* is a dark parody of Christian salvation myth. Back of Demogorgon is Shelley's difficult sense of divinity, an apocalyptic humanism like that of Blake's, and it is not possible therefore to characterize *Prometheus Unbound* as being either humanistic or theistic in its ultimate vision. Martin Price, writing of Blake's religion, observes that "Blake can hardly be identified as theist or humanist; the distinction becomes meaningless for him. God can only exist within man, but man must be raised to a perception of the infinite. Blake rejects both transcendental deity and natural man." The statement is equally true for the Shelley of *Prometheus Unbound*, if one modifies rejection of transcendental deity to a skeptical opening toward the possibility of such a Power. Though Demogorgon knows little more than does the Asia who questions him, that little concerns his relationship to a further Power, and the relationship is part of the imagelessness of ultimates, where poetry reaches its limit.

The events of *Prometheus Unbound* take place in the realm of mind, and despite his skepticism Shelley at this point in his career clung to a faith in the capacity of the human mind to renovate first itself, and then the outward world as well. The story of the lyrical drama is therefore an unfolding of renovation after renovation, until natural cycle itself is canceled in the rhapsodies of Act IV. Of actions in the traditional sense, I find only one, the act of pity that Prometheus extends toward Jupiter at line 53 of Act I. Frederick A. Pottle, in the most advanced essay yet written on the poem, insists that there is a second and as crucial action, the descent of Asia, with her subsequent struggle to attain to a theology of love: "Asia's action is to give up her demand for an ultimate Personal Evil, to combine an unshakable faith that the universe is sound at the core with a realization that, as regards man, Time is radically and incurably evil." Behind Pottle's reading is a drastic but powerful allegorizing of the poem, in which Prometheus and Asia occupy respectively the positions of head and heart: "The head must sincerely forgive, must willingly eschew hatred on purely experimental grounds ..." while the heart "must exorcize the demons of infancy." One can benefit from this provisional allegorizing even if one finds *Prometheus Unbound* to be less theistic in its implications than Pottle appears to do.

Further commentary on the complexities of the poem can be sought in works listed in the bibliography of this volume, but the aesthetic achievement needs to be considered here. Dr. Samuel Johnson still knew that invention was the essence of poetry, but this truth is mostly neglected in our contemporary criticism. It may be justly observed that Shelley had conquered the myth of Prometheus even as he had transformed it, and the conquest is the greatest glory of Shelley's poem. One power alone, Blake asserted, made a poet: the divine vision or imagination, by which he meant primarily the inventive faculty, the gift of making a myth or of so re-making a myth as to return it to the fully human truths of our original existence as unfallen men. If Johnson and Blake were right, then *Prometheus Unbound* is one of the greatest poems in the language, a judgment that will seem eccentric only to a kind of critic whose standards are centered in areas not in themselves imaginative.

IV

> Nature has appointed us men to be no base or ignoble animals, but when she ushers us into the vast universe ... she implants in our souls the unconquerable love of whatever is elevated and more divine than we. Wherefore not even the entire universe suffices for the thought and contemplation within the reach of the human mind.
>
> (Longinus, On the Sublime)

Published with *Prometheus Unbound* in 1820 were a group of Shelley's major odes, including "Ode to the West Wind," "To a Skylark," and "Ode to Liberty." These poems show Shelley as a lyricist deliberately seeking to extend the sublime mode, and are among his finest achievements.

Wallace Stevens, in one of the marvelous lyrics of his old age, hears the cry of the leaves and knows "it is the cry of leaves that do not transcend themselves," knows that the cry means no more than can be found "in the final finding of the ear, in the thing / Itself." From this it follows, with massive but terrible dignity, that "at last, the cry concerns no one at all." This is Stevens' modern reality of *decreation*, and this is the fate that Shelley's magnificent "Ode to the West Wind" seeks to avert. Shelley hears a cry of leaves that do transcend themselves, and he deliberately seeks a further transcendence that will metamorphosize "the thing itself" into human form, so that at last the cry will concern all men. But in Shelley's "Ode," as in Stevens, "there is a conflict, there is a resistance involved; / And being part is an exertion that declines." Shelley too feels the frightening strength of the *given*, "the life of that which gives life as it is," but here as elsewhere Shelley does not accept the merely "as it is." The function of his "Ode" is apocalyptic, and the controlled fury of his spirit is felt throughout this perfectly modulated "trumpet of a prophecy."

What is most crucial to an understanding of the "Ode" is the realization that its fourth and fifth stanzas bear a wholly antithetical relation to one another. The triple invocation to the elements of earth, air, and water occupies the first three stanzas of the poem, and the poet himself does not enter those stanzas; in them he is only a voice imploring the elements to hear. In the fourth stanza, the poet's ego enters the poem, but in the guise only of a battered job, seeking to lose his own humanity. From this nadir, the extraordinary and poignantly "broken" music of the last stanza rises up, into the poet's own element of fire, to affirm again the human dignity of the prophet's vocation, and to suggest a mode of imaginative renovation that goes beyond the cyclic limitations of nature. Rarely in the history of poetry have seventy lines done so much so well.

Shelley's other major odes are out of critical favor in our time, but this is due as much to actual misinterpretations as to any qualities inherent in these poems. "To a Skylark" strikes readers as silly when they visualize the poet staring at the bird and hailing it as nonexistent, but these readers have begun with such gross inaccuracy that their experience of what they take to be the poem may simply be dismissed. The ode's whole point turns on the lark's being out of sight from the start; the poet *hears* an evanescent song, but can see nothing, even as Keats in the "Ode to a Nightingale" never actually sees the bird. Flying too high almost to be heard, the lark is crucially compared by Shelley to his central symbol, the morning star fading into the dawn of an unwelcome day. What can barely be heard, and not seen at all, is still discovered to be a basis upon which to rejoice, and indeed becomes an inescapable motive for metaphor, a dark justification for celebrating the light of uncommon day. In the great revolutionary "Ode to Liberty," Shelley successfully adapts the English Pindaric to an abstract political theme, mostly by means of making the poem radically its own subject, as he does on a larger scale in *The Witch of Atlas* and *Epipsychidion*.

In the last two years of his life, Shelley subtly modified his lyrical art, making the best of his shorter poems the means by which his experimental intellectual temper and his more traditional social urbanity could be reconciled. The best of these lyrics would include "Hymn of Apollo," "The Two Spirits: An Allegory," "To Night," "Lines ... on ... the Death of Napoleon," and the final group addressed to Jane Williams, or resulting from the poet's love for her, including "When the lamp is shattered," "To

Jane: The Invitation," "The Recollection," "With a Guitar, to Jane," and the last completed lyric, the immensely moving "Lines written in the Bay of Lerici." Here are nine lyrics as varied and masterful as the language affords. Take these together with Shelley's achievements in the sublime ode, with the best of his earlier lyrics, and with the double handful of magnificent interspersed lyrics contained in *Prometheus Unbound* and *Hellas*, and it will not seem as if Swinburne was excessive in claiming for Shelley a rank as one of the two or three major lyrical poets in English tradition down to Swinburne's own time.

The best admonition to address to a reader of Shelley's lyrics, as of his longer poems, is to slow down and read very closely, so as to learn what Wordsworth could have meant when he reluctantly conceded that "Shelley is one of the best artists of us all: I mean in workmanship of style":

> There is no dew on the dry grass tonight,
>   Nor damp within the shadow of the trees;
> The wind is intermitting, dry and light;
>   And in the inconstant motion of the breeze
> The dust and straws are driven up and down,
> And whirled about the pavement of the town.
> ("Evening: Ponte Al Mare, Pisa")

This altogether characteristic example of Shelley's workmanship is taken from a minor and indeed unfinished lyric of 1821. I have undergone many unhappy conversations with university wits, poets, and critics, who have assured me that "Shelley had a tin ear," the assurance being given on one occasion by no less distinguished a prosodist than W.H. Auden, and I am always left wondering if my ears have heard correctly. The fashion of insisting that Shelley was a poor craftsman seems to have started with T.S. Eliot, spread from him to Dr. Leavis and the Fugitive group of Southern poets and critics, and then for a time became universal. It was a charming paradox that formalist and rhetorical critics should have become so affectively disposed against a poet as to be incapable of reading any of his verbal figures with even minimal accuracy, but the charm has worn off, and one hopes that the critical argument about Shelley can now move on into other (and more disputable) areas.

V

> Cruelty has a Human Heart,
> And Jealousy a Human Face;

Terror the Human Form Divine,
And Secrecy the Human Dress.
The Human Dress is forged Iron,
The Human Form a fiery Forge,
The Human Face a Furnace seal'd,
The Human Heart its hungry Gorge.
(Blake, "A Divine Image")

The Cenci occupies a curious place in Shelley's canon, one that is overtly apart from the sequence of his major works that goes from *Prometheus Unbound* to *The Triumph of Life*. Unlike the psuedo-Elizabethan tragedies of Shelley's disciple Beddoes, *The Cenci* is in no obvious way a visionary poem. Yet it is a tragedy only in a very peculiar sense, and has little in common with the stage-plays it ostensibly seeks to emulate. Its true companions, and descendants, are Browning's giant progression of dramatic monologues, *The Ring and the Book*, and certain works of Hardy that share its oddly effective quality of what might be termed dramatic solipsism, to have recourse to a desperate oxymoron. Giant incongruities clash in *Prometheus Unbound* as they do in Blake's major poems, but the clashes are resolved by both poets in the realms of a self-generated mythology. When parallel incongruities meet violently in *The Cenci*, in a context that excludes myth, the reader is asked to accept as human characters beings whose states of mind are too radically and intensely pure to be altogether human. Blake courts a similar problem whenever he is only at the borderline of his own mythical world, as in *Visions of the Daughters of Albion* and *The French Revolution*. Shelley's Beatrice and Blake's Oothoon are either too human or not human enough; the reader is uncomfortable in not knowing whether he encounters a Titaness or one of his own kind.

Yet this discomfort need not wreck the experience of reading *The Cenci*, which is clearly a work that excels in character rather than in plot, and more in the potential of character than in its realization. At the heart of *The Cenci* is Shelley's very original conception of tragedy. Tragedy is not a congenial form for apocalyptic writers, who tend to have a severe grudge against it, as Blake and D.H. Lawrence did. Shelley's morality was an apocalyptic one, and the implicit standard for *The Cenci* is set in *The Mask of Anarchy*, which advocates a nonviolent resistance to evil. Beatrice is tragic because she does *not* meet this high standard, though she is clearly superior to every other person in her world. Life triumphs over Beatrice because she does take violent revenge upon an intolerable oppressor. The tragedy Shelley develops is one of a heroic character "violently thwarted from her nature" by circumstances she ought to have defied. This allies Beatrice with a large group of Romantic heroes, ranging from the Cain of Byron's drama to the pathetic daemon of Mary Shelley's *Frankenstein* and, on the cosmic level, embracing Shelley's own Prometheus and the erring Zoas or demigods of Blake's myth.

To find tragedy in any of these, you must persuasively redefine tragedy, as Shelley implicitly did. Tragedy becomes the fall of the imagination, or rather the falling away from imaginative conduct on the part of a heroically imaginative individual.

Count Cenci is, as many critics have noted, a demonic parody of Jehovah, and has a certain resemblance therefore to Shelley's Jupiter and Blake's Tiriel and Urizen. The count is obsessively given to hatred, and is vengeful, anal-erotic in his hoarding tendencies, incestuous, tyrannical, and compelled throughout by a jealous possessiveness even toward those he abhors. He is also given to bursts of Tiriel-like cursing, and like Tiriel or Jupiter he has his dying-god aspect, for his death, symbolizes the necessity of revolution, the breaking up of an old and hopeless order. Like all heavenly tyrants in his tradition, Cenci's quest for dominion is marked by a passion for uniformity, and it is inevitable that he seek to seduce the angelic Beatrice to his own perverse level. His success is an ironic one, since he does harden her into the only agent sufficiently strong and remorseless to cause his own destruction.

The aesthetic power of *The Cenci* lies in the perfection with which it both sets forth Beatrice's intolerable dilemma and presents the reader with a parallel dilemma. The natural man in the reader exults at Beatrice's metamorphosis into a relentless avenger, and approves even her untruthful denial of responsibility for her father's murder. The imaginative man in the reader is appalled at the degeneration of an all-but-angelic intelligence into a skilled intriguer and murderess. This fundamental dichotomy *in the reader* is the theater where the true anguish of *The Cenci* is enacted. The overt theme becomes the universal triumph of life over integrity, which is to say of death-in-life over life.

The Cenci is necessarily a work conceived in the Shakespearean shadow, and it is obvious that Shelley did not succeed in forming a dramatic language for himself in his play. Dr. Leavis has seized upon this failure with an inquisitor's joy, saying that "it takes no great discernment to see that *The Cenci* is very bad and that its badness is characteristic." It takes a very little discernment to see that *The Cenci* survives its palpable flaws and that it gives us what Wordsworth's *The Borderers*, Byron's *Cain*, and Coleridge's *Remorse* give us also in their very different ways, a distinguished example of Romantic, experimental tragedy, in which a crime against nature both emancipates consciousness and painfully turns consciousness in upon itself, with an attendant loss of a higher and more innocent state of being. The Beatrice of Shelley's last scene has learned her full autonomy, her absolute alienation from nature and society, but at a frightful, and to Shelley a tragic, cost.

VI

> But were it not, that *Time* their troubler is,
>   All that in this delightful Gardin growes,
>   Should happie be, and have immortall blis
>   (Spenser)

In the spring of 1820, at Pisa, Shelley wrote *The Sensitive Plant*, a remarkably original poem, and a permanently valuable one, though it is little admired in recent years. As a parable of imaginative failure, the poem is another of the many Romantic versions of the Miltonic Eden's transformation into a wasteland, but the limitations it explores are not the Miltonic ones of human irresolution and disobedience. Like all of Shelley's major poems, *The Sensitive Plant* is a skeptical work, the skepticism here manifesting itself as a precariously poised suspension of judgment on the human capacity to perceive whether or not natural *or* imaginative values survive the cyclic necessities of change and decay.

The tone of *The Sensitive Plant* is a deliberate exquisitiveness, of a more-than-Spenserian kind. Close analogues to this tone can be found in major passages of Keats's *Endymion* and in Blake's *The Book of Thel*. The ancestor poet for all these visionary poems, including Shelley's *The Witch of Atlas* and the vision of Beulah in Blake's *Milton*, is of course Spenser, whose mythic version of the lower or earthly paradise is presented as the Garden of Adonis in *The Faerie Queene*, Book III, Canto VI, which is probably the most influential passage of poetry in English, if by "influential" we mean what influences other poets.

The dark melancholy of *The Sensitive Plant* is not Spenserian, but everything else in the poem to some extent is. Like many poems in this tradition, the lament is for mutability itself, for change seen as loss. What is lost is innocence, natural harmony, the mutual interpenetrations of a merely given condition that is nevertheless whole and beyond the need of justification. The new state, experiential life as seen in Part III of the poem, is the world without imagination, a tract of weeds. When Shelley, in the noblest quatrains he ever wrote, broods on this conclusion he offers no consolation beyond the most urbane of his skepticisms. The light that puts out our eyes is a darkness to us, yet remains light, and death may be a mockery of our inadequate imaginations. The myth of the poem—its garden, lady, and plant may have prevailed, while we, the poem's readers, may be too decayed in our perceptions to know this. Implicit in Shelley's poem is a passionate refutation of time, but the passion is a desperation unless the mind's imaginings can cleanse perception of its obscurities. Nothing in the poem proper testifies to the mind's mastery of outward sense. The "Conclusion" hints at what Shelley beautifully calls "a modest creed," but the poet is too urbane and skeptical to urge it upon either us or himself. The creed appears again in *The Witch of Atlas*, but with a playful and amiable disinterestedness that removes it almost entirely from the anguish of human desire.

The Witch of Atlas is Shelley's most inventive poem, and is by any just standards a triumph. In kind, it goes back to the English Renaissance epyllion, the Ovidian erotic-mythological brief epic, but in tone and procedure it is a new departure, except that for Shelley it had been prophesied by his own rendition of the Homeric "Hymn to Mercury." Both poems are in *ottava rima*, both have a Byronic touch, and both have been characterized accurately as possessing a tone of visionary cynicism. Hermes and the Witch of Atlas qualify the divine grandeurs among which they move, and remind us that the imagination unconfined respects no orders of being, however traditional or natural.

G. Wilson Knight first pointed to the clear resemblance between the tone of *The Witch of Atlas* and Yeats's later style, and there is considerable evidence of the permanent effect of the poem's fantastic plot and proper ties upon Yeats. Shelley's *Witch* is Yeats's "Byzantium" writ large; both poems deal with Phase 15 of Yeats's *A Vision*, with the phase of poetic incarnation, and so with the state of the soul in which art is created. In a comparison of the two poems, the immediate contrast will be found in the extraordinary relaxation that Shelley allows himself. The nervous intensity that the theme demands is present in the *Witch*, but has been transmuted into an almost casual acceptance of intolerable realities that art cannot mitigate.

The Witch of Atlas, as Shelley says in the poem's highly ironic dedicatory stanzas to his wife, tells no story, false or true, but is "a visionary rhyme." If the Witch is to be translated at all into terms not her own, then she can only be the mythopoeic impulse or inventive faculty itself, one of whose manifestations is the Hermaphrodite, which we can translate as a poem, or any work of art. The Witch's boat is the emblem of her creative desire, and like the Hermaphrodite it works against nature. The Hermaphrodite is both a convenience for the Witch, helping her to go beyond natural limitations, and a companion of sorts, but a highly inadequate one, being little more than a robot. The limitations of art are involved here, for the Witch has rejected the love of every mortal being, and has chosen instead an automaton of her own creation. In the poignant stanzas in which she rejects the suit of the nymphs, Shelley attains one of the immense triumphs of his art, but the implications of the triumph, and of the entire poem, are as deliberately chilling as the Byzantine vision of the aging Yeats.

Though the Witch turns her playful and antinomian spirit to the labor of upsetting church and state, in the poem's final stanzas, and subverts even the tired conventions of mortality as well as of morality, the ultimate impression she makes upon us is one of remoteness. The fierce aspirations of *Prometheus Unbound*, were highly qualified by a consciously manipulated prophetic irony, yet they retained their force, and aesthetic immediacy, as the substance of what Shelley passionately desired. The ruin that shadows love in *Prometheus Unbound*, the *amphisbaena* or two-headed serpent that could move downward and outward to destruction again, the warning made explicit in the closing stanzas spoken by Demogorgon; it is these antithetical hints that survived in Shelley longer than the vehement hope of his lyrical drama. *The Sensitive Plant* and *The Witch of Atlas* manifest a subtle movement away from that hope. *Epipsychidion*, the most exalted of Shelley's poems, seeks desperately to renovate that hope by placing it in the context of heterosexual love, and with the deliberate and thematic self-combustion of the close of *Epipsychidion* Shelley appears to have put all hope aside, and to have prepared himself for his magnificent but despairing last phase, of which the enduring monuments are *Adonais* and *The Triumph of Life*.

VII

> What man most passionately wants is his living wholeness and his living unison, not his own isolate salvation of his "soul." Man wants his physical fulfillment first and foremost, since now, once and once only, he is in the flesh and potent. For man, as for flower and beast and bird, the supreme triumph is to be most vividly, most perfectly alive. Whatever the unborn and the dead may know, they cannot know the beauty, the marvel of being alive in the flesh. The dead may look after the afterwards. But the magnificent here and now of life in the flesh is ours, and ours alone, and ours only for a time.
>
> (D.H. Lawrence, *Apocalypse*)

Except for Blake's *Visions of the Daughters of Albion*, which it in some respects resembles, *Epipsychidion* is the most outspoken and eloquent appeal for free love in the language. Though this appeal is at the heart of the poem, and dominates its most famous passage (lines 147–54), it is only one aspect of a bewilderingly problematical work. *Epipsychidion* was intended by Shelley to be his *Vita Nuova*, celebrating the discovery of his Beatrice in Emilia Viviani. It proved however to be a climactic and not an initiatory poem, for in it Shelley culminates the quest begun in *Alastor*, only to find after culmination that the quest remains unfulfilled and unfulfillable. The desire of Shelley remains infinite, and the only emblem adequate to that desire is the morning and evening star, Venus, at whose sphere the shadow cast by earth into the heavens reaches its limits. After *Epipsychidion*, in *Adonais* and *The Triumph of Life*, only the star of Venus abides as an image of the good. It is not Emilia Viviani but her image that proves inadequate in *Epipsychidion*, a poem whose most turbulent and valuable element is its struggle to record the process of image-making. Of all Shelley's major poems, *Epipsychidion* most directly concerns itself with the mind in creation. "Mont Blanc" has the same position among Shelley's shorter poems, and has the advantage of its relative discursiveness, as the poet meditates upon the awesome spectacle before him. *Epipsychidion* is continuous rhapsody, and sustains its lyrical intensity of a lovers' confrontation for six hundred lines. The mind in creation, here and in *A Defense of Poetry*, is as a fading coal, and much of Shelley's art in the poem is devoted to the fading phenomenon, as image after image recedes and the poet-lover feels more fearfully the double burden of his love's inexpressibility and its necessary refusal to accept even natural, let alone societal, limitations.

There is, in Shelley's development as a poet, a continuous effort to subvert the poetic image, so as to arrive at a more radical kind of verbal figure, which Shelley never altogether achieved. Tenor and vehicle are imported into one another, and the choice of natural images increasingly favors those already on the point of vanishing, just within the ken of eye and ear. The world is skeptically taken up into the mind, and there are suggestions and overtones that all of reality is a phantasmagoria. Shelley becomes an idealist totally skeptical of the metaphysical foundations of idealism, while he continues to entertain a skeptical materialism, or rather he becomes a fantasist pragmatically given to some materialist hypotheses that his imagination regards as absurd. This is not necessarily a self-contradiction, but it is a kind of psychic split, and it is exposed very powerfully in *Epipsychidion*. Who wins a triumph in the poem, the gambler with the limits of poetry and of human relationship, or the inexorable limits? Space, time, loneliness, mortality, wrong—all these are put aside by vision, yet vision darkens perpetually in the poem. "The world, unfortunately, is real; I, unfortunately, am Borges," is the ironic reflection of a great contemporary seer of phantasmagorias, as he brings his refutation of time to an unrefuting close. Shelley too is swept along by what destroys him and is inescapable, the reality that will not yield to the most relentless of imaginings. In that knowledge, he turns to elegy and away from celebration.

Adonais, Shelley's formal elegy for Keats, is a great monument in the history of the English elegy, and yet hardly an elegy at all. Nearly five hundred lines long, it exceeds in scope and imaginative ambition its major English ancestors, the *Astrophel* of Spenser and the *Lycidas* of Milton, as well as such major descendants as Arnold's Thyrsis and Swinburne's *Ave Atque Vale*. Only Tennyson's *In Memoriam* rivals it as an attempt to make the elegy a vehicle for not less than everything a particular poet has to say on the ultimates of human existence. Yet Tennyson, for all his ambition, stays within the bounds of elegy. *Adonais*, in the astonishing sequence of its last eighteen stanzas, is no more an elegy proper than Yeats's "Byzantium" poems are. Like the "Byzantium" poems (which bear a close relation to it), *Adonais* is a high song of poetic self-recognition in the presence of foreshadowing death, and also a description of poetic existence, even of a poem's state of being.

Whether Shelley holds together the elegiac and visionary aspects of his poem is disputable; it is difficult to see the full continuity that takes the poet from his hopeless opening to his more than triumphant close, from:

> I weep for Adonais—he is dead!
> O, weep for Adonais! though our tears
> Thaw not the frost which binds so dear a head!

to:

> I am borne darkly, fearfully, afar;
> Whilst, burning through the inmost veil of Heaven,
> The soul of Adonais, like a star,
> Beacons from the abode where the Eternal are.

From frost to fire as a mode of renewal for the self: that is an archetypal Romantic pattern, familiar to us from *The Ancient Mariner* and the *Intimations* Ode (see the contrast between the last line of stanza VIII and the first of stanza IX in that poem). But *Adonais* breaks this pattern, for the soul of Shelley's Keats burns through the final barrier to revelation only by means of an energy that is set against nature, and the frost that no poetic tears can thaw yields only to "the fire for which all thirst," but which no natural man can drink, for no living man can drink of the whole wine of the burning fountain. As much as Yeats's "All Souls' Night," *Adonais* reaches out to a reality of ghostly intensities, yet Shelley as well as Yeats is reluctant to leave behind the living man who blindly drinks his drop, and *Adonais* is finally a "Dialogue of Self and Soul," in which the Soul wins a costly victory, as costly as the Self's triumph in Yeats's "Dialogue." The Shelley who cries out, in rapture and dismay, "The massy earth and sphered skies are riven!", is a poet who has given himself freely to the tempest of creative destruction, to a reality beyond the natural, yet who movingly looks back upon the shore and upon the throng he has forsaken. The close of *Adonais* is a triumph of character over personality, to use a Yeatsian dialectic, but the personality of the lyric poet is nevertheless the dominant aesthetic element in the poem's dark and fearful apotheosis.

"Apotheosis is not the origin of the major man," if we are to credit Stevens, but the qualified assertions of Shelley do proclaim such an imaginative humanism in the central poems that preceded *Adonais*. In *Adonais* the imagination forsakes humanism, even as it does in the "Byzantium" poems.

Though *Adonais* has been extensively Platonized and Neoplatonized by a troop of interpreters, it is in a clear sense a materialist's poem, written out of a materialist's despair at his own deepest convictions, and finally a poem soaring above those convictions into a mystery that leaves a pragmatic materialism quite undisturbed. Whatever supernal apprehension it is that Shelley attains in the final third of *Adonais*, it is not in any ordinary sense a religious faith, for the only attitude toward natural existence it fosters in the poet is one of unqualified rejection, and indeed its pragmatic postulate is simply suicide. Nothing could be more different in spirit from Demogorgon's closing lines in *Prometheus Unbound* than the final stanzas of *Adonais*, and the ruthlessly skeptical Shelley must have known this.

He knew also though that we do not judge poems by pragmatic tests, and the splendor of the resolution to *Adonais* is not impaired by its implications of human defeat. Whether Keats lives again is unknown to Shelley; poets are among "the enduring dead," and Keats "wakes or sleeps" with them. The endurance is not then necessarily a mode of survival, and what flows back to the burning fountain is not necessarily the human soul, though it is "pure spirit." Or if it is the soul of Keats as well as "the soul of Adonais," then the accidents of individual personality have abandoned it, making this cold comfort indeed. Still, Shelley is not offering us (or himself) comfort; his elegy has no parallel to Milton's consolation in *Lycidas*:

> There entertain him all the Saints above,
> In solemn troops, and sweet Societies

That sing, and singing in their glory move,
And wipe the tears forever from his eyes.

To Milton, as a Christian poet, death is somehow unnatural. To Shelley, for all his religious temperament, death is wholly natural, and if death is dead, then nature must be dead also. The final third of *Adonais* is desperately apocalyptic in a way that *Prometheus Unbound*, Act IV, was not. For *Prometheus Unbound* ends in a Saturnalia, though there are darker implications also, but *Adonais* soars beyond the shadow that the earth casts into the heavens. Shelley was ready for a purgatorial vision of earth, and no longer could sustain even an ironic hope.

VIII

Mal dare, e mal tener lo mondo pulcro
    ha tolto loro, e posti a questa zuffa;
    qual ella sia, parole non ci appulcro.
                (*Inferno* 7:58–60)

        That ill they gave,
And ill they kept, hath of the beauteous world
Deprived, and set them at this strife, which needs
No labour'd phrase of mine to set it off.
                (Cary, *The Vision of Dante*)

There are elements in *The Triumph of Life*, Shelley's last poem, that mark it as an advance over all the poetry he had written previously. The bitter eloquence and dramatic condensation of the style are new; so is a ruthless pruning of invention. The mythic figures are few, being confined to the "Shape all light," the charioteer, and Life itself, while the two principal figures, Shelley and Rousseau, appear in their proper persons, though in the perspective of eternity, as befits a vision of judgment. The tone of Shelley's last poem is derived from Dante's *Purgatorio*, even as much in *Epipsychidion* comes from Dante's *Vita Nuova*, but the events and atmosphere of *The Triumph of Life* have more in common with the *Inferno*. Still, the poem is a purgatorial work, for all the unrelieved horror of its vision, and perhaps Shelley might have found some gradations in his last vision, so as to climb out of the poem's impasse, if he had lived to finish it, though I incline to doubt this. As it stands, the poem is in hell, and Shelley is there, one of the apparently condemned, as all men are, he says, save for "the sacred few" of Athens and Jerusalem, martyrs to vision like Socrates, Jesus, and a chosen handful, with whom on the basis of *Adonais* we can place Keats, as he too had touched the world with his living flame, and then fled back up to his native noon.

The highest act of Shelley's imagination in the poem, perhaps in all of his poetry, is in the magnificent appropriateness of Rousseau's presence, from his first entrance to his last speech before the fragment breaks off. Rousseau is Virgil to Shelley's Dante, in the sense of being his imaginative ancestor, his guide in creation, and also in prophesying the dilemma the disciple would face at the point of crisis in his life. Shelley, sadly enough, was hardly in the middle of the journey, but at twenty-nine he had only days to live, and the imagination in him felt compelled to face the last things. Without Rousseau, Shelley would not have written the "Hymn to Intellectual Beauty," and perhaps not "Mont Blanc" either. Rousseau, more even than Wordsworth, was the prophet of natural man, and the celebrator of the state of nature. Even in 1816, writing his hymns and starting the process that would lead to the conception of *Prometheus Unbound*, Shelley fights against the natural man and natural religion, but he fights partly against his own desires, and the vision of Rousseau haunts him still in the "Ode to the West Wind" and in the greatest chant of the apocalyptic fourth act of the lyrical drama, the song of the Earth beginning "It interpenetrates my granite mass." Shelley knew that the spirit of Rousseau was what had moved him most in the spirit of the age, and temperamentally (which counts for most in a poet) it makes more sense to name Shelley the disciple and heir of Rousseau than of Godwin, or Wordsworth, or any of the later French theorists of Revolution. Rousseau and Hume make an odd formula of heart and head in Shelley, but they are the closest parallels to be found to him on the emotional and intellectual sides respectively.

Chastened and knowing, almost beyond knowledge, Rousseau enters the poem, speaking not to save his disciple, but to show him that he cannot be saved, and to teach him a style fit for his despair. The imaginative lesson of *The Triumph of Life* is wholly present in the poem's title: life always triumphs, for life, our life, is after all what the preface to *Alastor* called it, a "lasting misery and loneliness." One Power only, the Imagination, is capable of redeeming life, "but that Power which strikes the luminaries of the world with sudden darkness and extinction, by awakening them to too exquisite a perception of its influences, dooms to a slow and poisonous decay those meaner spirits that dare to abjure its dominion." In *The Triumph of Life*, the world's luminaries are still the poets, stars of evening and morning, "heaven's living eyes," but they fade into a double light, the light of nature or the sun, and the harsher and more blinding light of Life, the destructive chariot of the poem's vision. The chariot of

Life, like the apocalyptic chariots of Act IV, *Prometheus Unbound*, goes back to the visions of Ezekiel and Revelation for its sources, as the chariots of Dante and Milton did, but now Shelley gives a demonic parody of his sources, possibly following the example of Spenser's chariot of Lucifera. Rousseau is betrayed to the light of life because he began by yielding his imagination's light to the lesser but seductive light of nature, represented in the poem by the "Shape all light" who offers him the waters of natural experience to drink. He drinks, he begins to forget everything in the mind's desire that had transcended nature, and so he falls victim to Life's destruction, and fails to become one of "the sacred few." There is small reason to doubt that Shelley, at the end, saw himself as having shared in Rousseau's fate. The poem, fragment as it is, survives its own despair, and stands with Keats's *The Fall of Hyperion* as a marvelously eloquent imaginative testament, fit relic of an achievement broken off too soon to rival Blake's or Wordsworth%, but superior to everything else in its own age.

IX

> The great instrument of moral good is the imagination.
>
> (A Defence of Poetry)

Anti-Shelleyans have come in all intellectual shapes and sizes, and have included distinguished men of letters from Charles Lamb and De Quincey down to T.S. Eliot, Allen Tate, and their school in our day. To distinguish between the kinds of anti-Shelleyans is instructive, though the following categories are by no means mutually exclusive. One can count six major varieties of anti-Shelleyans, whether one considers them historically or in contemporary terms:

1. The school of "common sense"
2. The Christian orthodox
3. The school of "wit"
4. Moralists, of most varieties
5. The school of "classic" form
6. Precisionists, or concretists.

It is evident that examples of (1), (2), and (4) need not be confuted, as they are merely irrelevant. We may deal with (3), (5), and (6) in their own terms, rather than in Shelley's, and still find Shelley triumphant.

The "wit" of Shelley's poetry has little to do with that of seventeenth-century verse, but has much in common with the dialectical vivacity of

Shaw, and something of the prophetic irony of Blake. If irony is an awareness of the terrible gap between aspiration and fulfillment, then the skeptical Shelley is among the most ironical of poets. If it is something else, as it frequently is in the school of Donne, one can observe that there are many wings in the house of wit, and one ought not to live in all of them simultaneously.

Form is another matter, and too complex to be argued fully here. The late C.S. Lewis justly maintained against the school of Eliot that Shelley was more classical in his sense of form, his balance of harmony and design, than Dryden. One can go further: Shelley is almost always a poet of the highest decorum, a stylist who adjusts his form and tone to his subject, whether it be the hammer-beat low style of *The Mask of Anarchy*, the urbane middle style of the *Letter to Maria Gisborne*, or the sublime inventiveness of the high style as it is renovated in *Prometheus Unbound*. Shelley was sometimes a hasty or careless artist, but he was always an artist, a poet who neither could nor would stop being a poet. Dr. Samuel Johnson would have disliked Shelley's poetry, indeed would have considered Shelley to be dangerously mad, but he would have granted that it was poetry of a high, if to him outmoded, order. Critics less classical than Johnson will not grant as much, because their notions of classical form are not as deeply founded.

The precisionist or concretist is probably Shelley's most effective enemy, since everything vital in Shelley's poetry deliberately strains away from the minute particulars of experience. But this is oddly true of Wordsworth as well, though Wordsworth usually insisted upon the opposite. The poetry of renovation in the United States, in our time, had its chief exemplars in William Carlos Williams and in Wallace Stevens, and it is Stevens who is in the line of both Wordsworth and of Shelley. Williams's famous adage, "no ideas but in things," is the self-justified motto of one valid kind of poetic procedure, but it will not allow for the always relevant grandeurs of the sublime tradition, with its "great moments" of ecstasy and recognition. Wordsworth on the mountainside looks out and finds only a sea of mist, an emblem of the highest imaginative vision, in which the edges of things have blurred and faded out. Stevens, opening the door of his house upon the flames of the Northern Lights, confronts an Arctic effulgence flaring upon the frame of everything he is, but does not describe the flashing auroras. Shelley, at his greatest, precisely chants an energetic becoming that cannot be described in the concrete because its entire purpose is to modify the concrete, to compel a greater reality to appear:

... the one Spirit's plastic stress
Sweeps through the dull dense world, compelling there,

All new successions to the forms they wear;
Torturing th' unwilling dross that checks its flight
To its own likeness, as each mass may bear;
And bursting in its beauty and its might
From trees and beasts and men into the Heaven's light.

Had Shelley been able to accept any known faith, he would have given us the name and nature of that "one Spirit." Unlike Keats, he would not have agreed with Stevens that the great poems of heaven and hell had been written, and that only the great poem of earth remained to be composed. His own spirit was apocalyptic, and the still unwritten poems of heaven and hell waited mute upon the answering swiftness of his own imaginings, when he went on to his early finalities:

As if that frail and wasted human form,
Had been an elemental god.

John Keats

(1795–1821)

ONE OF THE CENTRAL THEMES IN W. J. BATE'S DEFINITIVE *JOHN KEATS* IS the "large, often paralyzing embarrassment ... that the rich accumulation of past poetry, as the eighteenth century had seen so realistically, can curse as well as bless." As Mr. Bate remarks, this embarrassment haunted Romantic and haunts post-Romantic poetry, and was felt by Keats with a particular intensity. Somewhere in the heart of each new poet there is hidden the dark wish that the libraries be burned in some new Alexandrian conflagration, that the imagination might be liberated from the greatness and oppressive power of its own dead champions.

Something of this must be involved in the Romantics' loving struggle with their ghostly father, Milton. The role of wrestling Jacob is taken on by Blake in his "brief epic" *Milton*, by Wordsworth in *The Recluse* fragment, and in more concealed form by Shelley in *Prometheus Unbound* and Keats in the first *Hyperion*. The strength of poetical life in Milton seems always to have appalled as much as it delighted; in the fearful vigor of his unmatched exuberance the English master of the sublime has threatened not only poets, but the values once held to transcend poetry:

> ... the Argument
> Held me a while misdoubting his Intent,
> That he would ruin (for I saw him strong)
> The sacred Truths to Fable and old Song
> (So Sampson grop'd the Temple's Posts in spite)
> The World O'erwhelming to revenge his sight.

The older Romantics at least thought that the struggle with Milton had bestowed a blessing without a crippling; to the younger ones a consciousness of gain and loss came together. Blake's audacity gave him a Milton altogether fitted to his great need, a visionary prototype who could be dramatized as rising up, "unhappy tho' in heav'n," taking off the robe of the promise, and ungirding himself from the oath of God, and then descending into Blake's world to save the later poet and every man "from his Chain of Jealousy." Wordsworth's equal audacity allowed him, after praising Milton's invocatory power, to call on a greater Muse than Urania, to assist him in exploring regions more awful than Milton ever visited. The prophetic Spirit called down in *The Recluse* is itself a child of Milton's Spirit that preferred, before all temples, the upright and pure heart of the Protestant poet. But the child is greater than the father, and inspires, in a fine Shakespearean reminiscence:

> The human Soul of universal earth,
> Dreaming on things to come.

Out of that capable dreaming came the poetic aspirations of Shelley and of Keats, who inherited the embarrassment of Wordsworth's greatness to add to the burden of Milton's. Yielding to few in my admiration for Shelley's blank verse in *Prometheus*, I am still made uneasy by Milton's ghost hovering in it. At times Shelley's power of irony rescues him from Milton's presence by the argument's dissonance with the steady Miltonic music of the lyrical drama, but the ironies pass and the Miltonic sublime remains, testifying to the unyielding strength of an order Shelley hoped to overturn. In the lyrics of *Prometheus* Shelley is free, and they rather than the speeches foretold his own poetic future, the sequence of *The Witch of Atlas*, *Epipsychidion* and *Adonais*. Perhaps the turn to Dante, hinted in *Epipsychidion* and emergent in *The Triumph of Life*, was in part caused by the necessity of finding a sublime antithesis to Milton.

With Keats, we need not surmise. The poet himself claimed to have abandoned the first *Hyperion* because it was too Miltonic, and his critics have agreed in not wanting him to have made a poem "that might have been written by John Milton, but one that was unmistakably by no other than John Keats." In the Great Odes and *The Fall of Hyperion* Keats was to write poems unmistakably his own, as *Endymion* in another way had been his own. Individuality of style, and still more of conception, no critic would now deny to the odes, Keats's supreme poems, or to *The Fall of Hyperion*, which was his testament, and is the work future poets may use as Tennyson, Arnold and Yeats used the odes in the past.

That Keats, in his handful of great poems, surpassed the Milton-haunted poets of the second half of the eighteenth century is obvious to a critical age like our own, which tends to prefer Keats, in those poems, to even the best work of Blake, Wordsworth and Shelley, and indeed to most if not all poetry in the language since the mid-seventeenth century. Perhaps the basis for that preference can be explored afresh through a consideration of precisely how Keats's freedom of the negative weight of poetic tradition is manifested in some of his central poems. Keats lost and gained, as each of the major Romantics did, in the struggle with the greatness of Milton. Keats was perhaps too generous and perceptive a critic, too wonderfully balanced a humanist, not to have lost some values of a cultural legacy that both stimulated and inhibited the nurture of fresh values.

Mr. Bate finely says, commenting on Keats's dedication sonnet to Leigh Hunt, that "when the imagination looks to any past, of course, including one's own individual past, it blends memories and images into a denser, more massive unit than ever existed in actuality." Keats's confrontation with this idealized past is most direct from the *Ode to Psyche* on, as Mr. Bate emphasizes. Without repeating him on that ode, or what I myself have written elsewhere, I want to examine it again in the specific context of Keats's fight against the too-satisfying enrichments with which tradition threatens the poet who seeks his own self-recognition and expressive fulfillment.

Most readers recalling the *Ode to Psyche* think of the last stanza, which is the poem's glory, and indeed its sole but sufficient claim to stand near the poet's four principal odes. The stanza expresses a wary confidence that the true poet's imagination cannot be impoverished. More wonderfully, the poet ends the stanza by opening the hard-won consciousness of his own creative powers to a visitation of love. The paradise within is barely formed, but the poet does not hesitate to make it vulnerable, though he may be condemned in consequence to the fate of the famished knight of his own faery ballad. There is triumph in the closing tone of *To Psyche*, but a consciousness also I think of the danger that is being courted. The poet has given Psyche the enclosed bower nature no longer affords her, but he does not pause to be content in that poet's paradise. It is not Byzantium which Keats has built in the heretofore untrodden regions of his mind but rather a realm that is precisely not far above all breathing human passion. He has not assumed the responsibility of an expanded consciousness for the rewards of self-communing and solitary musing, in the manner of the poet-hero of *Alastor*, and of Prince Athanase in his lonely tower. He seeks "love" rather than "wisdom," distrusting a reality that must be approached apart from men. And he has written his poem, in however light a spirit, as an act of self-dedication and of freedom from the wealth of the past. He will be Psyche's priest and rhapsode in the proud conviction that she has had no others before him, or none at least so naked of external pieties.

The wealth of tradition is great not only in its fused massiveness, but in its own subtleties of internalization. One does poor service by sandbagging this profoundly moving poem, yet even the heroic innovators but tread the shadowy ground their ancestors found before them. Wordsworth had stood on that ground, as Keats well knew, and perhaps had chosen a different opening from it, neither toward love nor toward wisdom, but toward a plain recognition of natural reality and a more sublime recognition-by-starts of a final reality that seemed to contain nature. Wordsworth never quite named that finality as imagination, though Blake had done so and the young Coleridge felt (and resisted) the demonic temptation to do so. Behind all these were the fine collapses of the Age of Sensibility, the raptures of *Jubilate Agno* and the *Ode on the Poetical Character*, and the more forced but highly impressive tumults of *The Bard* and *The Progress of Poesy*. Farther back was the ancestor of all such moments of poetic incarnation, the Milton of the great invocations, whose spirit I think haunts the *Ode to Psyche* and the *Ode to a Nightingale*, and does not vanish until *The Fall of Hyperion* and *To Autumn*.

Hazlitt, with his usual penetration, praises Milton for his power to absorb vast poetic traditions with no embarrassment whatsoever: "In reading his works, we feel ourselves under the influence of a mighty intellect, that the nearer it approaches to others, becomes more distinct from them." This observation, which comes in a lecture Keats heard, is soon joined by the excellent remark that "Milton's learning has the effect of intuition." The same lecture, in its treatment of Shakespeare, influenced Keats's conception of the Poetical Character, as Mr. Bate notes. Whether Keats speculated sadly on the inimitable power of Milton's positive capability for converting the splendor of the past into a private expressiveness we do not know. But the literary archetype of Psyche's rosy sanctuary is the poet's paradise, strikingly developed by Spenser and Drayton, and brought to a perfection by Milton. I am not suggesting Milton as a "source" for Keats's *Ode to Psyche*. Poets influence poets in ways more profound than verbal echoings. The paradise of poets is a recurrent element in English mythopoeic poetry, and it is perhaps part of the critic's burden never to allow himself to yield to embarrassment when the riches of poetic tradition come crowding in upon him. Poets need to be selective; critics need the humility of a bad conscience when they exclude any part of the poetic past from "tradition," though humility is never much in critical fashion. Rimbaud put these matters right in one outburst: "On n'a jamais bien jugé le romantisme. Qui l'aurait jugé? Les Critiques!!"

Milton, "escap't the *Stygian* pool," hails the light he cannot see, and reaffirms his ceaseless wanderings "where the Muses haunt / clear Spring, or shady Grove," and his nightly visits to "*Sion* and the flow'ry Brooks beneath." Like Keats's nightingale, he "sings darkling," but invokes a light that can "shine inward, and the mind through all her powers / Irradiate." The light shone inward, the mind's powers were triumphant, and all the sanctities of heaven yielded to Milton's vision. For the sanctuary of Milton's psyche is his vast heterocosm, the worlds he makes and ruins. His shrine is built, not to the human soul in love, but to the human soul glorious in its solitude, sufficient, with God's aid, to seek and find its own salvation. If Keats had closed the casement, and turned inward, seeking the principle that could sustain his own soul in the darkness, perhaps he could have gone on with the first *Hyperion*, and become a very different kind of poet. He would then have courted the fate of Collins, and pursued the guiding steps of Milton only to discover the quest was:

> In vain—such bliss to one alone
> Of all the sons of soul was known,
> And Heav'n and Fancy, kindred pow'rs,
> Have now o'erturned th'inspiring bow'rs,
> Or curtain'd close such scene from ev'ry future view.

Yeats, in the eloquent simplicities of *Per Amica Silentia Lunae*, saw Keats as having "been born with that thirst for luxury common to many at the outsetting of the Romantic Movement," and thought therefore that the poet of *To Autumn* "but gave us his dream of luxury." Yeats's poets were Blake and Shelley; Keats and Wordsworth he refused to understand, for their way was not his own. His art, from *The Wanderings of Oisin* through the *Last Poems and Plays*, is founded on a rage against growing old, and a rejection of nature. The poet, he thought, could find his art only by giving way to an anti-self, which "comes but to those who are no longer deceived, whose passion is reality." Yeats was repelled by Milton, and found no place for him in *A Vision*, and certainly no poet cared so little as Milton to express himself through an anti-self. In Blake's strife of spectre and emanation, in Shelley's sense of being shadowed by the *alastor* while seeking the epipsyche, Yeats found precedent for his own quest towards Unity of Being, the poet as daimonic man taking his mask from. a phase opposite to that of his own will. Like Blake and Shelley, Yeats sought certainty, but being of Shelley's phase rather than Blake's, he did not find it. The way of Negative Capability, as an answer to Milton, Yeats did not take into account; he did not conceive of a poet "certain of nothing but of the holiness of the Heart's affections and the truth of Imagination." (There is, of course, no irritable reaching after mere fact and reason in Yeats: he reached instead for everything the occult sub-imagination had knocked together in place of fact and reason. But his motive was his incapability "of being in uncertainties, mysteries, doubts," and the results are more mixed than most recent criticism will admit.)

Keats followed Wordsworth by internalizing the quest toward finding a world that answered the poet's desires, and he hoped to follow Shakespeare by making that world more than a sublime projection of his own ego. Shakespeare's greatness was not an embarrassment to Keats, but the hard victories of poetry had to be won against the more menacing values of poetic tradition. The advance beyond the *Ode to Psyche* was taken in the *Ode to a Nightingale*, where the high world within the bird's song is an expansion of the rosy sanctuary of Psyche. In this world our sense of actuality is heightened simultaneously with the widening of what Mr. Bate terms "the realm of possibility." The fear of losing actuality does not encourage the dull soil of mundane experience to quarrel with the proud forests it has fed, the nightingale's high requiem. But to be the breathing garden in which Fancy breeds his flowers is a delightful fate; to become a sod is to suffer what Belial dreaded in that moving speech Milton himself and the late C.S. Lewis have taught too many to despise.

Milton, invoking the light, made himself at one with the nightingale; Keats is deliberate in knowing constantly his own separation from the bird. What is fresh in this ode is not I think a sense of the poet's dialogue with himself; it is surprising how often the English lyric has provided such an undersong, from Spenser's *Prothalamion* to Wordsworth's *Resolution and Independence*. Keats wins freedom from tradition here by claiming so very little for the imagination in its intoxicating but harsh encounter with the reality of natural song. The poet does not accept what is as good, and he does not exile desire for what is not. Yet, for him, what is possible replaces what is not. There is no earthly paradise for poets, but there is a time of all-but-final satisfaction, the fullness of lines 35 to 58 of this ode.

I do not think that there is, before Keats, so individual a setting-forth of such a time, anywhere in poetic tradition since the Bible. The elevation of Wordsworth in *Tintern Abbey* still trembles at the border of a theophany, and so derives from a universe centered upon religious experience. The vatic gift of Shelley's self to the elements, from *Alastor* on, has its remote but genuine ancestors in the sibylline frenzies of traditions as ancient as Orphism. Blake's moments of delight come as hard-won intervals of rest from an intellectual warfare that differs little if at all from the struggles towards a revelatory awareness in Ezekiel or Isaiah, and there is no contentment in them. What Keats so greatly gives to the Romantic tradition in the *Nightingale* ode is what no poet before him had the capability of giving—the sense of the human making choice of a human self, aware of its deathly nature, and yet having the will to celebrate the imaginative richness of mortality. The *Ode to a Nightingale* is the first poem to know and declare, wholeheartedly, that death is the mother of beauty. The *Ode to Psyche* still glanced, with high good humor, at the haunted rituals of the already-written poems of heaven; the *Ode to a Nightingale* turns, almost casually, to the unwritten great poem of earth. There is nothing casual about the poem's tone, but there is a wonderful lack of self-consciousness at the poem's freedom from the past, in the poem's knowing that death, our death, is absolute and without memorial.

The same freedom from the massive beliefs and poetic stances of the past is manifested in the *Ode on a Grecian Urn*, where the consolations of the spirit are afforded merely by an artifice of eternity, and not by evidences of an order of reality wholly other than our own. Part of this poem's strength is in the deliberate vulnerability of its speaker, who contemplates a world of values he cannot appropriate for his own, although nothing in that world is antithetical to his own nature as an aspiring poet. Mr. Bate states the poem's awareness of this vulnerability: "In attempting to approach the urn in its own terms, the imagination has been led at the same time to separate itself—or the situation of man generally—still further from the urn." One is not certain that the imagination is not also separating itself from the essential poverty of man's situation in the poem's closing lines. Mr. Bate thinks we underestimate Keats's humor in the Great Odes, and he is probably right, but the humor that apparently ends the *Grecian Urn* is a grim one. The truth of art may be all of the truth our condition can apprehend, but it is not a saving truth. If this is all we need to know, it may be that no knowledge can help us. Shelley was very much a child of Miltonic tradition in affirming the moral instrumentality of the imagination; Keats is grimly free of tradition in his subtle implication of a truth that most of us learn. Poetry is not a means of good; it is, as Wallace Stevens implied, like the honey of earth that comes and goes at once, while we wait vainly for the honey of heaven.

Blake, Wordsworth, and Shelley knew in their different ways that human splendors had no sources but in the human imagination, but each of these great innovators had a religious temperament, however heterodox, and Keats had not. Keats had a clarity in his knowledge of the uniqueness and finality of human life and death that caused him a particular anguish on his own death-bed, but gave him, before that, the imagination's gift of an absolute originality. The power of Keats's imagination could never be identified by him with an apocalyptic energy that might hope to transform nature. It is not that he lacked the confidence of Blake and of Shelley, or of the momentary Wordsworth of *The Recluse*. He felt the imagination's

desire for a revelation that would redeem the inadequacies of our condition, but he felt also a humorous skepticism toward such desire. He would
have read the prose testament of Wallace Stevens, Two *Or Three Ideas*, with
the wry approval so splendid a lecture deserves. The gods are dispelled in
mid-air, and leave "no texts either of the soil or of the soul." The poet does
not cry out for their return, since it remains his work to resolve life in his
own terms, for in the poet is "the increasingly human self."

Part of Keats's achievement is due then to his being perhaps the only
genuine forerunner of the representative post-Romantic sensibility.
Another part is centered in the *Ode on Melancholy* and *The Fall of Hyperion*,
for in these poems consciousness becomes its own purgatory, and the poet
learns the cost of living in an excitement of which he affirms "that it is the
only state for the best sort of Poetry—that is all I care for, all I live for."
From this declaration it is a direct way to the generally misunderstood
rigor of Pater, when he insists that "a counted number of pulses only is
given to us of a variegated, dramatic life," and asks: "How may we see in
them all that is to be seen in them by the finest senses?" Moneta, Keats's
veiled Melancholy, counted those pulses, while the poet waited, rapt in an
apprehension attainable only by the finest senses, nearly betrayed by those
senses to an even more premature doom than his destined one. What links
together *The Fall of Hyperion* and its modern descendants like Stevens's
Notes toward a Supreme Fiction is the movement of impressions set forth by
Pater, when analysis of the self yields to the poet's recognition of how dangerously fine the sells existence has become. "It is with this movement,
with the passage and dissolution of impressions, images, sensations, that
analysis leaves off—that continual vanishing away, that strange, perpetual
weaving and unweaving of ourselves."

Though there is a proud laughter implicit in the *Ode on Melancholy*,
the poem courts tragedy, and again makes death the mother of beauty.
Modern criticism has confounded Pater with his weaker disciples, and has
failed to realize how truly Yeats and Stevens are in his tradition. The *Ode
on Melancholy* is ancestor to what is strongest in Pater, and to what came
after in his tradition of aesthetic humanism. Pater's "Conclusion" to *The
Renaissance* lives in the world of the *Ode on Melancholy*:

> Great passions may give us this quickened sense of life, ecstasy
> and sorrow of love, the various forms of enthusiastic activity,
> disinterested or otherwise, which come naturally to many of us.
> Only be sure it is passion—that it does yield you this fruit of a
> quickened, multiplied consciousness.

The wakeful anguish of the soul comes to the courter of grief in the very shrine of pleasure, and the renovating powers of art yield the tragedy of their might only to a strenuous and joyful seeker. Keats's problem in *The Fall of Hyperion* was to find again the confidence of Milton as to the oneness of his self and theme, but with nothing of the Miltonic conviction that God had worked to fit that self and theme together. The shrines of pleasure and of melancholy become one shrine in the second *Hyperion*, and in that ruin the poet must meet the imaginative values of tradition without their attendant credences, for Moneta guards the temple of all the dead faiths.

Moneta humanizes her sayings to our ears, but not until a poet's courteous dialectic has driven her to question her own categories for mankind. When she softens, and parts the veils for Keats, she reveals his freedom from the greatness of poetic tradition, for the vision granted has the quality of a new universe, and a tragedy different in kind from the tragedy of the past:

> Then saw I a wan face,
> Not pined by human sorrows, but bright-blanch'd
> By an immortal sickness which kills not;
> It works a constant change, which happy death
> Can put no end to; deathwards progressing
> To no death was that visage; it had pass'd
> The lily and the snow; and beyond these
> I must not think now, though I saw that face.
> But for her eyes I should have fled away.
> They held me back with a benignant light,
> Soft mitigated by divinest lids
> Half closed, and visionless entire they seem'd
> Of all external things—

Frank Kermode finds this passage a prime instance of his "Romantic Image," and believes Moneta's face to be "alive only in a chill and inhuman way," yet Keats is held back from such a judgment by the eyes of his Titaness, for they give forth "a benignant light," as close to the saving light Milton invokes as Keats can ever get. Moneta has little to do with the Yeatsian concept of the poetic vision, for she does not address herself to the alienation of the poet. M.H. Abrams, criticizing Mr. Kermode, points to her emphasis on the poet as humanist, made restless by the miseries of mankind. Shelley's Witch of Atlas, for all her playfulness, has more to do with Yeats's formulation of the coldness of the Muse.

Moneta is the Muse of mythopoeia, like Shelley's Witch, but she contains the poetic and religious past, as Shelley's capricious Witch does not. Taking her in a limited sense (since she incarnates so much more than this), Moneta does represent the embarrassments of poetic tradition, a greatness it is death to approach. Moneta's perspective is close to that of the Rilkean Angel, and for Keats to share that perspective he would have to cease to depend on the visible. Moneta's is a perfect consciousness; Keats is committed still to the oxymoronic intensities of experience, and cannot unperplex joy from pain. Moneta's is a world beyond tragedy; Keats needs to be a tragic poet. Rilke dedicated himself to the task of describing a world regarded no longer from a human point of view, but as it is within the angel. Moneta, like this angel, does not regard external things, and again like Rilke's angel she both comforts and terrifies. Keats, like Stevens, fears the angelic imposition of any order upon reality, and hopes to discover a possible order in the human and the natural, even if that order be only the cyclic rhythm of tragedy. Stevens's definitive discovery is in the final sections of *Notes toward a Supreme Fiction*; Keats's similar fulfillment is in his perfect poem, *To Autumn*.

The achievement of definitive vision in *To Autumn* is more remarkable for the faint presence of the shadows of the poet's hell that the poem tries to exclude. Mr. Bate calls the *Lines to Fanny* (written, like *To Autumn*, in October 1819) "somewhat jumbled as well as tired and flat," but its nightmare projection of the imagination's inferno has a singular intensity, and I think considerable importance:

> Where shall I learn to get my peace again?
> To banish thoughts of that most hateful land,
> Dungeoner of my friends, that wicked strand
> Where they were wrecked and live a wrecked life;
> That monstrous region, whose dull rivers pour,
> Ever from their sordid urns unto the shore,
> Unown'd of any weedy-haired gods;
> Whose winds, all zephyrless, hold scourging rods,
> Iced in the great lakes, to afflict mankind;
> Whose rank-grown forests, frosted, black, and blind,
> Would fright a Dryad; whose harsh herbag'd meads
> Make lean and lank the starv'd ox while he feeds;
> There flowers have no scent, birds no sweet song,
> And great unerring Nature once seems wrong.

This may have begun as a fanciful depiction of an unknown America, where Keats's brother and sister-in-law were suffering, yet it develops into a vision akin to Blake's of the world of experience, with its lakes of menace and its forests of error. The moss-lain Dryads lulled to sleep in the forests of the poet's mind in his *Ode to Psyche*, can find no home in this natural world. This is Keats's version of the winter vision, the more powerful for being so unexpected, and clearly a torment to its seer, who imputes error to Nature even as he pays it his sincere and accustomed homage.

It is this waste land that the auroras of Keats's *To Autumn* transform into a landscape of perfection process. Does another lyric in the language meditate more humanly "the full of fortune and the full of fate"? The question is the attentive reader's necessary and generous tribute; the critical answer may be allowed to rest with Mr. Bate, who is moved to make the finest of claims for the poem: "Here at last is something of a genuine paradise." The paradise of poets bequeathed to Keats by tradition is gone; a tragic paradise of naturalistic completion and mortal acceptance has taken its place.

There are other Romantic freedoms won from the embarrassments of poetic tradition, usually through the creation of new myth, as in Blake and Shelley, or in the thematic struggle not to create a myth, as in the earlier work of Wordsworth and Coleridge. Keats found his dangerous freedom by pursuing the naturalistic implications of the poet's relation to his own poem, and nothing is more refreshing in an art so haunted by aspirations to surpass or negate nature. Shelley, still joined to Keats in the popular though not the critical consciousness, remains the best poet to read in counterpoint to the Great Odes and *The Fall of Hyperion*. There is no acceptance in Shelley, no tolerance for the limits of reality, but only the outrageous desire never to cease desiring, the unflagging intensity that goes on until it is stopped, and never is stopped. Keats did what Milton might have done but was not concerned to do; he perfected an image in which stasis and process are reconciled, and made of autumn the most human of seasons in consequence. Shelley's ode to autumn is his paean to the West Wind, where a self-destroying swiftness is invoked for the sake of dissolving all stasis permanently, and for hastening process past merely natural fulfillment into apocalyptic renewal. Whether the great winter of the world can be relieved by any ode Keats tended to doubt, and we are right to doubt with him, but there is a hope wholly natural in us that no doubt dispels, and it is of this hope that Shelley is the unique and indispensable poet.

Alexandr Pushkin

(1799–1837)

PUSHKIN IS SOMETHING OF AN AMIABLE PUZZLE TO AN AMERICAN CRITIC who has no Russian, if only because the poet, who all Russian critics insist is the foremost in their language, and essentially untranslatable, nevertheless seems to survive translation so extraordinarily well. I have just read *Eugene Onegin* in the very different versions of Charles Johnston and Vladimir Nabokov, and found the verse novel a fascination twice over, though so Nabokovian in that rendering as to make me believe, at moments, that I was reading *Pale Fire*. Byron's *Don Juan* and Jane Austen's novels seem to blend in *Onegin*, though John Bayley usefully cautions that Pushkin had never heard of Austen. Bayley also warns that "Onegin is not Don Juan, or anything like him. Most emphatically he is not on easy terms with the consciousness of his creator." Pushkin made the most useful of critical remarks upon his own verse-novel when he charmingly observed, "Do you know my Tatyana has rejected Onegin. I never expected it of her." These are hardly the accents of George Gordon, Lord Byron, gossiping about his own characters.

The example of Sterne's *Tristram Shandy* does seem to be nearly as decisive for *Onegin* as Byron was. Nabokov, himself a Shandean writer, notes that Pushkin knew Sterne only in French versions, even as he knew Byron in French paraphrases. Whether I can know Pushkin any better than he knew Byron and Sterne is open to doubt, since translation is a puzzling art. Just as nearly every generation of poets declares against "poetical diction" and insists that it (at last!) is bringing poetry closer to the common language, so nearly every fresh wave of translators proclaims triumph over all the malefactors who have gone before. Since most poets, and all translators, of every era, write a period style, a gracious skepticism ought to be maintained as to what it is that we actually are reading, at any time.

Here is the conclusion of *Eugene Onegin*, first as Johnston renders it, and then in Nabokov's diction:

XLVIII

She went—and Eugene, all emotion,
stood thunder-struck. In what wild round
of tempests, in what raging ocean
his heart was plunged! A sudden sound,
the clink of rowels, met his hearing;
Tatyana's husband, now appearing ...
But from the hero of my tale,
just at this crisis of his gale,
reader, we must be separating,
for long ... for evermore. We've chased
him far enough through wild and waste.
Hurrah! let's start congratulating
ourselves on our landfall. It's true,
our vessel's long been overdue.

XLIX

Reader, I wish that, as we parted—
whoever you may be, a friend,
a foe—our mood should be warm-hearted.
Goodbye, for now we make an end.
Whatever in this rough confection
you sought—tumultuous recollection,
a rest from toil and all its aches,
or just grammatical mistakes,
a vivid brush, a witty rattle
God grant that from this little book
for heart's delight, or fun, you took,
for dreams, or journalistic battle,
God grant you took at least a grain.
On this we'll part; goodbye again!

L

And my companion, so mysterious,
goodbye to you, my true ideal,
my task, so vivid and so serious
and yet so light. All that is real
and enviable for a poet,

in your pursuit I've come to know it:
oblivion of life's stormy ways,
sweet talk with friends. How many days
since, through the mist that dreams arise on,
young Tanya first appeared to me,
Onegin too—and there to see,
a free romance's far horizon,
still dim, through crystal's magic glass,
before my gaze began to pass.

LI

Of those who heard my opening pages
in friendly gatherings where I read,
as Sadi sang in earlier ages,
'some are far distant, some are dead'.
They've missed Eugene's completed etching
But she who modelled for the sketching
of Tanya's image ... Ah, how great
the toll of those borne off by fate!
Blest he who's left the hurly-burly
of life's repast betimes, nor sought
to drain its beaker down, nor thought
of finishing its book, but early
has wished it an abrupt goodbye—
and, with my Eugene, so have I.

XLVIII

She has gone. Eugene stands
as if by thunder struck.
In what a tempest of sensations
his heart is now immersed!
But a sudden clink of spurs has sounded,
and Tatiana's husband has appeared,
and here my hero,
at an unkind minute for him,
reader, we now shall leave
for long ... forever.... After him
sufficiently we on one path
roamed o'er the world. Let us congratulate
each other on attaining land. Hurrah!
It long (is it not true?) was time.

XLIX

Whoever you be, O my reader—
friend, foe—I wish with you
to part at present as a pal.
Farewell. Whatever you in my wake
sought in these careless strophes—
tumultuous recollections,
relief from labors,
live pictures or bons mots,
or faults of grammar—
God grant that you, in this book,
for recreation, for the daydream,
for the heart, for jousts in journals,
may find at least a crumb.
Upon which, let us part, farewell!

L

You, too, farewell, my strange traveling companion,
and you, my true ideal,
and you, my live and constant,
though small, work. I have known with you
all that a poet covets:
obliviousness of life in the world's tempests,
the sweet converse of friends.
Many, many days have rushed by
since young Tatiana,
and with her Onegin, in a blurry dream
appeared to me for the first time—
and the far stretch of a free novel
I through a magic crystal
still did not make out clearly.

LI

But those to whom at friendly meetings
the first strophes I read—
"Some are no more, others are distant,"
As erstwhiles Sadi said.
Finished without them is Onegin's portrait.
And she from whom is fashioned
the dear ideal of "Tatyana" ...
Ah, fate has much, much snatched away!

Blest who life's banquet early
left, having not drained to the bottom
the goblet full of wine;
who did not read life's novel to the end
and all at once could part with it
as I with my Onegin.

Johnston writes in the mode of W.H. Auden and Louis MacNeice. We might be in Auden's *Letter to Lord Byron* when we read, "Hurrah! Let's start congratulating / ourselves on our landfall," but not when Nabokov writes, "Let us congratulate / each other on attaining land. Hurrah!" But then, we hear Nabokov pure in "to part at present as a pal," "live pictures or bon mots," "jousts in journals," and "did not read life's novel to the end." Johnston's Audenesque style is appropriate for a Winchester and Balliol man who entered the diplomatic service in 1936, while Nabokov's style is of course his peculiar strength, far surpassing any dubious grasp of psychological realities he ever possessed. Where Pushkin is in either of these versions, I cannot know, but reading them side by side a common gusto emerges which does not seem to be secondhand Auden, or Nabokovian preciosity, and I would suppose that this gusto, this fine verve, somehow belongs to Pushkin.

Perhaps that is why I cannot find in Onegin the "superfluous man," archetype of all those Russian novelistic heroes who waste their lives in mock elegance, or in Tatyana the model for all those superb heroines who represent, for the major Russian novelists, the sincerely passionate virtues of Russian womanhood. Doubtless, to Russian readers these identifications are inevitable, but to an American reader in 1986, particularly to one who despises historicisms, old and new, Pushkin's center is neither in societal observation nor in national archetypes. The novel in verse I have just enjoyed in two rather different versions tells me a story of lovers who are out of phase with one another. That sad irony of experience, that we fall in love in varying rhythms even when with one another, is beautifully exemplified in *Eugene Onegin*. Tatyana first falls in love with Eugene, but he falls in love with her belatedly and only when their appropriate time is past. Call him the belated man rather than the superfluous man and you apprehend his ironic condition, and your own.

Of the prose tales of Pushkin, the most powerful (in translation) is clearly the novella *The Queen of Spades*, though the fuller length of *The Captain's Daughter* does reveal some of Pushkin's more varied narrative resources. Paul Debreczeny has culminated a Russian critical tradition of reading *The Queen of Spades* as a Kabbalistic parable, and to Debreczeny's intricate unpacking of the story's dense symbolism I desire to add nothing. But as a critical Kabbalist myself, I know that a Kabbalistic parable, whether in Pushkin or Kafka, shows us that rhetoric, cosmology, and psychology are not three subjects but three in one, and so I turn to the psychology of *The Queen of Spades*.

What is the secret misfortune that the Countess, Queen of Spades, signifies? Does Hermann frighten her to death, or does she pass on to him the curse of St. Germain and so only then is able to die? What we know most surely about the Countess is that she was, is, and will be rancid, a fit mistress for St. Germain (if that is what she was). What we know most surely about Hermann is that he is just as rancid, but unlike the Countess he is trapped in irony every time he speaks. His most extraordinary entrapments come in the first and last sentences we hear him speak: "The game fascinates me, but I am not in the position to sacrifice the essentials of life in the hope of acquiring the luxuries," and the insane, repetitious mutter, "Three, seven, ace! Three, seven, queen!" He of course does sacrifice the true essentials of life, and the identification of the Countess with the Queen of Spades or death-in-life ironically substitutes for the ace of occult success the Kabbalistic crown that is at once a pinnacle and the abyss of nothingness.

Psychologically Hermann and the Countess are very similar, each being compounded of worldly ambition and the diabolic, but the Countess refuses to accept Hermann as her initiate until after she is dead. While alive, all that she will say to Hermann is "It was a joke." It is again a diabolic irony that Hermann answers, "There's no joking about it," since her final joke will render him insane, the joke being the Kabbalistic substitution of the Queen of Spades for the ace. Yet the Countess's apparition speaks in terms that cannot be reconciled with much in the story's overdetermined symbolism:

> "I have come to you against my will," she said in a firm voice, "but I have been ordered to fulfill your request. Three, seven, ace, played in that order, will win for you, but only on condition that you play not more than one card in twenty-four hours, and that you never play again for the rest of your life. I'll forgive you my death if you marry my ward, Lisaveta Ivanovna."

Is it St. Germain or the Devil himself, each presumably on the other side of life, who compels her to come? Whose is the lie, as to the last card, hers or a power beyond her? Why would she wish the horrible Hermann upon poor Lisaveta Ivanovna? Is it because she now cares for her ward, or is it malice towards all concerned? Why three days for the card game rather than one? I do not think that there are aesthetic answers to these questions. What matters, aesthetically, is that we are compelled to try to answer them, that we also are swept into this Kabbalistic narrative of compulsions, deceptions, betrayals, Napoleonic drives. Pushkin has created an overdetermined cosmos and placed us firmly within it, subject to the same frightening forces that his protagonists have to endure.

The trope that governs the cosmos of *The Queen of Spades* is Dantesque, purgatorial exile: "You shall learn the salt taste of another's bread, and the hard path up and down his stairs." That is Dante at Ravenna and Lisaveta Ivanovna in the house of the Countess, but those purgatorial stairs are ascended also by Hermann and the Countess, both to ill effect. The power of *The Queen of Spades* is both purgatorial and infernal, and the reader, who is exposed to both realms, herself or himself chooses the path of the parable, a narrow, winding stair up, or the madness of Hermann's descent, outwards and downwards into wintry night.

Elizabeth Barrett Browning

(1806–1861)

Like the bright hair uplifted from the head
Of some fierce Maenad ...
                              —Shelley

IN THE UNIVERSITIES, COLLEGES AND SCHOOLS OF THE ENGLISH-SPEAKING
world, the canon wars in one sense are pragmatically over, since the academies, joined by the media, have replaced virtually all aesthetic and cognitive standards by considerations of gender, race, ethnicity, sexual orientation, social class, and other irreducible resentments. There is however no
necessary finality in this replacement. A considerable resistance still exists,
even in the ruined academies, and an aesthetic underground has formed in
many of those who staff the media. Much more important, as I have discovered throughout the last decade, there are hundreds of thousands of
common readers, outside of the academies and the media, who are not contaminated by what has become fashionable "cultural criticism." I have
given up all guest lecturing at academic institutions, and speak only on
book tours, which are not intended as aesthetic revival meetings, but which
hearten me nevertheless. One particularly mindless English Marxist cheer-
leader, waving his pom-poms, nastily compared me to Jimmy Swaggart, but
as an aesthetic evangelist I happily acknowledge the influence of the divine
Oscar Wilde, who would be rather startled to discover that Elizabeth
Barrett Browning has eclipsed her husband, the creator of the strongest
dramatic monologues in the English language.

I who have limped off too many canonical battlefields, acknowledge
defeat in the academies, and am content to carry on the war elsewhere,
and not in this essay. The partisans of Barrett Browning have much to say
in her behalf, and many of those reprinted here say it eloquently. I have

always loved Barrett Browning's "A Musical Instrument" best among her poems, so I will confine myself to an appreciation of its beauty, and a comparison of it to Shelley's "Hymn of Pan," a lyric at least equal in splendor.

II

Homer and Plato say that Pan, god of the woodlands, was the son of Hermes the messenger. As "panic" intimates, Pan has the effect of a sudden fear, like the night-terror he caused at Marathon, inducing the Persians to flee, and yet he was named "Pan" because, at his birth, he delighted all hearts, but particularly that of Dionysus, who recognized in the babe a kindred spirit of ecstasy. Attended by nymphs, Pan roams the wild places, and yet the other likely origin of his name means the "feeder" or herdsman, presumably of goats in Arcadia. Though sexually human, Pan has goats' ears and horns, and carries remarkably little mythology with him. His love affairs with Syrinx, Echo, and Pitys (nymph of the fir-tree) express his notorious amorousness, as does the music of his reed-pipe. Though Pan acquired no transcendental overtones, in the *Phaedrus* he is among the gods to whom Socrates appeals for an inward beauty.

Here is Barrett Browning's "A Musical Instrument," one of the best and most vitalizing lyrical poems in the language:

> What was he doing, the great god Pan,
>   Down in the reeds by the river?
> Spreading ruin and scattering ban,
> Splashing and paddling with hoofs of a goat,
> And breaking the golden lilies afloat
>   With the dragon-fly on the river.
>
> He tore out a reed, the great god Pan,
>   From the deep cool bed of the river;
> The limpid water turbidly ran,
> And the broken lilies a dying-lay,
> And the dragon-fly had fled away,
>   Ere he brought it out of the river.
>
> High on the shore sat the great god Pan
>   While turbidly flowed the river;
> And hacked and hewed as a great god can,
> With his hard bleak steel at the patient reed,

Till there was not a sign of the leaf indeed
    To prove it fresh from the river.

He cut it short, did the great god Pan
    (How tall it stood in the river!)
Then drew the pith, like the heart of a man.
Steadily from the outside ring,
And notched the poor dry empty thing
    In holes, as he sat by the river.

'This is the way,' laughed the great god Pan
    (Laughed while he sat by the river),
'The only way, since gods began
To make a sweet music, they could succeed.'
Then, dropping his mouth to a hole in the reed,
    He blew in power by the river.

Sweet, sweet, sweet, O Pan!
    Piercing sweet by the river!
Blinding sweet, O great god Pan!
The sun on the hill forgot to die,
And the lilies revived, and the dragon-fly
    Came back to dream on the river.

Yet half a beast is the great god Pan
    To laugh as he sits by the river,
Making a poet out of a man;
The true gods sigh for the cost and pain
For the reed which grows nevermore again
    As a reed with the reeds in the river.

Had she written often thus, she would be beyond praise, and I am puzzled that she did not cultivate her lyric powers. "A Musical Instrument" was published in 1860, a year before her death in Florence, and in it Barrett Browning rejoins the High Romantic vitalism of Shelley, Keats, the young Tennyson, and the young Browning. She knew Shelley's "Hymn of Pan," and I suspect she deftly writes an affectionate critique of it in her darker hymn of Pan:

        I.
From the forests and highlands
    We come, we come;

From the river-girt islands,
  Where loud waves are dumb
    Listening to my sweet pipings.
The wind in the reeds and the rushes,
    The bees on the bells of thyme,
The birds on the myrtle bushes,
    The cicale above in the lime,
And the lizards below in the grass,
Were as silent as ever old Tmolus was,
    Listening to my sweet pipings.

II.

Liquid Peneus was flowing,
  And all dark Tempe lay
In Pelion's shadow, outgrowing
  The light of the dying day,
    Speeded by my sweet pipings.
The Sileni, and Sylvans, and Fauns,
    And the Nymphs of the woods and the waves,
To the edge of the moist river-lawns,
    And the brink of the dewy caves,
And all that did then attend and follow,
Were silent with love, as you now, Apollo,
    With envy of my sweet pipings.

III.

I sang of the dancing stars,
I sang of the daedal Earth,
And of Heaven—and the giant wars,
    And Love, and Death, and Birth—
    And then I change my pipings—
Singing how down the vale of Maenalus
    I pursued a maiden and clasped a reed.
Gods and men, we are all deluded thus!
    It breaks in our bosom and then we bleed:
All wept, as I think both ye now would,
If envy or age had not frozen your blood,
    At the sorrow of my sweet pipings.

I love both hymns, and appreciate their differences and originalities.
Shelley's Pan chants in the first person, but sings also for the nymphs who

accompany him, and addresses two auditors, Apollo and the reader. Pan's tone is sublimely exuberant and self-confident, content as he is to have subdued (aesthetically) all nature with his sweet pipings, which are the envy of Apollo, god of Poetry. A music of earth challenges and overgoes the Olympian art. There is both a high Shelleyan irony and a universal male lament in the exquisite:

> I pursued a maiden and clasped a reed.
> Gods and men, we are all deluded thus!

This omits the perspective of the maiden Syrinx, whose metamorphosis saved her from Pan's lust, and thus provided him with a reed he transformed into his musical instrument. Barrett Browning, with her own superb irony, shows us Pan turning a male into a reed-pipe, and at the close reveals that her exquisite lyric is a parable of the incarnation of the poetic character itself:

> Yet half a beast is the great god Pan
>   To laugh as he sits by the river,
> Making a poet out of a man;
> The true gods sigh for the cost and pain
> For the reed which grows nevermore again
>   As a reed with the reeds by the river.

I read this as a profound fable of the denaturalization of the male poet, as opposed to the female, with the "true" or Olympian gods showing a very uncharacteristic sorrow, as if they too had been feminized. That Barrett Browning had the gifts that would have made her into a great lyric poet, I do not doubt. What diverted them, into narrative and sonnet sequence, is a complex matter, not to be discussed in this brief context, but she does seem to me most herself in ballads and dramatic lyrics. Yet the matter of her canonical eminence, or lack of it, remains to be resolved, perhaps when our age of ideology passes into another time.

Robert Browning

(1812–1889)

ONE OF THE PRINCIPLES OF INTERPRETATION THAT WILL ARISE OUT OF THE future study of the intricacies of poetic revisionism, and of the kinds of mis-reading that canon-formation engenders, is the realization that later poets and their critical followers tend to misread strong precursors by a fairly consistent mistaking of literal for figurative, and of figurative for literal. Browning misread the High Romantics, and particularly his prime precursor, Shelley, in this pattern, and through time's revenges most modern poets and critics have done and are doing the same to Browning. I am going to explore Browning, in this essay, as the master of misprision he was, by attempting to show our tendency to read his epiphanies or "good moments" as ruinations or vastations of quest, and our parallel tendency to read his darkest visions-of-failure as if they were celebrations.

I will concentrate on a small group of Browning's poems including *Cleon, Master Hugues of Saxe-Gotha, A Toccata of Galuppi's, Abt Vogler,* and *Andrea del Sarto,* but I cannot evade for long my own obsession with *Childe Roland to the Dark Tower Came,* and so it and its contrary chant, *Thamuris Marching,* will enter late into this discourse. Indeed, I want to end with a kind of critical self-analysis, and ask myself the question: why am I obsessed by the *Childe Roland* poem, or rather, what does it *mean* to be obsessed by that poem? How is it that I cannot conceive of an antithetical practical criticism of poetry without constantly being compelled to use *Childe Roland* as a test case, as though it were the modern poem proper, more even than say, *Tintern Abbey* or *Byzantium* or *The Idea of Order at Key West*? is there a way to make these questions center upon critical analysis rather than upon psychic self-analysis?

In Browning's prose *Essay on Shelley,* there is an eloquent passage that idealizes poetic influence:

There is a time when the general eye has, so to speak, absorbed its fill of the phenomena around it, whether spiritual or material, and desires rather to learn the exacter significance of what it possesses, than to receive any augmentation of what is possessed. Then is the opportunity for the poet of loftier vision, to lift his fellows.... The influence of such an achievement will not soon die out. A tribe of successors (Homerides) working more or less in the same spirit, dwell on his discoveries and reinforce his doctrine; till, at unawares, the world is found to be subsisting wholly on the shadow of a reality, on sentiments diluted from passions, on the tradition of a fact, the convention of a moral, the straw of last year's harvest.

Browning goes on to posit a mighty ladder of authentic poets, in an objective and subjective alternation, who will replace one another almost endlessly in succession, concerning which, "the world dares no longer doubt that its gradations ascend." Translated, this means: "Wordsworth to Shelley to Browning," in which Browning represents a triumph of what he calls the objective principle. Against Browning's prose idealization, I will set his attack upon the disciples of Keats in his poem *Popularity*:

> And there's the extract, flasked and fine,
>   And priced and saleable at last!
> And Hobbs, Nobbs, Stokes and Nokes combine
>   To paint the future from the past,
> Put blue into their line.

For "Hobbs, Nobbs, Stokes and Nokes" we might read Tennyson, Arnold, Rossetti, and whatever other contemporary Keatsian, whether voluntary or involuntary, that Browning wished to scorn. But the next stanza, the poem's last, would surely have cut against Browning himself if for "John Keats" we substituted "Percy Shelley":

> Hobbs hints blue,—straight he turtle eats:
>   Nobbs prints blue,—claret crowns his cup:
> Nokes outdares Stokes in azure feats,—
>   Both gorge. Who fished the murex up?
> What porridge had John Keats?

The vegetarian Shelley, according to his friend Byron, tended to dine on air and water, not fit fare for the strenuously hearty Browning, who in his later years was to become London's leading diner-out. But though Browning seems not to have had the slightest *personal* consciousness of an anxiety of influence, he wrote the most powerful poem ever to be explicitly concerned with the problem. This is the dramatic monologue *Cleon*, in which the imaginary jack-of-all-arts, Cleon, is in my judgment a kind of version of Matthew Arnold, whose *Empedocles on Etna* Browning had been reading. Arnold's Empedocles keeps lamenting his own and the world's belatedness, a lament that becomes a curious kind of inauthentic overconfidence in Cleon's self-defense:

> I have not chanted verse like Homer, no—
> Nor swept string like Terpander, no—nor carved
> And painted men like Phidias and his friend:
> I am not great as they are, point by point.
> But I have entered into sympathy
> With these four, running these into one soul,
> Who, separate, ignored each other's art.
> Say, is it nothing that I know them all?

Browning could enjoy the belatedness, of Arnold or Rossetti, because no poet ever felt less belated than this exuberant daemon. We remember the malicious epithet applied to him by Hopkins: "Bouncing Browning." I think we can surmise that poetic belatedness as an affliction, whether conscious or unconscious, always rises in close alliance with ambivalence towards the prime precursor. Browning felt no ambivalence towards Shelley, such as Yeats had towards Shelley, or Shelley towards Wordsworth, or Wordsworth towards Milton. Browning loved Shelley unbrokenly and almost unreservedly from the age of fourteen, when he first read him, until his own death at the age of seventy-seven. But ambivalence is not the only matrix from which the anxiety of influence rises. There is perhaps a darker source in the guilt or shame of identifying the precursor with the ego-ideal, and then living on in the sense of having betrayed that identification by one's own failure to have become oneself, by a realization that the ephebe has betrayed his own integrity, and betrayed also the covenant that first bound him to the precursor. That guilt unmistakably was Browning's, as Betty Miller and others have shown, and so the burden of belatedness was replaced in Browning by a burden of dissimulation, a lying-against-the-self, rather than a lying-against-time.

But is not that kind of shame only another mask for the guilt-of-indebtedness, the only guilt that ever troubles a poet-as-poet? Certainly, Shelley for Browning was precisely the "numinous shadow" or ancestor god whose baleful influence is stressed by Nietzsche. Rather than demonstrate this too obviously, whether by recourse to Browning's poem *Pauline* or by an examination of the unhappy episode in which the young Browning yielded to his stern mother's Evangelical will, I think it more interesting to seek out what is most difficult in Browning, which is the total contrast between his optimism, a quality both temperamental and theoretical, and the self-destructive peculiarities of his men and women. I want to start by puzzling over the grotesque and unique poem, *Master Hugues of Saxe-Gotha*, with its curious and central contrast between the charming organist who speaks the monologue and the heavy pseudo-Bachian composer, also invented by Browning, whose name is the poem's title. The relationship between performer and composer is the poem. This relationship is *not* a displaced form of the ambivalence between ephebe and precursor, because the performer's reading/misreading of the composer is very different from the later poet's interpretation of an earlier one, or anyone's reading/misreading of any poet. It is true that a performance is an interpretation, but a performance lacks the vital element of revisionism that makes for fresh creation. The charm of the poem *Master Hugues of Saxe-Gotha*, like the chill of the somewhat similar but greater poem, *A Toccata of Galuppi's*, is precisely that we are free of the burden of misprision and that the performer in each poem is more like a reciter of a text than he is like a critic of a text. Yet it remains true that you cannot recite any poem without giving some interpretation of it, though I would hazard the speculation that even the strongest recital, acting, or performance is at best a weak reading/misreading, in the technical antithetical senses of "weak" and "strong," for again there is no strength, poetic or critical, without the dialectics of revisionism coming into play.

The organist earnestly wants to understand Hugues without revising him, but evidently the world is right and the poor organist wrong, in that less is meant than meets the ear in Hugues' mountainous fugues. Hugues is a kind of involuntary musical nihilist, who in effect would rather have the void as purpose than be void of purpose. The organist is not only old-fashioned in his devotion to Hugues but, as we might say now, old-fashioned in his devotion to meaning. Yet skepticism, a suspicion concerning both meaning-in-Hugues and meaning-in-life, has begun to gain strength in the organist, despite himself. His quasi-desperate test-performance of Hugues, thematically racing the sacristan's putting-out of the light, moves from one sadly negative conclusion to a larger negation, from "But where's music, the dickens?" to:

Is it your moral of Life?
    Such a web, simple and subtle,
Weave we on earth here in impotent strife,
    Backward and forward each throwing his shuttle,
Death ending all with a knife?

The very reluctance of the organist's interpretation convinces us of its relevance to Hugues. Hugues will not "say the word," despite the organist's plea, and the organist lacks the strength to break out on his revisionary own and do what he wants to do, which is "unstop the full-organ, / Blare out the *mode Palestrina*," akin to the gentle simplicity of his own nature. Yet we must not take the organist too literally; after all, there is nothing whatsoever to prevent him from playing Palestrina to his own satisfaction in the moments of light that remain to him. But it is the problematical, cumbersome, absurdly intricate Hugues who obsesses him, whose secret or lack of a secret he is driven to solve. Despite himself, the organist is on an antithetical quest, like absolutely every other monologist in Browning. The luminous last line of the poem is to be answered, emphatically: "Yes!"

While in the roof, if I'm right there,
    ... Lo you, the wick in the socket!
Hallo, you sacristan, show us a fight there!
    Down it dips, gone like a rocket.
What, you want, do you, to come unawares,
Sweeping the church up for first morning-prayers,
And find a poor devil has ended his cares
At the foot of your rotten-runged rat-riddled stairs?
    Do I carry the moon in my pocket?

If the organist is right, then the gold in the gilt roof is a better emblem of a final reality than the spider web woven by Hugues. But fortunately the darkening of the light breaks in upon an uneasy affirmation, and leaves us instead with the realization that the organist is subject as well as object of his own quest for meaning. Hugues goes on weaving his intricate vacuities; the organist carries the moon in his pocket. Has the poem ended, however humorously, as a ruined quest or as a good moment? Does Browning make it possible for us to know the difference between the two? Or is it the particular achievement of his art that the difference cannot be known? Does the organist end by knowing he has been deceived, or does he end in the beautiful earliness of carrying imagination in his own pocket, in a transumptive allusion to the Second Spirit in one of Browning's favorite poems, Shelley's *The Two Spirits: An Allegory*? There the Second Spirit, overtly allegorizing desire, affirms that the "lamp of love," carried within, gives him the perpetual power to "make night day." Browning is more dialectical, and the final representation in his poem is deeply ambiguous. But that is a depth of repression that I want to stay with, and worry, for a space, if only because it bothers me that *Master Hugues of Saxe-Gotha*, like so many of Browning's poems, ends in an *aporia*, in the reader's uncertainty as to whether he is to read literally or figuratively. Browning personally, unlike Shelley, was anything but an intellectual skeptic, and that he should create figures that abide in our uncertainty is at once his most salient and his most challenging characteristic.

A Toccata of Galuppi's can be read as a reversal of this poem, since it appears to end in the performer's conscious admission of belatedness and defeat. But Browning was quite as multi-form a maker as poetic tradition affords, and the *Toccata* is as subtle a poem as ever he wrote. It invokes for us a grand Nietzschean question, from the Third Essay of *On the Genealogy of Morals*: "What does it mean when an artist leaps over into his opposite?" Nietzsche was thinking of Wagner, but Browning in the *Toccata* may be another instance. Nietzsche's ultimate answer to his own question prophesied late Freud, if we take the answer to be: "All great things bring about their own destruction through an act of self-overcoming." I think we can say rather safely that no one was less interested in *Selbstaufhebung* than Robert Browning; he was perfectly delighted to be at once subject and object of his own quest. Like Emerson, whom he resembles only in this single respect, he rejoiced always that there were so many of him, so many separate selves happily picnicking together in a single psyche. From a Nietzschean point of view, he must seem only an epitome of some of the most outrageous qualities of the British empirical and Evangelical minds, but he is actually more sublimely outrageous even than that. There are no dialectics that can subsume him, because he is not so much evasive as he is preternatural, wholly daemonic, with an astonishing alliance perpetual in him between an impish cunning and endless linguistic energy. I think we can surmise why he was so fascinated by poets like Christopher Smart and Thomas Lovell Beddoes, poets who represented the tradition of Dissenting Enthusiasm carried over into actual madness. With energies like Browning's, and self-confidence like Browning's, it took a mind as powerful as Browning's to avoid being carried by Enthusiasm into alienation, but perhaps the oddest of all Browning's endless oddities is that he was incurably sane, even as he imagined his gallery of pathological enthusiasts, monomaniacs, and marvelous charlatans.

There are at least four voices coldly leaping along in *A Toccata of Galuppi's*, and only one of them is more or less Browning's, and we cannot be certain even of that. Let us break in for the poem's conclusion, as the monologist first addresses the composer whose "touch-piece" he is playing, and next the composer answers back, *but only through the monologist's performance*, and finally the speaker-performer acknowledges his defeat by the heartlessly brilliant Galuppi:

> XI
>
> But when I sit down to reason, think to take my stand nor
>   swerve,
> While I triumph o'er a secret wrung from nature's close
>   reserve,
> In you come with your cold music till I creep through every
>   nerve.
>
> XII
>
> Yes, you, like a ghostly cricket, creaking where a house was
>   burned:
> 'Dust and ashes, dead and done with, Venice spent what Venice
>   earned.
> The soul, doubtless, is immortal—where a soul can be
>   discerned.
>
> XIII
>
> 'Yours, for instance: you know physics, something of geology,
> Mathematics are your pastime; souls shall rise in their degree;
> Butterflies may dread extinction,—you'll not die, it cannot be!
>
> XIV
>
> 'As for Venice and her people, merely born to bloom and drop,
> Here on earth they bore their fruitage, mirth and folly were the
>   crop:
> What of soul was left, I wonder, when,the kissing had to stop?
>
> XV
>
> 'Dust and ashes!' So you creak it, and I want the heart to scold.
> Dear dead women, with such hair, too—what's become of all
>   the gold
> Used to hang and brush their bosoms? I feel chilly and grown old.

The, "swerve" is the Lucretian *clinamen*, and we might say that Galuppi, like Lucretius, assaults the monologist-performer with the full strength of the Epicurean argument. One possible interpretation is that Browning, as a fierce Transcendentalist of his own sect, a sect of one, is hammering at the Victorian spiritual compromise, which his cultivated speaker exemplifies. That interpretation would confirm the poem's serio-comic opening:

> Oh Galuppi, Baldassaro, this is very sad to find!
> I can hardly misconceive you; it would prove me deaf and blind;
> But although I take your meaning, 'tis with such a heavy mind!

Galuppi's triumph, on this reading, would be the dramatic one of shaking up this cultivated monologist, who first half-scoffs at Galuppi's nihilism, but who ends genuinely frightened by the lesson Galuppi has taught which is a lesson of mortality and consequent meaninglessness. But I think that is to underestimate the monologist, who is a more consider-able temperament even than the organist who plays Hugues and can bear neither to give Hugues up nor accept Hugues' emptiness. Galuppi is no Hugues, but a powerfully sophisticated artist who gives what was wanted of him, but with a Dance-of-Death aspect playing against his audience's desires. And the speaker, who knows physics, some geology, a little math-ematics, and will not quite abandon his Christian immortality, is at least as enigmatic as the organist, and for a parallel reason. Why cannot he let Galuppi alone? What does he quest for in seeing how well he can perform that spirited and elegant art? Far more even than Galuppi, or Galuppi's audience, or than Browning, the speaker is obsessed with mortality:

> Then they left you for their pleasure: till in due time, one by one,
> Some with lives that came to nothing, some with deeds as well undone,
> Death stepped tacitly and took them where they never see the sun.

One of the most moving elements in the poem is its erotic nostalgia, undoubtedly the single sphere of identity between the monologist and Browning himself. Eros crowds the poem, with an intensity and poignance almost Shakespearean in its strength. Nothing in the poem is at once so moving and so shocking as the monologist's final "Dear dead women, with such hair, too—," for this spiritual trimmer is very much a sensual man, like his robust creator. It is the cold Galuppi who is more the dualist, more the artist fulfilling the Nietzschean insight that the ascetic ideal is a defen-sive evasion by which art preserves itself against the truth. But where, as readers, does that leave us, since this time Browning elegantly has cleared himself away? His overt intention is pretty clear, and I think pretty irrelevant also. He wants us—unlike the monologist, unlike Galuppi, unlike Galuppi's hard-living men and women—to resort to his ferocious version of an antithetical Protestantism, which is I think ultimately his misprision of Shelley's antithetical humanism. Yet Browning's art has freed us of Browning, though paradoxically not of Shelley, or at least of the strong Lucretian element in Shelley. Has the monologist quested after Galuppi's truth, only to end up in a vastation of his own comforting evasions of the truth? That would be the canonical reading, but it would overliteralize a metaleptic figuration that knowingly has chosen not to attempt a reversal of time. When the speaker ends by feeling "chilly and grown old," then he has introjected Galuppi's world and Galuppi's music, and projected his own compromise formulations. But this is an *illusio*, a metaleptic figuration that is on the verge of becoming an opening irony or reaction-formation again, that is, rejoining the tone of jocular evasion that began the poem. Nothing has happened because nothing has changed, and the final grimness of Browning's eerie poem is that its speaker is caught in a repetition. He will pause awhile, and then play a toccata of Galuppi's again.

Let us try a third music-poem or improvisation, the still more formidable Abt Vogler, where the daemonic performer is also the momentary composer, inventing fitfully upon an instrument of his own invention, grandly solitary because there is nothing for him to interpret except his own interpretation of his own creation. The canonical readings available here are too weak to be interesting, since they actually represent the poem as being pious. The historical Vogler was regarded by some as a pious fraud, but Browning's Vogler is too complex to be regarded either as an impostor or as sincerely devout. What matters most is that he is primarily an extemporizer, rather than necessarily an artist, whether as performer or composer. The poem leaves open (whatever Browning's intentions) the problem of whether Vogler is a skilled illusionist, or something more than that. At the least, Vogler is self-deceived, but even the self-deception is most complex. It is worth knowing what I must assume that Browning knew: Vogler's self-invented instruments sounded splendid only when played by Vogler. Though the great temptation in reading this poem is to interpret it as a good moment precariously attained, and then lost, I think the stronger or antithetical reading here will show that this is very nearly as much a poem of ruined quest, as *Childe Roland* or *Andrea del Sarto* is.

Abt Vogler is one of those poems that explain Yeats's remark to the effect that he feared Browning as a potentially dangerous influence upon him. If we could read *Abt Vogler* without interpretative suspicion (and I believe we cannot), then the poem would seem to be a way-station between the closing third of *Adonais* and Yeats's Byzantium poems. It establishes itself in a state of being that seems either to be beyond the antithesis of life and death, or else that seems to be the state of art itself. Yet, in the poem *Abt Vogler*, I think we have neither, but something more puzzling, a willed phantasmagoria that is partly Browning's and partly an oddity, a purely visionary dramatic monologue.

Vogler, we ought to realize immediately, does not seek the purposes of art, which after all is hard work. Vogler is daydreaming, and is seeking a magical power over nature or supernature, as in the debased Kabbalist myth of Solomon's seal. Vogler is not so much playing his organ as enslaving it to his magical purposes, purposes that do not distinguish between angel and demon, heaven and hell. Vogler is no Blakean visionary; he seeks not to marry heaven and hell, but merely to achieve every power that he can. And yet he has a moving purpose, akin to Shelley's in *Prometheus Unbound*, which is to aid earth's mounting into heaven. But, is his vision proper something we can grant the prestige of vision, or is there not a dubious element in it?

Being made perfect, when the subject is someone like Vogler, is a somewhat chancy phenomenon. Unlike the sublimely crazy Johannes Agricola, in one of Browning's earliest and most frightening dramatic monologues, Vogler is not a genuine Enthusiast, certain of his own Election. Stanza VI has a touch of *Cleon* about it, and stanza VII is clearly *unheimlich*, despite the miraculous line: "That out of three sounds he frame, not a fourth sound, but a star." But with stanzas VIII and IX, which are this poem's *askesis* or sublimation, it is not so easy to distinguish Vogler from Browning, or one of the beings always bouncing around in Browning, anyway:

VIII

Well, it is gone at last, the palace of music I reared;
　　Gone! and the good tears start, the praises that come too slow;
For one is assured at first, one scarce can say that he feared,
　　That he even gave it a thought, the gone thing was to go.
Never to be again! But many more of the kind
　　As good, nay, better perchance: is this your comfort to me?
To me, who must be saved because I cling with my mind
　　To the same, same self, same love, same God: ay, what was, shall be.

IX

Therefore to whom turn I but to thee, the ineffable Name?

Builder and maker, thou, of houses not made with hands!
What, have fear of change from thee who art ever the same?
    Doubt that thy power can fill the heart that thy power expands?
There shall never be one lost good! What was, shall live as before;
    The evil is null, is nought, is silence implying sound;
What was good shall be good, with, for evil, so much good more;
    On the earth the broken arcs; in the heaven, a perfect round.

The poem, from here to the end, in the three final stanzas, is suddenly as much Browning's Magnificat as the *Song to David*, which is deliberately echoed in the penultimate line, is Smart's. But what does that mean,
whether in this poem, or whether about Browning himself? Surely he
would not acknowledge, openly, that his is the art of the extemporizer, the
illusionist improvising? Probably not, but the poem may be acknowledging an anxiety that he possesses, to much that effect. Whether this is so or
not, to any degree, how are we to read the final stanza?

Well, it is earth with me; silence resumes her reign:
    I will be patient and proud, and soberly acquiesce.
Give me the keys. I feel for the common chord again,
    Sliding by semitones, till I sink to the minor,—yes,
And I blunt it into a ninth, and I stand on alien ground,
    Surveying awhile the heights I rolled from into the deep;
Which, hark, I have dared and done, for my resting-place is found,
    The C Major of this life: so now I will try to sleep.

This descent to C Major separates Vogler totally from Browning
again, since of the many keys in which the genuinely musical Browning
composes, his resting place is hardly a key without sharps or flats.
Browning has his direct imitation of Smart's *Song to David* in his own
overtly religious poem, *Saul*, and so we can be reasonably certain that
Vogler does not speak for Browning when the improviser belatedly stands
on alien ground, surveying the Sublime he had attained, and echoes
Smart's final lines:

Thou at stupendous truth believ'd;—
And now the matchless deed's achiev'd,
    DETERMINED, DARED, and DONE.

What Vogler has dared and done is no more than to have dreamed a
belated dream; where Browning is, in regard to that Promethean or

Shelleyan a dream, is an enigma, at least in this poem. What *Abt Vogler*, as a text, appears to proclaim is the impossibility of our reading it, insofar as reading means being able to govern the interplay of literal and figurative meanings in a text. Canonically, in terms of all received readings, this poem is almost an apocalyptic version of a Browningesque "Good Moment," a time of privilege or an epiphany, a sudden manifestation of highest vision. Yet the patterns of revisionary misprision are clearly marked upon the poem, and they tend to indicate that the poem demands to be read figuratively against its own letter, as another parable of ruined quest, or confession or imaginative failure, or the shame of knowing such failure.

I turn to *Andrea del Sarto*, which with *Childe Roland to the Dark Tower Came*, and the meditation entitled *The Pope* in *The Ring and the Book*, seems to me to represent Browning at his greatest. Here there would appear to be no question about the main issue of interpretation, for the canonical readings seem fairly close to the poem in its proclamation that this artist's quest is ruined, that Andrea stands self-condemned by his own monologue. Betty Miller has juxtaposed the poem, brilliantly, with this troubled and troublesome passage in Browning's *Essay on Shelley*:

> Although of such depths of failure there can be no question here we must in every case betake ourselves to the review of a poet's life ere we determine some of the nicer questions concerning his poetry,—more especially if the performance we seek to estimate aright, has been obstructed and cut short of completion by circumstances,—a disastrous youth or a premature death. We may learn from the biography whether his spirit invariably saw and spoke from the last height to which it had attained. An absolute vision is not for this world, but we are permitted a continual approximation to it, every degree of which in the individual, provided it exceed the attainment of the masses, must procure him a clear advantage. Did the poet ever attain to a higher platform than where he rested and exhibited a result? Did he know more than he spoke of?

On this juxtaposition, Andrea and Browning alike rested on a level lower than the more absolute vision they could have attained. Certainly Andrea tells us, perhaps even shows us, that he knows more than he paints. But Browning? If he was no Shelley, he was also no Andrea, which in part is the burden of the poem. But only in part, and whether there is some level of *apologia* in this monologue, in its patterning, rather than its overt content, is presumably a question that a more antithetical practical criticism ought to be capable of exploring.

Does Andrea overrate his own potential? If he does, then there is no poem, for unless his dubious gain-in-life has paid for a genuine loss-in-art, then he is too self-deceived to be interesting, even to himself. Browning has complicated this matter, as he complicates everything. The poem's subtitle reminds us that Andrea was called "The Faultless Painter," and Vasari, Browning's source, credits Andrea with everything in execution but then faults him for lacking ambition, for not attempting the Sublime. Andrea, in the poem, persuades us of a wasted greatness not so much by his boasting ("At any rate 'tis easy, all of it! / No sketches first, no studies, that's long past: / I do what many dream of, all their lives ..."), but by his frightening skill in sketching his own twilight-piece, by his showing us how "A common greyness silvers everything—." Clearly, this speaker knows loss, and clearly he is the antithesis of his uncanny creator, whose poetry never suffers from a lack of ambition, who is always Sublime where he is most Grotesque, and always Grotesque when he storms the Sublime. Andrea does not represent anything in Browning directly, not even the betrayed relationship of the heroic precursor, yet he does represent one of Browning's anxieties, an anxiety related to but not identical with the anxiety of influence. It is an anxiety of representation, or a fear of forbidden meanings, or in Freudian language precisely a fear of the return-of-the-repressed, even though such a return would cancel out a poem-as-poem, or is it because such a return would end poetry as such?

Recall that Freud's notion of repression speaks of an unconsciously *purposeful* forgetting, and remind yourself also that what Browning could never bear was a sense of *purposelessness*. It is purposelessness that haunts Childe Roland, and we remember again what may be Nietzsche's most powerful insight, which closes the great Third Essay of *On the Genealogy of Morals*. The ascetic ideal, Nietzsche said, by which he meant also the aesthetic ideal, was the only meaning yet found for human suffering, and mankind would rather have the void for purpose than be void of purpose. Browning's great fear, purposelessness, was related to the single quality that had moved and impressed him most in Shelley: the remorseless purposefulness of the Poet in *Alastor*, of Prometheus, and of Shelley himself questing for death in *Adonais*. Andrea, as an artist, is the absolute antithesis of the absolute idealist Shelley, and so Andrea is a representation of profound Browningesque anxiety.

But how is this an anxiety of representation? We enter again the dubious area of *belatedness*, which Browning is reluctant to represent, but is too strong and authentic a poet to avoid. Though Andrea uses another

vocabulary, a defensively evasive one, to express his relationship to
Michelangelo, Raphael, and Leonardo, he suffers the burden of the latecomer. His Lucrezia is the emblem of his belatedness, his planned excuse
for his failure in strength, which he accurately diagnoses as a failure in will.
And he ends in deliberate belatedness, and in his perverse need to be cuck-
olded:

> What would one have?
> In heaven, perhaps, new chances, one more chance—
> Four great walls in the New Jerusalem,
> Meted on each side by the angel's reed,
> For Leonard, Rafael, Agnolo and me
> To cover—the three first without a wife,
> While I have mine! So—still they overcome
> Because there's still Lucrezia,—as I choose.

> Again the Cousin's whistle! Go, my Love.

Can we say that Andrea represents what Shelley dreaded to become,
the extinguished hearth, an ash without embers? We know that Shelley
need not have feared, yet the obsessive, hidden fear remains impressive.
Browning at seventy-seven was as little burned out as Hardy at eighty-
eight, Yeats at seventy-four, or Stevens at seventy-five, and his *Asolando*, his
last book, fiercely prefigures Hardy's *Winter Words*, Yeats's *Last Poems*, and
Stevens's *The Rock*, four astonishing last bursts of vitalism in four of the
strongest modern poets. What allies the four volumes (*The Rock* is actually the last section of Stevens's *Collected Poems*, but he had planned it as a
separate volume under the title *Autumn Umber*) is their overcoming of
each poet's abiding anxiety of representation. "Representation," in poetry,
ultimately means self-advocacy; as Hartman says: "You justify either the
self or that which stands greatly against it: perhaps both at once." We could
cite Nietzsche here on the poet's Will-to-Power, but the more orthodox
Coleridge suffices, by reminding us that there can be no origination without discontinuity, and that only the Will can interrupt the repetition-compulsion that is nature. In the final phases of Browning, Hardy, Yeats, and
Stevens, the poet's Will raises itself against Nature, and this antithetical
spirit breaks through a final anxiety and dares to represent itself as what
Coleridge called self-determining spirit. Whether Freud would have compounded this self-realizing instinct with his "detours towards death" I do
not know, but I think it is probable. In this final phase, Browning and his
followers (Hardy and Yeats were overtly influenced by Browning, and I

would suggest a link between the extemporizing, improvising aspect of Stevens, and Browning) are substituting a transumptive representation for the still-abiding presence of Shelley, their common ancestor.

I want to illustrate this difficult point by reference to Browning's last book, particularly to its *Prologue*, and to the sequence called *Bad Dreams*. My model, ultimately, is again the Lurianic Kabbalah, with its notion of *gilgul*, of lifting up a precursor's spark, provided that he is truly one's precursor, truly of one's own root. *Gilgul* is the ultimate *tikkun*, as far as an act of representation can go. What Browning does is fascinatingly like the pattern of *gilgul*, for at the end he takes up precisely Shelley's dispute with Shelley's prime precursor, Wordsworth. By doing for Shelley what Shelley could not do for himself, overcome Wordsworth, Browning lifts up or redeems Shelley's spark or ember, and renews the power celebrated in the *Ode to the West Wind* and Act IV of *Prometheus Unbound*. I will try to illustrate this complex pattern, after these glances at *Asolando*, by returning for a last time (I hope) to my personal obsession with *Childe Roland to the Dark Tower Came*, and then concluding this discourse by considering Browning's late reversal of *Childe Roland* in the highly Shelleyan celebration, *Thamuris Marching*.

The *Prologue* to *Asolando* is another in that long series of revisions of the *Intimations* Ode that form so large a part of the history of nineteenth- and twentieth-century British and American poetry. But Browning consciously gives a revision of a revision, compounding *Alastor* and the *Hymn to Intellectual Beauty* with the parent poem. What counts in Browning's poem is not the Wordsworthian gleam, called here, in the first stanza, an "alien glow," but the far more vivid Shelleyan fire, that Browning recalls seeing for the first time, some fifty years before:

> How many a year, my Asolo,
> > Since—one step just from sea to land—
> I found you, loved yet feared you so—
> > For natural objects seemed to stand
> Palpably fire-clothed! No—
> No mastery of mine o'er these!
> > Terror with beauty, like the Bush
> Burning but unconsumed. Bend knees,
> > Drop eyes to earthward! Language? Tush!
> Silence 'tis awe decrees.
>
> And now? The lambent flame is—where?
> > Lost from the naked world: earth, sky,

Hill, vale, tree, flower,—Italia's rare
    O'er-running beauty crowds the eye—
But flame? The Bush is bare.

When Shelley abandoned the fire, then it was for the transumptive
trumpet of a prophecy, or in *Adonais* for the same wind rising ("The breath
whose might I have invoked in song / Descends on me") to carry him
beyond voice as beyond sight. Browning, as an Evangelical Protestant,
fuses the Shelleyan heritage with the Protestant God in a powerfully
incongruous transumption:

Hill, vale, tree, flower—they stand distinct,
    Nature to know and name. What then?
A Voice spoke thence which straight unlinked
    Fancy from fact: see, all's in ken:
Has once my eyelid winked?
    No, for the purged ear apprehends
Earth's import, not the eye late dazed:
The voice said 'Call my works thy friends!
    At Nature dost thou shrink amazed?
God is it who transcends.'

This is an absolute logocentrism, and is almost more than any poem
can bear, particularly at a time as late as 1889. Browning gets away with it
partly by way of a purged ear, partly because his Protestantism condenses
what High Romanticism normally displaces, the double-bind situation of
the Protestant believer whose God simultaneously says "Be Like Me in My
stance towards Nature" and "Do not presume to resemble Me in My
stance towards nature." The sheer energy of the Browningesque demonic
Sublime carries the poet past what ought to render him imaginatively
schizoid.

But not for long, of course, as a glance at *Bad Dreams* will indicate, a
glance that then will take us back to the greatest of Browning's nightmares,
the demonic romance of *Childe Roland*. *Bad Dreams III* is a poem in which
the opposition between Nature and Art has been turned into a double-
bind, with its contradictory injunctions:

This was my dream! I saw a Forest
    Old as the earth, no track nor trace
Of unmade man. Thou, Soul, explorest—
    Though in a trembling rapture—space

Immeasurable! Shrubs, turned trees,
Trees that touch heaven, support its frieze
Studded with sun and moon and star:
While—oh, the enormous growths that bar
Mine eye from penetrating past
    Their tangled twine where lurks—nay, lives
Royally lone, some brute-type cast
    In the rough, time cancels, man forgives.

On, Soul! I saw a lucid City
    Of architectural device
Every way perfect. Pause for pity,
    Lightning! Nor leave a cicatrice
On those bright marbles, dome and spire,
Structures palatial,—streets which mire
Dares not defile, paved all too fine
For human footstep's smirch, not thine—
Proud solitary traverser,
    My Soul, of silent lengths of way—
With what ecstatic dread, aver,
    Lest life start sanctioned by thy stay!

Ah, but the last sight was the hideous!
    A city, yes,—a Forest, true,—
But each devouring each. Perfidious
    Snake-plants had strangled what I knew
Was a pavilion once: each oak
Held on his horns some spoil he broke
By surreptitiously beneath
Upthrusting: pavements, as with teeth,
Griped huge weed widening crack and split
    In squares and circles stone-work erst.
Oh, Nature—good! Oh, Art—no whit
    Less worthy! Both in one—accurst!

In the sequence of *Bad Dreams*, Browning himself, as interpreter of his own text, identifies Nature with the husband, Art with the wife, and the marriage of Art and Nature, man and woman—why, with Hell, and a sado-masochistic sexual Hell, at that. But the text can sustain very diverse interpretations, as the defensive intensity of repression here is enormously strong. The City is of Art, but like Yeats's Byzantium, which it prophesies, it is also a City of Death-in-Life, and the previous vision of the forest is one of a Nature that might be called Life-in-Death. Neither realm can bear the other, in both senses of "bear"—"bring forth" or "tolerate." Neither is the other's precursor, and each devours the other, if they are brought together. This is hardly the vision of the *Prologue* to *Asolando*, as there seems no room for either Browning or God in the world of the final stanza. Granted that this is nightmare, or severe repression partly making a return, it carries us back to Browning at his most problematic and Sublime, to his inverted vision of the Center, *Childe Roland to the Dark Tower Came.*

As the author of two full-scale commentaries on this poem (in *The Ringers in the Tower*, 1971, and in *A Map of Misreading*, 1975) I reapproach the text with considerable wariness, fairly determined not only that I will not repeat myself, but also hopefully aiming not merely to uncover my own obsessional fixation upon so grandly grotesque a quest-romance. But I recur to the question I asked at the start of this discourse; is there an attainable critical knowledge to be gathered from this critical obsession?

Roland, though a Childe or ephebe on the road to a demonic version of the Scene of Instruction, is so consciously belated a quester that he seems at least as much an obsessive interpreter as anything else purposive that he might desire to become. He out-Nietzsches Nietzsche's Zarathustra in his compulsive will-to-power over the interpretation of his own text. It is difficult to conceive of a more belated hero, and I know of no more extreme literary instance of a quest emptying itself out. Borges accurately located in Browning one of the precursors of Kafka, and perhaps only Kafka's *The Castle* rivals *Childe Roland* as a Gnostic version of what was once romance. Nearly every figuration in the poem reduces to ruin, yet the poem, as all of us obscurely sense, appears to end in something like triumph, in a Good Moment carried through to a supreme representation:

> There they stood, ranged along the hill-sides, met
> > To view the last of me, a living frame
> > For one more picture! in a sheet of flame
> I saw them and I knew them all. And yet
> Dauntless the slug-horn to my lips I set,
> > And blew, '*Childe Roland to the Dark Tower came.*'

Surely it is outrageous to call this a Supreme or even a Good Moment? The stanza just before ends with the sound of loss: "one moment knelled the woe of years." Wordsworth and Coleridge had viewed the Imagination as compensatory, as trading off experiential loss for poetic gain, a formula that we can begin to believe was an unmitigated calamity.

It is the peculiar fascination of *Childe Roland*, as a poem, that it undoes every High Romantic formula, that it exposes the Romantic imagination as being merely an accumulative principle of repression. But such negation is itself simplistic, and evades what is deepest and most abiding in this poem, which is the representation of *power*. For here, I think, is the kernel of our critical quest, that Kabbalistic point which is at once *ayin*, or nothingness, and *ehyeh*, or the representation of Absolute Being, the rhetorical irony or *illusio* that always permits a belated poem to begin again in its quest for renewed strength. Signification has wandered away, and Roland is questing for lost and forgotten *meaning*, questing for *representation*, for a seconding or re-advocacy of his own self. Does he not succeed, far better than Tennyson's Ulysses and Percivale, and far better even than the Solitaries of the High Romantics, in this quest for representation? Let us grant him, and ourselves, that this is a substitute for his truly impossible original objective, for that was the *antithetical*, Shelleyan dream of rebegetting oneself, of breaking through the web of nature and so becoming one's own imaginative father. Substitution, as Roland shows, needs not be a sublimation, but can move from repression *through* sublimation to climax in a more complex act of defense.

Psychoanalysis has no single name for this act, unless we were willing (as we are not) to accept the pejorative one of paranoia for what is, from any point of view that transcends the analytic, a superbly valuable act of the will. Roland teaches us that what psychoanalysis calls "introjection" and "projection" are figurations for the spiritual processes of identification and apocalyptic rejection that exist at the outer borders of poetry. Roland learns, and we learn with him, that the representation of power *is* itself a power, and that this latter power or strength is the only purposiveness that we shall know. Roland, at the close, is re-inventing the self, but at the considerable expense of joining that self to a visionary company of loss, and loss means loss of *meaning* here. The endless fascination of his poem, for any critical reader nurtured upon Romantic tradition, is that the poem, more clearly than any other, nevertheless does precisely what any strong Romantic poem does, at once de-idealizes itself far more thoroughly than we can de-idealize it, yet points also beyond this self-deconstruction or limitation or reduction to the First Idea, on to a re-imagining, to a power-making that no other discursive mode affords. For Roland, as persuasively as any fictive being, warns us against the poisonous ravishments of truth itself. He and his reader have moved only through discourse together, and he and his reader are less certain about what they know than they were as the poem began, but both he and his reader have endured unto a representation of more strength than they had at the start, and such a representation indeed turns out to be a kind of restitution, a *tikkun* for repairing a fresh breaking-of-the-vessels. Meaning has been more curtailed than restored, but strength is revealed as antithetical to meaning.

I conclude with a great poem by Browning that is his conscious revision of *Childe Roland*: the marvelous late chant, *Thamuris Marching*, which is one of the finest unknown, unread poems by a major poet in the language. Twenty-two years after composing *Childe Roland*, Browning, not at the problematic age of thirty-nine, but now sixty-one, knows well that no spring has followed or flowered past meridian. But *Childe Roland* is a belated poem, except in its transumptive close, while all of *Thamuris Marching* accomplishes a metaleptic reversal, for how could a poem be more overwhelmingly early than this? And yet the situation of the quester is objectively terrible from the start of this poem, for Thamuris *knows* he is marching to an unequal contest, a poetic struggle of one heroic ephebe against the greatest of precursors, the Muses themselves. "Thamuris marching," the strong phrase repeated three times in the chant, expresses the *exuberance of purpose*, the Shelleyan remorseless joy in pure, self-destructive poetic quest, that Browning finally is able to grant himself.

Here is Browning's source, Iliad II, 594 ff:

> ... and Dorion, where the Muses
> encountering Thamyris the Thracian stopped him from
> singing, as he came from Oichalia and Oichalian Eurytos;
> for he boasted that he would surpass, if the very Muses,
> daughters of Zeus who holds the aegis, were singing against
> him.
> and these in their anger struck him maimed, and the voice of
> wonder
> they took away, and made him a singer without memory;
> (Lattimore version)

Homer does not say that Thamyris lost the contest, but rather that the infuriated Muses lost their divine temper, and unvoiced him by maiming his memory, without which no one can be a poet. Other sources, presumably known to Browning, mention a contest decided in the Muses' favor by Apollo, after which those ungracious ladies blinded Thamyris, and removed his memory, so as to punish him for his presumption. Milton, in the invocation to light that opens Book III of *Paradise Lost*, exalted Thamyris by coupling him with Homer, and then associated his own ambitions with both poets:

Nightly I visit: nor sometimes forget
Those other two equall'd with me in Fate,
So were I equall'd with them in renown,
Blind Thamyris and blind Maemonides.

Milton presumably had read in Plutarch that Thamyris was credited
with an epic about the war waged by the Titans against the Gods, the
theme that Browning would associate with Shelley and with Keats.
Browning's Thamuris marches to a Shelleyan terza rima, and marches
through a visionary universe distinctly like Shelley's, and overtly pro-
claimed as being early: "From triumph on to triumph, mid a ray / Of early
morn—." Laughing as he goes, yet knowing fully his own doom, Thamuris
marches through a landscape of joy that is the deliberate point-by-point
reversal of Childe Roland's self-made phantasmagoria of ordeal-by-land-
scape:

Thamuris, marching, laughed 'Each flake of foam'
(As sparklingly the ripple raced him by)
'Mocks slower clouds adrift in the blue dome!'

For Autumn was the season; red the sky
Held morn's conclusive signet of the sun
To break the mists up, bid them blaze and die.

Morn had the mastery as, one by one
All pomps produced themselves along the tract
From earth's far ending to near Heaven begun.

Was there a ravaged tree? it laughed compact
With gold, a leaf-ball crisp, high-brandished now,
Tempting to onset frost which late attacked.

Was there a wizened shrub, a starveling bough,
A fleecy thistle filched from by the wind,
A weed, Pan's trampling hoof would disallow?

Each, with a glory and a rapture twined
About it, joined the rush of air and light
And force: the world was of one joyous mind.
(19–36)

From Roland's reductive interpretations we have passed to the imagination's heightened expansions. And though this quest is necessarily for the fearful opposite of poetic divination, we confront, not ruin, but the Good Moment exalted and transfigured, as though for once Browning utterly could fuse literal and figurative:

> Say not the birds flew! they forebore their right—
> Swam, reveling onward in the roll of things.
> Say not the beasts' mirth bounded! that was flight—
>
> How could the creatures leap, no lift of wings?
> Such earth's community of purpose, such
> The ease of earth's fulfilled imaginings—
>
> So did the near and far appear to touch
> In the moment's transport—that an interchange
> Of function, far with near, seemed scarce too much;
> (37–45)

Roland's band of failures has become the glorious band of precursors among whom Thamuris predominates. The Shelleyan west wind of imagination rises, Destroyer and Creater, as Thamuris, eternally early, stands as the true ephebe, "Earth's poet," against the Heavenly Muse:

> Therefore the morn-ray that enriched his face,
> If it gave lambent chill, took flame again
> From flush of pride; he saw, he knew the place.
>
> What wind arrived with all the rhythms from plain,
> Hill, dale, and that rough wildwood interspersed?
> Compounding these to one consummate strain,
>
> It reached him, music; but his own outburst
> Of victory concluded the account,
> And that grew song which was mere music erst.
>
> 'Be my Parnassos, thou Pangaian mount!
> And turn thee, river, nameless hitherto!
> Famed shalt thou vie with famed Pieria's fount!
>
> 'Here I await the end of this ado:

Which wins—Earth's poet or the Heavenly Muse.'

There is the true triumph of Browning's art, for the ever-early Thamuris is Browning as he wished to have been, locked in a solitary struggle against the precursor-principle, but struggling in the visionary world of the precursor. Roland rode through a Gnostic universe in which the hidden God, Shelley, was repressed, a repression that gave Browning a negative triumph of the Sublime made Grotesque. In *Thamuris Marching*, the joyous struggle is joined overtly, and the repressed partly returns, to be repressed again into the true Sublime, as Browning lifts up the sparks of his own root, to invoke that great mixed metaphor of the Lurianic Kabbalah. There is a breaking-of-the-vessels, but the sparks are scattered again, and become Shelley's *and* Browning's words, mixed together, among mankind.

Charles Baudelaire

(1821-1867)

SARTRE ENDED HIS BOOK ON BAUDELAIRE BY INSISTING THAT THIS POET, like Emerson's ideal being, made his own circumstances:

> But we should look in vain for a single circumstance for which he was not fully and consciously responsible. Every event was a reflection of that indecomposable totality which he was from the first to the last day of his life. He refused experience. Nothing came from outside to change him and he learned nothing.

Could there have been such a person? Can any poet refuse the experience of reading his precursors? Was Victor Hugo a circumstance for which Baudelaire was fully and consciously responsible? Valéry, who was (unlike Sartre) a theorist of poetic influence, thought otherwise:

> Thus Baudelaire regarded Victor Hugo, and it is not impossible to conjecture what he thought of him. Hugo reigned; he had acquired over Lamartine the advantage of infinitely more powerful and more precise working materials. The vast range of his diction, the diversity of his rhythms, the superabundance of his images, crushed all rival poetry. But his work sometimes made concessions to the vulgar, lost itself in prophetic eloquence and infinite apostrophes. He flirted with the crowd, he indulged in dialogues with God. The simplicity of his philosophy, the disproportion and incoherence of the developments, the frequent contrasts between the marvels of detail and the fragility of the subject, the inconsistency of the whole—everything, in a word,

which could shock and thus instruct and orientate a pitiless young observer toward his future personal art—all these things Baudelaire was to note in himself and separate from the admiration forced upon him by the magic gifts of Hugo, the impurities, the imprudences, the vulnerable points in his work—that is to say, the possibilities of life and the opportunities for fame which so great an artist left to be gleaned.

With some malice and a little more ingenuity than is called for, it would be only too tempting to compare Victor Hugo's poetry with Baudelaire's, with the object of showing how exactly *complementary* the latter is to the former. I shall say no more. It is evident that Baudelaire sought to do what Victor Hugo had not done; that he refrained from all the effects in which Victor Hugo was invincible; that he returned to a prosody less free and scrupulously removed from prose; that he pursued and almost always captured the production of *unbroken charm*, the inappreciable and quasi-transcendent quality of certain poems—but a quality seldom encountered, and rarely in its pure state, in the immense work of Victor Hugo....

Hugo never ceased to learn by practice; Baudelaire, the span of whose life scarcely exceeded the *half* of Hugo's, developed in quite another manner. One would say he had to compensate for the probable brevity and foreshadowed insufficiency of the short space of time he had to live, by the employment of that critical intelligence of which I spoke above. A score of years were vouchsafed him to attain the peak of his own perfection, to discover his personal field and to define a specific form and attitude which would carry and preserve his name. Time was lacking to realize his literary ambitions by numerous experiments and an extensive output of works. He had to choose the shortest road, to limit himself in his gropings, to be sparing of repetitions and divergences. He had therefore to seek by means of analysis what he was, what he could do, and what he wished to do; and to unite, in himself, with the spontaneous virtues of a poet, the sagacity, the skepticism, the attention and reasoning faculty of a critic.

One can transpose this simply enough into very nearly any of the major instances of poetic influence in English. Attempt Wallace Stevens, a true peer of Valéry, but with a more repressed or disguised relation to Whitman than Baudelaire manifested towards Hugo:

It is evident that Wallace Stevens sought to do what Walt Whitman had not done; that he refrained from all the effects in which Walt Whitman was invincible; that he returned to a prosody less free and scrupulously removed from prose; that he pursued and almost always captured the production of *unbroken charm*, the inappreciable and quasi-transcendent quality of certain poems—but a quality seldom encountered, and rarely in its pure state, in the immense work of Walt Whitman.

Valéry, unlike both Formalist and Post-Structuralist critics, understood that Hugo was to French poetry what Whitman was to American poetry, and Wordsworth was to all British poetry after him: the inescapable precursor. Baudelaire's Hugo problem was enhanced because the already legendary poetic father was scarcely twenty years older than the gatherer of *Les Fleurs du Mal*. All French literary movements are curiously belated in relation to Anglo-American literature. Current French sensibility of the school of Derrida is merely a revival of the Anglo-American literary Modernism of which Hugh Kenner remains the antiquarian celebrant. "Post-Structuralist Joyce" is simply Joyce as we read and discussed him when I was a graduate student, thirty-five years ago. In the same manner, the French Romanticism of Hugo in 1830 repeated (somewhat unknowingly) the movement of British sensibility that produced Wordsworth and Coleridge, Byron and Shelley and Keats, of whom the first two were poetically dead, and the younger three long deceased, well before Hugo made his revolution.

Baudelaire started with the declaration that the Romanticism of 1830 could not be the Romanticism (or anything else) of 1845. T.S. Eliot, as was inevitable, cleansed Baudelaire of Romanticism, baptized the poet into an Original Sinner and a Neo-Classicist, and even went so far as to declare the bard of Lesbos a second Goethe. A rugged and powerful literary thinker, Baudelaire doubtless would have accepted these amiable distortions as compliments, but they do not help much in reading him now.

His attitude towards Hugo, always tinged with ambivalence, became at times savage, but a student of poetic influence learns to regard such a pattern as one of the major modes of misprision, of that strong misreading of strong poets that permits other strong poets to be born. *The Salon of 1845* blames the painter Boulanger on poor Hugo:

Here we have the last ruins of the old romanticism—this is what it means to come at a time when it is the accepted belief that inspiration is enough and takes the place of everything else; this is the abyss to which the unbridled course of Mazeppa has led. It is M. Victor Hugo that has destroyed M. Boulanger—after having destroyed so many others; it is the poet that has tumbled the painter into the ditch. And yet M. Boulanger can paint decently enough—look at his portraits. But where on earth did he win his diploma as history-painter and inspired artist? Can it have been in the prefaces and odes of his illustrious friend?

That Baudelaire was determined not to be destroyed by Hugo was clear enough, a determination confirmed by the rather invidious comparison of Delacroix to Hugo in *The Salon of 1846*:

Up to the present, Eugène Delacroix has met with injustice. Criticism, for him, has been bitter and ignorant; with one or two noble exceptions, even the praises of his admirers must often have seemed offensive to him. Generally speaking, and for most people, to mention Eugène Delacroix is to throw into their minds goodness knows what vague ideas of ill-directed fire, of turbulence, of hazardous inspiration, of confusion, even; and for those gentlemen who form the majority of the public, pure chance, that loyal and obliging servant of genius, plays an important part in his happiest compositions. In that unhappy period of revolution of which I was speaking a moment ago and whose numerous errors I have recorded, people used often to compare Eugène Delacroix to Victor Hugo. They had their romantic poet; they needed their painter. This necessity of going to any length to find counterparts and analogues in the different arts often results in strange blunders; and this one proves once again how little people knew what they were about. Without any doubt the comparison must have seemed a painful one to Eugène Delacroix, if not to both of them; for if my definition of romanticism (intimacy, spirituality and the rest) places Delacroix at its head, it naturally excludes M. Victor Hugo. The parallel has endured in the banal realm of accepted ideas, and these two preconceptions still encumber many feeble brains. Let us be done with these rhetorical ineptitudes once and for all. I beg all those who have felt the need to create some kind of aesthetic for their own use and to deduce causes from their results to make a careful comparison between the productions of these two artists.

M. Victor Hugo, whose nobility and majesty I certainly have no wish to belittle, *is* a workman far more adroit than inventive, a labourer much more correct than *creative*. Delacroix is sometimes clumsy, but he is essentially creative. In all his pictures, both lyric and dramatic, M. Victor Hugo lets one see a system of uniform alignment and contrasts. With him even eccentricity takes symmetrical forms. He is in complete possession of, and coldly employs, all the modulations of rhyme, all the resources of antithesis and all the tricks of apposition. He is a composer of the decadence or transition, who handles his tools with a truly admirable and curious dexterity. M. Hugo was by nature an academician even before he was born, and if we were still living in the time of fabulous marvels, I would be prepared to believe that often, as he passed before their wrathful sanctuary, the green lions of the *Institut* would murmur to him in prophetic tones, "Thou shalt enter these portals."

For Delacroix justice is more sluggish. His works, on the contrary, are poems—and great poems, *naïvely* conceived and executed with the usual insolence of genius. In the works of the former there is nothing left to guess at, for he takes so much pleasure in exhibiting his skill that he omits not one blade of grass nor even the reflection of a street-lamp. The latter in his works throws open immense vistas to the most adventurous imaginations. The first enjoys a certain calmness, let us rather say a certain detached egoism, which causes an unusual coldness and moderation to hover above his poetry—qualities which the dogged and melancholy passion of the second, at grips with the obstinacies of his craft, does not always permit him to retain. One starts with detail, the other with an intimate understanding of his subject; from which it follows that one only captures the skin, while the other tears out the entrails. Too earthbound, too attentive to the superficies of nature, M. Victor Hugo has become a painter in poetry; Delacroix, always respectful of his ideal, is often, without knowing it, a poet in painting.

This is grand polemical criticism, deliciously unfair to the greatest French poet ever. Hugo is now adroit, but not inventive; a correct laborer, but not creative. Few critical remarks are as effectively destructive as: "with him even eccentricity takes symmetrical forms." Hugo is somehow a mere, earthbound painter of nature, and an academic impostor, doomed from birth to be an institutional pillar. Baudelaire's stance towards Hugo over the next decade became yet more negative, so that it is at first something of a surprise to read his letters to the exiled Hugo in 1859. Yet the complex rhetoric of the letters is again wholly human, all too human, in the agon of poetic influence:

> So now I owe you some explanations. I know your works by heart and your prefaces show me that I've overstepped the theory you generally put forward on the alliance of morality and poetry. But at a time when society turns away from art with such disgust, when men allow themselves to be debased by purely utilitarian concerns, I think there's no great harm in exaggerating a little in the other direction. It's possible that I've protested too much. But that was in order to obtain what was needed. Finally, even if there were a little Asiatic fatalism mixed up in my reflections I think that would be pardonable. The terrible world in which we live gives one a taste for isolation and fatality.
>
> What I wanted to do above all was to bring the reader's thoughts back to that wonderful little age whose true king you were, and which lives on in my mind like a delicious memory of childhood....
>
> The lines I enclose with this letter have been knocking around in my brain for a long time. The second piece was written with the *aim of imitating you* (laugh at my absurdity, it makes me laugh myself) after I'd reread some poems in your collections, in which such magnificent charity blends with such touching familiarity. In art galleries I've sometimes seen wretched art students copying the works of the masters. Well done or botched, these imitations sometimes contained, unbeknownst to the students, something of their own character, be it great or common. Perhaps (perhaps!) that will excuse my boldness. When *The Flowers of Evil* reappears, swollen with three times as much material as the Court suppressed, I'll have the pleasure of inscribing at the head of these poems the name of the poet whose works have taught me so much and brought such pleasure to my youth.

"That wonderful little age" doubtless referred to the Romanticism of the Revolution of 1830, that enchanted moment when Victor Hugo was king. But the true reference is to the nine-year-old Baudelaire, who found in his precursor "a delicious memory of childhood," and no mere likeness. When Baudelaire goes on to speak of imitation he cannot forbear the qualification: "something of their own character, great or common." A few months later, sending his poem, "The Swan," to Hugo, he asked that the poem be judged "with your paternal eyes." But, a year later, Baudelaire again condemned Hugo for: "his concern with contemporary events ... the belief in progress, the salvation of mankind by the use of balloons, etc."

The whip of ambivalence lashed back and forth in Baudelaire. Though a believer in salvation through balloons, the bardic Hugo was also, in his bad son's estimate, a force of nature: "No other artist is so universal in scope, more adept at coming into contact with the forces of the universe, more disposed to immerse himself in nature." That might seem definitive, but later Baudelaire allowed himself this diatribe, which hardly dents the divine precursor:

> Hugo thinks a great deal about Prometheus. He has placed an imaginary vulture on a breast that is never lacerated by anything more than the flea-bites of his own vanity ...
>
> Hugo-the-Almighty always has his head bowed in thought; no wonder he never sees anything except his own navel.

It is painful to read this; more painful still to read the references to Hugo in Baudelaire's letters of 1865–66. One moment, in its flash of a healthier humor, renders a grand, partly involuntary tribute to the normative visionary who both inspired and distressed Baudelaire:

> It appears that he and the Ocean have quarreled! Either he has not the strength to bear the Ocean longer, or the Ocean has grown weary of his presence.

To confront, thus again, the rock-like ego of that force of nature, your poetic father, is to admit implicitly that he returns in his own colors, and not in your own.

II

Proust, in a letter to Jacques Rivière, compared Baudelaire to Hugo and clearly gave the preference to Baudelaire. What Wallace Stevens, following Baudelaire, called the profound poetry of the poor and of the dead, seemed to Proust wholly Baudelaire's, and not Hugo's. But as love poets, Hugo and Baudelaire seemed more equal, even perhaps with Hugo the superior. Proust said he preferred Hugo to Baudelaire in a great common trope:

Elle me regarda de ce regard suprême
Qui reste à la beauté quand nous en triômphons.

She gazed at me with that supreme look
Which endures in beauty even while it is vanquished.
(Hugo)

Et cette gratitude infinie et sublime
Qui sort de la paupière ainsi qu'un long soupir

And that sublime and infinite gratitude
which glistens under the eyelids like a sigh.
(Baudelaire)

Both tropes are superb; I too prefer Hugo's, but why did Proust have that preference, or pretend to have it? Both beauties have been vanquished, but Hugo's by the potent Victor himself, while Baudelaire's Hippolyta reflects the triumph of Delphine, who stares at her victim with the shining eyes of a lioness. Proust, perhaps rather slyly, says he prefers the heterosexual trope to the Lesbian one, but does not say why. Yet, superb critic that he was, he helps us to expand Valéry's insight. Resolving to do precisely what Hugo had not done, Baudelaire became the modern poet of Lesbos, achieving so complex a vision of that alternative convention of Eros as to usurp forever anyone else's representation of it:

Comme un bétail pensif sur le sable couchées,
Elles tournent leurs yeux vers l'horizon des mers,
Et leurs pieds se cherchant et leurs mains rapprochées
Ont de douces langueurs et des frissons amers.

Les unes, coeurs épris de longues confidences,
Dans le fond des bosquets où jasent les ruisseaux,
Vont épelant l'amour des craintives enfances
Et creusent le bois vert des jeunes arbrisseaux;

D'autres, comme des soeurs, marchent lentes et graves
A travers les rochers pleins d'apparitions,
Où saint Antoine a vu surgir comme des laves
Les seins nus et pourprés de ses tentations;

Il en est, aux lueurs des resines croulantes,

Qui dans le creux muet des vieux antres païens
T'appellent au secours de leurs fièvres hurlantes,
O Bacchus, endormeur des remords anciens!

Et d'autres, dont la gorge aime les scapulaires,
Qui, recélant un fouet sous leurs longs vêtements,
Mêlent, dans le bois sombre et les nuits solitaires,
L'écume du plaisir aux larmes des tourments.

O vierges, ô démons, ô monstres, ô martyres,
De la réalité grands esprits contempteurs,
Chercheuses d'infini, dévotes et satyres,
Tantôt pleines de cris, tantôt pleines de pleurs,

Vous que dans votre enfer mon âme a poursuivies,
Pauvres soeurs, je vous aime autant que je vous plains,
Pour vos mornes douleurs, vos soifs inassouvies,
Et les urnes d'amour dont vos grands coeurs sont pleins!

Pensive as cattle resting on the beach,
they are staring out to sea; their hands and feet
creep toward each other imperceptibly
and touch at last, hesitant then fierce.

How eagerly some, beguiled by secrets shared,
follow a talkative stream among the trees,
spelling out their timid childhood's love
and carving initials in the tender wood;

others pace as slow and grave as nuns
among the rocks where Anthony beheld
the purple breasts of his temptations rise
like lava from the visionary earth;

some by torchlight in the silent caves
consecrated once to pagan rites
invoke—to quench their fever's holocaust—
Bacchus, healer of the old regrets;

others still, beneath their scapulars,
conceal a whip that in the solitude

and darkness of the forest reconciles
tears of pleasure with the tears of pain.

Virgins, demons, monsters, martyrs, all
great spirits scornful of reality,
saints and satyrs in search of the infinite,
racked with sobs or loud in ecstasy,

you whom my soul has followed to your hell,
Sisters! I love you as I pity you
for your bleak sorrows, for your unslaked thirsts,
and for the love that gorges your great hearts!

Richard Howard's superb translation greatly assists my inner ear, inadequate for the nuances of Baudelaire's French, in the labor of apprehending what Erich Auerbach memorably spoke of as Baudelaire's aesthetic dignity, that all-but-unique fusion of Romantic pathos and classical irony, so clearly dominant in these immense quatrains. Yet I would place the emphasis elsewhere, upon that psychological acuity in which Baudelaire surpasses nearly all poets, Shakespeare excepted. Freud, speculating upon female homosexuality, uttered the grand and plaintive cry: "we find masculinity vanishing into activity and femininity into passivity, and that does not tell us enough." Baudelaire does tell us enough, almost more than enough, even as Melanie Klein came, after Freud and Karl Abraham, to tell us much more than enough. The "damned women," really little children, play at being masculine and feminine, for Baudelaire's great insight is that Lesbianism transforms the erotic into the aesthetic, transforms compulsion into a vain play that remains compulsive. "Scornful of reality," and so of the reality principle that is our consciousness of mortality, Baudelaire's great spirits search out the infinite, and discover that the only infinity is the hell of repetition. One thinks back to Delphine and Hippolyta; Baudelaire sees and shows that Delphine is the daughter revenging herself upon the mother, even as Hippolyta revenges herself upon the mother in quite another way. When Hippolyta cries out: "Let me annihilate myself upon / your breast and find the solace of a grave!" then we feel that Baudelaire has made Melanie Klein redundant, perhaps superfluous. The revenge upon the mother is doubtless Baudelaire's revenge upon his own mother, but more profoundly it is the aesthetic revenge upon nature. In Baudelaire's own case, was it not also the revenge upon that force of nature, too conversant with ocean, that victorious poetic father, the so-often reviled but never forgotten Victor Hugo?

Matthew Arnold

(1822-1888)

Arnold is a Romantic poet who did not wish to be one, an impossible conflict which caused him finally to abandon poetry for literary criticism and prose prophecy. From the middle 1850s on, Arnold was primarily a prose writer, and his influence has been largely as a literary critic.

Arnold was born on December 24, 1822, the eldest son of the formidable Dr. Thomas Arnold, who from 1828 on was to be Headmaster of Rugby School. Dr. Arnold, a historian of some limited distinction, was a Protestant moralist of the rationalizing kind. His son did well at Rugby but alarmed Dr. Arnold with a defensive posture of continuous gaiety, which became a mock-dandyism at Balliol College, Oxford, where his closest friend was the poet Arthur Hugh Clough. After a fellowship at Oriel College, Oxford, Arnold went to London in 1847, as private secretary to a high official. In 1849 his early poems were published as *The Strayed Reveller, and Other Poems*. The "Marguerite" of those poems is now known to have been inspired by a youthful infatuation with Mary Claude, a summertime neighbor in the Lake district. In 1850, he fell in love with a judge's daughter, whom he married in 1851, after being appointed an Inspector of Schools.

In 1852 Arnold published his principal poem, the ambitious and uneasy *Empedocles on Etna*. When he brought together his *Poems* in 1853, he excluded *Empedocles*, explaining in the volume's famous anti-Romantic Preface that passive suffering was not a fit theme for poetry. When in 1857 he was elected Professor of Poetry at Oxford, almost all his best poetry had been written. Thus, his next poem, *Merope, A Tragedy*, published in 1858, is rather frigid, and the outstanding poems of his last volume, *New Poems* (1867), were composed many years before.

Whatever his achievement as a critic of literature, society, or religion, his work as a poet may not merit the reputation it has continued to hold in the twentieth century. Arnold is, at his best, a very good but highly derivative poet, unlike Tennyson, Browning, Hopkins, Swinburne, and Rossetti, all of whom individualized their voices. As with Tennyson, Hopkins, and Rossetti, Arnold's dominant precursor was Keats, but this is an unhappy puzzle, since Arnold (unlike the others) professed not to admire Keats greatly, while writing his own elegiac poems in a diction, meter, imagistic procedure, that are embarrassingly close to Keats (any reader who believes that this judgment is too harsh ought to experiment immediately by reading side-by-side the odes of Keats and Arnold's "The Scholar-Gipsy" or "Thyrsis"). Tennyson, Hopkins, and D.G. Rossetti retain distinctive Keatsian elements in their mature styles, but these elements are subdued to larger effects. But Arnold in "The Scholar-Gipsy," his best poem of some length, uses the language and movement of Keats even though the effect is irrelevant to his poem's theme.

Still, it is not a mean distinction to have written lyrics as strong as the famous "To Marguerite—Continued" and "Dover Beach" or a meditative poem as profound as "The Buried Life." Arnold got into his poetry what Tennyson and Browning scarcely needed (but absorbed anyway), the main march of mind in his time. His frequently dry tone and flatness of statement may not have been, as he happily believed, evidences of Classicism, but of a lack of poetic exuberance, a failure in the vitality of his language. But much abides in his work, and he is usefully prophetic also of the anti-Romantic "Modernism" of our time, so much of which, like Arnold, has turned out to be Romantic in spite of itself.

Emily Dickinson

(1830–1886)

IT IS NOT A RARE QUALITY FOR GREAT POETS TO POSSESS SUCH COGNITIVE strength that we are confronted by authentic intellectual difficulties when we read them. "Poems are made by fools like me," yes, and by Dante, Milton, Blake and Shelley, but only God can make a tree, to reappropriate a rejoinder I remember making to W.H. Auden many years ago, when he deprecated the possibilities of poetry as compared with the awful truths of Christian theology. But there are certainly very grand poets who are scarcely thinkers in the discursive modes. Tennyson and Whitman are instances of overwhelming elegiac artists who make us fitful when they argue, and the subtle rhetorical evasions of Wallace Stevens do not redeem his unfortunate essay, "A Collect of Philosophy."

Of all poets writing in English in the nineteenth and twentieth centuries, I judge Emily Dickinson to present us with the most authentic cognitive difficulties. Vast and subtle intellect cannot in itself make a poet; the essential qualities are inventiveness, mastery of trope and craft, and that weird flair for intuiting significance through rhythm to which we can give no proper name. Dickinson has all these, as well as a mind so original and powerful that we scarcely have begun, even now, to catch up with her.

Originality at its strongest—in the Yahwists, Plato, Shakespeare and Freud—usurps immense spaces of consciousness and language, and imposes contingencies upon all who come after. These contingencies work so as to conceal authentic difficulty through a misleading familiarity. Dickinson's strangeness, partly masked, still causes us to wonder at her, as we ought to wonder at Shakespeare or Freud. Like them, she has no single, overwhelming precursor whose existence can lessen her wildness for us. Her agon was waged with the whole of tradition, but particularly with the Bible and with romanticism. As an agonist, she takes care to differ from any male model, and places us upon warning:

> I cannot dance upon my Toes—
> No Man instructed me—
> But oftentimes, among my mind,
> A Glee possesseth me,
>
> . . . .
> Nor any know I know the Art
> I mention—easy—Here—
> Nor any Placard boast me—
> It's full as Opera—
> [326]

The mode is hardly Whitmanian in this lyric of 1862, but the vaunting is, and both gleeful arts respond to the Emersonian prophecy of American Self-Reliance. Each responds with a difference, but it is a perpetual trial to be a heretic whose only orthodoxy is Emersonianism, or the exaltation of whim:

> If nature will not tell the tale
> Jehovah told to her
> Can human nature not survive
> Without a listener?
> [1748]

Emerson should have called his little first book, *Nature*, by its true title of Man, but Dickinson in any case would have altered that title also. Alas, that Emerson was not given the chance to read the other Titan that he fostered. We would cherish his charmed reaction to:

> A Bomb upon the Ceiling
> Is an improving thing—
> It keeps the nerves progressive
> Conjecture flourishing—
> [1128]

Dickinson, after all, could have sent her poems to Emerson rather than to the nobly obtuse Higginson. We cannot envision Whitman addressing a copy of the first *Leaves of Grass* to a Higginson. There is little reason to suppose that mere diffidence prevented Miss Dickinson of

Amherst from presenting her work to Mr. Emerson of Concord. In 1862, Emerson was still Emerson; his long decline dates from after the conclusion of the War. A private unfolding remained necessary for Dickinson, according to laws of the spirit and of poetic reason that we perpetually quest to surmise. Whereas Whitman masked his delicate, subtle and hermetic art by developing the outward self of the rough Walt, Dickinson set herself free to invest her imaginative exuberance elsewhere. The heraldic drama of her reclusiveness became the cost of her confirmation as a poet more original even than Whitman, indeed more original than any poet of her century after (and except) Wordsworth. Like Wordsworth, she began anew upon a *tabula rasa* of poetry, to appropriate Hazlitt's remark about Wordsworth. Whitman rethought the relation of the poet's self to his own vision, whereas Dickinson rethought the entire content of poetic vision. Wordsworth had done both, and done both more implicitly than these Americans could manage, but then Wordsworth had Coleridge as stimulus, while Whitman and Dickinson had the yet more startling and far wilder Emerson, who was and is the American difference personified. I cannot believe that even Dickinson would have written with so absolutely astonishing an audacity had Emerson not insisted that poets were as liberating gods:

> Because that you are going
> And never coming back
> And I, however absolute,
> May overlook your Track—
>
> Because that Death is final,
> However first it be,
> This instant be suspended
> Above Mortality—
>
> Significance that each has lived
> The other to detect
> Discovery not God himself
> Could now annihilate
>
> Eternity, Presumption
> The instant I perceive
> That you, who were Existence
> Yourself forgot to live—

These are the opening quatrains of poem 1260, dated by Thomas Johnson as about 1873, but it must be later, if indeed the reference is to the dying either of Samuel Bowles (1878) or of Judge Otis Lord (1884), the two men Richard Sewall, Dickinson's principal biographer, considers to have been her authentic loves, if not in any conventional way her lovers. The poem closes with a conditional vision of God refunding to us finally our "confiscated Gods." Reversing the traditional pattern, Dickinson required and achieved male Muses, and her "confiscated Gods" plays darkly against Emerson's "liberating gods." Of Emerson, whose crucial work (*Essays*, *The Conduct of Life*, *Society and Solitude*, the *Poems*) she had mastered, Dickinson spoke with the ambiguity we might expect. When Emerson lectured in Amherst in December 1857, and stayed next door with Dickinson's brother and sister-in-law, he was characterized by the poet: "as if he had come from where dreams are born." Presumably the Transcendental Emerson might have merited this, but it is curious when applied to the exalter of "Fate" and "Power" in *The Conduct of Life*, or to the dialectical pragmatist of "Experience" and "Circles," two essays that I think Dickinson had internalized. Later, writing to Higginson, she observed: "With the Kingdom of Heaven on his knee, could Mr. Emerson hesitate?" The question, whether open or rhetorical, is dangerous and wonderful, and provokes considerable rumination.

Yet her subtle ways with other male precursors are scarcely less provocative. Since Shelley had addressed *Epipsychidion* to Emilia Viviani, under the name of "Emily," Dickinson felt authorized to answer a poet who, like herself, favored the image of volcanoes. Only ten days or so before judge Lord died, she composed a remarkable quatrain in his honor (and her own):

> Circumference thou Bride of Awe
> Possessing thou shalt be
> Possessed by every hallowed Knight
> That dares to covet thee
> [1620]

Sewall notes the interplay with some lines in *Epipsychidion*:

> Possessing and possessed by all that is
> Within that calm circumference of bliss,
> And by each other, till to love and live
> Be one:—
> [549–52]

Shelley's passage goes on to a kind of lovers' apocalypse:

> One hope within two wills, one will beneath
> Two overshadowing minds, one life, one death,
> One heaven, one Hell, one immortality,
> And one annihilation...
> [584–87]

In his essay, "Circles," Emerson had insisted: "There is no outside, no inclosing wall, no circumference to us." The same essay declares: "The only sin is limitation." If that is so, then there remains the cost of confirmation, worked out by Dickinson in an extraordinary short poem that may be her critique of Emerson's denial of an outside:

> I saw no Way—The Heavens were stitched
> I felt the Columns close—
> The Earth reversed her Hemispheres—
> I touched the Universe—
>
> And back it slid—and I alone
> A Speck upon a Ball—
> Went out upon Circumference—
> Beyond the Dip of Bell—
> [378]

"My Business is Circumference—" she famously wrote to Higginson, to whom, not less famously, she described herself as "the only Kangaroo among the Beauty." When she wrote, to another correspondent, that "The Bible dealt with the Centre, not with the Circumference—," she would have been aware that the terms were Emerson's, and that Emerson also dealt only with the Central, in the hope of the Central Man who would come. Clearly, "Circumference" is her trope for the Sublime, as consciousness and as achievement or performance. For Shelley, Circumference was a Spenserian cynosure, a Gardens of Adonis vision, while for Emerson it was no part of us, or only another challenge to be overcome by the Central, by the Self-Reliant Man.

If the Bible's concern is Centre, not Circumference, it cannot be because the Bible does not quest for the Sublime. If Circumference or Dickinson is the bride of Awe or of the authority of Judge Lord, then Awe too somehow had to be detached from the Centre:

No man saw awe, nor to his house
Admitted he a man
Though by his awful residence
Has human nature been.

Not deeming of his dread abode
Till laboring to flee
A grasp on comprehension laid
Detained vitality.

Returning is a different route
The Spirit could not show
For breathing is the only work
To be enacted now.

"Am not consumed," old Moses wrote,
"Yet saw him face to face"—
That very physiognomy
I am convinced was this.
[1733]

This might be called an assimilation of Awe to Circumference, where "laboring to flee" and returning via "a different route" cease to be antithetical to one another. "Vitality" here is another trope for Circumference or the Dickinsonian Sublime. If, as I surmise, this undated poem is a kind of proleptic elegy for Judge Lord, then Dickinson identifies herself with "old Moses," and not for the first time in her work. Moses, denied entrance into Canaan, "wasn't fairly used—," she wrote, as though the exclusion were her fate also. In some sense, she chose this fate, and not just by extending her circumference to Bowles and to Lord, unlikely pragmatic choices. The spiritual choice was not to be post-Christian, as with Whitman or Emerson, but to become a sect of one, like Milton or Blake. Perhaps her crucial choice was to refuse the auction of her mind through publication. Character being fate, the Canaan she would not cross to was poetic recognition while she lived.

Of Dickinson's 1,775 poems and fragments, several hundred are authentic, strong works, with scores achieving an absolute aesthetic dignity. To choose one above all the others must reveal more about the critic than he or she could hope to know. But I do not hesitate in my choice, poem 627, written probably in her very productive year, 1862. What precedents are there for such a poem, a work of un-naming, a profound and shockingly original cognitive act of negation?

> The Tint I cannot take—is best—
> The Color too remote
> That I could show it in Bazaar—
> A Guinea at a sight—
>
> The fine—impalpable Array—
> That swaggers on the eye
> Like Cleopatra's Company—
> Repeated—in the sky—
>
> The Moments of Dominion
> That happen on the Soul
> And leave it with a Discontent
> Too exquisite—to tell—
>
> The eager look—on Landscapes—
> As if they just repressed
> Some Secret—that was pushing
> Like Chariots—in the West—
>
> The Pleading of the Summer—
> That other Prank—of Snow—
> That Cushions Mystery with Tulle,
> For fear the Squirrels—know.
>
> Their Graspless manners—mock us—
> Until the Cheated Eye
> Shuts arrogantly—in the Grave—
> Another way—to see—

It is, rugged and complete, a poetics, and a manifesto of Self-Reliance. "The poet did not stop at the color or the form, but read their meaning; neither may he rest in this meaning, but he makes the same objects exponents of his new thought." This Orphic metamorphosis is Emerson's, but is not accomplished in his own poetry, nor is his radical program of un-naming. Dickinson begins by throwing away the lights and the definitions, and by asserting that her jocular procreations are too sub-tle for the Bazaar of publication. The repetition of colors (an old word, after all, for tropes) remains impalpable and provokes her into her own Sublime, that state of Circumference at once a divine discontent and a series of absolute moments that take dominion everywhere. Better perhaps than any other poet, she knows and indicates that what is worth representing is beyond depiction, what is worth saying cannot be said. What she reads, on landscapes and in seasons, is propulsive force, the recurrence of perspectives that themselves are powers and instrumentalities of the only knowledge ever available.

The final stanza does not attempt to break out of this siege of perspectives, but it hints again that her eye and will are receptive, not plundering, so that her power to un-name is not Emersonian finally, but something different, another way to see. To see feelingly, yes, but beyond the arrogance of the self in its war against process and its stand against other selves. Her interplay of perspectives touches apotheosis not in a Nietzschean or Emersonian exaltation of the will to power, however receptive and reactive, but in suggestions of an alternative mode, less an interpretation than a questioning, or an othering of natural process. The poem, like so much of Dickinson at her strongest, compels us to begin again in rethinking our relation to poems, and to the equally troubling and dynamic relation of poems to our world of appearances.

Christina Rossetti

(1830–1894)

CHRISTINA ROSSETTI (1830–94) IS ONE OF A HANDFUL OF MAJOR ENGLISH devotional poets, together with John Donne, George Herbert, Richard Crashaw, Henry Vaughn, and her contemporary, the Jesuit Gerard Manley Hopkins. One might expect the beloved sister of Dante Gabriel Rossetti to manifest a marked difference from other poets of religious sensibility. Like the Pre-Raphaelites, her style and procedures stem from Keats and Tennyson, rather than Donne and Herbert, but then Hopkins also is Keatsian in mode.

Goblin Market doubtless is Christina Rossetti's masterpiece, and rightly has become a favorite text for feminist literary criticism. It fascinates and disturbs me, and though I have included it complete in two anthologies, I never have commented upon the poem, for reasons I can only surmise. In a sense it is poetry for children, though indeed they have to be extremely intelligent children of all ages. Thus they could resist the current academic interpretations: Marxist, feminist, lesbian-incestuous, or imagistic self-gratification, at once erotic, mercantile, and even vampiric.

There certainly is a struggle going on in *Goblin Market*, but it seems to me an agon for poetic incarnation, for the establishment of a strong poetic self. I don't suppose that Christina Rossetti would have accepted John Keats's Scene of Instruction less ambivalently if he had been a woman, since strong poets are not particularly given to communal quilt-making. What troubles *Goblin Market* is not only Keats's magnificent oxymoronic rhetoric but also his naturalistic humanism. Keatsian eroticism is totally free of the melancholy sound of church bells. Christina Rossetti's intense faith was intricately fused with an erotic temperament as exuberant as her brother Dante Gabriel Rossetti's, and her lifelong renunciation (so far as we know) of sexual experience testifies to a rather frightening strength of will, or of faith if you would have it so. The Tempter in *Goblin Market* is in any case John Keats and not John Keble, or Romanticism rather than the Oxford Movement of Anglican Revivalism.

I hasten to insist that I find it grotesque to identify the Goblins as male precursor poets: Milton, Keats, Tennyson, and D.G. Rossetti and his friends. The nursery rhyme stylistics of *Goblin Market* are wonderfully effective swerves away from Keatsian celebrations of natural abundance, but they defend against glories of language, and not against gendered dangers.

That *Goblin Market* is an open-ended allegory is its finest attribute. Such irony invests deeply in the fantastic, challenging us to behold our own idiosyncratic phantasmagorias. Perhaps Friedrich Schlegel's definition of irony as the "permanent parabasis of meaning" could not be better exemplified than by Christina Rossetti's most ambitious poem.

Gerard Manley Hopkins

(1844-1889)

OF ALL VICTORIAN POETS, HOPKINS HAS BEEN THE MOST MISREPRESENTED by modern critics. He has been discussed as though his closest affinities were with Donne on one side, and T.S. Eliot on the other. Yet his poetry stems directly from Keats and the Pre-Raphaelites, and the dominant influences upon his literary thought came from Ruskin and Pater. A disciple of Newman, he is as High Romantic as his master, and his best poetry, with all its peculiarities of diction and metric, is perhaps less of a departure from the Victorian norm than Browning's, or Swinburne's, or even Patmore's. His case is analogous to Emily Dickinson's. Published out of their own century, they became for a time pseudocontemporaries of twentieth-century poets, but perspectives later became corrected, and we learned to read both poets as very much involved in the literature and thought of their own generations. Hopkins was, in many of his attitudes, a representative Victorian gentleman; indeed he was as much a nationalistic jingo as Tennyson or Kipling, and his religious anguish is clearly related to a characteristic sorrow of his age. His more properly poetic anguish is wholly Romantic, like Arnold's, for it derives from an incurably Romantic sensibility desperately striving not to be Romantic, but to make a return to a lost tradition. Hopkins quested for ideas of order that were not available to his poetic mind, and as a poet he ended in bitterness, convinced that he had failed his genius.

Hopkins was born on July 28, 1844, at Stratford in Essex, the eldest of nine children, into a very religious High Anglican family, of comfortable means. He did not enjoy his early school years, but flowered at Balliol College, Oxford, where he studied Classics from 1863 to 1867, and became a student of Walter Pater, who corrected his essays. In the atmosphere of the continuing Oxford Movement, Hopkins underwent a crisis, which came in March 1865 and partly resulted from meeting an enthusiastic, young, religious poet, Digby Dolben, who was to drown in June 1867 at the age of nineteen.

In 1866, under Newman's sponsorship, Hopkins was received into the Roman Catholic Church. Two years later, he began his Jesuit novitiate, and continued faithful to the Order until he died. Ordained a priest in 1877, he preached in Liverpool, taught at Stonyhurst, a Jesuit seminary, and from 1884 until his death in 1889 served as Professor of Greek at the University College in Dublin. Though perfectly free to write poems and paint pictures, so far as his superiors in the Society of Jesus were concerned, Hopkins was a congenital self-torturer, and so much a Romantic that he found the professions of priest and poet to be mutually exclusive.

Austin Warren, one of Hopkins's best and most sympathetic critics, justly remarked that in Hopkins's most ambitious poems there is "a discrepancy between texture and structure: the copious, violent detail is matched by no corresponding intellectual or mythic vigor." Following Keats's advice to Shelley, that an artist must serve Mammon by loading every rift of his poem with ore, Hopkins sometimes went too far, and even a sympathetic reader can decide that the poems are overloaded.

What then is Hopkins's achievement as poet? It remains considerable, for the original, almost incredible, accomplishment of Hopkins is to have made Keatsian poetry into a devotional mode, however strained. In the "Subtle Doctor," the Scottish Franciscan philosopher Duns Scotus (1265–1308), also an Oxonian, Hopkins found doctrine to reconcile a concern for individual form, for the "thisness" of people and natural things, with the universal truths of the church. Following his own understanding of Scotus, Hopkins coined the word "inscape" for every natural pattern he apprehended. "Instress," another coinage, meant for him the effect of each pattern upon his own imagination. Taken together, the terms are an attempt at scholasticizing Keats's fundamental approach to perception: detachment, the poet's recourse to nonidentity, Negative Capability.

Hopkins remained unpublished until his friend, the poet Robert Bridges, brought out a first edition of the poems in 1918, nearly thirty years after Hopkins's death. By chance, this first publication almost coincided with the start of the aggressive literary modernism that dominated British and American poetry until the 1950s, and Hopkins was acclaimed by poets and critics as the true continuator of English poetry in the otherwise benighted nineteenth century, and as a precursor who could help justify modern experiments in diction, metrics, and imagistic procedure.

Hopkins's diction adds to its Keatsian and Pre-Raphaelite base a large stock of language derived from his study of Welsh and Old English, and from an amorphous group of Victorian philologists who sought a "pure English," less contaminated by the Latin and French elements that are incurably part of the language. Hopkins's metric was based, as he said, upon nursery rhymes, the choruses of Milton's *Samson Agonistes*, and Welsh poetry. Against what he called the "running" or "common" rhythm of nineteenth-century poetry, Hopkins espoused "sprung rhythm," which he insisted was inherent in the English language, the older, purely accentual meter of Anglo-Saxon verse. Evidently, Hopkins read Keats's odes as having this rhythm, despite Keats's Spenserian smoothness.

Though Hopkins came to the study of Old English late, his essential metrical achievement was to revive the schemes of Old English poetry. But the main traditions of English poetic rhythm go from Chaucer to Spenser and Milton and on to the major Romantics, and Hopkins's archaizing return to Cynewulf and Langland, though influential for a time, now seems an honorable eccentricity. Nevertheless, its expressive effectiveness is undeniable. The metrical basis of many of Hopkins's poems is a fixed number of primary-stressed syllables, surrounded by a variable number of unstressed ones, or "outrides" as he called them. The alliterations of early Germanic poetry also work powerfully to recast the poetic line into a chain of rhythmic bursts. Thus, in "The Windhover," the first two lines each have five of Hopkins's beats (as opposed to five regularized, alternating, accentual-syllabic ones):

> I caúght this mórning, mórning's minión, kíng-
> dom of dáylight's daúphin, dapple-dáwn-drawn Fálcon, in his
> ríding ...

But the first line has ten syllables, and might be mistaken for an iambic pentameter, while the second has sixteen; and we realize as we read through the poems that what is common to them, their *meter* rather than their individual rhythms, is the sequence of five major stresses. Moreover, the phrase "dapple-*dawn*-drawn" is so accented as to preserve the meaning "drawn by dappled dawn" through its interior rhyme and alliterative clusters. Hopkins's own invented metrical terminology is, like his other philosophical vocabulary, highly figurative: "hangers" or "outrides," "sprung rhythm," "counterpointing" (or superposition of rhythmic schemes), even the blended emotive-linguistic meanings of "stress" itself, all invoke the imagery of his poems, and are as subjective as are his metaphysical concepts, but like those concepts constitute an extraordinary approach to a Catholic poetic transcendentalism.

Alfred, Lord Tennyson

(1850–1892)

When I began to write I avowed for my principles those of Arthur Hallam in his essay upon Tennyson. Tennyson, who had written but his early poems when Hallam wrote, was an example of the school of Keats and Shelley, and Keats and Shelley, unlike Wordsworth, intermixed into their poetry no elements from the general thought, but wrote out of the impression made by the world upon their delicate senses.

—W.B. YEATS, *Art and Ideas*

So vivid was the delight attending the simple exertions of eye and ear, that it became mingled more and more with trains of active thought, and tended to absorb their whole being into the energy of sense.

—HALLAM on Shelley and Keats,
in his review of Tennyson's
Poems, Chiefly Lyrical (1830)

THE *LAUREATE OF DESPAIR* AND *THE ANCIENT SAGE* IS OF COURSE ONE OF the memorable disasters of poetic tradition, surpassing the Wordsworth of the *Ecclesiastical Sonnets* and even the Arnold of *Merope*. The whole being of Tennyson was at no single time absorbed into the energy of sense, and for this failure of experience the price was paid, alas even overpaid:

And more—think well! Do-well will follow thought,
And in the fatal sequence of this world
An evil thought may soil thy children's blood;
But curb the beast would cast thee in the mire,
And leave the hot swamp of voluptuousness
A cloud between the Nameless and thyself,

> And lay thine uphill shoulder to the wheel,
> And climb the Mount of Blessing, whence, if thou
> Look higher, then—perchance—thou mayest—beyond
> A hundred ever-rising mountain lines,
> And past the range of Night and Shadow-see
> The high-heaven dawn of more than mortal day
> Strike on the Mount of Vision!
>
> So, farewell.

There are still Tennyson scholars who can read this, or say they can, but the indefensible badness of it all is plain enough. Sixty years or so before this, as a boy of fourteen, Tennyson possessed the verbal exuberance of an absolute poetic genius, and manifested it in the splendid speeches of the Devil in *The Devil and the Lady*, and in the remarkable movement of an exercise like the *Ode: O Bosky Brook*. The extremes of a poet's values, if they are manifested merely as a chronological continuum, do not much matter. Vision darkens, life triumphs, the poet becomes the man whose pharynx is bad. So went Wordsworth, the founder of modern poetry, and where a Moses was lost, other losses must follow. Yeats and Wallace Stevens appear today to be the first and only poets in the Romantic tradition who flowered anew both in middle and in old age, and yet it can be questioned if either will rival Tennyson and Browning after the fogs of fashion have been dispelled.

At the center of Tennyson the problem is not whether or why he hardened and kept hardening in poetic character, or just how his vision darkened perpetually into the abysses of much of the later verse, but why and how the sensibility of a major Romantic poet was subverted even in his earlier years. What the most sympathetic reader can still find wanting in the best of Tennyson is a power of imagination shown forth uncompromisingly in *The Fall of Hyperion* and *The Triumph of Life*, in *Resolution and Independence* and *The Mental Traveller*, and on the largest scale in *The Prelude* and *Jerusalem*. Romance, lyric, epic were raised to greatness again in the two generations just before Tennyson. In a lyrical monologue like *Andrea del Sarto*, a romance like "Childe Roland to the Dark Tower Came," and in the curious epic of *The Ring and the Book* a poet of Tennyson's own generation comes close to approximating the Romantic achievement. Tennyson was as legitimately the heir of Keats as Browning was of Shelley, and as much a betrayal of Keats's imaginative honesty and autonomy as Browning was of Shelley's. To make such a point is to reveal in oneself an unreconstructed Romantic bias, like that of Swinburne, or Yeats, or Shaw or Hardy, to bring in four Shelleyans who were contemporaries of the older Browning and Tennyson. There are achievements in Tennyson that are not Romantic, but they are small enough. The Tennyson who counts for most, seen in the longest and clearest perspective we now can begin to recover, is certainly a Romantic poet, and not a Victorian anti-Romantic resembling the Arnold of *Merope* or the straining Hopkins of *The Wreck of the Deutschland*. He is a major Romantic poet, but not perhaps one of the greatest, though there is an antithetical storm-cloud drifting through the center of his work that sometimes shows us what his proper greatness should have been. His affinities in his own time were to no other poet but to Ruskin, a great ruin of a Romantic critic, and his value to us now is rather like Ruskin's, since he shows forth as a most crucial instance of the dilemma of post-Romantic art.

Hallam, who remains Tennyson's best critic, found "five distinctive excellences" in his friend's poetic manner: (1) the control of a luxuriant imagination; (2) accuracy of adjustment in "moods of character," so that narration and feeling naturally corresponded with each other; (3) skill in emotionally fusing a vivid, "picturesque" portrayal of objects ("picturesque" being opposed here to Wordsworthian descriptiveness); (4) modulation of verbal harmony; (5) "mellow soberness of tone," addressed to the understanding heart rather than the mere understanding. Yeats, in his old age, spoke of "the scientific and moral discursiveness of *In Memoriam*," but I cannot recognize the poem from that description. What lives in the elegies for Hallam are precisely the excellences that Hallam picked out in his friend's earlier manner, and the various tracts of discursiveness one learns to step over quickly. Discursiveness became a Tennysonian vice, but it did not in itself inhibit the development of Tennyson's poetry. Tennyson, like Browning, but to a still worse extent, never achieved even a pragmatic faith in the autonomy of his own imagination. Such a faith was a ruling passion in Blake, Shelley, and Keats, and such a faith, though held with earnest misgivings, for a while allowed Wordsworth and Coleridge to yield themselves to their greatest achievements. Though the overt Victorian Romantics of the Pre-Raphaelite group struggled back to a version of this faith, it was not held again with similar intensity in Tennyson's age except by Pater, who fostered Yeats even as he gave the more disjunctive and ironical Stevens a fresh point of departure in America. To trace the conflict in Tennyson's earlier poetry between a Romantic imagination and an emergent societal censor is hardly to conduct a fresh investigation, and I will not attempt it here. Such conflicts, whether found in a Spenser or even in a D.H. Lawrence, seem recurrent in the history of poetry, and belong more to the study of consciousness than to the study of poetic tradition. The more rewarding problem for pondering is the young Tennyson's profounder distrust of his own creative powers. A god spoke in him, or a demon, and a revulsion accompanied the maturing of this voice. No really magical poem by Tennyson ever became quite the work he intended it to be, and this gap between his intention and his actual achievement saved him as a poet, though it could not save him altogether. Most considerable poems by Tennyson do not mean what they meant to mean, and while this is true of all poets whatsoever to some degree, Tennyson is the most extreme instance I know of the imagination going one way and the will going quite another. Blake thought that the Milton of *Paradise Lost* had to be rescued from himself, an opinion that most recent Miltonists find dubious, perhaps without fully understanding it. But Tennyson's best poems are a much more radical version of Blake's paradox; they address themselves simultaneously and overtly to both a conventional and a "diabolic" reading.

Partly this is due to the prevalence in Tennyson's poetic mind of the "damned vacillating state" of the early *Supposed Confessions*. No lyric by Tennyson is more central to his sensibility than *Mariana*, entirely a poem of the autonomous imagination running down into isolated and self-destructive expectation. Wordsworth, in his sublime Tale of Margaret, wrote the contrary to Tennyson's poem, for Margaret is destroyed by an imaginative hope that will not take account of the mundane. The hope is all too willing to be fed, and the prevalence of the imagination could hardly be more dangerous. Wordsworth does, here and in *Michael*, what Tennyson could only approximate in *Dora*; the poet creates a consciousness narrower and purer than his own, and measures his own malady of self-concern by its distance from that pure intensity. Mariana, unlike Margaret, is a poetess, and she sings a Dejection ode that Tennyson scarcely ventured to write in his own person. Her disease is Romantic self-consciousness, and no bridegroom can come to heal her. "She could not look on the sweet heaven," for much the same cause as the singer of Blake's *Mad Song* turns his back to the east and rejects the comforts of the sun. Wilful and unwilling, she is poised between two states of being, one in which the world has been taken up into the mind (the mind of a Picturesque rather than Descriptive poet) and the other in which the solipsistic mind rejects the world as an unreal intruder; hence the landscape of her poem, which as a poetic achievement could not be overpraised. The poplar, seen as a phallic symbol by some recent Tennyson critics, is rather an indication of the border realm between the two states in which Mariana lives. She can neither absorb its presence nor utterly reject it, and it serves therefore to show how precarious her mode of existence is. The poem's strongest impulse is to see the world as phantasmagoria, in which case Mariana's lament would be transvalued and appear as an ironic cry of triumph for the autonomy of her vision. But there are other impulses in the poem, and "He cometh not" remains a lament.

The Shelleyan origins of Tennyson's female solitary, in *Mariana* and other poems, has been demonstrated ably by Lionel Stevenson, who unfortunately reduces this emblematic figure in both Shelley and Tennyson to Jung's archetype of the *anima*. The reduction is unnecessary in any case, since *Epipsychidion* demonstrates how consciously and deliberately Shelley used his epipsyche figure. Tennyson's use of his cynosure-female is presumably not as conscious or as deliberate, though no theory of the two Tennysons, and no prosaic psychoanalytic reduction, need be ventured in consequence. Tennyson's poetry is too many-sided for anyone to suggest plausibly that it was written by uneasy collaboration between a Shelley-Keats and a Victorian Christian humanist, and I intend no such notion in this essay. There is a profound sense of the limitations of poetry in both Keats and Shelley, but each learned how to convert this sense into an overt poetic strength. Tennyson wrote in an age of reform, both voluntary and involuntary, while the younger Romantics faced a time of apparent stasis, an exhaustion following an apocalyptic fervor. The temper of poetic imagination is peculiarly and favorably responsive to the thwarting of political hope, and Shelley and Keats and Byron gained immensely by their good fortune of having the era of Metternich and Castlereagh to contend against, little as they would appreciate so cynical a judgment. Like Beddoes and Darley, a half-generation before him, Tennyson found himself with a fiercely autonomous imagination confronting a time that neither challenged nor repelled such an imagination, yet also gave it no proper arena in which to function. Keats was of course not a political poet, indeed was far less one than Tennyson, but there still existed provocations for Keats's humanism and his naturalism to become combative. Browning found provocation enough in the Evangelicism of his parents, particularly his mother, but *Pauline* records too clearly how his Shelleyan sensibility failed guiltily before such a stimulus. Tennyson had no combative use to which an assertion of the imagination could be put, and no antidote therefore against any aesthetic corrosion that his moral doubts of imagination might bring about. The pride of imagination, and the distrust of it, had nowhere to go but within.

Sexual virginity for any poet, even a Jesuit, as Hopkins shows, is a kind of sickness unto action, a time of fear before the potential disorder of the strange. That Tennyson's Muse was (and always remained) Hallam has given Robert Graves occasion for innocent merriment, but need disturb no one any longer. The death of a beautiful young man strikes our social sense as a less appropriate theme for poetry than Poe's pervasive theme, but is of course much more traditional than Poe's preference in corpses. The sexual longings of a poet *qua* poet appear to have little relation to mere experience anyway, as for instance in the contrast between the sexually highly active Shelley, with his crucial antithetical theme of the inadequacy of nature to the imagination from *Alastor* on, and the probably virginal Keats of *Endymion*, with his profoundly primary sense of satisfaction in natural experience. Still, there is a line of poetry that goes from the complexly sensual aspirations of Spenser through the bitter sexual frustrations of Milton and Blake (particularly relevant to his Notebook poems and *Visions of the Daughters of Albion*), then to the curious argument between Shelley and Keats in *Alastor* and *Endymion*, and on to the astonishingly delayed entries into sexual experience of Tennyson and of Yeats. The analytical sophistication in aesthetic realms that would allow a responsible sexual history of English poetry to be written is not available to us, and yet such a history must and should come. The hidden fulfillment of Wordsworth is the aesthetic puzzle of *The Prelude*, since the 1805 version is marred by the inclusion of the Julia and Vaudracour episode, and the 1850 version suffers from its exclusion. The *malaise* of Tennyson's early poetry is very like that of *The Wanderings of Oisin*, and the existence of Shelley and Keats as ancestor-poets-in-common is insufficient to explain the likeness. The tragedy of sexual intercourse, according to the older Yeats, was the perpetual virginity of the soul. The comedy of sexual intercourse is presumably the initial virginity of the body, but in poetry poised before experience the comedy tends to be negated, or rather displaced into the phantasmagoria of a Mariana, whose poem would be destroyed by the slightest touch of a comic spirit.

I am not, I would hope, alone in my puzzlement as to why Tennyson has not had the prestige of the hieratic in our time, while the more limited but precisely similar Mallarmé has. Tennyson's poems of the *Mariana* kind, centered on a self-embowered consciousness, are not less artful or persuasive than Mallarmé's, and are rather more universal in their implications. The English Decadence has, as its true monument, not Swinburne, admirable poet as he certainly was, but the more masterful Tennyson, whose "metaphysics of night" go beyond Mallarmé's in their elaborately indeliberate subtleties. Hallam's is necessarily a theory of pure poetry (as H.M. McLuhan shows) and while Tennyson could not allow himself to share the theory overtly, he inspired it by his early practice, and fell back on it implicitly to save his poetry time and time again. In a way that *In Memoriam* does not apprehend, the dead Hallam remained Tennyson's guardian angel.

Mariana is too pure a poem to test any argument by, so that an overview of its neighbors in early Tennyson seems likely to be helpful. *Recollections of the Arabian Nights* is a clearly Shelleyan poem, more confident indeed in its Shelleyan faith of imagination than anything else of Tennyson's. It echoes *Kubla Khan* also, but not the third part of that poem in which Coleridge to some degree withdraws from the full implications of his own vision. Like the Poet-hero of *Alastor*, Tennyson voyages through nature in search of a center transcending nature, and he finds it in a pleasure-dome like that of *Kubla Khan* or *The Palace of Art* or *The Revolt of Islam*:

> The fourscore windows' all alight
> As with the quintessence of flame,
> A million tapers flaring bright
> From twisted silvers look'd to shame
> The hollow-vaulted dark, and stream'd
> Upon the mooned domes aloof
> In inmost Bagdat, till there seem'd
> Hundreds of crescents on the roof
>   Of night new-risen ...

This is the young Tennyson's Byzantium, and perhaps it lingered in the mind of the old Yeats, though more likely both poets were recalling, however involuntarily, visions seen by Coleridge and by Shelley. Reasonable sophisticates will smile at my connecting Tennyson's playful *Recollections* to Yeats's supreme lyric, but there is a great deal legitimately to claim (or reclaim) for *Recollections of the Arabian Nights*. It was Hallam's favorite among the 1830 *Poems*, and his choice was a justified one, for the lyric is a complete and perfected miniature of Tennyson's poetic mind, and is even an *In Memoriam* in little. A very great, a consummate poet is at work in the full strength of his sensibility, and can be felt with especial power from the fifth line of this stanza on:

> Far off, and where the lemon grove
> In closest coverture upsprung,
> The living airs of middle night
> Died round the bulbul as he sung;
> Not he: but something which possess'd
> The darkness of the world, delight,
> Life, anguish, death, immortal love,
> Ceasing not, mingled, unrepress'd,

> Apart from place, withholding time,
> But flattering the golden prime
>   Of good Haroun Alraschid.

This stanza is at the poem's center of vision, and properly recalls the song of Keats's nightingale, also sung to a poet in darkness, and like this chant an overcoming of the limitations of space and time. The companion poem to *Recollections* is the impressive *Ode to Memory*, and it is palpable that both lyrics are love poems addressed to Hallam. Palpable to us and not presumably to Tennyson and Hallam, I suppose I ought to add, but then the *Ode to Memory* ends:

> My friend, with you to live alone,
> Were how much better than to own
> A crown, a sceptre, and a throne!

> O strengthen me, enlighten me!
> I faint in this obscurity,
> Thou dewy dawn of memory.

The *Recollections* opens with an inspiriting breeze that takes the poet back to what Hart Crane in *Passage* beautifully called "an improved infancy." In that unitary joy, Tennyson emulates the Poet-hero of *Alastor* and sets forth on his quest for the good Haroun Alraschid, who is already the supernatural Hallam of *In Memoriam*, a poet-king dwelling at the center of vision, a type of god-man still to come. To reach this absolute being, the poet-voyager sails, with "a majesty of slow motion in every cadence," as Hallam observed, until he enters "another night in night," an "imbower'd" world of "imprisoning sweets." The voyage suggests not only the quest of *Alastor*, but also the journey to the Bower of Bliss in Book II of *The Faerie Queene*. Tennyson, as many critics by now have noted, is the most discreetly powerful erotic poet in the language, and this early lyric is a masterpiece of subdued erotic suggestiveness. The penultimate stanza, with its confectioner's delight of a Persian girl, is merely an erotic evasion, but the final stanza, directly celebrating Hallam, is sustained by a lyric rapture remarkable even in the younger Tennyson.

In section CIII of *In Memoriam*, Tennyson finds an after-morn of content because of another voyage-vision in which Hallam is again at the center, the Muse presiding over a realized quest. But the playfulness of *Recollections of the Arabian Nights* is now gone, that poem's greatest admirer being dead. Perhaps remembering how much Hallam had loved the poem, *Tennyson* returns to its design at one of the climaxes in his book of elegies, in which his grief is assuaged by the compensatory imagination, and Hallam is resurrected as a Titan capable of reviving Tennyson's lesser Muses. In itself, section CIII has rightly been judged to be one of Tennyson's great lyrics, but one can wonder how many of the poet's readers have seen how very little the poem has to do with the supposed faith of *In Memoriam*. Bradley, the definitive commentator on the elegies for Hallam, interpreted the dream of section CHI with his usual good sense, but declined to see its clearly Promethean pattern of *consolation*. In Numbers 13:32–33, the spies of Moses report on the Anakim, "which come of the giants," and the report appals the murmuring Israelites. Like the Titans, the Anakim testify to a time when there were giants in the earth, when men walked with gods as equals. In the titanic section CIII Tennyson dreams "a vision of the sea" during his last sleep in the house of his childhood, and in the vision he leaves behind him not only childhood, but all that precedes a rising Prometheanism as well. The poet's lesser Muses, his Daughters of Beulah as Blake patronizingly would have named them, sing "of what is wise and good / And graceful" to a veiled statue of Hallam, the unknown god who must lead them to a greater music. A dove summons Tennyson to an apocalyptic sea, an outward-flowing tide on which he will be reunited with "him I loved, and love / For ever." The weeping Muses sail with the poet:

> And still as vaster grew the shore
>   And rolled the floods in grander space,
>   The maidens gather'd strength and grace
> And presence, lordlier than before;
> And I myself, who set apart
>   And watch'd them, wax'd in every limb;
>   I felt the thews of Anakim,
> The pulses of a Titan's heart.

Watching the ministering spirits of his own creativity, Tennyson suddenly shares their participation in a daemonic possession, an influx of power as the poet rises in the body to be one again with the giants in the earth. With this transformation his Muses sing not of what is, but ought to be: the death of war, the great race that is to come, and a new cosmos—the shaping of a star. The New Man, the first of the crowning race, Tennyson's Albion "appearing ere the times were ripe," and so dying an early and unnatural death, is necessarily Hallam, whose epiphany "thrice as large as man" is the saving culmination of section CIII, and indeed of all the elegies. The ship of the reunited lovers, both now Titans and accompanied by the nervous Muses, fearful lest their function be gone, sails at last toward a land of crimson cloud, a realm where vapor, sea, and earth come together, a world out of space and time and free of all merely human moralities.

One never ceases to be puzzled that *In Memoriam*, an outrageously personal poem of Romantic apotheosis, a poem indeed of vastly eccentric mythmaking, should have been accepted as a work of consolation and moral resolution in the tradition of Christian humanism. *In Memoriam*, viewed as one poem, is rather a welter of confusions, but its main movement is clear enough, and establishes the work as having considerably less relation to a Christian elegy than even *Adonais* has. Whatever Tennyson thought he was doing, the daemon of imaginative autonomy got hold of the poem's continuity, and made the poem an argument for a personal love about as restrained and societal as Heathcliff's passion, or Blake's in *Visions of the Daughters of Albion* or Shelley's in *Epipsychidion*. The vision of Hallam in sections CXXVI to CXXX for instance is a more extreme version of the transfiguration of Keats in the final stanzas of Adonais, and is a victory for everything in Tennyson that could accept neither God nor nature as adequate to the imaginative demands of a permanently bereaved lover who was also a professional poet.

No poet in English seems to me as extreme and fortuitous as Tennyson in his sudden moments of recognition of his own powers, bursts of radiance against a commonplace conceptual background that cannot accommodate such radiance. The deeply imaginative reader learns instinctively to listen to the song and not the singer, for Lawrence's adage is perfectly relevant to Tennyson. More relevant still was the prophetic warning of Hallam, in one sentence of his review that one wishes Tennyson had brooded upon daily, and so perhaps saved for poetry more fully than he did one of the major Romantic sensibilities:

> That delicate sense of fitness which grows with the growth of artist feelings, and strengthens with their strength, until it acquires a celerity and weight of decision hardly inferior to the correspondent judgments of conscience, is weakened by every indulgence of heterogeneous aspirations, however pure they may be, however lofty, however suitable to human nature.

Had Tennyson heeded this, he might have ended like the sinful soul of his own *The Palace of Art*, howling aloud "I am on fire within." One cannot be sure it would not have been the fitting end his imagination required.

Arthur Rimbaud

(1854–1891)

RIMBAUD, HEIR OF BOTH HUGO AND BAUDELAIRE, WAS POTENTIALLY A stronger poet than either, just as Hart Crane, influenced by Eliot and Stevens, possessed poetic gifts that could have transcended the work of both precursors. Crane's identification with Rimbaud takes on a particular poignancy in this context, reminding us of imaginative losses as great as those involved in the early deaths of Shelley and of Keats. The scandal of Rimbaud, which would have been considerable in any nation's poetic tradition, was magnified because of the relative decorum in terms of form and rhetoric of French Romantic poetry, let alone of the entire course of French poetic tradition. A crisis in French poetry would seem a ripple in the Anglo-American tradition, which is endlessly varied and heterodox.

Except for Rimbaud, and a few more recent figures, French poetry does not have titanic eccentrics who establish entirely new norms. Rimbaud was a great innovator within French poetry, but he would have seemed less so had he written in the language of William Blake and William Wordsworth, of Robert Browning and Walt Whitman. *A Season in Hell* comes more than eighty years after *The Marriage of Heaven and Hell*, and the *Illuminations* do not deconstruct the poetic self any more radically than do the Browning monologues and *Song of Myself*. One must be absolutely modern, yes, and a century after Rimbaud it is clear that no one ever is going to be more absolutely modern that the poet of *The Prelude* and the crisis lyrics of 1802. I once believed that the true difference between English and French poetry was the absence of French equivalents of Chaucer and Spenser, Shakespeare and Milton. A larger difference, I now believe, is Wordsworth, whose astonishing originality ended a continuous tradition that had gone unbroken between Homer and Goethe.

Rimbaud had strong precursors in the later Hugo and in Baudelaire, but so great was Rimbaud's potential that he would have benefited by an even fiercer agon, like the one Wordsworth conducted with Milton, and to a lesser extent with Shakespeare. The strongest French poets, down to Valéry, finally seem to confront a composite precursor, Boileau-Descartes, part classical critic, part philosopher. That develops very different urgencies from those ensuing when you must wrest your literary space from Milton or Wordsworth. The difference, even in the outcast Rimbaud, sets certain limits both to rhetoric and to vision.

Those limits, critics agree, come closest to being transcended, in very different ways, in *Une Saison en enfer* and *Les Illuminations*. Leo Bersani, impressively arguing for the "simplicity" of the *Illuminations*, affirms that Rimbaud's greatness is in his negations. Making poetry mean as little as possible is thus seen as Rimbaud's true ambition. If Rimbaud's "The I is another" is the central formula, then the *Illuminations* becomes the crucial work. But since poetry, like belief, takes place between truth and meaning, the Rimbaldian-Bersanian dream of literary negation may be only a dream. What would a poem be if it were, as Bersani hopes, "nonreferential, non-relational, and devoid of attitudes, feelings and tones"? Bersani is the first to admit that the *Saison* is anything but that; it overwhelmingly reveals a coherent self, though hardly one of durable subjectivity. The trope and topos we call "voice" is so strong in *Saison* that we must judge it to be a High Romantic prose poem, whatever we take the *Illuminations* to be.

Saison, far more than Blake's *Marriage*, is always in danger of falling back into the normative Christianity that Rimbaud wants to deny, and that he evidently ceased to deny only upon his death bed. Kristin Ross, in a brilliant exegesis, reads *Saison* as opening out onto a sociohistorical field of which presumably Marcuse, in the name of Freud, was a prophet. I hear *Eros and Civilization* in Ross's eloquent summation of Rimbaud's stance as: "I *will* be a worker—but only at the moment when work, as we know it, has come to an end." If Bersani beautifully idealizes Rimbaud's aesthetic ambition, then Ross nobly idealizes his supposed socialization, though in a post-apocalyptic beyond. I am condemned to read Rimbaud from the perspective of Romanticism, as does John Porter Houston, and the poet I read has all the disorders of Romantic vision, but much of the meanings as well, and they hardly seem to me social meanings.

So much the worse for the wood that finds it is a violin, or the brass that finds it is a bugle, or the French boy of yeoman stock who at sixteen could write "Le Bateau ivre," transuming Baudelaire's "Le Voyage." Rimbaud's violent originality, from "Le Bateau ivre" on, drives not against meaning but against anyone whatsoever, even Baudelaire, bequeathing Rimbaud any meaning that is not already his own. More even than the later Victor Hugo, to whom he grudgingly granted the poetic faculty of Vision, Rimbaud could tolerate no literary authority. Perhaps, if you could combine the visionary Hugo and Baudelaire into a single poet, Rimbaud would have had a precursor who might have induced in him some useful anxiety, but the Anglo-American poetic habit of creating for oneself an imaginary, composite poetic forerunner was not available to Rimbaud.

Barely two years after "Le Bateau ivre," Rimbaud had finished *Une Saison en enfer*. Blake is supposed to have written "How Sweet I Roam'd from Field to Field" before he was fourteen, but except for Blake there is no great poet as precocious as Rimbaud in all of Western literary history. Like Blake, a poet of extraordinary power at fourteen, Rimbaud quite unlike Blake abandoned poetry at nineteen. A trader and gunrunner in Africa, dead at thirty-seven, having written no poetry in the second half of his life, Rimbaud necessarily became and remains the mythical instance of the modern poet as the image of alienation. The myth obscures the deeper traditionalism of *Saison* in particular. Despite the difference implicit in the belated Romanticism of France, Rimbaud is as High Romantic as Blake or Shelley, or as Victor Hugo.

II

Une Saison en enfer has been called either a prose poem or a *récit*; it could also be named a miniature "anatomy" in Northrop Frye's sense of that genre. Perhaps it ought to be regarded as a belated Gnostic Gospel, like its hidden model, the canonical Gospel of John, a work which I suspect was revised away from its original form, one where the Word became, not flesh, but *pneuma*, and dwelt among us. Of all Rimbaud's writings, the *Saison* is most like a Hermetic Scripture. Rimbaud had never heard of Blake, who had promised the world his Bible of Hell, but *Saison* in its form always reminds me of *The Marriage of Heaven and Hell*, though it is very different in spirit from that curiously genial instance of apocalyptic satire.

In no way is it condescending to call *Saison* also the Gospel of Adolescence, particularly when we remember that Rousseau had invented that interesting transition, since literature affords no traces of it before him. To think of Rousseau reading *Saison* is grotesque, but in a clear sense Rimbaud indeed is one of Rousseau's direct descendants. Rimbaud doubtless attempted to negate every inheritance, but how could Rimbaud negate Romanticism? His negation of Catholicism is nothing but Romantic, particularly in its ambivalences.

The pattern unfolded in the nine sections of *Saison* would have been familiar to any Alexandrian Gnostic of the second century A.D. Rimbaud begins with a Fall that is also a catastrophic Creation, abandoning behind him the feast of life, and yet remembering "la clef du festin ancien," the key of charity. The feast must therefore be a communion table, the *pleroma* or Fullness from which Rimbaud has fallen away into the Gnostic *kenoma*, or emptiness of Hell that is simple, everyday bodily existence. Satan, in *Saison*, is the Gnostic Demiurge rather than the Catholic Devil, but then it is soon clear enough that Rimbaud himself, insofar as there is "himself," is a Demiurge also, a peasant or serf Demiurge, as it were. Perhaps Rimbaud's largest irony is his: "Je ne puis comprendre la révolte," since the serfs rose up only to plunder. The medieval yearnings of the "Mauvais sang" section all resemble the rapaciousness of wolves against an animal they have not killed, and so the wolf Rimbaud, his pagan blood returning, is now passed by:

> Le sang païen revient! L'Esprit est proche, pourquoi Christ ne m'aide-t-il pas, en donnant à mon âme noblesse et liberté. Hélas! l'Évangile a passe! l'Évangile! l'Évangile.
>
> J'attends Dieu avec gourmandise. Je suis de race inférieure de toute éternité.

The Holy Ghost is near, but the gluttonous waiting-for-God only guarantees Christ's withholding of charity. Nobility and freedom do not come to the serf lusting for a preternatural salvation. A riot of barbarism is therefore preferable to a supposed civilization in a world bereft of revelation. This is the dialectic of libertine Gnosticism, and reminds me that the American work closest to Rimbaud in spirit is Nathanael West's *Miss Lonelyhearts*, with its superbly squalid version of the ancient Gnostic doctrine that Gershom Scholem grimly called: "Redemption through Sin." Rimbaud peals throughout the rest of his "Bad Blood" section the iron music of atavism, in a full-scale justification of his own systematic derangement of the senses, only to collapse afterwards into the night of a real hell. Rimbaud's Hell is shot through with glimpses of divinity, and seems to be married to Heaven in a literal way, very different from Blake's ironic dialectic. God and Satan appear to be different names for one and the same spirit of lassitude, and Rimbaud thus prepares himself for his deepest descent, into delirium and its memories of his life of intimacy with Verlaine.

When I think of *Saison* I remember first the sick brilliance of Verlaine, the Foolish Virgin, addressing Rimbaud, the Infernal Bridegroom. If *Saison* has any common readers, in the Johnsonian sense, what else would they remember? Rimbaud, had he wished to, could have been the most consistently savage humorist in the French language. Poor

Verlaine is permanently impaled as that masochistic trimmer, the Foolish Virgin, unworthy either of salvation or damnation. The authority of this impaling is augmented by the portrait of the Infernal Bridegroom's forays into poetic alchemy, which are surely to be read as being just as ridiculous as the Foolish Virgin's posturings. So strong is the Rimbaud myth that his own repudiations of divinity and magic do not altogether persuade us. Thinking back to *Saison*, we all grimace wryly at Verlaine as Foolish Virgin, while remembering with aesthetic respect those verbal experiments that Rimbaud renounces so robustly.

To climb out of Hell, Rimbaud discovers that he must cast off his own Gnostic dualism, which means his not wholly un-Johannine Gnostic Christianity. Much of the sections, "L'Impossible" and "L'Éclair," are given to the quest away from Christianity, or rather the only Christianity that seems available. But since the quest involves those two great beasts of Nineteenth Century Europe, Transcendental Idealism and the Religion of Science, Rimbaud discovers that neither God nor Rimbaud is safely mocked. "Matin," following these dismissed absurdities, first restores Rimbaud's Gnosticism, his sense that what is best and oldest in him goes back to before the Creation-Fall. Hailing the birth of the new labor, the new wisdom, Rimbaud moves into his remarkable "Adieu," with its notorious motto: "Il faut être absolument moderne," the epigraph to the life's work of Rimbaud's Gnostic heir, Hart Crane. No longer a magus or an angel, Rimbaud is given back to the earth, a peasant again, like his ancestors. To think of the earth hardly seems a Gnostic formulation, and the famous closing passage of *Saison* abandons Gnosticism once and for all in an extraordinary breakthrough into visionary monism:

> —j'ai vu l'enfer des femmes là-bas;—et il me sera loisible de *posséder la vérité dans une âme et un corps.*

I take it that Rimbaud saw *down there*—in his relation with Verlaine—"the hell of women," precisely the Oedipal romance that he sought to flee. Possessing the truth in a single mind and a single body—one's own—is a narcissistic revelation akin to that of Walt Whitman's at the close of *Song of Myself*. Christianity *and* Gnosticism alike are rejected, and so are both heterosexuality and homosexuality. *Saison* ends with an inward turning closer to Whitman than to Hugo or to Baudelaire:

> Cependant c'est la veille. Recevons tous les influx de vigueur et de tendresse réelle. Et à l'aurore, armés d'une ardente patience, nous entrerons aux splendides villes.

It is a passage worthy of the poet whom the late James Wright called: "our father, Walt Whitman." We can hardly murmur: "our father, Arthur Rimbaud," but we can remember Hart Crane's equal devotion to Whitman and to Rimbaud, and we can be grateful again to Crane for teaching us something about our ancestry.

A.E. Housman

(1859-1936)

EDMUND WILSON WAS A REMARKABLE CRITIC, BUT NOT NECESSARILY OF modern poetry. In the decline of his former lover, the Byronic Edna Millay, Wilson found the debacle of modern verse. Against A.E. Housman, Wilson got off the grim shot: "Housman has managed to grow old without in a sense knowing maturity." Cyril Connolly was a touch nastier: "He will live as long as the B.B.C." Tom Stoppard, in his *The Birth of Love*, has juxtaposed Housman with Oscar Wilde, much to Wilde's favor.

As a reader of Housman's poetry since childhood, I tend to be surprised by critical dislike of his work. Housman palpably is not a poet of the eminence of Thomas Hardy and D.H. Lawrence, of Edward Thomas and Wilfred Owen, of T.S. Eliot and Geoffrey Hill, and W.B. Yeats is a mountain range of excellence away. But I greatly prefer Housman to many poets who support critical industries (Pound, Auden, et al.), and I am puzzled how any lover of poetry could fail to respond to this:

> Into my heart an air that kills
>   From yon far country blows:
> What are those blue remembered hills,
>   What spires, what farms are those?
>
> That is the land of lost content,
>   I see it shining plain,
> The happy highways where I went
>   And cannot come again.

The first line: "Into my heart an air that kills" is almost a poem in itself, and is a superb irony. It seems strange that Housman should be so undervalued as an ironist. As a classicist, he tends to favor the irony that says one thing while meaning another, but he is also a Romantic ironist, with a keen sense that meaning breaks under the strain of the irony of irony. "The Land of Lost Content" is precisely what cannot be seen, but Housman risks the Blakean line: "I see it shining plain."

Housman, though he can have a superficial resemblance to the earlier Blake, is anything but a visionary poet. Tom Stoppard, in his brilliant *The Invention of Love*, tells us that Housman's life was a failure, in contrast to Oscar Wilde's. Housman probably would have agreed with Stoppard, but recovering from an open heart operation makes me very wary of terming anyone's life a failure.

Do failures write uncanny poems? I have been upset with one of Housman's poems for longer than I can remember:

> Her strong enchantments failing,
>   Her towers of fear in wreck,
> Her limbecks dried of poisons,
>   And the knife at her neck,
>
> The Queen of air and darkness
>   Begins to shrill and cry,
> 'O young man, O my slayer,
>   To-morrow you shall die.'
>
> O Queen of air and darkness,
>   I think 'tis truth you say,
> And I shall die to-morrow;
>   But you will die to-day.

The Queen of air and darkness is no ordinary witch, and her young slayer is grimmer than any irony. What is the poem for? What did Housman do for himself, whether as person or as poet, by composing this poem? He was not susceptible to female enchantments, however strong, and this morbid little masterpiece of a lyric appears to have no sexual element, as it would if we found it in Kipling or in William Morris, or in the sadomasochistic Swinburne: One feels that Housman is exorcising something, something he cannot quite confront.

If I had to choose only one poem by Housman, it would be the superbly savage "Epitaph upon an Army of Mercenaries." But his subtlest and most beautiful poem probably is this:

Tell me not here, it needs not saying,
  What tune the enchantress plays
In aftermaths of soft September
  Or under blanching mays,
For she and I were long acquainted
  And I knew all her ways.

On russet floors, by waters idle,
  The pine lets fall its cone;
The cuckoo shouts all day at nothing
  In leafy dells alone;
And traveller's joy beguiles in autumn
  Hearts that have lost their own.

On acres of the seeded grasses
  The changing burnish heaves;
Or marshalled under moons of harvest
  Stands still all night the sheaves;
Or beeches strip in storms for winter
  And stain the wind with leaves.

Possess, as I possessed a season,
  The countries I resign,
Where over elmy plains the highway
  Would mount the hills and shine,
And full of shade the pillared forest
  Would murmer and be mine.

For nature, heartless, witless nature,
  Will neither care nor know
What stranger's feet may find the meadow
  And trespass there and go,
Nor ask amid the dews of morning
  If they are mine or no.

Had Ben Jonson lived to read this, he might have said: "Had the poet intended an actual mistress, it would have been something." The poem's language is certainly the most heteroerotic in all of Housman, who nevertheless follows Wordsworthian convention by personifying nature as a beloved woman. Yet Housman's enchantress is "heartless, witless," and this is a poem of loss, of intimations of mortality. But there is magnificence in the loss, and an erotic music of the unlived life.

Edwin Arlington Robinson

(1869–1935)

Emerson himself was a product of New England and a man of strong moral habits.... He gave to American romanticism, in spite of its irresponsible doctrine, a religious tone which it has not yet lost and which has often proved disastrous.... there is a good deal of this intellectual laziness in Robinson; and as a result of the laziness, there is a certain admixture of Emersonian doctrine, which runs counter to the principles governing most of his work and the best of it.

—YVOR WINTERS

THE TORRENT AND THE NIGHT BEFORE (PUBLISHED LATE IN 1896 BY Robinson himself) remains one of the best first volumes in our poetry. Three of its shorter poems—"George Crabbe," "Luke Havergal," "The Clerks"—Robinson hardly surpassed, and three more—"Credo," "Walt Whitman" (which Robinson unfortunately abandoned), and "The Children of the Night" (reprinted as title-poem in his next volume)—are memorable works, all in the earlier Emersonian mode that culminates in "Bacchus." The stronger "Luke Havergal" stems from the darker Emersonianism of "Experience" and "Fate," and has a relation to the singular principles of *Merlin*. It prophesies Robinson's finest later lyrics, such as "Eros Turannos" and "For a Dead Lady," and suggests the affinity between Robinson and Frost that is due to their common Emersonian tradition.

In *Captain Craig* (1902) Robinson published "The Sage," a direct hymn of homage to Emerson, whose *The Conduct of Life* had moved him profoundly at a first reading in August 1899. Robinson had read the earlier Emerson well before, but it is fascinating that he came to essays like "Fate" and "Power" only after writing "Luke Havergal" and some similar poems, for his deeper nature then discovered itself anew. He called "Luke Havergal" "a piece of deliberate degeneration," which I take to mean what an early letter calls "sympathy for failure where fate has been abused and self demoralized." Browning, the other great influence upon Robinson, is obsessed with "deliberate degeneration" in this sense; Childe Roland's and Andrea del Sarto's failures are wilful abuses of fate and demoralizations of self. "The Sage" praises Emerson's "fierce wisdom," emphasizes Asia's influence upon him, and hardly touches his dialectical optimism. This Emerson is "previsioned of the madness and the mean," fit seer for "the fiery night" of "Luke Havergal":

> But there, where western glooms are gathering,
> The dark will end the dark, if anything:
> God slays Himself with every leaf that flies,
> And hell is more than half of paradise.

These are the laws of Compensation, "or that nothing is got for nothing," as Emerson says in "Power." At the depth of Robinson is this Emersonian fatalism, as it is in Frost, and even in Henry James. "The world is mathematical," Emerson says, "and has no casualty in all its vast and flowing curve." Robinson, brooding on the end of "Power," confessed: "He really gets after one," and spoke of Emerson as walloping one "with a big New England shingle," the cudgel of Fate. But Robinson was walloped too well, by which I do not mean what Winters means, since I cannot locate any "intellectual laziness" in Emerson. Unlike Browning and Hardy, Robinson yielded too much to Necessity.... Circumstances and temperament share in Robinson's obsession with Nemesis, but poetic misprision is part of the story also, for Robinson's *tessera* in regard to Emerson relies on completing the sage's fatalism. From Emerson's categories of power and circumstance, Robinson fashions a more complete single category, in a personal idealism that is a "philosophy of desperation," as he feared it might be called. The persuasive desperation of "Luke Havergal" and "Eros Turannos" is his best expression of this nameless idealism that is also a fatalism, but "The Children of the Night," for all its obtrusive echoes of Tennyson and even Longfellow, shows more clearly what Robinson found to be a possible stance:

> It is the crimson, not the gray,
> That charms the twilight of all time;
> It is the promise of the day
> That makes the starry sky sublime;

It is the faith within the fear
   That holds us to the life we curse;
So let us in ourselves revere
   The Self which is the Universe!

The bitter charm of this is that it qualifies so severely its too-hope-
ful and borrowed music. Even so early, Robinson has "completed"
Emersonian Self-Reliance and made it his own by emphasizing its Stoic as
against its Transcendental or Bacchic aspect. When, in "Credo," Robinson
feels "the coming glory of the Light!" the light nevertheless emanates from
unaware angels who wove "dead leaves to garlands where no roses are." It
is not that Robinson believed, with Melville, that the invisible spheres were
formed in fright, but he shrewdly suspected that the ultimate world,
though existent, was nearly as destitute as this one. He is an Emersonian
incapable of transport, an ascetic of the Transcendental spirit, contrary to
an inspired saint like Jones Very or to the Emerson of "The Poet," but a
contrary, not a negation, to use Blake's distinction. Not less gifted than
Frost, he achieves so much less because he gave himself away to Necessity
so soon in his poetic life. Frost's Job quotes "Uriel" to suggest that confusion is "the form of forms," the way all things return upon themselves, like
rays:

   Though I hold rays deteriorate to nothing,
   First white, then red, then ultra red, then out.

This is cunning and deep in Frost, the conviction that "all things
come round," even the mental confusions of God as He morally blunders.
What we miss in Robinson is this quality of savagery, the strength that can
end "Directive" by saying:

   Here are your waters and your watering place.
   Drink and be whole again beyond confusion.

To be beyond confusion is to be beyond the form of forms that is
Fate's, and to be whole beyond Fate suggests an end to circlings, a resolu-
tion to all the Emersonian turnings that see unity, and yet behold divisions.
Frost will play at [yielding to Necessity], many times, but his wariness
saved him from Robinson's self-exhaustions.
   There is a fine passage in "Captain Craig" where the talkative cap-
tain asks: "Is it better to be blinded by the lights, / Or by the shadows?"
This supposes grandly that we are to be blinded in any case, but Robinson

was not blinded by his shadows. Yet he was ill-served by American Romanticism, though not for the reasons Winters offers. It demands the exuberance of a Whitman in his fury of poetic incarnation, lest the temptation to join Ananke come too soon and too urgently to be resisted. Robinson was nearly a great poet, and would have prospered more if he had been chosen by a less drastic tradition.

Paul Valéry

(1871–1945)

IN THE PREFACE TO HIS *LEONARDO POE MALLARMÉ*, VALÉRY CALLS THESE precursors "three masters of the art of abstraction." "Man fabricates by abstraction" is a famous Valéryan formula, reminding us that this sense of abstraction is Latin: "withdrawn, taken out from, removed." *It Must Be Abstract*, the first part of Stevens's *Notes toward a Supreme Fiction*, moves in the atmosphere of an American version of Valéry's insight, but the American is Walt Whitman and not Edgar Poe:

> The weather and the giant of the weather,
> Say the weather, the mere weather, the mere air:
> An abstraction blooded, as a man by thought.

Valéry fabricates by withdrawing from a stale reality, which he refuses to associate with the imaginings of his masters. These "enchanted, dominated me, and—as was only fitting—tormented me as well; the beautiful is that which fills us with despair." Had Valéry spoken of pain, rather than despair, he would have been more Nietzschean. The genealogy of imagination is not truly Valéry's subject. Despair is not a staleness in reality, or an absence of it; it is the overwhelming presence of reality, of the reality-principle, or the necessity of death-in-life, or simply of dying. Valéry's beautiful "Palme" concludes with a metaphor that seems central to all of his poetry:

> Pareille à celui qui pense
> Et dont l'âme se dépense
> A s'accroître de ses dons!

The palm is the image of a mind so rich in thinking that the gifts of its own soul augment it constantly. That may be one of the origins of Stevens's death-poem, "Of Mere Being," but Valéry's palm is less pure and less flickering than Stevens's final emblem. The two poets and poetic thinkers do not much resemble one another, despite Stevens's yearning regard for Valéry. Perhaps the largest difference is in the attitudes towards precursors. Valéry is lucid and candid, and he confronts Mallarmé. Stevens insists that he does not read Whitman, condemns Whitman for his tramp *persona*, and yet he cannot cease revising Whitman's poems in his own poems. But then that is how Whitman came to discuss his relation to Ralph Waldo Emerson—clearly they order these matters differently in America.

In a meditation of 1919 on "The Intellectual Crisis," Valéry memorably depicted the European Hamlet staring at millions of ghosts:

> But he is an intellectual Hamlet. He meditates on the life and death of truths. For phantoms he has all the subjects of our controversies; for regrets he has all our titles to glory; he bows under the weight of discoveries and learning, unable to renounce and unable to resume this limitless activity. He reflects on the boredom of recommencing the past, on the folly of always striving to be original. He wavers between one abyss and the other, for two dangers still threaten the world: order and disorder.

This retains its force nearly seventy years later, just as it would baffle us if its subject were the American Hamlet. Valéry's fear was that Europe might "become *what she is in reality*: that is, a little cape of the Asiatic continent." The fear was prophetic, though the prophecy fortunately is not yet wholly fulfilled. When Valéry writes in this mode, he is principally of interest to editorial writers and newspaper columnists of the weightier variety. Yet his concern for European culture, perhaps a touch too custodial, is a crucial element in all his prose writing. Meditating upon Descartes, the archetypal French intellect, Valéry states the law of his own nature: "Descartes is above all, a man of intentional action." Consciousness was for Valéry an intentional adventure, and this sense of deliberate quest in the cultivation of consciousness is partly what makes Valéry a central figure of the Western literary intellect.

Valéry deprecated originality, but his critical insights are among the most original of our century. His *Analects* are crowded with the darker truths concerning literary originality:

The value of men's works is not in the works themselves but in their later development by others, in other circumstances.

Nothing is more "original," nothing more "oneself" than to feed on others. But one has to digest them. A lion is made of assimilated sheep.

The hallmark of the greatest art is that imitations of it are legitimate, worthwhile, tolerable; that it is not demolished or devoured by them, or they by it.

Any production of the mind is important when its existence resolves, summons up, or cancels other works, whether previous to it or not.

An artist wants to inspire jealousy till the end of time.

Valéry's central text on originality is his "Letter about Mallarmé" of 1927 where his relation to his authentic precursor inspired dialectical ironies of great beauty;

> We say that an author is *original* when we cannot trace the hidden transformations that others underwent in his mind; we mean to say that the dependence of *what he does* on *what others have done* is excessively complex and irregular. There are works in the likeness of others, and works that are the reverse of others, but there are also works of which the relation with earlier productions is so intricate that we become confused and attribute them to the direct intervention of the gods.
>
> (To go deeper into the subject, we should also have to discuss the influence of a mind on itself and of a work on its author. But this is not the place.)

Everywhere else in Valéry, in prose and verse, is the place, because that was Valéry's true topos, the influence of Paul Valéry's mind upon itself. Is that not the true subject of Descartes and of Montaigne, and of all French men and women of sensibility and intellect? What never ceases to engage Valéry is the effect of his thought and writings upon himself. Creative misunderstandings induced in others were not without interest, but Valéry's creative misunderstandings of Valéry ravished his heart away. Texts of this ravishment abound, but I choose one of the subtlest and most evasive, the dialogue *Dance and the Soul*. Socrates is made by Valéry to speak of "that poison of poisons, that venom which is opposed to all nature," the reduction of life to things as they are that Stevens called the First Idea:

PHAEDRUS

What venom?

SOCRATES

Which is called: the tedium of living? I mean, understand me, not the passing ennui, the tedium that comes of fatigue, or the tedium of which we can see the germ or of which we know the limits; but that perfect tedium, that pure tedium that is not caused by misfortune or infirmity, that is compatible with apparently the happiest of all conditions—that tedium, in short, the stuff of which is nothing else than life itself, and which has no other second cause than the clearsightedness of the living man. This absolute tedium is essentially nothing but life in its nakedness when it sees itself with unclouded eyes.

ERYXIMACHUS

It is very true that if our soul purges itself of all falseness, strips itself of every fraudulent addition to *what is*, our existence is endangered on the spot by the cold, exact, reasonable and moderate view of human life *as it is*.

PHAEDRUS

Life blackens at the contact of truth, as a suspicious mushroom blackens, when it is crushed, at the contact of the air.

SOCRATES

Eryximachus, I asked you if there were any cure?

ERYXIMACHUS

Why cure so reasonable a complaint? There is nothing, no doubt, nothing more essentially morbid, nothing more inimical to nature than to *see things as they are*. A cold and perfect light is a poison it is impossible to combat. Reality, unadulterated, instantly puts a stop to the heart. One drop of that icy lymph suffices to slacken all the springs of the soul, all the throbbing of desire, to exterminate all hopes and bring to ruin all the gods that inhabited our blood. The Virtues and the noblest colors are turned pale by it in a gradual and devouring consumption. The past is reduced to a handful of ashes, the future to a tiny icicle. The soul appears to itself as an empty and measurable form. Here then are things as they are—a rigorous and deadly chain, where each link joins and limits the next.... O Socrates, the universe cannot endure for a single instant to be only what it is. It is strange to think that that which is the Whole cannot suffice itself! ... Its terror of being what it is has induced it to create and paint for itself thousands of masks; there is no other reason for the existence of mortals. What are mortals for?—Their business is *to know*. Know? And what is *to know*?—*It is assuredly not to be what one is.*—So here are human beings raving and thinking, introducing into nature the principle of unlimited errors and all these myriads of marvels!

The mistakes, the appearances, the play of the mind's dioptric give depth and animation to the world's miserable mass. The idea introduces into what is, the leaven of what is not.... But truth sometimes shows itself, and sounds a discord in the harmonious system of phantasmagorias and errors.... Everything straightway is threatened with perdition, and Socrates in person comes to beg of me a cure for this desperate case of clearsightedness and ennui!...

We are close again to Stevens's appropriations from Valéry in *Notes toward a Supreme Fiction*. The "clearsightedness of the living man" does not belong to Stevens or to us; it is the particular gift of the reductively lucid Valéry, who is capable of seeing "life in its nakedness." If Socrates here is Valéry the writer, then Eryximachus is Valéry the reader of—Valéry! "A cold and perfect light" is what Valéry has taught himself to see—in Valéry. Reality here is not so much the reality principle of Freud, as it is the next step after the nothingness of the abyss or final void in French Poe and in Mallarmé. A pragmatic Gnosticism, implicit in Poe and developed by Mallarmé, triumphs in Valéry's ironic sermon about "what is to *know*." The universe's terror of its own nothingness causes it to proliferate mortals, as if each one of us were only another desperate figuration. Our errors, our marvels, introduce "into what is, the leaven of what is not."

We encounter here again the vision of "Palme," since we hear the influence upon Valéry himself of

Parfois si l'on désespère,
Si l'adorable rigueur
Malgré tes larmes n'opère
Que sous ombre de langueur.

"There is a strict law in literature that we must never go to the bottom of anything." Valéry almost did not take his own counsel in his endless quest to explain the preternatural prevalence of his intentional self-awareness. He seems now the last person-of-letters in the French tradition to have been capable of reconciling acute consciousness of one's own consciousness with the grand fabrications made possible only by abstraction, by a withdrawal from heightened rhetoricity. Compared to him, Sartre and Blanchot, let alone Derrida, come to creation only in the accents of a severe belatedness.

Paul Laurence Dunbar

(1872–1906)

PAUL LAURENCE DUNBAR WAS THE FIRST MAJOR AFRICAN AMERICAN POET, and in my judgment remains one of the truly authentic poets of his American generation, which included Edwin Arlington Robinson, Trumbull Stickney, Edgar Lee Masters, James Weldon Johnson, and the earlier work of Robert Frost. Dead at thirty-five (tuberculosis augmented by alcoholism), Dunbar essentially wrote in the skeptical strain of Shelley, except in dialect poems. He inherited from Shelley an agonistic spirit, expressed strongly in "The Mystery," one of his undervalued poems, where he deliberately echoes "To a Skylark": "I fain would look before / and after, but can neither do." Caught in an unhappy present for a black poet, Dunbar concludes "The Mystery" with memorable eloquence:

> I question of th'eternal bending skies
> That seem to neighbor with the novice earth;
> But they roll on and daily shut their eyes
> On me, as I one day shall do on them,
> And tell me not the secret that I ask.

The secret is the mystery of being an eternal novice, a kind of Promethean complaint, which leads to what may be Dunbar's best poem, "'Ere Sleep Comes Down to Soothe the Weary Eyes." The fifth of the six stanzas is an epitome of how intensely Dunbar can transcend his situation and its limitations:

> Ere sleep comes down to soothe the weary eyes,
>   How questioneth the soul that other soul,—
> The inner sense which neither cheats nor lies,

But self exposes unto self, a scroll
Full writ with all life's acts unwise or wise,
    In characters indelible and known;
So, trembling with the shock of sad surprise,
    The soul doth view its awful self alone,
Ere sleep comes down to soothe the weary eyes.

"That other soul" or "awful self" is what the early African American Baptists called "the little me inside the big me," a spark or breath that is no part of nature or history. After eleven repetitions of: "Ere sleep comes down to soothe the weary eyes," we are startled by the poem's closing line, where "seal" replaces "soothe." In his perpetual struggle between bitterness and the Shelleyan wisdom of casting out personal remorse, Dunbar most frequently yields to a bitterness that transcends his personal sorrows.

One of the lucid voicings of that bitterness is Dunbar's memorial sonnet to Robert Gould Shaw, the Harvard College colonel who commanded the black 54th Massachusetts Regiment in its suicidal attack upon Fort Wagner (near Charleston) in July 1863. The sonnet's sestet laments the sacrifice of Shaw and his African American recruits, in a skepticism still relevant in 2001:

Far better the slow blaze of Learning's light,
    The cool and quiet of her dearer fane,
Than this hot terror of a hopeless fight,
    This cold endurance of the final pain,—
Since thou and those who with thee died for right
    Have died, the Present teaches, but in vain!

Dunbar's emblematic poem remains "Sympathy," popularized by Maya Angelou's autobiographical appropriation of "I know why the caged bird sings!" Though Dunbar's High Romantic lyricism has long been unfashionable, his achievement in it remains considerable.

Robert Frost

(1874–1963)

FROST—AT HIS FREQUENT BEST—RIVALS WALLACE STEVENS AS THE GREAT American poet of this century. He does not much resemble Stevens, ultimately for reasons that have little to do with the "essential gaudiness" of much early Stevens, or even with the austere clairvoyance of the later Stevens, poet of "The Auroras of Autumn" and "The Rock." Both of those aspects of Stevens rise from a powerful, barely repressed influence-relationship to Whitman, a poet who scarcely affected Frost. Indeed, Frost's uniqueness among modern American poets of real eminence partly stems from his independence of Whitman. Eliot, Stevens, Pound, Hart Crane, W.C. Williams, Roethke—all have complex links to Whitman, covert in Eliot and in Stevens. Frost (in this like Whitman himself) is the son of Emerson, of the harsher Emerson that we begin only now to recover. Any deep reader of Frost understands why the poet of "Two Tramps in Mud Time" and "Directive" seriously judged Emerson's "Uriel" to be "the greatest Western poem yet." "Uriel's voice of cherub scorn," once referred to by Frost as "Emersonian scorn," is the essential mode of irony favored throughout Frost's poetry.

"Uriel" is Emerson's own irreverent allegory of the controversy set off by his "Divinity School Address." There are certainly passages in the poem that seem to have been written by Frost and not by Emerson:

> The young deities discussed
> Laws of form, and metre just,
> Orb, quintessence, and sunbeams,
> What subsisteth, and what seems.
> One, with low tones that decide,
> And doubt and reverend use defied,

> With a look that solved the sphere,
> And stirred the devils everywhere,
> Gave his sentiment divine
> Against the being of a line.
> "Line in nature is not found;
> Unit and universe are round;
> In vain produced, all rays return;
> Evil will bless, and ice will burn."

At the center of this is Emerson's law of Compensation: "Nothing is got for nothing," as Emerson phrased it later, in the remorseless essay "Power," in his *The Conduct of Life*. The darker Emersonian essays—"Experience," "Power," "Circles," "Fate," "Illusions"—read like manifestos for Frost's poetry. Richard Poirier has demonstrated this in some detail, and I follow him here in emphasizing how pervasive and crucial the affinity between Emerson and Freud tends to be. If there is a particular motto that states the dialectic of Frost's best poems, then it is to be found in a formulation of Emerson's "Self-Reliance."

> Life only avails, not the having lived. Power ceases in the instant
> of repose; it resides in the moment of transition from a past to a
> new state, in the shooting of the gulf, in the darting to an aim.

One thinks of the extraordinary early poem "The Wood-Pile" (1914), where the poet, "out walking in the frozen swamp one gray day," comes upon "a cord of maple, cut and split / and piled" and then abandoned:

> I thought that only
> Someone who lived in turning to fresh tasks
> Could so forget his handiwork on which
> He spent himself, the labor of his ax,
> And leave it there far from a useful fireplace
> To warm the frozen swamp as best it could
> With the slow smokeless burning of decay.

That "slow smokeless burning" is the metaphor for Emerson's "instant of repose," where power ceases. Frost's restless turnings are his most Emersonian moments, American and agonistic. His Job, in *A Masque of Reason*, puzzling over God's Reason, deliberately relates Jehovah's dialectic to that of Emerson's "Uriel":

Yet I suppose what seems to us confusion
Is not confusion, but the form of forms,
The serpent's tail stuck down the serpent's throat,
Which is the symbol of eternity
And also of the way all things come round,
Or of how rays return upon themselves,
To quote the greatest Western poem yet.
Though I hold rays deteriorate to nothing:
First white, then red, then ultrared, then out.

Job's last two lines here mark Frost's characteristic swerve away from
Emerson, except that Emerson is the most difficult of fathers to evade,
having been always so subtly evasive himself. Frost's authentic nihilism is
considerable, but is surpassed by "Fate" in *The Conduct of Life*, and by a
grand more-than-Frostian late entry in Emerson's journals, set down in the
autumn of 1866, when the sage felt burned to the socket by the intensities
he had experienced during the Civil War:

There may be two or three or four steps, according to the
genius of each, but for every seeing soul there are two absorbing facts, *I and the Abyss*.

Frost's religion, as a poet, was the American religion that Emerson
founded. A latecomer exegete of that religion, I once offered its credo as
Everything that can be broken should be broken, a Gnostic motto that emi-
nently suits Frost's poetry, where God, whether in *A Masque of Reason*, *A
Masque of Mercy*, or in "Once by the Pacific," is clearly animated neither by
reason nor mercy but only by the blind necessities of being the Demiurge:

It looked as if a night of dark intent
Was coming, and not only a night, an age.
Someone had better be prepared for rage.
There would be more than ocean-water broken
Before God's last *Put out the Light* was spoken.

A God who echoes Othello at his most murderous is himself also
crazed by jealousy. Frost's celebrated negativity is a secularized negative
theology, almost wholly derived from Emerson, insofar as it was not purely temperamental. Slyly aware of it, Frost used it as the occasion for lovely jokes, as in the marvelous "Two Tramps in Mud Time":

The water for which we may have to look
In summertime with a witching wand,
In every wheelrut's now a brook,
In every print of a hoof a pond.
Be glad of water, but don't forget
The lurking frost in the earth beneath
That will steal forth after the sun is set
And show on the water its crystal teeth.

"Two Tramps in Mud Time" hymns the Emersonian negativity of refusing to identify yourself with any work, in order instead to achieve the Gnostic identity of the knower with what is known, when the sparks of the Alien God or true Workman stream through you. A shrewd Gnostic, Frost refuses to lament confusion, though he also will not follow Whitman in celebrating it. In Emerson's "Uriel," confusion precedes the dimming of that Miltonic archangel of the sun, who withers from a sad self-knowledge. Uriel-Emerson (for which read Frost) is himself not responsible for engendering the confusion, which results from the failure of nerve suffered by the heavenly powers when they hear Uriel proclaim that "all rays return; Evil will bless, and ice will burn":

As Uriel spoke with piercing eye,
A shudder ran around the sky;
The stern old war-gods shook their heads,
The seraphs frowned from myrtle-beds;
Seemed to the holy festival
The rash word boded ill to all;
The balance-beam of Fate was bent;
The bounds of good and ill were rent;
Strong Hades could not keep his own,
But all slid to confusion.

"Confusion" is a mixing or pouring together of entities that would be better off if kept apart. Whether instinctively or overtly, both Emerson and Frost seem to have known that the Indo-European root of "confusion" originally meant "to pour a libation," as if to the gods. Frost's "form of forms," or confusion which is not confusion, identified by him with the Emersonian rays returning upon themselves, is a kind of libation poured out to the Alien God, as in the trope that concludes his great poem "Directive":

Here are your waters and your watering place.
Drink and be whole again beyond confusion.

II

"Directive" is Frost's poem of poems or form of forms, a meditation
whose rays perpetually return upon themselves. "All things come round,"
even our mental confusion as we blunder morally, since the Demiurge is
nothing but a moral blunderer. Frost shares the fine Emersonian wildness
or freedom, the savage strength of the essay "Power" that suggests a way
of being whole beyond Fate, of arriving at an end to circlings, at a resolution to all the Emersonian turnings that see unity, and yet behold divisions:
"The world is mathematical, and has no casualty, in all its vast and flowing
curve." "Directive" appears to be the poem in which Frost measures the
lot, and forgives himself the lot, and perhaps even casts out remorse. In
some sense, it was the poem he always wrote and rewrote, in a revisionary
process present already in *A Boy's Will* (1913) but not fully worked out until
Steeple Bush (1947), where "Directive" was published, when Frost was sev-
enty-three. "The Demiurge's Laugh" in *A Boy's Will* features a mocking
demonic derision at the self-realization that "what I hunted was no true
god."

North of Boston (1914) has its most memorable poem in the famous
"After Apple-Picking," a gracious hymn to the necessity of yielding up the
quest, of clambering down from one's "long two-pointed [ladder] sticking
through a tree / Toward heaven still." Frost's subtlest of perspectivizings is
the true center of the poem:

I cannot rub the strangeness from my sight
I got from looking through a pane of glass
I skimmed this morning from the drinking trough
And held against the world of hoary grass.
It melted, and I let it fall and break.

The sheet of ice is a lens upon irreality, but so are Frost's own eyes,
or anyone's, in his cosmos. This supposed nature poet represents his harsh
landscapes as a full version of the Gnostic *kenoma*, the cosmological emptiness into which we have been thrown by the mocking Demiurge. This is
the world of *Mountain Interval* (1916), where "the broken moon" is preferred to the dimmed sun, where the oven bird sings of "that other fall we
name the fall," and where the birches:

> shed crystal shells
> Shattering and avalanching on the snow crust
> Such heaps of broken glass to sweep away
> You'd think the inner dome of heaven had fallen.

Mountain Interval abounds in images of the shattering of human ties, and of humans, as in the horrifying "Out, Out—." But it would be redundant to conduct an overview of all Frost's volumes in pursuit of an experiential darkness that never is dispelled. A measurer of stone walls, as Frost names himself in the remarkable "A Star in a Stoneboat," is never going to be surprised that life is a sensible emptiness. The demiurgic pattern of "Design," with its "assorted characters of death and blight," is the rule in Frost. There are a few exceptions, but they give Frost parodies, rather than poems.

Frost wrote the concluding and conclusive Emersonian irony for all his work in the allegorical "A Cabin in the Clearing," the set-piece of *In the Clearing* (1962), published for his eighty-eighth birthday, less than a year before his death. Mist and Smoke, guardian wraiths and counterparts, eavesdrop on the unrest of a human couple, murmuring in their sleep. These guardians haunt us because we are their kindred spirits, for we do not know where we are, since who we are "is too much to believe." We are "too sudden to be credible," and so the accurate image for us is "an inner haze," full kindred to mist and smoke. For all the genial tone, the spirit of "A Cabin in the Clearing" is negative even for Frost. His final letter, dictated just before his death, states an unanswerable question as though it were not a question: "How can we be just in a world that needs mercy and merciful in a world that needs justice." The Demiurge's laugh lurks behind the sentence, though Frost was then in no frame of spirit to indulge a demiurgic imagination.

Frost would have been well content to give his mentor Emerson the last word, though "content" is necessarily an inadequate word in this dark context. Each time I reread the magnificent essay, "Illusions," which concludes and crowns *The Conduct of Life*, I am reminded of the poetry of Robert Frost. The reminder is strongest in two paragraphs near the end that seem to be "Directive" writ large, as though Emerson had been brooding upon his descendant:

> We cannot write the order of the variable winds. How can we penetrate the law of our shifting moods and susceptibility? Yet they differ as all and nothing. Instead of the firmament of yesterday, which our eyes require, it is to-day an eggshell which

coops us in; we cannot even see what or where our stars of destiny are. From day to day, the capital facts of human life are hidden from our eyes. Suddenly the mist rolls up, and reveals them, and we think how much good time is gone, that might have been saved, had any hint of these things been shown. A sudden rise in the road shows us the system of mountains, and all the summits, which have been just as near us all the year, but quite out of mind. But these alternations are not without their order, and we are parties to our various fortune. If life seem a succession of dreams, yet poetic justice is done in dreams also. The visions of good men are good; it is the undisciplined will that is whipped with bad thoughts and bad fortunes. When we break the laws, we lose our hold on the central reality. Like sick men in hospitals, we change only from bed to bed, from one folly to another; and it cannot signify much what becomes of such castaways,—wailing, stupid, comatose creatures,—lifted from bed to bed, from the nothing of life to the nothing of death.

In this kingdom of illusions we grope eagerly for stays and foundations. There is none but a strict and faithful dealing at home, and a severe barring out of all duplicity or illusion there. Whatever games are played with us, we must play no games with ourselves, but deal in our privacy with the last honesty and truth. I look upon the simple and childish virtues of veracity and honesty as the root of all that is sublime in character. Speak as you think, be what you are, pay your debts of all kinds. I prefer to be owned as sound and solvent, and my word as good as my bond, and to be what cannot be skipped, or dissipated, or undermined, to all the *éclat* in the universe. This reality is the foundation of friendship, religion, poetry, and art. At the top or at the bottom of all illusions, I set the cheat which still leads us to work and live for appearances, in spite of our conviction, in all sane hours, that it is what we really are that avails with friends, with strangers, and with fate or fortune.

Wallace Stevens

(1879-1955)

POETS INFLUENCE US BECAUSE WE FALL IN LOVE WITH THEIR POEMS. ALL love unfortunately changes, if indeed it does not end, and since nothing is got for nothing, we also get hurt when we abandon, or are abandoned by, poems. Criticism is as much a series of metaphors for the acts of loving what we have read as for the acts of reading themselves. Walter Pater liked to use the word "appreciations" for his critical essays, and I present this particular series of metaphors as an appreciation of Wallace Stevens. Precisely, I mean to appreciate his success in writing the poems of our climate more definitively than any American since Whitman and Dickinson. What justifies an estimate that sets him higher than Frost, Pound, Eliot and Williams? If he is, as so many readers now believe, a great poet, at least the equal of such contemporaries as Hardy, Yeats, Rilke and Valéry, what are the qualities that make for greatness in him? How and why does he move us, enlighten us, enlarge our existences, and help us to live our lives?

Though the admirers of Stevens are a mighty band these days, they have not convinced all skeptics or detractors. We have had some difficulty in exporting him to the British, who with a few noble exceptions continue to regard him as a rather luxurious and Frenchified exquisite, a kind of upper-middle-class mock-Platonist who represents at best an American Aestheticism, replete with tropical fruits and aroma-laden invitations to the voyage. Their Stevens is the celebrator of Florida and of pre-Castro Havana, a vulgarian-in-spite-of-himself. Some American apostles of the Pound-Eliot-Williams-Olson axis are holdouts also; thus we find Hugh Kenner growling, in his recent *The Pound Era*, that all Stevens comes to is the ultimate realization of the poetics of Edward Lear. We can find also, apart from different adherents of the Gorgeous Nonsense school, those critics who complain that Stevens increasingly became desiccated and mock-philosophical; here one can remember Jarrell's crack about G.E. Moore at the spinet. Finally, sometimes we can hear the complaint of those who insist they are weary of poems about poetry, and so are rendered weariest by the recorder of *Notes Toward a Supreme Fiction*. Probably new fault-findings, more soundly based upon Stevens' actual limitations, will arrive as the decades pass. Someone will rise to ask the hard question: How many qualifications can you get into a single poem and still have a poem? Do we not get more than enough of these interjections that Stevens himself describes as "a few words, an and yet, and yet, and yet—"?

But an appreciation does not address itself to answering negative critics, or to proposing fresh negations. The reader who loves Stevens learns a passion for Yes, and learns also that such a passion, like the imagination, needs to be indulged. "It must give pleasure," Stevens says, following a supreme tradition, and his poems do give pleasure. This pleasure, though naturalistic, essentially helps to satisfy the never-satisfied mind, and to the pursuit of the meaning of that satisfaction I now turn. Courageously waving before me the gaudy banners of the Affective Fallacy, I ask myself what it is that reading Stevens does for me, and what is it that I then attempt to do for other readers of Stevens? Is it an effectual though reduced Romantic Humanism that is rekindled for us? Is it a last splendid if willfully grotesque triumph of the American Sublime? Is it, O glorious if this be so, an achieved survival of the Genteel Tradition, another final hedge against the barbarians who are, as we all know, not only within the gates but also indistinguishable, alas, except upon certain moonlit nights, from our very selves? Is the prudential Seer of Hartford only the most eloquent elaborator of our way of life, the Grand Defender of our sanctified evasions, our privileged status as the secular clergy of a society we cannot serve, let alone save? Have we committed the further and grievous sin of making a Stevens in our own image, a poet of professors as Auden and Eliot and Arnold used to be? Having employed Stevens as a weapon in the mimic wars of criticism against the anti-Romantic legions of the Eliotics and Arnoldians, are we now confronted by his poems as so many statues in the formal parks of our university culture? Are his poems still Spirit to us, or are they only what Emerson, most prudential of New England seers, shrewdly called Commodity? Have we made him too into Literature? Do we need now to defend him against ourselves?

Several critics have regarded Stevens as essentially a comic poet. I think this characterization is not adequate to even his more sardonic aspect, but at least it reminds us of how humorous he could be. One of my favorite poems in *Harmonium*, which I rarely persuade anyone else to like, is called "Two Figures in Dense Violet Light." I take it as being a superbly

American kind of defeated eroticism, the complaint of a would-be lover who is ruefully content to be discontent, because he rather doubts that high romance can be domesticated anyway in a world still so ruggedly New. One might think of this poem's speaker as being a decadent Huckleberry Finn dressed up to play the part of Romeo:

> I had as lief be embraced by the porter at the hotel
> As to get no more from the moonlight
> Than your moist hand.
>
> Be the voice of night and Florida in my ear.
> Use dusky words and dusky images.
> Darken your speech.
>
> Speak, even, as if I did not hear you speaking,
> But spoke for you perfectly in my thoughts,
> Conceiving words,
>
> As the night conceives the sea-sounds in silence,
> And out of their droning sibilants makes
> A serenade.
>
> Say, puerile, that the buzzards crouch on the ridge-pole
> And sleep with one eye watching the stars fall
> Below Key West.
>
> Say that the palms are clear in a total blue,
> Are clear and are obscure; that it is night;
> That the moon shines.

Though more than usually mocking and self-mocking, this is surely another of Stevens' hymns to the Interior Paramour, another invocation of his Muse, his version of Whitman's Fancy. But Whitman's Fancy, though she rarely emanated very far out from him, did have a touch or two of an exterior existence. Stevens' Paramour, poor girl, is the most firmly Interior being in Romantic tradition. Compared to her, the epipsyches of Nerval, Poe, Shelley and the young Yeats are buxom, open-air, Renoir-like ladies. Stevens knows this, and the violet light of his poem is so dense that the two figures might as well be one. "What a love affair!" we cannot help exclaiming, as the Grand Solipsist murmurs to his Paramour: "Speak, even, as if I did not hear you speaking, / But spoke for you perfectly in my thoughts."

This is a delicious Dialogue of One, all right, and we find its true father in some of Emerson's slyly bland observations on the Self-Reliance of Spheral Man. Recalling one Boscovich, an Italian Newtonian who had formulated a more-than-usually crazy version of the molecular theory of matter, Emerson mused: "Was it Boscovich who found that our bodies never come in contact? Well, souls never touch their objects. An innavigable sea washes with silent waves between us and the things we aim at and converse with."

In Stevens, this "innavigable sea" is called "the dumbfoundering abyss / Between us and the object," and no poet has been more honestly ruthless about the actual dualism of our everyday perceptions and imperceptions. Except for a peculiar roster of fabulistic caricatures, there aren't any *people* in Stevens' poems, and this exclusion is comprehensive enough to include Stevens himself as whole man or as person. But the "whole man" or "person" in a poem is generally only another formalizing device or dramatizing convention anyway, a means of self-presentation that Stevens did not care to employ. In the difficult poem, "The Creations of Sound," written against Eliot, who appears in it as X, Stevens declares himself as:

> ... a separate author, a different poet,
> An accretion from ourselves, intelligent
> Beyond intelligence, an artificial man
>
> At a distance, a secondary expositor,
> A being of sound, whom one does not approach
> Through any exaggeration.

For all his antimythological bias, the old Stevens turned to Ulysses, "symbol of the seeker," to present his own final quest for a transcendental self. Unlike the Ulysses of Tennyson, at once somewhat Homeric, Dantesque, Shakespearean and Miltonic, the Ulysses of Stevens is not seeking to meet anything even partly external to himself. What other Ulysses would start out by saying: "As I know, I am and have / The right to be"? For Stevens, "the right to know / And the right to be are one," but his Ulysses must go on questing because:

> Yet always there is another life,
> A life beyond this present knowing,
> A life lighter than this present splendor,
> Brighter, perfected and distant away,
> Not to be reached but to be known,

Not an attainment of the will
But something illogically received,
A divination, a letting down
From loftiness, misgivings dazzlingly
Resolved in dazzling discovery.

There is, despite so many of his critics, no doubt concerning the precursor of this ultimate Stevens. For that "something illogically received," we can recall the divinations of the inescapable father of the American Sublime, who uttered the grand formula: "All I know is reception; I am and I have: but I do not get, and when I have fancied I had gotten anything, I found I did not." In the same essay, the superb "Experience," Emerson mused: "I am very content with knowing, if only I could know." Both Emerson and Stevens hold hard to what both call "poverty," imaginative need, and they believe that holding hard long enough will compel the self to attain its due sphericity. Between the skeptically transcendental grandfather and the transcendentally skeptical grandson came the heroic father, spheral man himself, unqualified in his divinations, who tells us what we miss in Emerson and Stevens alike, and what we cannot resist in him:

Encompass worlds, but never try to encompass me,
I crowd your sleekest and best by simply looking toward you.

Writing and talk do not prove me,
I carry the plenum of proof and every thing else in my face,
With the hush of my lips I wholly confound the skeptic.

For the absolutely transcendental self, the man-god, we read Whitman only, but I am astonished always how much of it abides in Stevens, despite nearly all his critics, and despite the Idiot Questioner in Stevens himself. His evasive glory is hardly distinguishable from his imperfect solipsism, or from ours. And there I verge upon what I take as the clue to his greatness; in the curiously esoteric but centrally American tradition of Emerson, Whitman, Thoreau and Dickinson, Stevens is uniquely the twentieth century poet of that solitary and inward glory we can none of us share with others. His value is that he describes and even celebrates (occasionally) our selfhood-communings as no one else can or does. He knows that "the sublime comes down / To the spirit and space," and though he keeps acknowledging the spirit's emptiness and space's vacancy, he keeps demonstrating a violent abundance of spirit and a florabundance of the consolations of space. He is the poet we always needed, who would speak for the solitude at our center, who would do for us what his own "Large Red Man Reading" did for those ghosts that returned to earth to hear his phrases, "and spoke the feeling for them, which was what they had lacked." Or, to state this function positively, Stevens, more even than Wordsworth, is the essential poet who can recognize that:

> There is a human loneliness,
> A part of space and solitude,
> In which knowledge cannot be denied,
> In which nothing of knowledge fails,
> The luminous companion, the hand,
> The fortifying arm, the profound
> Response, the completely answering voice,
> That which is more than anything else
> The right within us and about us,
> Joined, the triumphant vigor, felt,
> The inner direction on which we depend,
> That which keeps us the little that we are,
> The aid of greatness to be and the force.

There is nothing communal here. Stevens celebrates an apprehension that has no social aspect whatsoever and that indeed appears resistant to any psychological reductions we might apply. As no one is going to be tempted to call Stevens a mystical poet, or in any way religious, we rightly *confront* a considerable problem in description whenever Stevens is most himself. His True Subject appears to be his own sense of glory, and his true value for his readers appears to be that he reminds us of our own moments of solipsistic bliss, or at least of our aspirations for such moments.

The Stevens I begin to sketch has little in common with the poet of "decreation" most of his better critics have described for us. There is indeed a Stevens as seen by Hillis Miller, a poet of the almost-Paterian flux of *sensations*, of a cyclic near-nihilism returning always upon itself. There is also truly a Stevens as seen by Helen Vendler: Stevens the venerable ironist, apostle of "the total leaflessness." I do not assert that these are merely peripheral aspects of the poet, but they seem to me aspects only, darker saliences that surround the central man, shadows flickering beyond that crucial light cast by the single candle of Stevens' self-joying imagination, his version of "A Quiet Normal Life":

His place, as he sat and as he thought, was not
In anything that he constructed, so frail,
So barely lit, so shadowed over and naught,

As, for example, a world in which, like snow,
He became an inhabitant, obedient
To gallant notions on the part of cold.

It was here. This was the setting and the time
Of year. Here in his house and in his room,
In his chair, the most tranquil thought grew peaked

And the oldest and the warmest heart was cut
By gallant notions on the part of night—
Both late and alone, above the crickets' chords,

Babbling, each one, the uniqueness of its sound.
There was no fury in transcendent forms.
But his actual candle blazed with artifice.

Stevens' customary anxiety about transcendent forms is evident, yet
it is also evident that his actual candle is precisely a transcendent form.
Wordsworth was sanely English in refusing to go too far into his True
Subject, which was his own sense of actual sublimity. Emerson, deliberately and wildly American, made possible for all his descendants the outrageous True Subject of the American Sublime. Mocking as always where he
is most vulnerable and most involved, here is Stevens' "The American
Sublime":

How does one stand
To behold the sublime,
To confront the mockers,
The mickey mockers
And plated pairs?

When General Jackson
Posed for his statue
He knew how one feels.
Shall a man go barefoot
Blinking and blank?

But how does one feel?
One grows used to the weather,
The landscape and that;
And the sublime comes down
To the spirit itself,

The spirit and space,
The empty spirit
In vacant space.
What wine does one drink?
What bread does one eat?

Juxtapose this to one of the pure versions of the American Sublime:

> In the highest moments, we are a vision. There is nothing that
> can be called gratitude nor properly joy. The soul is raised over
> passion. It seeth nothing so much as Identity. It is a Perceiving
> that Truth and Right ARE. Hence it becomes a perfect Peace
> out of the knowing that all things will go well. Vast spaces of
> nature, the Atlantic Ocean, the South Sea; vast intervals of
> time, years, centuries, are annihilated to it; this which I think
> and feel underlay that former state of life and circumstances, as
> it does underlie my present, and will always all circumstance,
> and what is called life and what is called death.

This excerpt from Emerson's 1838 Journal was modified into one of
the most famous passages in the essay, "Self-Reliance." Nervous as Stevens
is at confronting possible mockers, his American Sublime is no appreciable distance from Emerson's. One doesn't see Stevens posing for his statue, but he still admits that the Sublime comes down to what one feels and
what one sees, and his emptiness of spirit and vacancy of space were part
of the weather, inner and outer, and not permanent metaphysical reductions. That which he was, that only could he see, and he never wearied of
affirming his version of Self-Reliance:

> ... What
> One believes is what matters. Ecstatic identities
> Between one's self and the weather and the things
> Of the weather are the belief in one's element,
> The casual reunions, the long-pondered
> Surrenders, the repeated sayings that

There is nothing more and that it is enough
To believe in the weather and in the things and men
Of the weather and in one's self, as part of that
And nothing more.

How can a solipsism present itself in the accents of glory, we may be uneasy enough to ask, and again, can a solipsism be a possible humanism? I begin an answer with the dark Wittgensteinian aphorism: What the solipsist *means* is right. For, though solipsism is refutable by its status as tautology, this is what Wittgenstein means when he speaks of a *deep* tautology, which leads to a true realism. Stevens too knows, as Emerson knew, that what he *says* is wrong, but that his meaning is right. The European Sublime had a communal aspect, however solitary its stimulus, but we are of an even more displaced Protestant national sensibility, and, accordingly, we come to reality only through knowing first the scandalous reality of our own selves. Or, as Stevens said:

The lean cats of the arches of the churches,
That's the old world. In the new, all men are priests.

Stevens is a priest, not of the invisible, but of that visible he labors to make a little hard to see. He serves that visible, not for its own sake, but because he wants to make his own sublimity more visible to himself. Endlessly qualifying his sense of his own greatness, he still endlessly returns to rest upon such a sense. Yet he knows that he needs us, his possible read-ers, to do for him "what he cannot do for himself, that is to say, receive his poetry." As he proudly tells us, he addresses us as an elite, being in this one respect, at least, more honest than a far more esoteric and difficult poet, Whitman. In *The Noble Rider and the Sound of Words*, Stevens says:

> ... all poets address themselves to someone and it is of the essence of that instinct, and it seems to amount to an instinct, that it should be to an elite, not to a drab but to a woman with the hair of pytoness, not to a chamber of commerce but to a gallery of one's own, if there are enough of one's own to fill a gallery. And that elite, if it responds, not out of complaisance, but because the poet has quickened it, because he has educed from it that for which it was searching in itself and in the life around it and which it had not yet quite found, will thereafter do for the poet what he cannot do for himself, that is to say, receive his poetry.

There are two questions to be asked of this passage: What is it in this poet that gives him the instinct to address himself not to a drab but to a woman with the hair of a pythoness, and what is it that we keep searching for in ourselves that Stevens would quicken in us, that he would educe from us? The answer to both questions must be the same answer: a quality that Stevens calls "nobility." As he knew, it is hardly a word that now moves us, and I suspect he chose the word defiantly and therefore wrongly. Stevens says, in the same essay, that "It is one of the peculiarities of the imagination that it is always at the end of an era." Certainly Stevens now seems peculiarly to have been at the end of an era, where he himself could still be visualized as a *noble* rider moving to the sound of words. I myself have come to think that the principal peculiarity of the imagination is that it does not exist, or to state my thought another way, that people talking about the arts do better when they begin to talk as though the imagination did not exist. Let us reduce to the rocky level, and say, as Hobbes did, that "decaying sense" most certainly does exist. Stevens had then a decaying sense of nobility, which he called an imagination of nobility. "Noble," in its root, means to be knowing or seeing, and Stevens had therefore a decaying sense of a certain seeing that was also a knowing. I turn again to Stevens' central precursor for the inevitable vision of this nobility in its American variety:

> ... This insight, which expresses itself by what is called Imagination, is a very high sort of seeing, which does not come by study, but by the intellect being where and what it sees; by sharing the path or circuit of things through forms, and so making them translucid to others.

"Leave the many and hold the few," Emerson also advises in his late poem, "Terminus," thus sanctioning the democratic poet, like Whitman, in the pragmatic address to an actual elite. Stevens needed little sanctioning as to audience, but he was rather anxious about his own constant emphasis upon the self as solitary "scholar," and his recourse was to plead "poverty." He cannot have been unaware that both "scholar" and "poverty" in his rather precise senses were Emersonian usages. A great coverer of traces, Stevens may be judged nevertheless to have turned more to a tradition than to a man. American Romanticism found its last giant in Stevens, who defines the tradition quite as strongly as it informs him. "The prologues are over.... It is time to choose," and the Stevens I think we must choose writes the poems not of an empty spirit in vacant space, but of a spirit so full of itself that there is room for nothing else. This description hardly appears to flatter Stevens, yet I render it in his praise. Another of his still neglected poems, for which my own love is intense, is entitled simply, "Poem With Rhythms":

> The hand between the candle and the wall
> Grows large on the wall.
>
> The mind between this light or that and space,
> (This man in a room with an image of the world,
> That woman waiting for the man she loves,)
> Grows large against space:
>
> *There the man sees the image clearly at last.*
> *There the woman receives her lover into her heart*
> *And weeps on his breast, though he never comes.*
>
> It must be that the hand
> Has a will to grow larger on the wall,
> To grow larger and heavier and stronger than
> The wall; and that the mind
> Turns to its own figurations and declares,
> *"This image, this love, I compose myself*
> *Of these. In these, I come forth outwardly.*
> *In these, I wear a vital cleanliness,*
> *Not as in air, bright-blue-resembling air,*
> *But as in the powerful mirror of my wish and will."*

The principal difference between Stevens and Whitman appears to be that Stevens admits his mind is alone with its own figurations, while Whitman keeps inaccurately but movingly insisting he wants "contact" with other selves. His "contact" is an Emersonian term, and we know, as Whitman's readers, that he actually cannot bear "contact," any more than Emerson, Dickinson, Frost or Stevens can tolerate it. "Poem With Rhythms," like so much of Stevens, has a hidden origin in Whitman's "The Sleepers," particularly in a great passage apparently describing a woman's disappointment in love:

> I am she who adorn'd herself and folded her hair expectantly,
> My truant lover has come, and it is dark.
> Double yourself and receive me darkness,
> Receive me and my lover too, he will not let me go without him.

I roll myself upon you as upon a bed, I resign myself to the
    dusk.

He whom I call answers me and takes the place of my lover,
He rises with me silently from the bed.

Darkness, you are gentler than my lover, his flesh was sweaty
    and panting,
I feel the hot moisture yet that he left me.

My hands are spread forth, I pass them in all directions.
I would sound up the shadowy shore to which you are journeying.

Be careful, darkness! already, what was it touch'd me?
I thought my lover had gone, else darkness and he are one,
I hear the heart-beat, I follow, I fade away.

This juxtaposition of major Whitman to relatively minor Stevens is
not altogether fair, but then I don't think I hurt Stevens by granting that
Whitman, upon his heights, is likely to make his descendant seem only a
dwarf of disintegration. Whitman-as-Woman invokes the darkness of
birth, and blends himself into the mingled Sublimity of death and the
Native Strain. Stevens-as-Interior-Paramour invokes only his mind's own
figurations, but he sees himself cleansed in the vitalizing mirror of will as
he could never hope to see himself in the mere outwardness of air.
Whitman oddly but beautifully persuades us of a dramatic poignance that
his actual solipsism does not earn, while Stevens rather less beautifully
knows only the nondramatic truth of his own fine desperation.

What then is Stevens giving us? What do we celebrate with and in
him when he leads us to celebrate? His vigorous affirmation, "The Well
Dressed Man With a Beard," centers on "a speech / Of the self that must
sustain itself on speech." Is eloquence enough? I turn again to the fountain
of our will, Emerson, who had the courage to insist that eloquence was
enough, because he identified eloquence with "something unlimited and
boundless," in the manner of Cicero. Here is Stevens mounting through
eloquence to his individual sense of "something unlimited and boundless,"
a "something" not beyond our apprehension:

Last night at the end of night his starry head,
Like the head of fate, looked out in darkness, part
Thereof and part desire and part the sense

Of what men are. The collective being knew
There were others like him safely under roof.

The captain squalid on his pillow, the great
Cardinal, saying the prayers of earliest day;
The stone, the categorical effigy;
And the mother, the music, the name; the scholar,
Whose green mind bulges with complicated hues:

True transfigurers fetched out of the human mountain,
True genii for the diminished, spheres,
Gigantic embryos of populations,
Blue friends in shadows, rich conspirators,
Confiders and comforters and lofty kin.

To say more than human things with human voice,
That cannot be; to say human things with more
Than human voice, that, also, cannot be;
To speak humanly from the height or from the depth
Of human things, that is acutest speech.

A critic who has learned, ruefully, to accept the reductive view that
the imagination is only decaying sense, must ask himself. Why is he so
moved by this transfiguration of language into acutest speech? He may
remember, in this connection, the prose statement by Stevens that moves
him most:

> Why should a poem not change in sense when there is a fluc-
> tuation of the whole of appearance? Or why should it not
> change when we realize that the indifferent experience of life is
> the unique experience, the item of ecstasy which we have been
> isolating and reserving for another time and place, loftier and
> more secluded....

The doctrinal voice of Walter Pater, another unacknowledged ancestor, is heard in this passage, as perhaps it must be heard in any modern
Epicureanism. Stevens, I suggest, is the Lucretius of our modern poetry,
and like Lucretius seeks his truth in mere appearances, seeks his spirit in
things of the weather. Both poets are beyond illusions, yet both invest their
knowing of the way things are with a certain grim ecstasy. But an American
Lucretius, coming after the double alienation of European Romanticism

and domestic Transcendentalism, will have lost all sense of the communal in his ecstasy. Stevens fulfilled the unique enterprise of a specifically American poetry by exposing the essential solipsism of our Native Strain. No American feels free when he is not alone, and every American's passion for Yes affirms a hidden belief that his soul's substance is no part of the creation. We are mortal gods, the central strain in our poetry keeps saying, and our aboriginal selves are forbidden to find companionship in one another. Our ecstasy comes only from self-recognition, yet cannot be complete if we reduce wholly to "the evilly compounded, vital I ... made ... fresh in a world of white." We need "The Poems of Our Climate" because we are, happily, imperfect solipsists, unhappy in a happily imperfect and still external world—which is to say, we need Stevens:

> There would still remain the never-resting mind,
> So that one would want to escape, come back
> To what had been so long composed.
> The imperfect is our paradise.
> Note that, in this bitterness, delight,
> Since the imperfect is so hot in us,
> Lies in flawed words and stubborn sounds.

William Carlos Williams

(1883–1963)

IN HIS CRITICAL BIOGRAPHY *WILLIAM CARLOS WILLIAMS: A NEW WORLD Naked*, Paul Mariani wisely asserts the lasting influence of John Keats's poetry upon even the late phases of Williams:

> The voice he was listening to, and the voice that struck paydirt for him, was a matter of a complex crossing with Keats, especially the Keats of the *Hyperion* fragments and the odes. Why this should have been so is difficult to say with any exactness, for Williams himself probably did not understand why. What *he* thought he was "capturing" was the voice of the classics—the stately rhythms and sharp straightforward idiom of the Greeks as he thought they must sound should they be discovered walking the streets of his Paterson. But there was something more, a kinship Williams had felt with Keats for over half a century, the plight of the romantic poet who would have spoken as the gods speak if only he had had the power to render their speech in the accents of his own debased language. *Hyperion* is in part the portrait of the dying of the ephebe into the life of the major poet, and Keats had aborted it at the very moment that his poet was undergoing that transformation.
>
> And so with Williams, opting for the step-down line as his "classic" signature as he surfaced from the realization of his mortality, the new rhythm providing a stately, slow saraband to echo Keats's Miltonic and Dantesque phase with a difference. The crossing with Keats is there too in the nature of Williams's late iconography, in the stasis of his late images, frozen for eternity in the realized artifact, as in Williams's translation from

Theocritus's first idyll, with its images limned on a "two-eared bowl / of ivy-wood," a girl and two young men, an ancient fisherman, and a small boy preoccupied with "plaiting a pretty / cage of locust stalks and asphodel." The images of *Asphodel* too belong to the same strain: sharply realized but without Williams's earlier breathlessness and jagged line cuttings.

Poetic influence, an intensely problematical process, normally brings together a strong poet's earliest and final phases. Williams's true precursor, necessarily composite and in some sense imaginary, was a figure that fused Keats with Walt Whitman. Such a figure has in it the potential for a serious splitting of the poetic ego in its defense against the poetic past. The "negative capability" of Keats sorts oddly with Whitman's rather positive capability for conveying the powerful press of himself. "Memory is a kind / of accomplishment," Williams wrote in "The Descent," a crucial poem in his *The Desert Music* (1954). The descent to dying beckons to a return of the dead precursors in one's own colors, even as Keats and Whitman beckoned Williams to ascend into his own poetry. But the poem "The Descent" Williams shrewdly quarried from Book 2 of his own major long poem, *Paterson*, a quarrying that suggests his pride in his own continuities.

Those continuities are massive throughout Williams's best work, which can be cataloged (against the numerous Williams idolators) as a limited yet still remarkably diverse canon: *Paterson* (Book I), *Kora in Hell*, *Spring and All*, "The Widow's Lament in Springtime," "To Waken an Old Lady," "The Trees," "The Yachts," "A Coronal," "These," "The Poor," "A Marriage Ritual," "Raleigh Was Right," "Burning the Christmas Greens," "A Unison," and the grand return of Keats-as-Williams in *Asphodel, That Greeny Flower*. Every critic I have chosen for this volume would select more, much more, but I am of the school of Wallace Stevens, rather than of Williams, and the Williams I honor is the author of about a dozen shorter poems, and four remarkable long poems and prose or verse sequences. I write this introduction not to dissent, but as an experiment. If you believe—as I do—that Williams is not of the eminence of Stevens and Robert Frost, of Hart Crane and even of T.S. Eliot, then what is the irreducible achievement that survives even an extreme skepticism as to Williams's poetic greatness?

Of the volumes that collect Williams, I return most often to *Imaginations*, edited by Webster Schott (1979), which gathers together four weird American originals—*Kora in Hell*, *Spring and All*, *The Great American Novel*, *The Descent of Winter*—as well as some miscellaneous prose. *Kora in Hell* was subtitled *Improvisations* by Williams, who had a particular fondness

for it. He analogized its astonishing "Prologue" to *On the Sublime* by the
pseudo-Longinus, a comparison not so farfetched as he himself asserted it
to be. Essentially it, and all of *Kora*, is a collection of what Emerson (following Plutarch and Cudworth) called "lustres" (Ezra Pound's *lustra*),
aphoristic impressions drawn either from others or from the self. Its center is in Williams's characteristic polemic against Pound and Eliot, with an
ironizing boost from Stevens:

> E.P. is the best enemy United States verse has. He is inter-
> ested, passionately interested—even if he doesn't know what he
> is talking about. But of course he does know what he is talking
> about. He does not, however, know everything, not by more
> than half. The accordances of which Americans have the parts
> and the colors but not the completions before them pass
> beyond the attempts of his thought. It is a middle-aging blight
> of the imagination.
>
> I praise those who have the wit and courage, and the con-
> ventionality, to go direct toward their vision of perfection in an
> objective world where the signposts are clearly marked, viz., to
> London. But confine them in hell for their paretic assumption
> that there is no alternative but their own groove.
>
> Dear fat Stevens, thawing out so beautifully at forty! I was
> one day irately damning those who run to London when
> Stevens caught me up with his mild: "But where in the world
> will you have them run to?"

The shrewd link to *On the Sublime* is that Williams (admirably and
accurately) shares the conviction of Longinus that the Sublime or strong
poetry either is agonistic or it is nothing. Williams too seeks to persuade
the reader to forsake easier pleasures (Eliot and Pound) for more difficult
pleasures (*Kora in Hell*). And his quest is frankly Emersonian, an overt
instance of American cultural nationalism. Unfortunately, *Kora*'s considerable verve and vivacity is shadowed by the immense power of James Joyce's
Ulysses, still incomplete then, but appearing in magazine installments even
as Williams wrote and read. Williams's use of mythology is essentially
Joyce's, and to fight Joyce on any ground, let alone his prepared killing
field, was beyond Williams's talents:

> Giants in the dirt. The gods, the Greek gods, smothered in
> filth and ignorance. The race is scattered over the world.
> Where is its home? Find it if you've the genius. Here Hebe

with a sick jaw and a cruel husband,—her mother left no place for a brain to grow. Herakles rowing boats on Berry's Creek! Zeus is a country doctor without a taste for coin jingling. Supper is of a bastard nectar on rare nights for they will come—the rare nights! The ground lifts and out sally the heroes of Sophokles, of Æschylus. They go seeping down into our hearts, they rain upon us and in the bog they sink again down through the white roots, down—to a saloon back of the railroad switch where they have that girl, you know, the one that should have been Venus by the lust that's in her. They've got her down there among the railroad men. A crusade couldn't rescue her. Up to jail—or call it down to Limbo—the Chief of Police our Pluto. It's all of the gods, there's nothing else worth writing of. They are the same men they always were—but fallen. Do they dance now, they that danced beside Helicon? They dance much as they did then, only, few have an eye for it, through the dirt and fumes.

The question becomes: who shall describe the dance of the gods as it is danced now in America? The answer is: Dr. Williams, who brings American babies into the world, and who sees exquisitely what we cannot see without him, which is how differently the gods come to dance here in America:

This is a slight stiff dance to a waking baby whose arms have been lying curled back above his head upon the pillow, making a flower—the eyes closed. Dead to the world! Waking is a little hand brushing away dreams. Eyes open. Here's a new world.

This dance figures again in the concluding improvisation of *Kora in Hell*, as an American seasonal rhythm akin to the natural year of Stevens's "Credences of Summer" and Emerson's "Experience":

Seeing the leaves dropping from the high and low branches the thought rises: this day of all others is the one chosen, all other days fall away from it on either side and only itself remains in perfect fullness. It is its own summer, of its leaves as they scrape on the smooth ground it must build its perfection. The gross summer of the year is only a halting counterpart of those fiery days of secret triumph which in reality themselves paint the year as if upon a parchment, giving each season a mockery of the warmth or frozenness which is within ourselves. The

true seasons blossom or wilt not in fixed order but so that many of them
may pass in a few weeks or hours whereas sometimes a whole life pass-
es and the season remains of a piece from one end to the other.

The world is largest in the American summer, for Williams and Stevens, even as it was for their forefather, Emerson. *Spring and All* cele-brates not this world, but the more difficult American skepticism of a hard spring, imperishably rendered in its magnificent opening lyric, "By the road to the contagious hospital," with its harsh splendor of inception, at once of vegetation, infants, and of Whitmanian or American poems:

Lifeless in appearance, sluggish
dazed spring approaches—

They enter the new world naked,
cold, uncertain of all
save that they enter. All about them
the cold, familiar wind—

Now the grass, tomorrow
the stiff curl of wildcarrot leaf
one by one objects are defined—
It quickens: clarity, outline of leaf

But now the stark dignity of
entrance—Still, the profound change
has come upon them: rooted, they
grip down and begin to awaken

The ancient fiction of the leaves, a continuous tradition from Homer and Virgil, through Dante and on to Spenser and Milton, Shelley and Whitman, receives one culmination in Stevens, and a very different apoth-eosis here in Williams. In the prose of *Spring and All*, Williams protests too emphatically that: "THE WORLD IS NEW," a protest that has been taken too much at its own self-mystifying evaluation by the most distin-guished of the deconstructive critics of Williams, J. Hillis Miller and Joseph Riddel. But when the best poems in *Spring and All* unfold them-selves, the reader can be persuaded that Williams has invented freshly the accurate metaphors for our American sense of imaginative belatedness: "There is / an approach with difficulty from / the dead—," and: "The rose is obsolete / but each petal ends in / an edge." Except for "By the road to the contagious hospital," the best poems in *Spring and All* are the justly famous ones: "The pure products of America / go crazy—," and "so much depends / upon / a red wheel / barrow."

More problematical are *The Great American Novel* and *The Descent of Winter*, pugnacious assaults upon Williams's own formal limits, yet assaults masked as ironies directed against the literary conventionalities of others. I prefer *The Descent of Winter*, where the authentic anxiety of belatedness, the only legitimate point of origin for any American literature, is expressed in relation to that most impossible of all influences, Shakespeare:

> By writing he escaped from the world into the natural world of his mind. The unemployable world of his fine head was unnaturally useless in the gross exterior of his day—or any day. By writing he made this active. He melted himself into that grossness, and colored it with his powers. The proof that he was right and they passing, being that he continues always and naturally while their artificiality destroyed them. A man unable to employ himself in his world.
>
> Therefore his seriousness and his accuracies, because it was not his play but the drama of his life. It is his anonymity that is baffling to nitwits and so they want to find an involved explanation—to defeat the plainness of the evidence.
>
> When he speaks of fools he is one; when of kings he is one, doubly so in misfortune.
>
> He is a woman, a pimp, a prince Hal—
>
> Such a man is a prime borrower and standardizer— No inventor. He lives because he sinks back, does not go forward, sinks back into the mass—
>
> He is Hamlet plainer than a theory—and in everything.
>
> You can't buy a life again after it's gone, that's the way I mean.
>
> He drinks awful bad and he beat me up every single month while I was carrying this baby, pretty nearly every week.

As an overview of Shakespeare, this is unquestionably the weakest commentary available since Tolstoy; but as a representation of Williams's dilemmas, it has a curious force, including the weird parody of Hemingway's agonistic stance in the last sentence I have just quoted. Despite his army of hyperbolic exegetes, Williams's nakedness in relation to the literary past is not so much that of "a new world naked" as it is that of a no longer so very new world awkwardly wrapped round by too many fine rags.

II

The best lyrics and Book I of *Paterson* are of a higher order, though they also betray darker anxieties of influence than even Williams's defiances dared to confront. They display also another kind of agon, the anxiety as to contemporary rivals, not so much Pound and Eliot as Wallace Stevens and Hart Crane, heirs to Keats and to Whitman, even as Williams was. No two readers are likely to agree upon just which shorter poems by Williams are his strongest, but the one that impresses and moves me most is "A Unison," where the title seems to comprehend most of the dictionary meanings of "unison": an identity of pitch in music; the same words spoken simultaneously by two or more speakers; musical parts combined in octaves; a concord, agreement, harmony. Thomas R. Whitaker, one of Williams's best and most sympathetic critics but no idolator, gives the best introduction to "A Unison":

> It is like an improvisation from *Kora in Hell*—but one with the quiet maturity of vision and movement that some three decades have brought.... As the implicit analogies and contrasts accumulate, we discover (long before the speaker tells us) that we are attending a "unison and a dance." This "death's festival"—*memento mori* and celebration of the "*Undying*"—evades neither the mystery of transience nor that of organic continuance, though neither can be "parsed" by the analytical mind.... In this composed testament of acceptance, Williams's saxifrage ("through metaphor to reconcile / the people and the stones") quietly does its work.... Not since Wordsworth has this natural piety been rendered so freshly and poignantly.

I would not wish to quarrel with Whitaker's judgment, yet there is very little Wordsworth and (inevitably) much Whitman and considerable Keats in "A Unison." Indeed, the poem opens with what must be called an echo from Whitman, in what I assume was a controlled allusion:

> The grass is very green, my friend,
> And tousled, like the head of—
> your grandson, yes?

We hear one or the uncanniest passages in Whitman, from *Song of Myself* 6:

This grass is very dark to be from the white heads of old mothers,
Darker than the colorless beards of old men,
Dark to come from under the faint red roofs of mouths.

Whitman's great fantasia answers a child's question: *"What is the grass?"* As an Epicurean materialist, Whitman believed that the *what* was unknowable, but his remarkable troping on the grass takes a grand turn after his Homeric line: "And now it seems to me the beautiful uncut hair of graves." Williams simply borrows the trope, and even his "very green" merely follows Whitman's hint that a "very green" becomes a "very dark" color, in the shadow of mortality. "A Unison" insists upon:

—what cannot be escaped: the
mountain riding the afternoon as
it does, the grass matted green,
green underfoot and the air—
rotten wood. *Hear! Hear them!*
the Undying. The hill slopes away,
then rises in the middleground,
you remember, with a grove of gnarled
maples centering the bare pasture,
sacred, surely—for what reason?

Williams does not know whether he can or cannot say the reason, but the allusion is to Keats's characteristic, Saturnian shrine in *Hyperion*. For Williams it is "a shrine cinctured there by / the trees," the girdling effect suggested by the natural sculpture of Keats's shrine. Where Keats as the quester in *The Fall of Hyperion* pledges "all the mortals of the world, / And all the dead whose names are in our lips," and where Whitman insists, "The smallest sprout shows there is really no death," Williams neither salutes the living and the dead, nor folds the two into a single figuration. Rather, he *hears* and urges us to: *"Hear the unison of their voices...."* How are we to interpret such an imaginative gesture? Are we hearing more, or enough more, than the unison of the voices of John Keats and Walt Whitman? Devoted Williamsites doubtless would reject the question, but it always retains its force, nevertheless. It is not less true of *The Waste Land* than it is of Williams. Eliot revises Whitman's "When Lilacs Last in the Dooryard Bloom'd" by fusing it with Tennyson (among others, but prime among those others). Image of voice or the trope of poetic identity then becomes a central problem.

Whitman once contrasted himself to Keats by rejecting "negative capability" and insisting instead that the great poet gave us the "powerful press of himself." Admirable as *Paterson* is (particularly its first book), does even it resolve the antithesis in Williams between his "objectivism" or negative capability, and his own, agonistic, powerful press of himself? Mariani ends his vast, idealizing biography by asserting that Williams established "an American poetic based on a new measure and a primary regard for the living, protean shape of the language as it was actually used." Hillis Miller, even more generously, tells us that Williams gave us a concept of poetry transcending both Homer and Wordsworth, both Aristotle and Coleridge:

> The word is given reality by the fact it names, but the independence of the fact from the word frees the word to be a fact in its own right and at the same time "dynamizes" it with meaning. The word can then carry the facts named in a new form into the realm of imagination.

Mariani and Miller are quite sober compared to more apocalyptic Williamsites. Not even Whitman gave us "a new measure," and not Shakespeare himself freed a single word "to be a fact in its own right." William Carlos Williams was, at his best, a strong American poet, far better than his hordes of imitators. Like Ezra Pound's, Williams's remains a fairly problematical achievement in the traditions of American poetry. Some generations hence, it will become clear whether his critics have canonized him permanently, or subverted him by taking him too much at his own intentions. For now he abides, a live influence, and perhaps with even more fame to come.

H.D. (Hilda Doolittle)

(1886–1961)

LIKE EZRA POUND, HER CLOSE FRIEND AND POETIC COLLEAGUE, H.D. seems to me essentially an American pre-Raphaelite poet, a naming that I intend as a compliment since I deeply love the poetry of the Rossettis, Morris, Meredith, and Swinburne. Even as Pound assimilates Dante Gabriel Rossetti to Walt Whitman, so H.D. compounds Christina Rossetti with Emily Dickinson, and both together with the male sequence of Dante Gabriel Rossetti, William Morris, Pound, and D.H. Lawrence.

Louis L. Martz, in his "Introduction" to H.D.'s *The Collected Poems 1912–1944*, sensitively sketches the relation between the psychosexual and the poetic crises that kept her from publishing any volumes of poetry between 1931 and 1944. Her brief analysis with Freud himself (about three months in 1933, and some five weeks in 1934) issued not only in her *Tribute to Freud* but in a number of fairly strong if problematic poems, three in particular, which Martz reports she grouped in the order of "The Dancer," "The Master," and "The Poet." "The Dancer" is the most problematic of these and perhaps would not matter much, except that it informs a powerful return of its central trope in the midst of "The Master," which is a moving tribute to Freud. Martz shrewdly calls "The Poet" a calm and measured tribute to D.H. Lawrence, and while it is not as distinguished a poem as "The Master," it has its own value and place in H.D.'s achievement.

Tribute to Freud is a rather overpraised book, particularly dear to Freudian literalists from Ernest Jones to the present since it is a kind of hagiography. H.D. herself chats on rapturously, while the old Professor somehow never does get to say anything remotely memorable. Precisely how he clarifies either the poet's bisexuality or her creative inhibitions may escape even the most assiduous and skilled reader. Section 10 of "Writing on the Wall," the first part of the *Tribute*, is both famous and typical:

So much for the Princess, Hanns Sachs, and Walter Schmideberg, the one-time Rittmeister of the 15th Imperial Austro-Hungarian Hussars of His Royal Highness, Archduke Francis Salvator. For myself, I veer round, uncanonically seated stark upright with my feet on the floor. The Professor himself is uncanonical enough; he is beating with his hand, with his fist, on the head-piece of the old-fashioned horsehair sofa that had heard more secrets than the confession box of any popular Roman Catholic father-confessor in his heyday. This was the homely historical instrument of the original scheme of psychotherapy, of psychoanalysis, the science of the unravelling of the tangled skeins of the unconscious mind and the healing implicit in the process. *Consciously*, I was not aware of having said anything that might account for the Professor's outburst. And even as I veered around, facing him, my mind was detached enough to wonder if this was some idea of *his* for speeding up the analytic content or redirecting the flow of associated images. The Professor said, "The trouble is—I am an old man—*you do not think it worth your while to love me*." ("Writing on the Wall")

Presumably such a shock tactic was intended to speed up the transference, but if Freud actually said anything like this, then he was mistaken, as clearly H.D. loved him beyond measure. "But the Professor insisted I myself wanted to be Moses; not only did I want to be a boy but I wanted to be a hero." That certainly sounds like Freud, or by now like a self-parody on his part. There is something quaintly archaic about *Tribute to Freud*, where the Professor's interventions are so accurate, his spiritual efficacy so instantaneous, as to suggest the advent of a new age of faith, the Freud era. A prose memorial provokes our resistances when it seems too pious or too amiably earnest. The pre-Raphaelite aura, hieratic and isolated, with its characteristic effect of a hard-edged phantasmagoria, rescues "The Master" from the cloying literalism of the *Tribute*. "The old man" of the poem is God's prophet, since "the dream is God," and Freud therefore is heard as one who speaks with authority: "his command / was final" and "his tyranny was absolute, / for I had to love him then." The command, at least as H.D. interpreted it, was to accept her own bisexuality as being one with her poethood:

I do not know what to say to God,
for the hills

answer his nod,
and the sea
when he tells his daughter,
white Mother
of green
leaves
and green rills
and silver,
to still
tempest
or send peace
and surcease of peril
when a mountain has spit fire:

I did not know how to differentiate
between volcanic desire,
anemones like embers
and purple fire
of violets
like red heat,
and the cold
silver
of her feet:
I had two loves separate;
God who loves all mountains,
alone knew why
and understood
and told the old man
to explain
the impossible,
which he did.
("The Master")

The phallic or volcanic is evidently preferred by this male God, at
least rhetorically, but of the "two loves separate" the "cold / silver / of her
feet" triumphs with the re-entry of the dancer in section 5. The force that
comes with celebration of the dancer depends upon H.D.'s vision of herself as wrestling Jacob, arguing till daybreak, and of Freud as God or His
angel, giving further rhetorical primacy to "the man-strength" rather than
to the dancer's leapings:

I was angry with the old man
with his talk of the man-strength,
I was angry with his mystery, his mysteries,
I argued till day-break;

O, it was late,
and God will forgive me, my anger,
but I could not accept it.

I could not accept from wisdom
what love taught,
woman is perfect.
("The Dancer")

That would appear to have meant that a woman's bisexuality or her perfection (in the sense of completeness) was of a different and more acceptable order than a man's bisexuality. The ecstasy of section 5 gently mocks the Freudian "man-strength" even as it salutes the dancer for needing no male, since at least as dancer (or poet) woman is indeed pragmatically perfect. Section 5 has a kind of uncanny force, akin to Yeatsian celebrations of the dancer as image. But the authentic strength of the poem centers elsewhere, in its elegiac identifications of the dead father, Freud, with the earth, and with all the dead fathers. Freud is Saturn, ancient wisdom, and the rock that cannot be broken—a new earth. His temples will be everywhere, yet H.D. cries out: "only I, I will escape," an escape sanctioned by Freud as the freedom of the woman poet. Though D.H. Lawrence is not even alluded to in "The Master," he enters the poem by negation, since it is transformed into a fierce hymn against Lawrence's vision of sexual release:

no man will be present in those mysteries,
yet all men will kneel,
no man will be potent,
important,
yet all men will feel
what it is to be a woman,
will yearn,
burn,
turn from easy pleasure
to hardship
of the spirit,

men will see how long they have been blind,
poor men
poor man-kind
how long
how long
this thought of the man-pulse has tricked them.
has weakened them,
shall see woman,
perfect.
("The Master")

The blindness is precisely Lawrence's in H.D.'s judgment, and it is
hinted at, in muted form, in "The Poet," not so much an elegy for
Lawrence as for her failed friendship with him. What seems clear is that
her sexual self-acceptance, whether Freudian or not, gave her the creative
serenity that made possible the wonderfully controlled, hushed resignation
of her wisely limited farewell to Lawrence:

No,
I don't pretend, in a way, to understand,
nor know you,
nor even see you;

I say,
"I don't grasp his philosophy,
and I don't understand,"

but I put out a hand, touch a cold door,
(we have both come from so far);
I touch something imperishable;
I think,
why should he stay there?
why should he guard a shrine so alone,
so apart,
on a path that leads nowhere?

he is keeping a candle burning in a shrine
where nobody comes,
there must be some mystery
in the air
about him,

he couldn't live alone in the desert,
without vision to comfort him,
there must be voices somewhere.
("The Poet")

The wistfulness of that tribute, if it is a tribute, veils the harshness of the critique. A woman can be perfect, but a man cannot, though Lawrence would not learn this. One can imagine his response to H.D.; it would have been violent, but that perhaps would have confirmed her stance, whether sanctioned or unsanctioned by her father and master, Freud.

Marianne Moore

(1887–1972)

For Plato the only reality that mattered is exemplified best for us in the
principles of mathematics. The aim of our lives should be to draw ourselves away as much as possible from the unsubstantial, fluctuating
facts of the world about us and establish some communion with the
objects which are apprehended by thought and not sense. This was the
source of Plato's asceticism. To the extent that Miss Moore finds only
allusion tolerable she shares that asceticism. While she shares it she
does so only as it may be necessary for her to do so in order to establish a particular reality or, better, a reality of her own particulars.

—WALLACE STEVENS

ALLUSION WAS MARIANNE MOORE'S METHOD, A METHOD THAT WAS HER SELF.
One of the most American of all poets, she was fecund in her progeny—
Elizabeth Bishop, May Swenson, and Richard Wilbur being the most gift-
ed among them. Her own American precursors were not Emily Dickinson
and Walt Whitman—still our two greatest poets—but the much slighter
Stephen Crane, who is echoed in her earliest poems, and in an oblique way
Edgar Poe, whom she parodied. I suspect that her nearest poetic father, in
English, was Thomas Hardy, who seems to have taught her lessons in the
mastery of incongruity, and whose secularized version of Biblical irony is
not far from her own. If we compare her with her major poetic contemporaries—Frost, Stevens, Eliot, Pound, Williams, Aiken, Ransom,
Cummings, H.D., Hart Crane—she is clearly the most original American
poet of her era, though not quite of the eminence of Frost, Stevens, Crane.
A curious kind of devotional poet, with some authentic affinities to George
Herbert, she reminds us implicitly but constantly that any distinction
between sacred and secular poetry is only a shibboleth of cultural politics.

Some day she will remind us also of what current cultural politics obscure: that any distinction between poetry written by women or poetry by men is a mere polemic, unless it follows upon an initial distinction between good and bad poetry. Moore, like Bishop and Swenson, is an extraordinary poet-as-poet. The issue of how gender enters into her vision should arise only after the aesthetic achievement is judged as such.

Moore, as all her readers know, to their lasting delight, is the visionary of natural creatures: the jerboa, frigate pelican, buffalo, monkeys, fish, snakes, mongooses, the octopus (actually a trope for a mountain), snail, peacock, whale, pangolin, wood-weasel, elephants, race horses, chameleon, jellyfish, arctic ox (or goat), giraffe, blue bug (another trope, this time for a pony), all of La Fontaine's bestiary, not to mention sea and land unicorns, basilisks, and all the weird fabulous roster that perhaps only Borges also, among crucial modern writers, celebrates so consistently. There is something of Blake and of the Christopher Smart of *Jubilate Agno* in Moore, though the affinity does not result from influence, but rather is the consequence of election. Moore's famous eye, like that of Bishop after her, is not so much a visual gift as it is visionary, for the beasts in her poems are charged with a spiritual intensity that doubtless they possess, but which I myself cannot see without the aid of Blake, Smart, and Moore.

I remember always in reading Moore again that her favorite poem was the Book of Job. Just as I cannot read Ecclesiastes without thinking of Dr. Johnson, I cannot read certain passages in Job without recalling Marianne Moore:

> But ask now the beasts, and they shall teach thee; and the fowls
> of the air, and they shall tell thee:
>   Or speak to the earth, and it shall teach thee: and the fishes
> of the sea shall declare unto thee.
>   Who knoweth not in all these that the hand of the Lord hath
> wrought this?
>   In whose hand is the soul of every living thing.

This, from chapter 12, is the prelude to the great chant of Yahweh, the Voice out of the whirlwind that sounds forth in the frightening magnificence of chapters 38 through 41, where the grand procession of beasts comprehends lions, ravens, wild goats, the wild ass, the unicorn, peacocks, the ostrich, the sublime battle-horse who "saith among the trumpets, Ha, ha," the hawk, the eagle, and at last behemoth and leviathan. Gorgeously celebrating his own creation, Yahweh through the poet of job engendered another strong poet in Marianne Moore. Of the Book of job, she remarked that its agony was veracious and its fidelity of a force "that contrives glory for ashes."

"Glory for ashes" might be called Moore's ethical motto, the basis for the drive of her poetic will toward a reality of her own particulars. Her poetry, as befitted the translator of La Fontaine, and the heir of George Herbert, would be in some danger of dwindling into moral essays, an impossible form for our time, were it not for her wild allusiveness, her zest for quotations, and her essentially anarchic stance, the American and Emersonian insistence upon seeing everything in her own way, with "conscientious inconsistency." When her wildness or freedom subsided, she produced an occasional poetic disaster like the patriotic war poems "In Distrust of Merits" and "'Keeping Their World Large.'" But her greatest poems are at just the opposite edge of consciousness: "A Grave," "Novices," "Marriage," "An Octopus," "He 'Digesteth Harde Yron,'" "Elephants," the deceptively light "Tom Fool at Jamaica."

Those seven poems by themselves have an idiosyncratic splendor that restores my faith, as a critic, in what the language of the poets truly is: diction, or choice of words, playing endlessly upon the dialectic of denotation and connotation, a dialectic that simply vanishes in all Structuralist and post-Structuralist ruminations upon the supposed priority of "language" over meaning. "The arbitrariness of the signifier" loses its charm when one asks a Gallic psycholinguistifier whether denotation or connotation belongs to the signifier, as opposed to the signified, and one beholds blank incredulity as one's only answer. Moore's best poems give the adequate reply: the play of the signifier is answered always by the play of the signified, because the play of diction, or the poet's will over language, is itself constituted by the endless interchanges of denotation and connotation. Moore, with her rage to order allusion, echo, and quotation in ghostlier demarcations, keener sounds, helps us to realize that the belated Modernism of the Gallic proclamation of the death of the author was no less premature than it was, always already, belated.

II

Marriage, through which thought does not penetrate, appeared to Miss Moore a legitimate object for art, an art that would not halt from using thought about it, however, as it might want to. Against marriage, "this institution, perhaps one should say enterprise"—Miss Moore launched her thought not to have it appear arsenaled as in a textbook on psychology, but to stay among apples and giraffes in a poem.

—WILLIAM CARLOS WILLIAMS

If I had to cite a single poem by Moore as representing all of her powers working together, it would be "Marriage" (1923), superficially an outrageous collage but profoundly a poignant comic critique of every society's most sacred and tragic institution. As several critics have ventured, this is Moore's *The Waste Land*, a mosaic of fragments from Francis Bacon, the *Scientific American*, Baxter's *The Saint's Everlasting Rest*, Hazlitt on Burke, William Godwin, Trollope, *The Tempest*, a book on *The Syrian Christ*, the Bible, Ezra Pound, and even Daniel Webster (from an inscription on a statue!), and twenty sources more. Yet it is a poem, and perhaps is more ruggedly unified than any other poem of such ambition by Moore.

The poet's own headnote to "Marriage" could not be more diffident: "Statements that took my fancy which I tried to arrange plausibly." The arrangement is more than plausible; it is quite persuasive, though it begins with a parody of the societal *apologia* for marriage:

This institution,
perhaps one should say enterprise
out of respect for which
one says one need not change one's mind
about a thing one has believed in,
requiring public promises
of one's intention
to fulfil a private obligation.

No one, I believe, could interpret that opening stance with any exactitude. The substitution of "enterprise" for "institution" qualifies the wryness of "public promises / of one's intention / to fulfil a private obligation," but adds a note both of commerce and of the human virtue of taking an initiative. Who could have anticipated that the next movement of the poem would be this?

I wonder what Adam and Eve
think of it by this time,
this fire-gilt steel
alive with goldenness;
how bright it shows—
"of circular traditions and impostures,
committing many spoils,"
requiring all one's criminal ingenuity
to avoid!

Like nearly every other quotation in this poem, the two lines from Sir Francis Bacon gain nothing for Moore's own text by being restored to their own context. Steel burned by fire does not exactly brighten into a golden bough, so the "gilt" is there partly as anticipation of "criminal ingenuity." Yet "gilt" is in cognitive sequence with "goldenness" and "bright," even if we rightly expect to behold blackened steel. All who have known marriage (as Moore declined to do) will register an unhappy shudder at the force the Baconian phrases take on when Moore appropriates them. Traditions as treasons become circular, and together with impostures can be read here either as performing many despoilments or as investing many gains of previous despoilments. Either way, it might seem as though an ingenuity avoiding this equivocal enterprise could only be taken as criminal by some dogmatist, whether societal or theological.

The poem proceeds to dismiss psychology, since to explain everything is to explain nothing, and then meditates upon the beauty, talents, and contrariness of Eve, a meditation that suddenly achieves Paterian intensity:

Below the incandescent stars
below the incandescent fruit,
the strange experience of beauty;
its existence is too much;
it tears one to pieces
and each fresh wave of consciousness
is poison.

The detachment of Moore as watcher is not totally lost, but seems (by design) never fully recovered again in the poem. A woman's fine bitterness against the West's endless assault upon Eve is felt in Moore's description of the universal mother as "the central flaw" in the experiment of Eden, itself "an interesting impossibility" ecstatically described by Richard Baxter as "the choicest piece of my life." If Baxter's ecstasy (though not his eloquence) is qualified shrewdly by Moore's contextualizations, Eden is nowhere near so scaled down by her as is Adam, whose male pomp is altogether undermined. He is pretty well identified with Satan, and like Satan is: "alive with words, / vibrating like a cymbal / touched before it has been struck."

Moore's genius at her method allows her the joy of exemplifying her borrowings even as she employs them in a corrective polemic against male slanderings of women:

"Treading chasms
on the uncertain footing of a spear,"
forgetting that there is in woman
a quality of mind
which as an instinctive manifestation
is unsafe,
he goes on speaking
in a formal customary strain.

In the first quotation, Hazlitt is praising his precursor Edmund Burke for a paradoxically certain footing: for power, energy, truth set forth in the Sublime style. Burke is a chasm-treader, sure-footed as he edges near the abyss. But men less given to truth than Burke have very uncertain footing indeed, whether they forget or remember their characteristic brutalities in regard to a woman's "quality of mind." The poem's "he" therefore goes on speaking of marriage in Richard Baxter's ecstatic terms, as though marriage itself somehow could become "the saints' everlasting rest." Fatuously joyous, the male is ready to suffer the most exquisite passage in the poem, and perhaps in all of Moore:

Plagued by the nightingale
in the new leaves,
with its silence—
not its silence but its silences,
he says of it:
"It clothes me with a shirt of fire."
"He dares not clap his hands
to make it go on
lest it should fly off;
if he does nothing, it will sleep;
if he cries out, it will not understand."
Unnerved by the nightingale
and dazzled by the apple,
impelled by "the illusion of a fire
effectual to extinguish fire,"
compared with which
the shining of the earth
is but deformity—a fire
"as high as deep
as bright as broad
as long as life itself,"

he stumbles over marriage,
"a very trivial object indeed"
to have destroyed the attitude
in which he stood—.

I hardly know of a more unnerving representation of the male fear
and distrust of the female, uncannily combined with the male quandary of
being obsessed with, fascinated by, not only the female but the enterprise
of marriage as well. Moore imperishably catches the masterpiece of male
emotive ambivalence towards the female, which is the male identification
of woman and the taboo. Here the nightingale, perhaps by way of Keats's
erotic allusions, becomes an emblem of the female, while the male speaker, ravished by the silences of the emblem, becomes Hercules suicidally
aflame with the shirt of Nessus. The poor male, "unnerved by the nightingale / and dazzled by the apple," stumbles over the enterprise that is
Adam's experiment, marriage:

its fiddlehead ferns,
lotus flowers, opuntias, white dromedaries,
its hippopotamus—
nose and mouth combined
in one magnificent hopper—
its snake and the potent apple.

We again receive what might be called Moore's Paradox: marriage,
considered from either the male or female perspective, is a dreadful disaster, but as a poetic trope gorgeously shines forth its barbaric splendors.
The male, quoting Trollope's *Barchester Towers*, returns us to the image of
Hercules, and commends marriage "as a fine art, as an experiment, / a duty
or as merely recreation." I myself will never get out of my memory
Moore's subsequent deadpan definition of marriage as "the fight to be
affectionate." With a fine impartiality, the poet has a vision of the agonists
in this eternal dispute:

The blue panther with black eyes,
the basalt panther with blue eyes,
entirely graceful—
one must give them the path—.

But this mutual splendor abates quickly, and a rancorous humor emerges:

He says, "What monarch would not blush
to have a wife
with hair like a shaving brush?"
The fact of woman
is "not the sound of the flute
but very poison."
She says, "Men are monopolists
of 'stars, garters, buttons
and other shining baubles'—
unfit to be the guardians
of another person's happiness."
He says, "These mummies
must be handled carefully—
'the crumbs from a lion's meal,
a couple of shins and the bit of an ear';
turn to the letter M
and you will find
that 'a wife is a coffin.'

This marvelous exchange of diatribes is weirdly stitched together from outrageously heterogeneous "sources," ranging from a parody of *The Rape of the Lock* (in which Moore herself took a hand) to a women's college president's denunciation of the male love of awards and medals on to a surprising misappropriation of a great moment in the prophet Amos, which is then juxtaposed to a brutal remark of Ezra Pound's. Amos associates the lion with Yahweh:

> The lion hath roared, who will not fear? the Lord GOD hath spoken, who can but prophesy?
> Thus saith the LORD; As the shepherd taketh out of the mouth of the lion two legs, or a piece of an ear; so shall the children of Israel be taken out that dwell in Samaria in the corner of a bed, and in Damascus in a couch.

Moore slyly revises the roaring prophet, making the lion every male, and the children of Israel every woman. Pound's dictum, that "a wife is a coffin" is presumably placed under the letter M for "male," and sorts well with Moore's unfair but strong revision of Amos, since the revision suggests that a wife is a corpse. In order to show that her revisionary zeal is savagely if suavely directed against both sexes (or rather their common frailties), Moore proceeds to dissect the narcissism of men

and women alike, until she concludes with the most ironic of her visions
in the poem:

> "I am such a cow,
> if I had a sorrow
> I should feel it a long time;
> I am not one of those
> who have a great sorrow
> in the morning
> and a great joy at noon";

> which says: "I have encountered it
> among those unpretentious
> protégés of wisdom,
> where seeming to parade
> as the debater and the Roman,
> the statesmanship
> of an archaic Daniel Webster
> persists to their simplicity of temper
> as the essence of the matter:

> 'Liberty and union
> now and forever';

> the Book on the writing table;
> the hand in the breast pocket."

Webster, hardly unpretentious, and wise only in his political cunning, is indeed the message inscribed upon his statue: "Liberty and union
/ now and forever." As a judgment upon marriage, it would be a hilarious
irony, if we did not wince so much under Moore's not wholly benign tute-
lage. That Book on the writing table, presumably the Bible, is precisely like
Webster's hand in the breast pocket, an equivocal emblem, in this context,
of the societal benediction upon marriage. Moore's own *The Waste Land*,
"Marriage," may outlast Eliot's poem as a permanent vision of the West in
its long, ironic decline.

Claude McKay

(1889–1948)

THE JAMAICAN CLAUDE MCKAY, WHO WENT FROM MARXISM TO ROMAN Catholicism, was a fierce spirit, whose sonnets have a formalist, baroque intensity that is also now undervalued, as here in "Saint Isaac's Church, Petrograd":

Bow down my soul in worship very low
And in the holy silences be lost.
Bow down before the marble man of woe,
Bow down before the singing angel host.

What jewelled glory fills my spirit's eye!
What golden grandeur moves the depths of me!
The soaring arches lift me up on high
Taking my breath with their rare symmetry.

Bow down my soul and let the wondrous light
Of Beauty bathe thee from her lofty throne
Bow down before the wonder of man's might.
Bow down in worship, humble and alone;
Bow lowly down before the sacred sight
Of man's divinity alive in stone.

This is still the admirer of Leon Trotsky, but the poem's complexity arises out of McKay's repressed awareness that something in his spirit is moving towards conversion. The sestet retreats from the octave's spirituality, and overtly hymns an aesthetic humanism. And yet "The marble man of woe," a representation of the Russian Christ, is not wholly consonant with "man's divinity alive in stone."

The most rugged of McKay's poems is "The Desolate City," a Romantic lament for the lost innocence of the spirit, and another indication of this poet's road to Rome. It may be that McKay, poetically speaking, was born at the wrong time, but too late rather than too early. For all his political anger, which has an authority difficult to withstand, he would have been culturally at home in the Catholicism of Gerard Manley Hopkins and Francis Thompson, a generation earlier than his own.

E.E. cummings

(1894–1962)

THE POET'S FATHER, EDWARD CUMMINGS, WAS BY ALL ACCOUNTS AN impressive person: Unitarian minister, Harvard sociologist, an athlete and outdoorsman, an exuberant personality. He died in a locomotive–automobile collision in the autumn of 1926. "my father moved through dooms of love" was published as number 34 of the *50 Poems* (1934).

Any ambivalence between son and father overtly vanishes in this celebratory poem, though doubtless it remains between the lines, as it were. What renders this elegiac lyric so poignant is its identification with the dead father, and a wonderfully open expression of filial love:

> my father moved through dooms of love
> through sames of am through haves of give,
> singing each morning out of each night
> my father moved through depths of height
>
> this motionless forgetful where
> turned at his glance to shining here;
> that if (so timid air is firm)
> under his eyes would stir and squirm
>
> newly as from unburied which
> floats the first who, his April touch
> drove sleeping selves to swarm their fates
> woke dreamers to their ghostly roots
>
> and should some why completely weep
> my father's fingers brought her sleep:

vainly no smallest voice might cry
for he could feel the mountains grow.

Lifting the valleys of the sea
my father moved through griefs of joy;
praising a forehead called the moon
singing desire into begin

joy was his song and joy so pure
a heart of star by him could steer
and pure so now and now so yes
the wrists of twilight would rejoice

keen as midsummer's keen beyond
conceiving mind of sun will stand,
so strictly (over utmost him
so hugely) stood my father's dream

The characteristic flaw in Cummings is his flagrant sentimentalism, but who would find emotion in excess of the object in this poem? Hyperbolical flaws begin to appear after these first seven stanzas—"his anger was as right as rain" and "his shoulders marched against the dark." Still, the lively metric of the poem partly obscures these banalities. The two final stanzas are pitched so high that they ought not to work, but they do. The father, who preached the social gospel and believed in the potential divinity of all people, returns in the spirit to elevate the son's rhetoric:

though dull were all we taste as bright,
bitter all utterly things sweet,
maggoty minus and dumb death
all we inherit,all bequeath

and nothing quite so least as truth
—I say though that were why men breathe—
because my father lived his soul
love is the whole and more than all

Partly this is effective because Cummings is *not* his father: his own myth did not stress universal love, or potential divinity, but rather isolation, the difficulty of love, the reality of death. That makes more vivid and valuable the transcendence of his filial tribute.

Jean Toomer

(1894–1967)

JEAN TOOMER'S REMARKABLE *CANE* (1923), A SUBTLY INTERWOVEN MEDLEY of prose-poem and verse, was never matched by him again in the more than forty years remaining. *The Blue Meridian* (1929) fades away in contrast with Hart Crane's *The Bridge* (1930), though Toomer and Crane were friends, and some mutual influence was involved. Toomer's immersion in quack spiritualities was fatal both to his work and his sense of identity. And yet, in his brief flowering, he became the authentic poet of what would have to be called black pastoral, as in his marvelous "November Cotton Flower":

> Boll-weevil's coming, and the winter's cold,
> Made cotton-stalks look rusty, seasons old,
> And cotton, scarce as any southern snow,
> Was vanishing; the branch, so pinched and slow,
> Failed in its function as the autumn rake;
> Drouth fighting soil had caused the soil to take
> All water from the streams; dead birds were found
> In wells a hundred feet below the ground—
> Such was the season when the flower bloomed.
> Old folks were startled, and it soon assumed
> Significance. Superstition saw
> Something it had never seen before:
> Brown eyes that loved without a trace of fear,
> Beauty so sudden for that time of year.

This extraordinary lyric is both beautifully wrought and humanly profound. The late blooming of the flower becomes emblematic of a freedom from psychic dearth, the freedom to love.

Robert Graves

(1895–1985)

In 1948, I was one of many young enthusiasts for poetry who fell in love with *The White Goddess: A Historical Grammar of Poetic Myth* by the lyric poet and popular novelist Robert Graves. Graves died December 8, 1985, at his home in Deya, Majorca, and I began writing this introduction some seven months later, in July 1986, after having reread *The White Goddess* for the first time in many years. Nearly four decades after first reading Graves's remarkable phantasmagoria, I cannot recover the enchantment that the book held for me when I was eighteen. What replaces mystery, and intellectual desire, is the puzzled impression I remember recording back in 1969, the last time I reread *The White Goddess*:

> The shamanism of Empedocles, so strangely reborn in Yeats's *A Vision*, Lawrence's *Fantasia of the Unconscious*, and Graves's *The White Goddess*, proposes a preternatural catharsis to heal a magical spirit in us....
>
> Romantic poetry, in its long history, has been saved ... by its sense of its own tradition, by the liberating burden of poetic influence. Yeats, Lawrence, Graves—despite their varied and real poetic successes—willfully placed their First Romantics too freely and too far away, and.were saved from too crippling a freedom by the relative proximity of their true Romantic ancestors: Blake and Shelley for Yeats, Whitman and Hardy for Lawrence, Keats and Hardy for Graves....
>
> When we turn to the major descendants of Romanticism in modern poetry, we behold a competition to drink of Circe's cup, with only a few notable exceptions. The *daimon* is our destiny, Yeats says, and our destiny is even a kind of justice, but then we

discover that this justice means only the exhaustion of every possible illusion, the completion of every possible emotional relationship. Or, to descend to a lower comedy, Graves tells us that Freud projected a private fantasy upon the world and then Graves offers us the assurance that true poetry worships a barbaric lunar Muse. Both Yeats and Graves show us the nightmare cyclic world of Blake's *The Mental Traveller*, but what Blake tells us is mere unnecessary masochism, Yeats and Graves affirm as imaginative truth, though only Graves insists also on the mutual rendings of poet and Muse as being true love.

Patrick J. Keane, who impresses me as Graves's most persuasive critical defender, argues against this judgment by observing, "it is equally true that Gravesian wildness is tempered by stoicism and a stress on limitation." Yet *ethos* or character does not seem to me the issue. What calls *The White Goddess* and many of the poems founded upon it into question is Graves's curious literalism, which prevents the reader from regarding the White Goddess or Muse as a metaphor for the Gravesian imagination. What cheerfully kept Graves a good minor poet, despite authentic genius, was his distrust of figurative language, and his powerfully reductive tendency to historicize and literalize every manifestation of the Goddess he could discover, whether in life or literature. Just before the end of *The White Goddess*, Graves states his credo, which I am afraid requires both critical correction and experiential skepticism:

> True poetic practice implies a mind so miraculously attuned and illuminated that it can form words, by a chain of more-than-coincidences, into a living entity—a poem that goes about on its own (for centuries after the author's death, perhaps) affecting readers with its stored magic. Since the source of poetry's creative power is not scientific intelligence, but inspiration—however this may be explained by scientists—one may surely attribute inspiration to the Lunar Muse, the oldest and most convenient European term for this source? By ancient tradition, the White Goddess becomes one with her human representative— a priestess, a prophetess, a queen-mother. No Muse-poet grows conscious of the Muse except by experience of a woman in whom the Goddess is to some degree resident; just as no Apollonian poet can perform his proper function unless he lives under a monarchy or a quasi-monarchy. A Muse-poet falls in love, absolutely, and his true love is for him the embodiment of

the Muse. As a rule, the power of absolutely falling in love soon vanishes; and, as a rule, because the woman feels embarrassed by the spell she exercises over her poet-lover and repudiates it; he, in disillusion, turns to Apollo who, at least, can provide him with a livelihood and intelligent entertainment, and reneges before his middle twenties. But the real, perpetually obsessed Muse-poet distinguishes between the Goddess as manifest in the supreme power, glory, wisdom and love of woman, and the individual woman whom the Goddess may make her instrument for a month, a year, seven years, or even more. The Goddess abides; and perhaps he will again have knowledge of her through his experience of another woman.

This is Gravesian autobiography, and as such has a certain limited authority. If the greatest poets in English include Milton, Blake, and Wordsworth, then we can imagine the grim comedy of their reactions to Graves's assurance that they were inspired by the Lunar Muse. Graves had a lifelong contempt for Milton, the butt of his nasty novel *Wife to Mr. Milton*, and had little liking also for Wordsworth, while he managed to so weakly misread Blake's *The Mental Traveller* as not to hear its horror at the dreadful cycle it depicted. "Muse-poets," as Graves describes them, are rather rare. John Keats certainly is the clearest instance of what Graves thinks he means, but that would be the Keats of *Endymion*, not the mature poet of *The Fall of Hyperion* and the great Odes. Graves's favorite lyric, Keats's "La Belle Dame sans Merci," is hardly a celebration of enchantment by the Muse, since the "wretched wight" is starving to death, and cannot be saved. But *The White Goddess*, as Keane admits, loses sight of the reality of human suffering, a loss totally un-Keatsian. Its dedicatory poem, marvelous with bravura, is the purest Graves:

In Dedication

All saints revile her, and all sober men
Ruled by the God Apollo's golden mean—
In scorn of which I sailed to find her
In distant regions likeliest to hold her
Whom I desired above all things to know,
Sister of the mirage and echo.

It was a virtue not to stay,
To go my headstrong and heroic way

Seeking her out at the volcano's head,
Among pack ice, or where the track had faded
Beyond the cavern of the seven sleepers:
Whose broad high brow was white as any leper's,
Whose eyes were blue, with rowan-berry lips,
With hair curled honey-coloured to white hips.

Green sap of Spring in the young wood a-stir
Will celebrate the Mountain Mother,
And every song-bird shout awhile for her;
But I am gifted, even in November
Rawest of seasons, with so huge a sense
Of her nakedly worn magnificence
I forget cruelty and past betrayal,
Careless of where the next bright bolt may fall.

When Graves reprinted this, under the title of "The White Goddess," as the first poem in *Poems and Satires 1951*, he changed its "I" and "my" to "we" and "our," rather ruining it, at least for me, since its point is the Keatsian assertion of poethood in one's own generation. Behind Graves is Keats's declaration to the scornful Muse, Moneta, in *The Fall of Hyperion*: "I sure should see / Other men here; but I am here alone." Yeats appropriated Keats's assertion for *A Full Moon in March*, and Yeats, as Keane rightly argues, is Graves's true rival as a Muse-poet in our century. To engage Yeats in a poetic agon simply was beyond Graves's powers, and led to some inadequate posturings, and a number of lyrics weaker than perhaps they had to be.

What survives rereading in *The White Goddess* is neither its spurious history nor its tendentious mythmaking, which increasingly seems Graves's romance with Laura Riding writ large (and according to Miss Riding, writ wrong indeed). Nor can many readers tolerate the book's interminable speculations on tree-alphabets, which read like John Ruskin gone even madder than in his weirdest phase:

The thumb of Venus is connected with the palm-tree by its sacredness to the orgiastic goddess Isis, Latona or Lat. Lat was the mother of Nabatean Dusares the vine-god, worshipped in Egypt, and the lowest consonant on the thumb was the vine.

The Jupiter-finger is connected with the furze, or gorse, by the Spring gorse-fires burned in his honour as god of shepherds.

The connexion of the Mercury-finger with the yew is made by Mercury's conducting of souls to the place presided over by the death-goddess Hecate, alias his mother Maia, to whom the yew was sacred.

Fortunately there is a very different Graves who also inhabits the mythographic chapters of *The White Goddess*. Call his an authentic religious sensibility that writes best in negation, and you have him at his strongest:

> What ails Christianity today is that it is not a religion squarely based on a single myth; it is a complex of juridical decisions made under political pressure in an ancient law-suit about religious rights between adherents of the Mother-goddess who was once supreme in the West, and those of the usurping Father-god. Different ecclesiastical courts have given different decisions, and there is no longer a supreme judicature. Now that even the Jews have been seduced into evading the Mosaic Law and whoring after false gods, the Christians have drifted farther away than ever from the ascetic holiness to which Ezekiel, his Essene successors, and Jesus, the last of the Hebrew prophets, hoped to draw the world. Though the West is still nominally Christian, we have come to be governed, in practice, by the unholy triumdivate of Pluto god of wealth, Apollo god of science, and Mercury god of thieves. To make matters worse, dissension and jealousy rage openly between these three, with Mercury and Pluto blackguarding each other, while Apollo wields the atomic bomb as if it were a thunderbolt; for since the Age of Reason was heralded by his eighteenth-century philosophers, he has seated himself on the vacant throne of Zeus (temporarily indisposed) as Triumdival Regent.

Two years before *The White Goddess* appeared, Graves published his most effective novel, *King Jesus* (1946), and eventually risked *The Nazarene Gospel Restored* (with Joshua Podro, 1953). Though the return of matriarchal religion, which is the positive program of Graves's polemic, is now a fashionable notion in certain sects and covens, Graves is not taken as a prophet by current literary feminists. His quest for his kind of historical Jesus may however prove more lasting and disturbing than his celebration of the White Goddess.

II

Graves's curious literalism, which weakens *The White Goddess* and all but a double handful of his poems, constitutes the strength of *King Jesus*. Certain that he tells us the story as it must have been, Graves persuades us at least that he has persuaded himself. Convinced that he had suspended time, Graves insisted that he had recovered the truth about Jesus, and therefore the truth about the origin and meaning of Christianity. Yet *The Nazarene Gospel Restored*, seven years after *King Jesus*, recovers a totally contrary truth, in a clean contradiction that Graves charmingly shrugged off. What *King Jesus* and the *Nazarene Gospel* have in common is a very Jewish, indeed properly Pharisaic Jesus, who takes the Law of Moses to be "sacred and immutable." Graves and Podro divide early Christianity into three factions: the Nazarenes, headed by James and the other surviving disciples of Jesus, who remained loyal to the normative Pharisees; the Alexandrians, essentially Gnostics; Paul and his Gentile churches, who circulated the slander that Jesus condemned the Pharisees rather than some charlatans pretending to be Pharisees. Whether the reader agrees with Graves and Podro that the Nazarenes, rather than the Gnostics or the triumphant Paulines, were the true Christians, is not likely to make much difference. Far more interesting is the authors' contention that Jesus survived the cross, an assertion they share with the ill-assorted literary company of George Moore, Samuel Butler, and D.H. Lawrence.

King Jesus, though hardly one of the neglected masterpieces of narrative in our time, remains far more vital than *The Nazarene Gospel Restored*. Its Jesus is a grandson of Herod the Great, which is at variance with the *Nazarene Gospel*, and indeed only can be called the Gospel according to Graves, since the Nazarenes hardly would have hailed as Messiah an abominable Edomite of the House of Herod. Yet the Herodian Jesus of Graves's novel is the only successful and attractive representation of a personality and moral character to appear anywhere in Graves's prose fiction. Claudius, though newly popular because of a recent television series, is merely a droning voice, scarcely distinguishable from Graves's own. King Jesus speaks a voice of his own, as in the dialogue with the synagogue elders of Capernaum:

> They asked him: "Do you dishonour the memory of the learned Hillel from whom we learned these 'absurd legal fictions', as you call them, these 'falsifications of the Law'?"
>
> "Hillel was a carpenter who never ceased to labour with his hands and remained a poor man to the last. If any man now pleads poverty as an excuse for not studying the Law, it is asked

of him: 'Are you poorer even than Hillel was?' He interpreted the Law in the spirit of love and laid no burden on the people that he would not himself undertake with joy. It is written that when Moses died all the men of Israel mourned for him; but at the death of Hillel, as at Aaron's death, not only men but women and children also mourned. Honouring his memory, I say: Sell your profitable business, merchants, distribute the proceeds to the poor, return to the boats and nets that you foolishly abandoned, and as you labour on the waters of the Lake remember again your duty towards your neighbour! For is it not written: 'Six days *shalt* thou labour'? And the learned Shammai, who received from Simeon son of Shetach, said: 'Love work, and hate lordship.' And others of the wise have said: 'A man should hire himself out to a stranger rather than sit idle; let him flay a carcase in the street to earn his bread rather than say: "I am a priest", or "I am a great and learned man".'"

"You are called Jesus the carpenter. Where then are your hammer, saw, chisel and mallet?"

"From a carpenter I have become a shepherd." He displayed his pastoral staff and mantle. "Let no man envy me my laborious new trade."

"And these idle disciples of yours?"

"Let no man envy them their laborious apprenticeship."

The elders took their leave of him without another word; and he received no more invitations to preach in any synagogue of Capernaum.

The vigorous, plain style is Graves at his best, and the portrayal of his Jesus carries dignity, persuasiveness, and an authentic ethical force. These are, I think, the virtues of Graves's poetry at its very best. The Muse-poems, celebrations of the sadistic and vengeful White Goddess, are less likely to live than what I take to be the best and most bitter love poems in the language since Hardy:

The Foreboding

Looking by chance in at the open window
  I saw my own self seated in his chair
With gaze abstracted, furrowed forehead,
  Unkempt hair.

I thought that I had suddenly come to die,
   That to a cold corpse this was my farewell,
Until the pen moved slowly upon paper
   And tears fell.

He had written a name, yours, in printed letters:
   One word on which bemusedly to pore
No protest, no desire, your naked name,
   Nothing more.

Would it be to-morrow, would it be next year?
   But the vision was not false, this much I knew;
And I turned angrily from the open window
   Aghast at you.

Why never a warning, either by speech or look,
   That the love you cruelly gave me could not last?
Already it was too late: the bait swallowed,
   The hook fast.

Allen Tate

(1899-1979)

I MET ALLEN TATE ONLY TWICE, AND WAS MOVED BY THE POIGNANCE OF his memories of Hart Crane, his exact contemporary and close friend. Tate's literary criticism was very much in the mode of T.S. Eliot, and I always greatly preferred Tate's own poetry to his work as a critic. Northrop Frye, reviewing Tate's collected essays, found in them what Frye called the Eliotic myth of the Great Western Butterslide, in which a grand slab of classical, Catholic, and royalist butter slides down the centuries and melts, until it congeals again in Eliot's *The Waste Land*.

Though a resolute New Critic, in Eliot's wake, Tate ultimately was as much a late Romantic poet as Eliot proved to be. Though Tate increasingly repudiated Hart Crane's *The Bridge* while hailing Eliot's *The Waste Land*, the idiom of Crane never abandoned the would-be classicist. Crane's pentameter quatrains easily can be mistaken for Tate's while Eliot's fascinating blend of Tennyson and Whitman (his true precursors) yielded a very different mode.

Tate's "Ode to the Confederate Dead" strives to be Eliotic, yet the voice of Hart Crane keeps breaking in:

> The brute curiosity of an angel's stare
> Turns you, like them, to stone,
> Transforms the heaving air
> Till plunged to a heavier world below
> You shift your sea-space blindly
> Heaving, turning like the blind crab.
>
> Dazed by the wind, only the wind
> The leaves flying, plunge

This would be at home anywhere in Crane's first volume, *White Buildings*. Even closer to Crane are the majestic quatrains that conclude "The Mediterranean", to me Tate's best poem:

> Let us lie down once more by the breathing side
> Of Ocean, where our live forefathers sleep
> As if the Known Sea still were a month wide—
> Atlantic howls but is no longer steep!
>
> What country shall we conquer, what fair land
> Unman our conquest and locate our blood?
> We've cracked the hemispheres with careless hand!
> Now, from the Gates of Hercules we flood
>
> Westward, westward till the barbarous brine
> Whelms us to the tired land where tasseling corn,
> Fat beans, grapes sweeter than muscadine
> Rot on the vine: in that land were we born.

Tate is a permanent poet, though not of the eminence either of Eliot or of Hart Crane. The savage energy of "Aeneas at Washington" is Tate's own, even if the elegiac splendor of "The Mediterranean" always returns me to the somber and stately quatrains that conclude the canto of *The Bridge* titled "The River".

Sterling A. Brown

(1901–1989)

STERLING BROWN, AT HIS FREQUENT BEST, WAS ABLE TO ASSIMILATE THE strong influences of A.E. Housman, Thomas Hardy, and Robert Frost, and to fuse them in a mode of his own. I should say "modes," for this eclectic poet had several voices, very much his own. The Frostian "Idyll" juxtaposes a sheltered woodland cranny with an intrusive hawk, and sees the deep peace return after the hawk's kill, giving the reader the burden of the final irony: "The stream purred listlessly along, / And all grew quite as peaceful as before."

In another mode developed from Hardy, Brown gives us the poignant "Rain," a remarkable transformation of the sonnet form:

> Outside the cold, cold night; the dripping rain ...
> The water gurgles loosely in the eaves,
> The savage lashes stripe the rattling pane
> And beat a tattoo on November leaves.
> The lamp wick gutters, and the last log steams
> Upon the ash-filled hearth. Chill grows the room.
> The ancient clock ticks creakily and seems
> A fitting portent of the gathering gloom.
>
> This is a night we planned. This place is where
> One day, we would be happy; where the light
> Should tint your shoulders and your wild flung hair.—
> Whence we would—oh, we planned a merry morrow—
> Recklessly part ways with the old hag, Sorrow ...
>
> Outside dripping rain; the cold, cold night.

After that wonderfully gloomy octave, there is the fine poetic shock of "This is a night we planned." The speaker is solitary, erotic loss is overwhelming, and yet everything proceeds by indirection. Thomas Hardy, with his acute sense of life's ironies, might have admired Sterling Brown's "Rain," which precedes Robert Penn Warren in reviving Hardy's spirit.

Langston Hughes

(1902–1967)

TWENTIETH-CENTURY BLACK AMERICAN LITERATURE IS SO VARIED THAT adequate critical generalization is scarcely possible, at least at this time. A literary culture that includes the fiction of Ellison and Hurston, the moral essays of Baldwin, and the extraordinary recent poetry of Jay Wright is clearly of international stature. Langston Hughes may be the most poignant and representative figure of that culture, more so even than Richard Wright. Clearly an authentic poet, Hughes nevertheless seems to lack any definitive volume to which we can turn for rereading. His best book of poems is certainly *Fine Clothes to the Jew* (1927), which retains some freshness and yet has palpable limitations. Ideological defenses of Hughes's poetry are now common and necessarily are represented in this volume. Folk traditions ranging from blues to spirituals to jazz songs to work chants to many other modes do get into Hughes's poetry, but his poems on the whole do not compare adequately to the best instances of those cultural models. Other critics find Hughes Whitmanian, but the subtle, evasive, and hermetic Whitman—still the most weakly misread even as he is the greatest of our poets—had little real effect upon Hughes's poetry. The authentic precursor was Carl Sandburg, and Hughes, alas, rarely surpassed Sandburg.

Social and political considerations, which doubtless will achieve some historical continuity, will provide something of an audience for Hughes's poetry. His first autobiography, *The Big Sea*, may be his most lasting single book, though its aesthetic values are very mixed. Rereading it, plus his second autobiography, *I Wonder as I Wander*, his *Selected Poems*, and *The Langston Hughes Reader*, I come to the sad conclusion that Hughes's principal work was his life, which is to say his literary career. This conclusion is partly founded upon the contrast between Hughes's own writings and the admirable biography by Arnold Rampersad, *The Life of Langston Hughes, Volume 1, 1902–1941* (1986). Reading Rampersad's *Life* is simply a more vivid and valuable aesthetic and human experience than reading the rather faded verse and prose of Hughes himself. Hughes's courage and his persistence made the man more crucial as a representative figure than his intrinsic strength as a writer by itself might have allowed him to have become.

Rampersad, a biographer of uncommon distinction, memorably condenses the essence of Hughes's personal vision in the fifth paragraph of his *Life*:

> As successful as his life seemed to be by its end, with honors and awards inspired by more than forty books, and the adulation of thousands of readers, Hughes's favorite phonograph record over the years, spun in his bachelor suite late into the Harlem night, remained Billie Holiday's chilly moaning of "God Bless the Child That's Got His Own." Eventually he had gotten his own, but at a stiff price. He had paid in years of nomadic loneliness and a furtive sexuality; he would die without ever having married, and without a known lover or a child. If by the end he was also famous and even beloved, Hughes knew that he had been cheated early of a richer emotional life. Parents could be so cruel! "My theory is," he wrote not long before he died, "children should be born without parents—if born they must be."

Most of Hughes's writing, like his overt stances in life, is a reaction-formation away from that origin. Rampersad's skilled devotion uncovers the trace of sorrow that moves remorselessly from a grim family romance (or lack of it) through a refusal to abide or end in alienation. The refusal may be ascribed to Hughes's profound, almost selfless love for his own people, and makes him an authentic and heroic exemplar for many subsequent black American writers. Whatever the inadequacies of Hughes's various styles, his place in literary history is an assured one.

Rampersad, in his essay on Hughes's poetic origins reprinted in this volume, shrewdly notes the mixture of will and passivity that combines in Hughes's art, and relates the passivity to Hughes's apparent asexuality. I wish only that the poetic will in Hughes had been stronger, as it was in Whitman and is now in John Ashbery and Jay Wright, among other contemporaries. What Hughes lacked, perhaps, was a sufficient sense of what Nietzsche called the will's revenge against time, and time's "It was."

Absorbing his own plangencies, Hughes chose not to take revenge upon his familial past. His pride in his family and in his race was too great for that, but what made him a hero of a pioneering black literary life may also have weakened his actual achievement as a poet. Rampersad defends Hughes by comparing him to Whitman, who also had the sense that his life was a larger poem than any he could write. But the poet of "Crossing Brooklyn Ferry" and "As I Ebb'd with the Ocean of Life" could afford that sense better than could the poet of "The Weary Blues" and "Reverie on the Harlem River."

Yet there are moments in Hughes that are unique and testify to a mode of irony almost his own. In *The Big Sea*, Hughes recalls an exchange with his friend of Harlem Renaissance days, the black writer Wallace Thurman. The brief sketch of Thurman, followed by the wise passivity of Hughes's self-revelation, is like a fragment of an art, humorous and wise, that cultural and personal circumstances did not permit Hughes to perfect. Still, it remains a strong testament:

> Wallace Thurman laughed a long bitter laugh. He was a strange kind of fellow, who liked to drink gin, but *didn't* like to drink gin; who liked being a Negro, but felt it a great handicap; who adored bohemianism, but thought it wrong to be a bohemian. He liked to waste a lot of time, but he always felt guilty wasting time. He loathed crowds, yet he hated to be alone. He almost always felt bad, yet he didn't write poetry.
>
> Once I told him if I could feel as bad as he did *all* the time, I would surely produce wonderful books. But he said you had to know how to *write*, as well as how to feel bad. I said I didn't have to know how to feel bad, because, every so often, the blues just naturally overtook me, like a blind beggar with an old guitar:
>> You don't know,
>> You don't know my mind—
>> When you see me laughin',
>> I'm laughin' to keep from cryin'.

Countee Cullen

(1903–1946)

I HAVE A PARTICULAR FONDNESS FOR COUNTEE CULLEN, AS I DO FOR Edwin Arlington Robinson, who was a benign influence upon Cullen's art, showing him how to be at once Keatsian and oneself. Like Robinson and Keats, Cullen was a highly self-conscious artist who knew that moral concerns could sink a poem without trace. Answering those who would make him only a "protest poet," Cullen eloquently prophesied for the best African American poets after him in his "To Certain Critics":

> No radical option narrows grief,
> Pain is no patriot,
> And sorrow plaits her dismal leaf
> For all as lief as not.

That wry pun upon "leaf" and "lief" is wonderfully typical of Countee Cullen, and is part of his legacy.

Pablo Neruda

(1904–1973)

IN 1930, THE YEAR THAT HART CRANE PUBLISHED *THE BRIDGE*, FEDERICO García Lorca completed the composition of his *Poet in New York*, which includes his "Ode to Walt Whitman." The "Ode to Walt Whitman" of Pablo Neruda was written much later, in 1956, and has very little in common with Lorca's poem, a difference surely deliberate on Neruda's part. Lorca's English, at least in 1930, was nonexistent, and his Walt Whitman was a marvelous phantasmagoria. Neruda translated Whitman, and in some ways knew Whitman, and how Whitman influenced other poets, better than some of Neruda's best exegetes have known. Not that Neruda's "Ode to Walt Whitman" is a good poem, but then paradoxically it is one of his least Whitmanian poems. Insofar as I can judge, Neruda is not only a poet of extraordinarily diverse styles, but of very mixed achievement, ranging from bathos to the high Sublime. Whatever the reader's political sympathies, the last phases of Neruda's life, personal and political, and of his poetry, possess a noble pathos, constantly augmented for us by the hideous survival of the barbaric regime that came into power by murdering Allende, and sacking the home and possessions of the dying national poet. Neruda's directly political poetry, even in much of his *Canto general* (1950), some day may be judged as a generous error, human and humane, but aesthetically inadequate. His later political poetry seems to me scarcely readable, but that is the usual fate of nearly all political poetry of any century. Very little American poetry written in English, and that is overtly political, has survived, or is likely still to join the canon. There is Emerson's fine Channing Ode, written against the Mexican War, and William Vaughn Moody's "An Ode in Time of Hesitation," concerning our land-grab in the Spanish-American War. The poems inspired by our Vietnamese debacle are themselves an aesthetic debacle, as is so much current verse of an ideological kind, reflecting the various passions of our composite School of Resentment. No Victor Hugo has come out of us in North, South, or Central America, or the islands of the Caribbean. American political poetry is perhaps too belated, and Neruda is hardly an exception, nor ought he to have been.

Walt Whitman, despite the ways all too many lame verse writers attempt to see him, was not the ancestor of Allen Ginsberg and other contemporary shamans. Whitman, at his most Sublime, is an immensely difficult and hermetic poet: subtle, evasive, ineluctable, withdrawn, defensive, shy, and endlessly metamorphic. His truest poetic descendants were Wallace Stevens and T.S. Eliot, each of whom repressed him, but the return of the repressed poetic father, partly in the son's own colors, produced their finest poetry. True, deep, poetic influence, a matter I have studied obsessively all my life and attempted to think through as that one thought each of us can hope to think, seems to me to depend upon unconscious or purposive forgetting. As such, it tends to take place in the language in which the poet actually writes his own mature poems. America is not Europe, but American English is also not American Spanish, and Whitman therefore is not the actual precursor of Neruda or Borges, Vallejo or Paz. Whitman is the strongest American poet, and the major figure in American Romanticism, but his language is the language of Shakespeare and of the English Bible. Hispanic poetry, like French, came to Romanticism belatedly, and until our century rather weakly. That must be anyone's impression, but I rely here upon *Children of the Mire* by Octavio Paz, and upon the recent criticism of Roberto González Echevarría, particularly his essay on Nicolás Guillén and the Baroque. The strong Spanish poets before our century were Quevedo, Góngora, and Calderón, a very different grouping from the English line of Chaucer, Spenser, Shakespeare, and Milton, and the descendants of that great fourfold in the High Romantics: Blake, Wordsworth, Shelley and Keats in England, Whitman and Dickinson in America. Neruda's crucial turn, to Blake and Whitman, was clearly an almost desperate effort to find what the Spanish tradition could not give him. Yet Quevedo and not Whitman is clearly his true ancestor, just as his near precursor, who caused him some discomfort, was Vicente Huidobro. T.S. Eliot tried to find ancestors in Dante, Baudelaire, even the rather minor Laforgue, yet remained always the child of Whitman and Tennyson. Neruda's case of poetic influence was not wholly dissimilar.

Neruda, excessive and expressionistic, overtly rhetorical, necessarily delighted in Quevedo, a poet neither Blakean nor Whitmanian. González Echevarría catches the precise dilemma of Neruda's poetic stance, as the

critic sets the background for his own investigation into the poetics of
Afro-Antilleanism in Nicolás Guillén:

> A central feature of that revision is a return to the Baroque, that
> is to say, to the work of the major poets of the language,
> Góngora, Quevedo, and Calderón, and to the Baroque aesthet-
> ics formulated by Baltasar Gracián. The inversion of the con-
> cept of representation from mimesis to expression envisioned
> by the Romantics was already implicit in the Spanish Baroque.
> As the Spanish and Spanish-American Romantics were a mere
> echo of their European counterparts, the great Hispanic poets
> of the avant-garde had to search for their poetic foundation not
> in the Romantics, as their English and German counterparts
> did, but in the Baroque. While it is a commonplace of Spanish
> literary history to say that the Generation of '27 in Spain
> looked to Góngora for inspiration, the fact is that the revision
> which brought about Góngora's rediscovery began in Spanish
> America with the *modernistas*—José Martí and Rubén Darío in
> particular—and continued in the writings of the Mexican
> Alfonso Reyes during the teens. It also has not been made suf-
> ficiently clear that both the Spanish-American and the Spanish
> writers looked to the Baroque poets because there were no
> Spanish language romantics worthy of rediscovery or rejection:
> no Goethe, no Coleridge, no Wordsworth, no Schiller, no
> Leopardi, only Espronceda, Bécquer, and in Spanish America
> Heredia, Echeverría, all minor poets, no matter how much we
> strain to find traces of originality in their works. The great
> Spanish-language poetic tradition that begins with the *mod-*
> *ernistas* and makes yet another start in the twenties with the
> Generation of '27 has as foundation a rewriting of the
> Baroques.

Implicit here is a realization that runs counter to the overt assumptions of Formalist, Anglo-American literary Modernism: productively
accepted contingency must come out of the poetic traditions of one's own
language. We cannot choose those whom we are free to love, and poets
cannot choose their own precursors. Overdetermination may be much the
same process in the erotic and the literary realms. We demand liberty in
both, and yet we must compound with the past in both. And in neither
past do we confront the universal, but always what is closest at or to home.
In Neruda, the place to discover what was closest is in his *Memoirs*

(posthumously published, 1974; translated into English by Hardie St. Martin, 1977).

An aspiring poet by the age of six, if we are to credit his account, Neruda had a memory (or a fantasy) of his first poem that is a very dark version of the Enlightenment myth of the birth of what then was called the Poetic Character:

> I have often been asked when I wrote my first poem, when poetry was born in me.
>
> I'll try to remember. Once, far back in my childhood, when I had barely learned to read, I felt an intense emotion and set down a few words, half rhymed but strange to me, different from everyday language. Overcome by a deep anxiety, something I had not experienced before, a kind of anguish and sadness, I wrote them neatly on a piece of paper. It was a poem to my mother, that is, to the one I knew, the angelic stepmother whose gentle shadow watched over my childhood. I had no way at all of judging my first composition, which I took to my parents.
>
> They were in the dining room, immersed in one of those hushed conversations that, more than a river, separate the world of children and the world of grownups. Still trembling after this first visit from the muse, I held out to them the paper with the lines of verse. My father took it absentmindedly, read it absentmindedly, and returned it to me absentmindedly, saying: "Where did you copy this from?" Then he went on talking to my mother in a lowered voice about his important and remote affairs.
>
> That, I seem to remember, was how my first poem was born, and that was how I had my first sample of irresponsible literary criticism.

Like Whitman before him, Neruda came to associate the genesis of his poetry with the death of the father. Lincoln, particularly in the magnificent elegy, "When Lilacs Last in the Dooryard Bloom'd," became a surrogate father for Whitman, as Neruda understood, and that was Neruda's own placement of Walt Whitman, a knowing substitution of the greatest poet of the Western Hemisphere for José del Carmen Reyes, the trainman, the first and most important of Neruda's irresponsible literary critics. The "deep anxiety ... a kind of anguish and sadness" testifies to what might be called a Primal Scene of Instruction, in which the poem to the mother meets the father's indifference, and a second narcissistic, scar is formed.

Neruda's poem, "The Father," hardly can be termed an elegy, and its
fiercely effective conclusion chills the reader:

Mi pobre padre duro
allí estaba, en el eje de la vida,
la viril amistad, la copa llena.
Su vida fue una rápida milicia
y entre su madrugar y sus caminos,
entre llegar para salir corriendo,
un dia con más lluvia que otros dias
el conductor José del Carmen Reyes
subio al tren de la muerte y hasta ahora no ha vuelto.

(My poor, hard father,
there he was at the axis of existence,
virile in friendship, his glass full.
His life was a running campaign,
and between his early risings and his traveling,
between arriving and rushing off,
one day, rainier than other days,
the railwayman, Jose del Carmen Reyes,
climbed aboard the train of death, and so far has not come back.)
(tr. Alastair Reid)

The irony, as Neruda must have known, is that the hard father was the
best gift that the poet's genius could have received, just as the substitution of the
figure of Whitman as idealized father must be a knowing irony also. Frank
Menchaca shrewdly observes that: "Neruda also must have understood that the
self which claims to be everywhere freely available in Whitman's poetry is
nowhere to be found." The sublime evasions that constitute *Song of Myself* offer
Whitman to everyone, and on what do not seem to be Whitman's own terms,
though they are. This is the phenomenon that Doris Sommer wittily terms
"supplying demand" in her essay on the fatherhood of Whitman in Neruda,
Borges, and Paz. She argues that: "Neruda's admiration for the master may have
displaced Whitman's narcissism with love for others; but ... ironically, by re-
placing self-love with the hierarchy-producing secondary narcissism of hero
worship." I think Sommer describes part of the normal process of poetic influence, and I myself would suggest that Borges and Paz, lesser poets than Neruda
(though Borges is of similar eminence in his fictions, and Paz as a man-of-letters), actually benefited more from Whitman because they understood him far
less well than Neruda did. An idealized father is best misunderstood.

Neruda's misreadings (in what I think I can call the Bloomian sense) of Whitman were creative only when they were deliberate, a process that Sommer again depicts accurately:

> Ironically, an heir such as Pablo Neruda seems indifferent to the problem; he will destroy his teacher by resuscitating older models that never even tempted the reader with a promise of equality and the like of whom Whitman had kissed off in the Preface to his poems. Neruda's colossal *Canto general* (1950) writes in and closes off the spaces for the poet's interlocutor by returning the model of America's new fragmented "epic" to a familiar tradition of apparently seamless romantic narrative. It sets Whitman's rawness right; it tames the earlier and more revolutionary aesthetic until what is left of Whitman is the figure of the father, something Whitman claimed he never wanted to be. Neruda thus reaffirms the political usefulness of representative romance over a poetry of "pure possibility" and reestablishes the hierarchy of poet over people that Whitman had managed (however briefly) to level.

I disagree only with "Whitman's rawness," since that is merely Whitman's deception of his reader; no poetry could be more delicate and finished, while pretending to be tough and raw, and *Canto general* is far rawer than Whitman even pretends to be. Compare to the end of *Song of Myself* the conclusion of *The Heights of Macchu Picchu*, the crown of *Canto general*:

> contadme todo, cadena a cadena,
> eslabón a eslabón, y paso a Paso,
> afilad los cuchillos que guardasteis,
> ponedlos en mi pecho y en mi mano,
> como un río de rayos amarillos,
> como un río de tigres enterrados,
> y dejadme llorar, horas, días, años,
> edades ciegas, siglos estelares.
>
> Dadme el silencio, el agua, la esperanza.
>
> Dadme la lucha, el hierro, los volcanes.
>
> Apegadme los cuerpos como imanes.

Acudid a mis venas y a mi boca.

Hablad por mis palabras y mi sangre.

(tell me everything, chain by chain,
link by link, and step by step,
file the knives you kept by you,
drive them into my chest and my hand
like a river of riving yellow light,
like a river where buried jaguars lie,
and let me weep, hours, days, years,
blind ages, stellar centuries.

Give me silence, water, hope.

Give me struggle, iron, volcanoes.

Fasten your bodies to me like magnets.

Hasten to my veins to my mouth.

Speak through my words and my blood.)
(tr. John Felstiner)

Like Whitman, Neruda addresses the multitudes, multitudes in the valley of decision. His expressionistic tropes are true to the High Baroque: river of light, buried jaguars, "struggle, iron, volcanoes," and the dead workmen magnetizing Neruda's language and the very drives within him. This is intensely moving, but perhaps rather strenuous when juxtaposed to the quiet authority of our father, Walt Whitman:

I depart as air.... I shake my white locks at the runaway sun,
I effuse my flesh in eddies and drift it in lacy jags.
I bequeath myself to the dirt to grow from the grass I love,
If you want me again look for me under your bootsoles.

You will hardly know who I am or what I mean,
But I shall be good health to you nevertheless,
And filter and fibre your blood.

Failing to fetch me at first keep encouraged,

Missing me one place search another,
I stop some where waiting for you.

Walt is out there, up ahead of us, but patiently waiting, somewhere. The reader is anxious to catch up, but Walt is beyond anxiety, since he is early, while the reader is belated: "Will you speak before I am gone? Will you prove already too late?" At the close of *Heights of Macchu Picchu*, we wonder if the poet is not oppressed by belatedness, even as he urges the dead workers to speak through him. But Neruda, who meditated upon Whitman throughout a lifetime, learned the lesson beautifully, in the superb Whitmanian conclusion of his justly famous poem, "The People":

Por eso nadie se moleste cuando
parece que estoy solo y no estoy solo,
no estoy con nadie y hablo para todos:

Alguien me está escuchando y no to saben,
pero aquellos que canto y que to saben
siguen naciendo y llenarán el mundo.

(So let no one be perturbed when
I seem to be alone and am not alone;
I am not without company and I speak for all.

Someone is hearing me without knowing it,
but those I sing of, those who know,
go on being born and will overflow the world.)
(tr. Alastair Reid)

The direct model is clearly the two uncanny tercets that end *Song of Myself*. I might not have believed anyone could come so close to Whitman's splendor as Neruda does here, in a poetic act at once bold and generous. Whitman's grand closure is superbly interpreted by Neruda's self-valediction. Neruda and Whitman together seem to be alone and are not alone; they keep each other company and each speaks for all. Someone among us, or within us, is hearing Neruda and Whitman without knowing it, without knowing who they are, but they are good health to us nevertheless. Here, at least, Neruda too stops somewhere waiting for us.

Robert Penn Warren

(1905–1989)

ROBERT PENN WARREN, BORN APRIL 24, 1905, IN GUTHRIE, KENTUCKY, AT
the age of eighty is our most eminent man of letters. That truism is vital-
ized by his extraordinary persistence of development into a great poet. A
reader thinks of the handful of poets triumphant in their later or last phases: Browning, Hardy, Yeats, Stevens, Warren. Indeed, "Myth of Mountain
Sunrise," the final poem among the new work in the fifth Warren *Selected
Poems*, will remind some readers of Browning's marvelous "Prologue" to
Asolando, written when the poet was seventy-seven. Thinking back fifty
years to the first time he saw Asolo (a village near Venice), Browning burns
through every sense of loss into a final transcendence:

> How many a year, my Asolo,
> Since—one step just from sea to land—
> I found you, loved yet feared you so—
> For natural objects seemed to stand
> Palpably fire-clothed! No—

"God is it who transcends," Browning ends by asserting. Warren,
older even than Browning, ruggedly remains the poet of immanence, of
something indwelling and pervasive, though not necessarily sustaining, that
can be sensed in a mountain sunrise:

> The curdling agony of interred dark strives dayward, in stone
> strives though
> No light here enters, has ever entered but
> In ageless age of primal flame. But look! All mountains want
> slow-

ly to bulge outward extremely. The leaf, whetted on light, will cut
Air like butter. Leaf cries: "I feel my deepest filament in dark rejoice.
I know the density of basalt has a voice."

Two primal flames, Browning's and Warren's, but at the close of
"Myth of Mountain Sunrise" we receive not "God is it who transcends,"
but: "The sun blazes over the peak. That will be the old tale told." The
epigraph to the new section of this *Selected Poems* is from Warren's favorite
theologian, St. Augustine: "Will ye not now after that life is descended
down to you, will not you ascend up to it and live?" One remembers another epigraph Warren took from the *Confessions*, for the book of poems *Being
Here* (1980): "I thirst to know the power and nature of time." Warren now
has that knowledge, and his recent poems show him ascending up to living
in the present, in the real presence of time's cumulative power. Perhaps no
single new poem here quite matches the extraordinary group of visions and
meditations by Warren that includes "Red-Tail Hawk and Pyre of Youth,"
"Heart of Autumn," "Evening Hawk," "Birth of Love," "The Leaf,"
"Mortmain," "To a Little Girl, One Year Old, in a Ruined Fortress" and so
many more. But the combined strength of the eighty-five pages of new
poems that Warren aptly calls *Altitudes and Extensions* is remarkable, and
indeed extends the altitudes at which our last poet of the Sublime continues to live, move and have his being.

II

Warren's first book was *John Brown: The Making of a Martyr* (1929).
I have just read it, for the first time, and discovered, without surprise, that
it made me very unhappy. The book purports to be history, but is Southern
fiction of Allen Tate's ideology, and portrays Brown as a murderous
nihilist, fit hero for Ralph Waldo Emerson. Indeed I find it difficult to
decide, after suffering the book, whether the young Warren loathed Brown
or Emerson more. Evidently, both Brown and his intellectual supporter
seemed, to Warren, instances of an emptiness making ruthless and passionate attempts to prove itself a fullness. But *John Brown*, if read as a first
fiction, does presage the Warren of *Night Rider* (1939), his first published
novel, which I have just re-read with great pleasure.

Night Rider is an exciting and remorseless narrative, wholly characteristic of what were to be Warren's prime virtues as a novelist: good story-
telling and intensely dramatic unfolding of the moral character of his
doom-eager men and women. Mr. Munn, upon whom *Night Rider* centers,
is as splendidly unsympathetic as the true Warren heroes continued to be:

Jerry Calhoun and Slim Sarrett in *At Heaven's Gate* (1943), Jack Burden and Willie Stark in *All the King's Men* (1946), Jeremiah Beaumont and Cassius Fort in *World Enough and Time* (1950). When Warren's crucial personages turned more amiable, starting with poor Amanda Starr in *Band of Angels* (1955), the books alas turned much less interesting. This unfortunate phenomenon culminated in Warren's last novel (so far), *A Place to Come To* (1977), which Warren himself ranks with *All the King's Men* and *World Enough and Time*. I wish I could agree, but re-reading *A Place to Come To* confirms an earlier impression that Warren likes his hero, Jed Tewksbury, rather too much. Without some real moral distaste to goad him, Warren tends to lose his narrative drive. I find myself wishing that Tewksbury had in him a touch of what might be called Original John Brown.

Warren's true precursor, as a novelist, was not Faulkner but Conrad, the dominant influence upon so many of the significant American novelists of Warren's generation. In one of his best critical essays, written in 1951 on Conrad's *Nostromo*, Warren gave an unknowing clue as to why all his own best work, as a novelist, already was over:

> There is another discrepancy, or apparent discrepancy, that we must confront in any serious consideration of Conrad—that between his professions of skepticism and his professions of faith ...
>
> Cold unconcern, an "attitude of perfect indifference" is, as he says in the letter to Galsworthy, "the part of creative power." But this is the same Conrad who speaks of Fidelity and the human communion, and who makes Kurtz cry out in the last horror and Heyst come to his vision of meaning in life. And this is the same Conrad who makes Marlow of "Heart of Darkness" say that what redeems is the "idea only" ...
>
> It is not some, but all, men who must serve the "idea." The lowest and the most vile creature must, in some way, idealize his existence in order to exist, and must find sanctions outside himself ...

Warren calls this a reading of Conrad's dual temperament, skepticism struggling with a last-ditch idealism, and remarks, much in T.S. Eliot's spirit:

> We must sometimes force ourselves to remember that the act of creation is not simply a projection of temperament, but a criticism and a purging of temperament.

This New Critical shibboleth becomes wholly Eliotic if we substitute the word "personality" for the word "temperament." As an analysis of Conrad's dramatism in his best novels, and in *Nostromo* in particular, this has distinction, but Warren is not Conrad, and like his poetic and critical precursor, Eliot, Warren creates by projecting temperament, not by purging it. There is no "cold unconcern," no "attitude of perfect indifference," no escape from personality in Eliot, and even more nakedly Warren's novels and poems continually reveal his passions, prejudices, convictions. Conrad is majestically enigmatic, beyond ideology; Warren, like Eliot, is an ideologue, and his temperament is far more ferocious than Eliot's.

What Warren accurately praises in Conrad is not to be found in Warren's own novels, with the single exception of *All the King's Men*, which does balance skepticism against belief just adroitly enough to ward off Warren's moralism. *World Enough and Time*, Warren's last stand as a major novelist, is an exuberant work marred finally by the author's singular fury at his own creatures. As a person who forgives himself nothing, Warren abandons the Conradian skepticism and proceeds to forgive his hero and heroine nothing. Re-reading *World Enough and Time*, I wince repeatedly at what the novelist inflicts upon Jeremiah Beaumont and Rachel Jordan. Warren, rather like the Gnostics' parody of Jehovah, punishes his Adam and Eve by denying them honorable or romantic deaths. Their joint suicide drug turns into an emetic, and every kind of degradation subsequently is heaped upon them. Warren, a superb ironist, nevertheless so loves the world that he will forgive it nothing, a stance more pragmatically available to a poet than to a novelist.

III

Warren's poetry began in the Modernist revival of the Metaphysical mode, as a kind of blend of Eliot's *The Waste Land* with the gentler ironies of Warren's own teacher at Vanderbilt, John Crowe Ransom. This phase of the poetry took Warren up to 1943, and then came to an impasse and, for a decade, an absolute stop. *At Heaven's Gate*, *All the King's Men* and *World Enough and Time* belong to that silent poetic decade, and perhaps the major sequence of his fiction usurped Warren's greater gift. But he was certainly unhappy in the later stages of his first marriage, which ended in divorce in 1950, and it cannot be accidental that his poetry fully resumed in the late summer of 1954, two years after his marriage to the writer Eleanor Clark, and a year after the birth of his daughter, the accomplished poet Rosanna Warren.

The book-length poem, *Brother to Dragons* (1953, revised version

1979), formally began Warren's return to verse, and is undoubtedly a work of considerable dramatic power. I confess to admiring it only reluctantly and dubiously, ever since 1953, because its ideological ferocity is unsurpassed even elsewhere in Warren. Much improved in revision, it remains unnerving, particularly if the reader, like myself, longs to follow Emerson in forgiving himself, if not everything, then at least as much as possible. But Warren—unlike Emerson, Nietzsche, Yeats—does not wish us to cast out remorse. Like his then master Eliot, though in a more secular way, Warren was by no means reluctant to remind us that we *are* Original Sin. *Brother to Dragons* is rendered no weaker by its extraordinary tendentiousness, but is not necessarily persuasive, if you happen not to share its moral convictions.

Warren's shorter poems, his lyrics and meditations, evolved impressively through three subsequent volumes: *Promises* (1957), *You, Emperors and Others* (1960) and a *Selected Poems* (1966), where the new work was grouped as *Tale of Time*. I recall purchasing these volumes, reading them with grudging respect, and concluding that Warren was turning into a poet rather like Melville (whom he was to edit in a *Selected Poems of Herman Melville*, in 1970) or the earlier Hardy. Warren's poems of 1934 through 1966 seemed interestingly ungainly in form, highly individual in genre and rhetoric, and not fundamentally a departure from Eliot's High Modernist mode. A poetry of belief, I would have judged, rather dismissively, and not of overwhelming concern if a reader was devoted to Hart Crane and Wallace Stevens, and to contemporary volumes such as Elizabeth Bishop's *Questions of Travel* (1965) and John Ashbery's *Rivers and Mountains* (1967). I could not foresee the astonishing breakthrough that Warren, already past the age of sixty, was about to accomplish with *Incarnations* (1968) and *Audubon: A Vision* (1969). Other critics of Warren's poetry see more continuity in its development than I do. But in 1968 I was a belated convert, transported against my will by reading *Incarnations*, and able at least to offer the testimony of a very reluctant believer in a poetic greatness now become indisputable and maintained by Warren throughout these nearly two decades since he began to write the poems of *Incarnations* in 1966.

IV

Incarnations opens with a closely connected sequence of fifteen poems called *Island of Summer*, which is the volume's glory. Unfortunately, Warren has included only five of these in his new *Selected Poems*, but they are the best of a strong group, and I will discuss only those five here, since Warren subtly has created a new sequence or a condensed *Island of*

Summer. Like the original work, the sequence is a drama of poetic incarnation, or the death and rebirth of Warren's poethood. In what is now the opening meditation, "Where the Slow Fig's Purple Sloth," Warren associates the fig with fallen human consciousness and so with an awareness of mortality:

> When you
> Split the fig, you will see
> Lifting from the coarse and purple seed, its
> Flesh like flame, purer
> Than blood.
> It fills
> The darkening room with light.

This hard, substantive riddling style is now pure Warren, and has very little in common with the Eliotic evocations of his earlier verse. "Riddle in the Garden" even more oddly associates fruits, peach and plum, with negative human yearnings, suicidal and painful, and with a horror of inwardness. A violent confrontation, "The Red Mullet," juxtaposes the swimming poet and the great fish, eye to eye, in a scene where "vision is armor, he sees and does not / Forgive." In a subsequent vision of "Masts of Dawn," the optical effect of how "The masts go white slow, as light, like dew, from darkness / Condensed on them" leads to what in some other poet might be an epiphany, but here becomes a rather desperate self-admonition, less ironic than it sounds: "We must try / To love so well the world that we may believe, in the end, in God." This reversed Augustinianism preludes an overwhelming conflagration of Warren's poetic powers in the most ambitious poem he has yet written, "The Leaf."

When he was fifteen, Warren was blinded in one eye by a sharp stone playfully thrown by a younger brother, who did not see that Warren was lying down on the other side of a hedge. Only after graduating from Vanderbilt, did Warren get round to having the ruined eye removed and replaced by a glass eye. Until then, the young poet suffered the constant fear of sympathetic blindness in his good eye. There may be some complex relation between that past fear and Warren's most remarkable and prevalent metaphor of redemption, which is to associate poetic vision both with a hawk's vision and with a sunset hawk's flight. This trope has appeared with increasing frequency in Warren's poetry for more than half a century and even invades the novels. So, in *A Place to Come To*, Jed Tewksbury endures the same vision as he loses consciousness after being stabbed:

I remember thinking how beautiful, how redemptive, all
seemed. It was as though I loved him. I thought how beautifully he had moved, like Ephraim, like a hawk in sunset flight. I
thought how all the world was justified in that moment.

"The Leaf" centers itself upon the image of a hawk's redemptive
flight, with the difference from earlier Warren being in the nature of the
redemption. Opening with a renewed vision of the fig as emblem of human
mortality and guilt, and of "the flaming mullet" as an encounter in the
depths, the poem proceeds to an episode of shamanistic force:

> Near the nesting place of the hawk, among
> Snag-rock, high on the cliff, I have seen
> The clutter of annual bones, of hare, vole, bird, white
>
> As chalk from sun and season, frail
> As the dry grass stem. On that
>
> High place of stone I have lain down, the sun
> Beat, the small exacerbation
> Of dry bones was what my back, shirtless and bare, knew. I saw
>
> The hawk shudder in the high sky, he shudders
> To hold position in the blazing wind, in relation to
> The firmament, he shudders and the world is a metaphor, his eye
> Sees, white, the flicker of hare-scut, the movement of vole.
>
> Distance is nothing, there is no solution, I
> Have: opened my mouth to the wind of the world like wine, I wanted
> To taste what the world wind dried up
>
> The live saliva of my tongue, my tongue
> Was like a dry leaf in my mouth.

Nothing in Warren's earlier poetry matches this in dramatic intensity, or in the accents of inevitability, as the poetic character is reincarnated
in him by his sacrificial self-offering "near the nesting place of the hawk."
Much of Warren's earlier guilt and sorrow comes together here, with beautiful implicitness: the fear of blindness, the decade of poetic silence, the failure of the first marriage, and most mysteriously, a personal guilt at poetic
origins. The mystery is partly clarified in the poem's next movement:

The world is fruitful, In this heat
The plum, black yet bough-bound, bursts, and the gold ooze is,
Of bees, joy, the gold ooze has striven
Outward, it wants again to be of
The goldness of air and—blessedly—innocent. The grape
Weakens at the juncture of the stem. The world

Is fruitful, and I, too,
In that I am the father
Of my father's father's father. I,
Of my father, have set the teeth on edge. But
By what grape? I have cried out in the night.

From a further garden, from the shade of another tree,
My father's voice, in the moment when the cicada ceases, has
     called to me.

Warren's father had died in 1955, at the age of eighty-six. Robert
Franklin Warren, who wanted above everything to be a poet, became a
banker instead, solely to support not only his own children, but also a family of young children bequeathed to him by his own father, who had married again and then died. Reflecting upon all this, Warren has said: "It's as
if I've stolen my father's life," somberly adding: "If he had had the opportunity I did, with his intelligence and energy, he'd have done a lot better
than I did."

This is probably part of the sorrow heard in: "I, / Of my father, have
set the teeth on edge." Experientially, it would be the larger part, but imaginatively it may yield to the burden of a more strictly poetic inheritance,
the Eliotic influence, which Warren almost involuntarily here disavows
and surmounts. Eliot's "not the cicada" from *The Waste Land* becomes here
the moment when Eliot's presence in Warren's voice ceases, to be replaced
by the poetic voice that Robert Franklin Warren had to abandon. The
return of the father's voice becomes the blessing of Warren's new style, the
gift given by Warren in his father's name. By reversing the Biblical trope
from Jeremiah 31:29–30, in which the children's teeth are set on edge,
Warren ironically celebrates the harshness of his new style:

The voice blesses me for the only
Gift I have given: *teeth set on edge*.

In the momentary silence of the cicada,

I can hear the appalling speed,
In space beyond stars, of
Light. It is

A sound like wind.

From this poem on, Warren rarely falters, whether in *Audubon: A Vision* or in the half dozen books of shorter poems (or new sections in selected volumes) that have followed. The achievement throughout these books necessarily is mixed, but there are several scores of poems that manifest all the stigmata of permanence.

V

I want to look at. just one of these poems, because it raises again, for me and for others, the ancient problem of poetry and belief. The poem is "A Way to Love God" from *Can I See Arcturus From Where I Stand?*, the sheaf of new poems in the *Selected Poems* before the one under review. I quote only the poem's final vision, which is no grislier than the ones preceding it:

But I had forgotten to mention an upland
Of wind-tortured stone white in darkness, and tall, but when
No wind, mist gathers, and once on the Sarré at midnight,
I watched the sheep huddling. Their eyes

Stared into nothingness. In that mist-diffused light their eyes
Were stupid and round like the eyes of fat fish in muddy water,
Or of a scholar who has lost faith in his calling.

Their jaws did not move. Shreds
Of dry grass, gray in gray mist-light, hung
From the side of a jaw, unmoving.

You would think that nothing would ever again happen.

That may be a way to love God.

By loving God, Warren always appears to mean loving the truth, in all its dreadfulness. This is an ancient polemic in all his work, poetry and prose, and does not beg the questions of truth but rather asserts a necessarily personal conviction as to the truth. Warren, despite the critical

efforts of his more pious exegetes, is a skeptic and not a believer, but a
Bible-soaked skeptic. His way of loving God is to forgive himself nothing,
and to forgive God nothing. The aesthetic consequences of this stance, in
a poetry written since 1966, seem to me wholly admirable, while the spiritual grimness involved remains a formidable challenge for many readers,
myself among them. Missing from this new *Selected Poems* is a notorious
sequence, "Homage to Emerson, On Night Flight to New York," to be
found in the *Tale of Time* section of *Selected Poems: 1923–1975*. I don't
regret its deletion, but it has a cognitive value in clarifying Warren's lifelong distaste for Emerson. Here is its first part, "His Smile":

> Over Peoria we lost the sun:
> The earth, by snow like sputum smeared, slides
> Westward. Those fields in the last light gleam. Emerson—
>
> The essays, on my lap, lie. A finger
> Of light, in our pressurized gloom, strikes down,
> Like God, to poke the page, the page glows. There is
> No sin. Not even error. Night,
>
> On the glass at my right shoulder, hisses
> Like sand from a sand-blast, but
> The hiss is a sound. that only a dog's
> Ear could catch, or the human heart. My heart
>
> Is as abstract as an empty
> Coca-Cola bottle. It whistles with speed.
> It whines in that ammoniac blast caused by
> The passages of stars, for
> At 38,000 feet Emerson
>
> Is dead right. His smile
> Was sweet as he walked in the greenwood.
> He walked lightly, his toes out, his body
> Swaying in the dappled shade, and
> His smile never withered a violet. He
>
> Did not even know the violet's name, not having
> Been introduced, but he bowed, smiling,
> For he had forgiven God everything, even the violet.

When I was a boy I had a wart on the right forefinger.

The final line is perhaps redundant, since the entire poem vigorously thrashes Emerson for his supposedly deficient sense of fact. Accusing Emerson of an abstract heart is not original with Warren, but I wince properly at the effective anti-transcendentalism of: "At 38,000 feet Emerson / Is dead right." At ground level, I believe Emerson to be dead right also. "His Smile" is a good polemic, and should be admired as such. The vexed issue of poetry and belief rises rather when I re-read a poem like "A Way to Love God," which is a sublime nightmare from my perspective, but a truth from Warren's. A secularized conviction of sin, guilt, and error is an obsessive strand in all of Warren's work, and for him it helps constitute a stance which is more than rhetorical. However, the effect is only to increase his *otherness*, the rich strangeness of a kind of poetic strength wholly different from the best living poets of my own generation: Ashbery, Merrill, Ammons and others, and from their precursor, Stevens.

Ideological ferocity never abandons Warren, but he passionately dramatizes it, and he has developed an idiom for it that is now entirely his own. He would appear to be, as I have intimated elsewhere, a sunset hawk at the end of a great tradition. I doubt that we will ever again have a poet who can authenticate so heroic a stance. He has earned, many times over, his series of self-identifications with aspects of the truth. The second new poem in the *Selected Poems*, "Mortal Limit," is a sonnet celebrating again his great image of the hawk:

> I saw the hawk ride updraft in the sunset over Wyoming.
> It rose from coniferous darkness, past gray jags
> Of mercilessness, past whiteness, into the gloaming
> Of dream-spectral light above the last purity of snow-snags.
>
> There—west—were the Tetons. Snow-peaks would soon be
> In dark profile to break constellations. Beyond what height
> Hangs now the black speck? Beyond what range will gold eyes see
> New ranges rise to mark a last scrawl of light?
>
> Or, having tasted that atmosphere's thinness, does it
> Hang motionless in dying vision before
> It knows it will accept the mortal limit.
> And swing into the great circular downwardness that will restore

The breath of earth? Of rock? Of rot? Of other such
Items, and the darkness of whatever dream we clutch?

So long as he abides, there will be someone capable of asking that grand and unanswerable question: "Beyond what range will gold eyes see / New ranges rise to mark a last scrawl of light?"

W.H. Auden

(1907–1973)

> Attacking bad books is not only a waste of time but also bad for the character.
>
> —AUDEN

> While an author is yet living we estimate his powers by his worst performance, and when he is dead we rate them by his best.
>
> —JOHNSON

SECONDARY WORLDS IS A BAD BOOK, AND AUDEN'S WORST PERFORMANCE. These four lectures in memory of T.S. Eliot deal in turn with *Thomas Cranmer*, a pious verse drama by Charles Williams; Icelandic sagas; the three opera libretti by Auden and Chester Kallman; the relation between Christian belief and the writing of poetry. Since the title, *Secondary Worlds*, refers to works of art as against "the primary world of our everyday social experience," the rationale for printing these four talks as a book must be their linked relevance to what has long been Auden's overt polemic against the Romantic view of poetry. Coleridge's ill-chosen terms, Primary and Secondary Imagination, are here subverted by Auden's wit, since by secondary Auden, unlike Coleridge, does mean "inferior."

Of all Auden's writings, *Secondary Worlds* comes most directly out of the neo-Christian matrix of modern Anglo-Catholic letters: Eliot, Williams, C.S. Lewis, Tolkien. I search in vain only for references to Dorothy Sayers. Auden comp ensates with a quotation from *The Future of Belief*, by Leslie Dewart, a book one might not otherwise know:

> The Christian God is not *both* transcendent and immanent. He is a reality other than being Who is present to being, by which presence He makes being to be.

"To believe this," Auden modestly says, "is to call into question the art of poetry and all the arts." In *The Dyer's Hand*, an admirable performance, Auden remarked that "the imagination is a natural human faculty and therefore retains the same character whatever a man believes." In his new book, the imagination of a humane man-of-letters and talented comic poet appears to be hardening, which would be a loss.

Johnson definitively stated the difficulties of devotional verse when he observed that the good and evil of Eternity were too ponderous for the wings of wit. The mind sinks under them, and must be content with calm belief and humble adoration, attitudes admirable in themselves but perhaps not conducive to the writing of poems. One of Auden's many virtues is that, unlike Eliot and other literary Christians, he has spared us, and mostly refrained from devotional verse. *For the Time Being*, a work dear to many churchwardenly critics, is a long and unhappy exception, but even it, unlike much Eliot, does not offer us the disciplined humility of the poet as our aesthetic experience.

It is of course one thing to deprecate the possibility of Christian poetry, or of poetry being Christian, and quite another to deprecate poetry itself, all poetry. In Auden's criticism, and particularly *Secondary Worlds*, the two are not always kept apart. When this happens, I find it is bad for my character. On a higher level the experience of reading Auden then becomes rather like reading Kilmer's *Trees*. "Poems are made by fools like me," yes, and by Dante, Milton, Blake, and Homer, but only God makes primary worlds. Or, as Auden says:

> it is possible that artists may become both more modest and more self-assured, that they may develop both a sense of humour about their vocation and a respect for that most admirable of Roman deities, the god *Terminus*. No poet will then produce the kind of work which demands that a reader spend his whole life reading it and nothing else. The claim to be a "genius" will become as strange as it would have seemed to the Middle Ages.

It is possible that other artists may become more like Auden. It is likelier that other critics may become more like him for, with Arnold and Eliot, he is a poet-critic who appeals greatly to critics, little as the splendor of becoming a "poet of professors" appeals to him. Books about Auden all tend to be fairly good, just as books about, say Wallace Stevens, tend to be quite bad. This is probably not because admirers of Stevens love him less well than the lovers of Auden, but because more genuinely difficult poets do not reduce to structures of ideas and images so readily as Auden does.

Auden's poetry now maintains a general esteem among academic critics. If one's judgment of Auden's poetry is more eccentric, one needs to take up the sad burden of literary dissent. Auden has been accepted as not only a great poet but also a Christian humanist sage not because of any conspiracy among moralizing neo-Christian academicians, but because the age requires such a figure. Eliot is gone, and Auden now occupies his place, though with a difference. The difference is refreshing; Auden is wittier, gentler, much less dogmatic, and does not feel compelled to demonstrate the authenticity of his Christian humanism by a judicious anti-Semitism. He has more wisdom and more humor than Eliot, and his talent is nowhere near so sparse, as the enormous range of his lyrics shows. I think it unfortunate that he should find himself in apostolic succession to Eliot, but *Secondary Worlds* seems to indicate that the succession is not unwelcome to him.

Much of *The Dyer's Hand*, despite its generosity as criticism, is darkened by Auden's obsessive doubts about the value of art in the context of Christianity. Similar doubts have maimed many writers, Tolstoi and Hopkins in particular. Insofar as Auden's uneasiness has prevented him from devotional poetry, he has gained by it, but unfortunately the effect upon him has been larger, and has resulted in a trivialization of his art. As a songwriter he remains supreme, being certainly the best in English in the century, but as a reflective poet he suffers from the continual evanescence of his subject matter. As a satirist, he may have been aided, yet the staple of his poetry is neither song nor satire but rumination on the good life, and his notion of the relation between Christianity and art has troubled that rumination. Auden is one of the massive modern sufferers from the malady of Poetic Influence, a variety of melancholy or anxiety-principle that our studies have evaded. Poetic Influence, in this sense, has little to do with the transmission of ideas and images from an earlier poet to a later one. Rather, it concerns the poet's sense of his precursors, and of his own achievement in relation to theirs. Have they left him room enough, or has their priority cost him his art? More crucially, where did they go wrong, so as to make it possible for him to go right? In this revisionary sense, in which the poet creates his own precursors by necessarily misinterpreting them, Poetic Influence forms and malforms new poets, and aids their art at the cost of increasing, finally, their already acute sense of isolation. Auden, like Byron, gives the continual impression of personal sincerity in his poetry, but again like Byron this sincerity is the consequence of a revisionary swerve away from the sincerity of the precursor. In Byron's case of Poetic

Influence the great precursor was Pope, with his highly dialectical sincerity; with Auden the prime precursor is Hardy, and the poetic son's sincerity is considerably more dialectical than the father's.

Auden, in his very fine *New Year Letter* (1 January 1940, at the height of his poetic power), wrote an important poem about Poetic Influence. His precursors are invoked there as a summary tribunal sitting in perpetual session:

> Though
> Considerate and mild and low
> The voices of the questioners,
> Although they delegate to us
> Both prosecution and defence,
> Accept our rules of evidence
> And pass no sentence but our own,
> Yet, as he faces them alone,
> O who can show convincing proof
> That he is worthy of their love?

He names these fathers and judges: Dante, Blake, Rimbaud, Dryden, Catullus, Tennyson, Baudelaire, Hardy, and Rilke, connecting this somewhat miscellaneous ninefold (except for Dryden, there for his mastery of the middle style) by their common sense of isolation, fit companions "to one unsocial English boy." Of all these, Auden's most characteristic poetry is closest to Hardy's, not merely in its beginnings, and like Hardy Auden remains most convincing as a ruminator upon human incongruities, upon everything valuable that somehow will not fit together. Auden's best poems, such as the justly esteemed *In Praise of Limestone*, brood upon incongruities, swerving from Hardy's kind of poem into a more double-natured sense of ruinous circumstance and thwarted love, yet retaining their family resemblance to Hardy. But where Hardy's strenuous unbelief led him to no worse redundancies than an occasional sharp striving after too palpable an irony, Auden's self-conscious belief and attendant doubt of poetry mar even *In Praise of Limestone* with the redundancy of uneasy and misplaced wit:

> But if
> Sins can be forgiven, if bodies rise from the dead,
>   These modifications of matter into
> Innocent athletes and gesticulating fountains,
>   Made solely for pleasure, make a further point;

The blessed will not care what angle they are regarded from,
   Having nothing to hide,

The blessed, as Auden says so often in prose, need neither to read nor to write poems, and poems do not describe their sanctity with much success, as Auden also sadly notes, contemplating the verse of Charles Williams. Close thy Auden, open thy Stevens, and read:

> If, then, when we speak of liberation, we mean an exodus; if when we speak of justification, we mean a kind of justice of which we had not known and on which we had not counted; if when we experience a sense of purification, we can think of the establishing of a self, it is certain that the experience of the poet is of no less a degree than the experience of the mystic and we may be certain that in the case of poets, the peers of saints, those experiences are of no less a degree than the experiences of the saints themselves. It is a question of the nature of the experience. It is not a question of identifying or relating dissimilar figures; that is to say, it is not a question of making saints out of poets or poets out of saints.

Theodore Roethke

(1908–1963)

THEODORE ROETHKE SHARES WITH ELIZABETH BISHOP AND ROBERT PENN Warren the distinction of having emerged as the strongest survivors of what could be called the middle generation of modern American poets, which included Robert Lowell, John Berryman, Delmore Schwartz, and Randall Jarrell. This generation came after the succession from E.A. Robinson and Frost through Pound, Eliot, Moore, Stevens, Williams, and Crane, and before the group that includes Ashbery, Merrill, Ammons, James Wright, Snyder, Merwin, Hollander, Kinnell, and others. The fate of a middle generation is hard, particularly when its older contemporaries included half a dozen poets of authentic greatness. The shadows of Stevens and of Eliot still hover in Roethke's last poems in *The Far Field* (1964), which seems to me as derivative a volume as his first, *Open House* (1941).

Dead much too soon, at fifty-five, Roethke did not have time to work through to another achievement as original as his best book, *The Lost Son* (1948), published at the crucial age of forty. My own sense of Roethke's eminence is founded almost entirely on *The Lost Son*. Elizabeth Bishop was unwaveringly strong, from first to last, while Warren became a great poet at the age of sixty, and maintained this eminence for fully two decades after. Roethke is upon his heights, in my judgement, only in *The Lost Son*, but the book is so marvelous that it justifies placing Roethke with Bishop and Warren in his own generation.

The Lost Son is alive in every poem, but the most memorable include "Big Wind," "Frau Bauman, Frau Schmidt, and Frau Schwartze," "The Waking," and four remarkable sequences: "The Lost Son," "The Long Alley," "A Field of Light," and perhaps the most distinguished, "The Shape of the Fire." Since "The Shape of the Fire" is the Roethke I love best, I choose it for an introductory commentary here. Resenting insinuations that the sequence was too much influenced by Dylan Thomas, Roethke rather eagerly took up a suggestion of W.H. Auden's, and asserted that Thomas Traherne was his true source. The source sensibly can be found in Walt Whitman, the most benign of influences upon Roethke, and the hidden influence upon Eliot and Stevens, two of Roethke's masters. Unlike say Yeats, whose effect upon Roethke was overwhelming and destructive, Whitman worked deep within Roethke to help bring to birth what was best in Roethke's own imagination.

The shape of the fire is the shape or form of Roethke's inspiration, and is the dominant if implicit trope of the sequence, until it becomes explicit in the sunlight of section 5. I take it that the title helps guide us to the realization that the poem is not about the first or natural birth, but instead concerns the second birth into poetic vision. The painful birth imagery of section 1 is more a farewell to mothering nature than a celebration of her function.

> What's this? A dish for fat lips.
> Who says? A nameless stranger.
> Is he a bird or a tree? Not everyone can tell.

Water recedes to the crying of spiders.
An old scow bumps over black rocks.
A cracked pod calls.

> Mother me out of here. What more will the bones allow?
> Will the sea give the wind suck? A toad folds into a stone.
> These flowers are all fangs. Comfort me, fury.
> Wake me, witch, we'll do the dance of rotten sticks.

Shale loosens. Marl reaches into the field. Small birds pass
    over water.

Spirit, come near. This is only the edge of whiteness.
I can't laugh at a procession of dogs.

> In the hour of ripeness the tree is barren.
> The she-bear mopes under the hill.
> Mother, mother, stir from your cave of sorrow.

A low mouth laps water. Weeds, weeds, how I love you
The arbor is cooler. Farewell, farewell, fond worm.
The warm comes without sound.

Roethke was reluctant to associate himself with Rimbaud; there is a Notebook comment of 1944 in which he oddly remarks: "The error of Rimbaud: the world is chaotic, therefore I must be." Hart Crane was the American Rimbaud, as he meant to be; Roethke will not survive a poetic comparison with either. But "The Shape of the Fire" is the most Rimbaldian of Roethke's poems, in its aggressivity and its deep rebellion against nature. The aggressivity subverts the referential aspect of the poem, while the rebellion dissolves any clear sense of a unified subjectivity in Roethke's use of "I." "What's this?" dismisses nature as the "dish for fat lips" that the poem's voice declines to devour. The "nameless stranger," whether bird or tree, is a messenger from beyond nature guiding the poet's Rimbaldian drunken boat over the black rocks of an intransigent nature, to the music of a call from "a cracked pod," also now beyond natural process.

An immense ambivalence in this poet, longing for the maternal even as he is guided out of it, is impelled to fall back on the rejected image of mothering in order to accomplish the new emergence into a vision antithetical to nature's. The prayer to be mothered out of the mother is accompanied by parallel antitheses: a sea nursing the wind, toad folding into a stone, flowers that are fangs, a fury that comforts. Even the contra-natural is viewed dialectically, as the awakening patroness is addressed under the name of witch, and the dance of deliverance from process becomes one of rotten sticks.

If the spirit beckoned near is identified as Whitman's, then the highly Whitmanian affirmation is wholly contextualized: "Weeds, weeds, how I love you." The fat lips of the opening are replaced now by the low mouth lapping water, emblem here of the rebirth into the incarnation of what the eighteenth century called the Poetical Character. Perhaps the most brilliant stroke in section 1 is the final trope, where the soundless warm of the shaping fire replaces the fond warm of what Blake called the state of Generation.

After the relative clarity of this first section, Roethke gives us the most difficult movement, not only of "The Shape of the Fire," but of any poem he ever published. It yields a surreal coherence to repeated rereadings, while defying the heresy of any paraphrase. To me it seems a total success, representing as it does the startled awakening to the poetic condition, a state of origins where every prior expectation has been twisted askew. Eye, ear, nose, foot have relocated themselves, and the nameless stranger of annunciation has been replaced by an hallucinatory listener, Roethke's version of Blake's Idiot Questioner, flat-headed, replete with platitudes and rubber doughnuts, and greeted by the poet with a question one might ask of Satan: "Have you come to unhinge my shadow?"

A poignant tentativeness attends the poet's new state, near allied, as

it must have been for Roethke himself, to the disorders of schizophrenia.
After a child-like nonsense song of this new innocence, Roethke cries out:
"Who waits at the gate?" The answer does not seem to be the abandoned
"mother of quartz" with her renewal of the whispers of family romance,
but the wasp and other emblems of antithetical redemption of section 3:

> The wasp waits.
> > The edge cannot eat the center.
> The grape glistens.
> > The path tells little to the serpent.
> An eye comes out of the wave.
> > The journey from flesh is longest.
> A rose sways least.
> > The redeemer comes a dark way.

The center, being prolific, will hold against the devouring edge or
circumference. If the long journey from flesh to poetic incarnation is
longest, this is because, as St. John of the Cross suggested, you must go by
a dark way, wherein there is no knowing. Roethke indeed does get back to
where he does not know, to the childhood world of section 4: "Death was
not. I lived in a simple drowse." Dylan Thomas's "Fern Hill" and much of
Traherne are doubtless analogues, but Wordsworth is closer, as James
Applewhite has indicated. These intimations of immortality guide us to the
fifth and final section, the strongest passage in. all of Roethke, an epiphany
both Whitmanian and Wordsworthian:

> To have the whole air!—
> The light, the full sun
> Coming down on the flowerheads,
> The tendrils turning slowly,
> A slow snail-lifting, liquescent;
> To be by the rose
> Rising slowly out of its bed,
> Still as a child in its first loneliness;
> To see cyclamen veins become clearer in early sunlight,
> And mist lifting out of the brown cat-tails;
> To stare into the after-light, the glitter left on the lake's surface,
> When the sun has fallen behind a wooded island;
> To follow the drops sliding from a lifted oar,
> Held up, while the rower breathes, and the small boat drifts
> > quietly shoreward;

To know that light falls and fills, often without our knowing,
As an opaque vase fills to the brim from a quick pouring,
Fills and trembles at the edge yet does not flow over,
Still holding and feeding the stem of the contained flower.

Certainly one of the most American of visions, this splendor is extraordinary for its gentle but taut control of the nearly ineffable. What the sequence gives us is truly the shape of the fire, the shape of the movement: to have, to be, to see, to stare, to follow, and at last to know. To know what? A falling, a filling to the brim, a trembling at the edge that will not flow over: these are the shapes of the creative fire transformed into a sustaining light. Roethke concludes with the image of a light still holding and feeding, a mothering light that contains the flower of restored consciousness as its child. The trope, almost Dantesque, achieves an aesthetic dignity worthy of Wordsworth or Whitman, true founders of the tradition that chose Roethke, at his rare best, as its own.

Elizabeth Bishop

(1911–1979)

THE PRINCIPAL POETS OF ELIZABETH BISHOP'S GENERATION INCLUDED
Roethke, Lowell, Berryman, Jarrell, and, in a different mode, Olson.
Whether any of these articulated an individual rhetorical stance with a skill
as sure as hers may be questioned. Her way of writing was closer to that of
Stevens and Marianne Moore, in the generation just beyond, than to any of
her exact contemporaries. Despite the differences in scale, her best poems
rival the Stevens of the shorter works, rather than the perhaps stronger
Stevens of the sequences.

Bishop stands, then, securely in a tradition of American poetry that
began with Emerson, Very, and Dickinson, and culminated in aspects of
Frost as well as of Stevens and Moore. This tradition is marked by firm
rhetorical control, overt moral authority, and sometimes by a fairly strict
economy of means. The closing lines in *Geography III* epitomize the tradition's self-recognition:

> He and the bird know everything is answered,
> all taken care of,
> no need to ask again.
> —Yesterday brought to today so lightly!
> (A yesterday I find almost impossible to lift.)

These poignant lines have more overt pathos than the poet ever
allowed herself elsewhere. But there is a paradox always in the contrast
between a poetry of deep subjectivity, like Wordsworth's or Stevens's or
Bishop's, and a confessional poetry, like Coleridge's or that of Bishop's principal contemporaries. When I read, say, "The Poems of Our Climate," by
Stevens, or "The End of March," by Bishop, I encounter eventually the

overwhelming self-revelation of a profoundly subjective consciousness. When I read, say, "Skunk Hour" by Lowell or one of Berryman's sonnets, I confront finally an opacity, for that is all the confessional mode can yield. It is the strength of Bishop's tradition that its clarity is more than a surface phenomenon. Such strength is cognitive, even analytical, and surpasses philosophy and psychoanalysis in its power to expose human truth.

There are grander poems by Bishop than the relatively early "The Unbeliever," but I center upon it here because I love it best of all her poems. It does not compare in scope and power to "The Monument," "Roosters," "The Fish," "The Bight," "At the Fishhouses," "Brazil, January 1, 1502," "First Death in Nova Scotia," or the extraordinary late triad of "Crusoe in England," "The Moose," and "The End of March." Those ten poems have an authority and a possible wisdom that transcend "The Unbeliever." But I walk around, certain days, chanting "The Unbeliever" to myself, it being one of those rare poems you never evade again, once you know it (and it knows you). Its five stanzas essentially are variations upon its epigraph, from Bunyan: "He sleeps on the top of a mast." Bunyan's trope concerns the condition of unbelief; Bishop's does not. Think of the personae of Bishop's poem as exemplifying three rhetorical stances, and so as being three kinds of poet, or even three poets: cloud, gull, unbeliever. The cloud is Wordsworth or Stevens. The gull is Shelley or Hart Crane. The unbeliever is Dickinson or Bishop. None of them has the advantage; the spangled sea wants to destroy them all. The cloud, powerful in introspection, regards not the sea but his own subjectivity. The gull, more visionary still, beholds neither sea nor air but his own aspiration. The unbeliever observes nothing, but the sea is truly observed in his dream:

> which was, "I must not fall.
> The spangled sea below wants me to fall.
> It is hard as diamonds; it wants to destroy us all."

I think that is the reality of Bishop's famous eye. Like Dickinson's, its truest precursor, it confronts the truth, which is that what is most worth seeing is impossible to see, at least with open eyes. A poetry informed by that mode of observation will station itself at the edge where what is most worth saying is all but impossible to say. I will conclude here by contrasting Bishop's wonderful trope of the lion, in "The End of March," to Stevens's incessant use of the same figure. In Stevens, the lion tends to represent poetry as a destructive force, as the imposition of the poet's will-to-power over reality. This image culminates in "An Ordinary Evening in New Haven":

Say of each lion of the spirit

It is a cat of a sleek transparency
That shines with a nocturnal shine alone.
The great cat must stand potent in the sun.

Against that destructive night in which all cats are black, even the
transparent ones, Stevens sets himself as a possible lion, potent in the light
of the idea-of-ideas. Here, I take it, Bishop's affectionate riposte:

They could have been teasing the lion sun,
except that now he was behind them
—a sun who'd walked the beach the last low tide,
making those big, majestic paw-prints,
who perhaps had batted a kite out of the sky to play with.

A somewhat Stevensian lion sun, clearly, but with something better
to do than standing potent in itself. The path away from poetry as a
destructive force can only be through play, the play of trope. Within her
tradition so securely, Bishop profoundly plays at trope. Dickinson, Moore,
and Bishop resemble Emerson, Frost, and Stevens in that tradition, with a
difference due not to mere nature or mere ideology but to superb art.

Robert Hayden

(1913-1980)

I MET ROBERT HAYDEN ONLY ONCE, WHEN SOMETIME IN THE EARLY 1970S I lectured at Ann Arbor, and had the privilege of a personal conversation with him for rather more than an hour or so. We talked about the Baha'i gardens in Haifa, which I had visited in the later 1950s, and also about the poetry of W.B. Yeats, on which I had recently published a long book, and of Hart Crane, who still seems to me an unexamined presence in several of Hayden's strongest poems.

Like Jay Wright, Hayden is a major modern American poet, as well as forming a quartet, together with Ralph Ellison, Toni Morrison, and Jay Wright, one that seems to me the crown of African American literary achievement up to this moment (I write in May 2004). Hayden (1913–1980) is a permanent poet, canonical in a sense that current politicism continues to deride. Cultural fashions fade away, and literary survival always depends upon three criteria: aesthetic splendor, cognitive power, and wisdom. If the United States emerges from the triumphalism of George W. Bush, a time will come when much current rant and cant will dwindle into period pieces, at best. Hayden, a maker and not an image of political correctness, will be read long after louder voices have vanished into the void.

Hayden was at his best in poetic sequences, though some of his lyrical poems are as rewarding. Like Yeats and Hart Crane (and the young Jay Wright of *The Homecoming Singer*), at his most memorable, Hayden is an incantatory poet. His characteristic rhetorical movement is invocation, rather as Yeats invokes his Tower or Hart Carne, Brooklyn Bridge. Most of Hayden's critics regard him as invoking black history, but they oversimplify the basis for his rhetorical art. You can be a very bad poet no matter how incessantly you call upon the West African past, or the horrific sadism of the English, Spanish, and Portuguese slave traders and owners of the Americas. Hayden matters because he is an authentic poet, one of the best of his generation (which included Elizabeth Bishop, Theodore Roethke, May Swenson, and the still overesteemed Robert Lowell). He told me, with a reticence worthy of his best poems, that he was fascinated by the *impacted* quality of Hart Crane's rhetoric, and in some respects he resembles Crane more than he does Yeats, whom his teacher W.H. Auden had commended to him as a model.

Like Crane, who hymned an Unknown God, Hayden was a religious poet, but of the highly eclectic Baha'i persuasion, a heresy from Iranian Islam. Inwardness and aesthetic elitism mark Hayden's highest achievements, as they do the Pindaricism of Jay Wright, for whom Hayden's freedom from spuriously black ideological "criticism" provided a beacon. Hayden's poetic integrity, like Jay Wright's, was absolute, and invariably courageous, in the mode of Ralph Ellison, who insisted that the American and European literary traditions were as much his possession as was the example of Richard Wright.

All this is merely preamble to a rather rapid survey of a few of Hayden's superb sequences, of which *Middle Passage* is the most famous. Both Hart Crane and T.S. Eliot are both drawn upon and evaded in Section III in particular, where an Eliotic allusion, in *The Waste Land*, to Shakespeare's *The Tempest*, fuses with the high rhetoric of Crane's Columbus approaching the New World in the "Ave Maria" canto of *The Bridge*:

> Shuttles in the rocking loom of history,
> the dark ships move, the dark ships move,
> their bright ironical names
> like jests of kindness on a murderer's mouth;
> plough through thrashing glister toward
> fata morgana's lucent melting shore,
> weave toward New World littorals that are
> mirage and myth and actual shore.
>
> Voyage through death,
>   voyage whose chartings are unlove.
>
> A charnel stench, effluvium of living death
> spreads outward from the hold,
> where the living and the dead, the horribly dying,
> lie interlocked, lie foul with blood and excrement.

Deep in the festering hold thy father lies,
the corpse of mercy rots with him,
rats eat love's rotten gelid eyes.

The dispassionate tonalities of this extraordinary passage stem from Hayden's poetic reticence, his characteristic rhetoric of litotes or understatement, in a reaction-formation against Crane's ecstatic hyperboles and Eliot's hyperbolic ironies. For Crane, Columbus is a mystical (if cruel) disciple of the prophet Isaiah, while Eliot's Tiresias is death-in-life desperately waiting for the grace of Anglican conversion. Hayden, a black Baha'i, longs for a more universal salvation. His Cinquez, hero of the *Amistad* Mutiny, is the emblem of all those, of whatever origin, who sought the Blessing that America ought to constitute, however far from that ideal it continues to fall:

Voyage through death
                              to life upon these shores.

Runagate Runagate is not as intricate and fully written as *Middle Passage*, but it too dares and sustains a high rhetoric:

Tell me, Ezekiel, oh tell me do you see
mailed Jehovah coming to deliver me?

My late friend, the great poet-novelist Robert Penn Warren, fiercely hated John Brown, upon whom he had written his first book. One day, at lunch with Warren, I commended John Brown as a prophet, though violent in the extreme, yet in the best of causes. Warren, too urbane to argue, presented me at the next week's lunch with a copy of his *John Brown: The Making of a Martyr*. Loving and honoring Warren's memory, I still follow Emerson and Thoreau and vote for Hayden's sequence, *John Brown*, which honestly admits the prophet's responsibility for "Bleeding Kansas":

Doing The Lord's work with saber
sharpened on the grindstone
of The Word:
                              Bleeding Kansas:

the cries of my people the cries
of their oppressors harrowed
hacked—poison meat for Satan's
maw.

>   I slew no man but blessed
> the Chosen, who in the name
> of justice killed at my command.
>
> Bleeding Kansas:
>
>   a son martyred
> there: I am tested I am trued
> made worthy of my servitude.
>
> Oh the crimes of this guilty
> guilty land:
>
>   let Kansas bleed.

Of John Brown, Hayden says simply: "he died/for us." Few American poets have understood so well their hopelessly paradoxical country. Hayden, in the concluding stanza of his *American Journal*, joins Walt Whitman in apprehending what may be beyond comprehension:

> confess i am curiously drawn   unmentionable   to
> the americans   doubt i could exist among them for
> long however   psychic demands far too severe
> much violence   much that repels   i am attracted
> none the less   their variousness their ingenuity
> their elan vital   and that some thing   essence
> quiddity   i cannot penetrate or name

John Berryman

(1914–1972)

"I BEGAN WORK IN VERSE-MAKING AS A BURNING, TRIVIAL DISCIPLE OF THE great Irish poet William Butler Yeats, and I hope I have moved off from there." That is John Berryman in 1965, and he added: "Then came Yeats, whom I didn't so much wish to resemble as to *be*." Then came Auden, by Berryman's own testimony. "Winter Landscape" was cited by Berryman as his first poem in his own voice, and *Homage to Mistress Bradstreet* as his true breakthrough. That there are breakthroughs in the development or unfolding of a strong poet cannot be denied; the burden for literary criticism always must be to determine which poets inevitably compel the canon to make place for them. Roethke in his two best volumes achieved strength and then fell away from it. Robert Lowell, concerning whom I seem to be the only dissenter in our nation, did not achieve it, either in the manner of Eliot and Tate, or in that of W.C. Williams. Berryman I find the largest puzzle of his poetic generation, though I believe he will be judged at last only by *The Dream Songs*. To compare them, as some admirers do, to *Song of Myself*, is palpably an error; they are neither of that mode nor anywhere close to that astonishing eminence.

Berryman, like Lowell, continues to be overpraised in Britain, where both are associated with Anne Sexton and Sylvia Plath. This is hardly fair to Berryman, but British critics such as John Bayley and A. Alvarez seem to like their American poets to be suicidal, mentally ill, and a touch unruly, "beyond the Gentility Principle," as Alvarez phrases it. Wallace Stevens, in the judgment of Bayley, is inferior to Berryman and Lowell, which is roughly akin to my proclaiming that Alice Meynell and Charlotte Mew wrote better poems than Thomas Hardy, which I am not about to proclaim. Perhaps Berryman has some permanent poems, but they are hard to locate if you start out with his admirers' hyperbolical guides, which have little actual relation to the terrain of the work itself.

Yeats never left Berryman, who made extraordinary efforts to stop *sounding* like Yeats. That is a perfectly normal procedure in severe cases of poetic influence; Browning's remarkable diction and syntax resulted from his need to stop being Shelley, and the Browning dramatic monologue, with its purported objectivity, was a swerve away from the flamboyant subjectivity of the Shelleyan lyric, or the autobiographical romance of the *Alastor* variety. It would be wonderful if Berryman had become the American Browning, but alas he did not. *The Dream Songs* are not *Men and Women*, and *Love & Fame* is not *Asolando*. In the spirit of having named Lowell as our William Mason, and Plath as our Felicia Hemans, I could call Berryman our "Festus" Bailey or our Alexander Smith, creator of that other masterpiece of the Spasmodic School, *A Life Drama*. Berryman's similarity to Bailey and Smith is quite uncanny, and like Mason and Hemans in their eras, the Spasmodics had critical admirers as profusely enthusiastic as Alvarez, Bayley, Mendelson, and other loyal Berrymanians. Contemporary acclaim is sometimes a very bad indication of a poet's future canonicity.

The poem by Berryman I love best is the proper answer to me, or to anyone else who has the temerity to worry the issue of poetic survival. Here is the last stanza of his superb "A Professor's Song":

> Alive now–no–Blake would have written prose,
> But movement following movement crisply flows,
> So much the better, better the much so,
> As burbleth Mozart. Twelve. The class can go.
> Until I meet you, then, in Upper Hell
> Convulsed, foaming immortal blood: farewell.

Yes, yes indeed, a more than palpable hit, but there precisely is the maddening and necessary question: among the poets, whose blood is immortal? No one likes the question, poets least of all, but it has to be asked, and answered. The cost of belatedness is not a shrinking of literary space, but of the reader's time. I have had the experience of being denounced in this regard, in print and out, by a vociferous bevy of literary journalists, inchoate rhapsodes, and academic impostors, but they too must choose whom they will read in the time they have, and even they must recognize that we cannot reread everyone. Berryman's poetry does not repress this dilemma, no poetry wholly can, however implicitly the sorrow is addressed, and Berryman, even more than most of his contemporaries, was obsessed with this burden. Elizabeth Kaspar Aldrich is particularly shrewd in noting how central this anxiety was to Berryman's imagination. She

quotes his splendid remark, from the same 1965 interview that acknowledged the influence of Yeats and Auden: "A poem's force may be pivoted
on a missing or misrepresented element in an agreed-upon or imposed
design." Someone indeed is always missing, or misrepresented. Aldrich,
who loves *Homage to Mistress Bradstreet* more than I do, though I must
acknowledge it an ambitious and admirable poem, catches the precise
function of crossing over that it fulfilled:

> The "more" that Berryman's poem attempts seems to me, final-
> ly, a foredoomed willing-into-being of a burdensome past (the
> "present" of Anne's world against which she rebels, to which
> she finally submits) the real burden of which is its quality of
> absence. Thus, extreme identification with his heroine repre-
> sents an attempted appropriation of a past from which he is—
> by the very fact of a literary ancestor like Hawthorne—all the
> more displaced. But the very hopelessness of the effort is the
> extraordinary power of *Homage to Mistress Bradstreet*. This is a
> poem which celebrates impossibilities. The impossibility of liv-
> ing in the faithless void of the present time, the impossibility of
> being an American poet at all—these are celebrated in this
> most American of poems in verse Berryman equalled but never
> surpassed. And it is the nearly impossible intensity of the poet's
> emotion—need, rage, longing, grief—that this verse contains,
> and that his Muse/mistress/subject is able to embody. Anne
> Bradstreet could, paradoxically, embody for Berryman the very
> weaknesses and absences from which his poetic effort had hith-
> erto suffered—his breakthrough, at what he described as enor-
> mous cost; thereafter, *The Dream Songs* and Henry.

I find this persuasive and poignant, though I am uneasy as to all that
celebration of impossibilities. "The impossibility of being an American
poet at all"—but we have had Whitman, Dickinson, Frost, Stevens,
Marianne Moore, Hart Crane, R.P. Warren, Elizabeth Bishop, John
Ashbery, James Merrill, A.R. Ammons and, if you will, Eliot, Pound, W.C.
Williams and more. Are we to say of *The Dream Songs* also that the very
hopelessness of the effort is their extraordinary power? Poetic ambition is
vital to poetic strength, and is commendable, and perhaps (*pace* Allen Tate)
the poetic will *can* perform the work of the imagination. Like *Homage, The
Dream Songs* would move even the stoniest of critics, but the question cannot be one of pathos alone. Mad songs are a major lyric genre in our language, and Yeats excelled in them, in and for our century. Late Yeats always

hovers nearby in *The Dream Songs*, by which I do not mean the Yeatsian *persona* of Crazy Jane and Tom the Lunatic but the mask of Yeats himself, the wild old wicked man, sometimes appearing as Ribh. What is absent in *The Dream Songs*, inevitably, is the strongest Yeats, the poet who could end almost his last poem by discarding all his own mythologies and personae, and cry aloud in a perfection of agnostic recognition of dying and death:

> O Rocky Voice
> Shall we in that great night rejoice?
> What do we know but that we face
> One another in this place?

Berryman, confronted by that, as all of us are, could only yield, as all of us yield. His own achieved mode, as here in the first stanza of *Dream Song* 88, remained Yeatsian, but without enough perhaps of a swerve into individual difference:

> In slack times visit I the violent dead
> and pick their awful brains. Most seem to feel
> nothing is secret more
> to my disdain I find, when we who fled
> cherish the knowings of both worlds, conceal
> more, beat on the floor,

The violent dead poet here, whose brain is picked, necessarily is Yeats. Berryman, who fled the living world while cherishing the knowings of both the living and the dead, conceals more than Yeats, beats on the floor (a trope taken from Yeats), and finds by rereading Yeats that his own deepest secrets are revealed there, to his own disdain. This has the power of sincerity, but not enough is missing, not enough is misrepresented, and the design is manifestly imposed.

Octavio Paz

(1914-1998)

PAZ RECEIVED THE NOBEL PRIZE FOR LITERATURE IN 1990, ONE OF THE sounder choices. He possessed, and retains, a unique eminence in Mexican literature up to this time. Primarily a poet-critic, nevertheless his most influential books are likely to be *The Labyrinth of Solitude* (1950), which is a quest for the Mexican identity, and *Sor Juana Or, The Traps of Faith* (1988), a critical biography of the poet Juana Ramírez, who became Sor Juana Inés De La Cruz (1651–1695), the major literary figure of the City of Mexico in seventeenth-century New Spain.

An eclectic and idiosyncratic international poet-critic, and certainly one of the principal Spanish-language poets of the twentieth century, Paz paradoxically is most original in his exploration of the very vexed question of Mexican national identity. Doubtless there are and will be rival attempts to define what might be called the genius of Mexico, and some Mexican feminists already denounce *The Labyrinth of Solitude* for implicitly taking the side of what it exposes and criticizes, the Mexican male myth that their women first betrayed them to, and with, the invading Spaniards. And yet I cannot see how Paz could have been clearer:

> In contrast to Guadalupe, who is the Virgin Mother, the *Chingada* is the violated Mother. Neither in her nor in the Virgin do we find traces of the darker attributes of the great goddesses: the lasciviousness of Amaterasu and Aphrodite, the cruelty of Artemis and Astarte, the sinister magic of Circe or the bloodlust of Kali. Both of them are passive figures. Guadalupe is pure receptivity, and the benefits she bestows are of the same order: she consoles, quiets, dries tears, calms passions. The *Chingada* is even more passive. Her passivity is abject: she does

not resist violence, but is an inert heap of bones, blood and dust. Her taint is constitutional and resides, as we said earlier, in her sex. This passivity, open to the outside world, causes her to lose her identity: she is the *Chingada*. She loses her name; she is no one; she disappears into nothingness; she *is* Nothingness. And yet she is the cruel incarnation of the feminine condition.

If the *Chingada* is a representation of the violated Mother, it is appropriate to associate her with the Conquest, which was also a violation, not only in the historical sense but also in the very flesh of Indian women. The symbol of this violation is Doña Malinche, the mistress of Cortés. It is true that she gave herself voluntarily to the conquistador, but he forgot her as soon as her usefulness was over. Doña Marina [The name given to La Malinche by the Spaniards.] becomes a figure representing the Indian women who were fascinated, violated or seduced by the Spaniards. And as a small boy will not forgive his mother if she abandons him to search for his father, the Mexican people have not forgiven La Malinche for her betrayal. She embodies the open, the *chingado*, to our closed, stoic, impassive Indians. Cuauhtémoc and Doña Marina are thus two antagonistic and complementary figures. There is nothing surprising about our cult of the young emperor—"the only hero at the summit of art," an image of the sacrificed son—and there is also nothing surprising about the curse that weighs against La Malinche. This explains the success of the contemptuous adjective *malinchista* recently put into circulation by the newspapers to denounce all those who have been corrupted by foreign influences. The *malinchistas* are those who want Mexico to open itself to the outside world: the true sons of La Malinche, who is the *Chingada* in person. Once again we see the opposition of the close and the open.

The Mexicans thus see themselves as the sons of La Malinche, and regard her as the *Chingada* personified. Since Paz was writing as a poet, he received all the misunderstandings that he risked: "an elegant insult against Mexican mothers." More accurately, as Paz remarked, *"The Labyrinth of Solitude* was an attempt to describe and understand certain myths; at the same time, insofar as it is a literary work, it has in turn become another myth." Involved here is a disagreement on Paz's part with Claude Lévi-Strauss, set forth in a wise little book (1967):

... Lévi-Strauss affirms that there is a real kinship between myth and music and not between myth and poetry. Myth as distinguished from poetry can be translated without any appreciable loss in the translation ...

Paz adds that translation, for a poem, "implies transmutation or resurrection." A poem by Paz, translated into English by Elizabeth Bishop or Mark Strand is another poem and yet the same poem. This is a version of the Mexicans respecting their President, while behind the respect is the traditional image of the Father. Yet Paz ends his *Labyrinth* on an ominous note:

> Every moribund or sterile society attempts to save itself by creating a redemption myth which is also a fertility myth, a creation myth ... The sterility of the bourgeois world will end in suicide or a new form of creative participation.

Paz has been dead for more than two years, and his Mexico currently is becoming both more bourgeois and more Catholic. A superb Surrealist poet, whether in verse or prose, Paz founders in prophecy, as everyone has done in opposing the endlessly driven onward march of bourgeois societies. But that does not lessen the insight nor the visionary power of *The Labyrinth of Solitude*. Himself of mixed Spanish and Indian ancestry, Paz explains Mexican "solitude" by the original trauma of the Spanish Conquest, though as a diplomat and world-traveler he came to know that there are different modes of "solitude" in every national culture.

The starting-points for Paz in defining the difference between the United States and Mexico is that the Native Americans were essentially nomads, while the native Mexicans were settled peoples, farmers rather than hunters. To this was added the differences between Protestant England and the Spain of the Counter-Reformation. So far, that seems obvious enough; Paz manifests his particular genius for locating differences by passing beyond historical origins to spiritual insight:

> The Mexicans' vision of death, which is also the hope of resurrection is as profoundly steeped in Catholic eschatology as in Indian naturalism. The Mexican death is of the body, exactly the opposite of the American death, which is abstract and disembodied. For Mexicans, death sees and touches itself; it is the body emptied of the soul, the pile of bones that somehow, as in the Aztec poem, must bloom again. For Americans, death is what is not seen: absence, the disappearance of the person. In

the Puritan consciousness, death was always present, but as a moral entity, an idea. Later on, scientism pushed death out of the American consciousness. Death melted away and became unmentionable. Finally, in vast segments of the American population of today, progressive rationalism and idealism have been replaced by neo-hedonism. But the cult of the body and of pleasure implies the recognition and acceptance of death. The body is mortal, and the kingdom of pleasure is that of the moment, as Epicurus saw better than anyone else. American hedonism closes its eyes to death and has been incapable of exorcising the destructive power of the moment with a wisdom like that of the Epicureans of antiquity. Present-day hedonism is the last recourse of the anguished and the desperate, and expression of the nihilism that is eroding the West.

Capitalism exalts the activities and behavior patterns traditionally called virile: aggressiveness, the spirit of competition and emulation, combativeness. American society made these values its own. This perhaps explains why nothing like the Mexicans' devotion to the Virgin of Guadalupe appears in the different versions of Christianity professed by Americans, including the Catholic minority. The Virgin unites the religious sensibilities of the Mediterranean and Mesoamerica, both of them regions that fostered ancient cults of feminine divinities, Guadalupe-Tonantzin is the mother of all Mexicans—Indians, mestizos, whites—but she is also a warrior virgin whose image has often appeared on the banners of peasant uprising. In the Virgin of Guadalupe we encounter a very ancient vision of femininity which, as was true of the pagan goddesses, is not without a heroic tint.

There is much here to acknowledge, and much to argue. Paz had a limited understanding of the American Religion, which he identified with Puritan New England. But the United States, since about 1800, has not been Protestant in the European way, and instead has developed a complex configuration of new faiths that are more than sects: Southern Baptists, Adventists, Mormons, Pentecostalists, and others. Our hedonists are not that different from those of other nations, and our denial of death has something to do with the astonishing national belief (eighty-nine percent, according to Gallup) that God loves each of us on a personal and individual basis. Sane Mexicans do not walk and talk with Jesus; an astonishing number of ordinary citizens of the United States do.

And yet Paz troubles me when he opposes Mexico's vision of femininity to that of the United States, though in this area someone regularly condemned as a "patriarchal critic" had better exercise wariness. The myth of La Malinche or the *Chingada*, unforgettably expounded by Paz, is alien to the United States, yet it is the center of *The Labyrinth of Solitude*, which on rereading flowers into a two hundred page prose-poem, rather than what Paz himself describes as "a book of social, political and psychological criticism."

Halfway through his *Labyrinth*, Paz gives us a remarkable excursus upon Sor Juana, which decades later exfoliated into his superb biography of the first major Hispanic poet in the New World:

> Despite the brilliance of her career, the pathos of her death, and the admirable geometry that shapes her best poetic creations, there is something unrealized and fragmentary in the life and work of Sor Juana. We can sense the melancholy of a spirit who never succeeded in forgiving herself for her boldness and her condition as a woman. Her epoch did not provide her with the intellectual nourishment her appetite required, and she herself could not—and who can?—create a world of ideas in which to live alone. An awareness of her singularity was always very alive in her: "What can women know except the philosophy of the kitchen?" she asked with a smile. But the wound hurt her: "Who would not believe, hearing such general applause, that I have voyaged full-sail on the handclaps of popular acclamation?" Sor Juana was a solitary figure. Indecisive and smiling, she lived an ambiguous life; she was conscious of the duality of her condition and the impossibility of her task. We often hear reproaches against men who have not fulfilled their destinies. Should we not grieve, however, for the ill fortune of a woman who was superior both to her society and her culture?

Eloquently plangent, this still would not have prepared me for Paz's *Sor Juana*, which is a baroque masterwork, and though a critical biography in form, fulfills the project of *The Labyrinth of Solitude*, and perfects Paz's lifelong meditation upon Mexican identity. What emerges most vividly from *Sor Juana*, aside from its depiction of the culture of later seventeenth-century Mexico, is the poetic splendor and final personal tragedy of Sor Juana, destroyed by "the traps of faith," the spiritual tyranny of a Church resisting all enlightenment, and obliterating a woman poet of genius for the sole sake of eliminating an anomaly, an autonomous creative spirit:

It is scarcely necessary to point out the similarities between Sor Juana's personal situation and the obstacles we Mexicans have experienced during the process of modernization. There was an insoluble contradiction between Sor Juana and her world. This contradiction was not merely intellectual; it was fundamental, and can be located in three main areas. The first was the opposition between her literary vocation and the fact that she was a nun. At other moments, although not in New Spain, the Church had been tolerant and had harbored writers and poets who, often in blatant disregard of their religious responsibilities, had devoted themselves exclusively to letters. Their cases, however—the most notable being those of Góngora, Lope de Vega, Tirso de Molina, and Mira de Amescua—differ from that of Sor Juana in an essential point: they were poets and dramatists but not intellectuals. Both vocations, poet and intellectual, converged in Sor Juana. In late seventeenth-century Spain and its domains, a priest or nun with an intellectual vocation was restricted to theology and sacred studies. This incompatibility was aggravated by the fact that Sor Juana's extraordinary intellectual restlessness and her encyclopedic curiosity—Sigüenza's also—coincided with a moment of paralysis in the Church and exhaustion in Hispanic culture.

The second area of discord was Sor Juana's gender. The fact that a woman—what is more, a nun—should devote herself so single-mindedly to letters must have both astounded and scandalized her contemporaries. She was called the "Tenth Muse" and the "Phoenix of America": sincere expressions of admiration that must have set her head spinning at times. She tells us in the *Response* that no lack of criticism and censure accompanied this praise. The censure came from influential prelates and was founded on a point of doctrine. It was not by chance that in his appeal to Sor Juana asking her to forsake secular letters the Bishop of Puebla quoted St. Paul. It was one thing to be tolerant with Lope de Vega and Góngora, both bad priests, and another to be lenient with Sor Juana Inés de la Cruz. Although her conduct was beyond reproach, her attitudes were not. She was guilty of the sin of pride, a sin to which the vain feminine sex is particularly susceptible. Pride was the ruin of Lucifer, because hubris leads to rebelliousness. Sor Juana's critics saw a causal relationship between letters, which lead a woman from her natural state of obedience, and rebelliousness. Sor Juana had disproved the inferiority of women in intellectual and literary matters and made her attainments a source of admiration and public applause; to the prelates this was sin, and her obstinacy was rebellion. That is why they demanded a total abdication.

As Paz shows, Sor Juana's great, Hermetic poem, *First Dream*, differs profoundly from the visions of St. John of the Cross and of St. Teresa. John of the Cross quested to get to a point where there was no knowing, and St. Teresa wished to be possessed by God's light. Both were impatient with reason, but Sor Juana, sublimely reasonable, desired to illuminate all things, in a quest both more Neoplatonic and more encyclopedic than it was specifically Christian. She was the last great poet of Spain's Baroque Age, and that the Church violated her creative integrity was its own sin against the spirit.

Paz, an eclectic religionist, more Hindu and Buddhist than Christian, had an instinctive empathy for Sor Juana's doomed Hermeticism. She stands in his work as the other personification of the scapegoated *Chingada*, at the other end of the historical and spiritual world from the reviled La Malinche. It fascinates me that Octavio Paz, a great erotic poet and universal critic of poetry, composes his two major prose achievements upon two victims of what has to be called the vision of Mexican masculinity, the nature of which remains so resistant to change.

Gwendolyn Brooks

(1917–2000)

GWENDOLYN BROOKS SAYS OF HER PRE-1967 POETRY: "I WASN'T WRITING consciously with the idea that blacks *must address* blacks, *must write* about blacks." Certainly, her work after 1967 is very different from her poems composed before she turned fifty. I prefer the earlier achievement, a judgment (if it is one) that is harmless since every essayist in this volume, except for Langston Hughes, centers upon the later Brooks.

The famous lyric, "The Bean Eaters" ironically and memorably celebrates:

> Two who are Mostly Good,
> Two who have lived their day,
> But keep on putting on their clothes
> And putting things away.

This wry turn upon the universal still seems to me Brooks's strength, as does "The Crazy Woman," an eloquent extension of the Mad Song tradition:

> I'll wait until November.
> That is the time for me.
> I'll go out in the frosty dark
> And sing most terribly.

If I contrast these with the poem of 1969, "The Riot," I come to see that I am not yet competent to judge the poet who was reborn in 1967. The satiric eye is still there, and the dominant stylistic influence remains T.S. Eliot. Yet the style and the stance seem not to cohere:

Because the Poor were sweaty and unpretty
(not like Two Dainty Negroes in Winnetka)
and they were coming toward him in rough ranks.
In seas. In windsweep. They were black and loud.
And not detainable. And not discreet.

I like that: "In sea. In windsweep," and I grant that the poem's sentiments are admirable, if you believe (as most of us really do) that only violence is the valid answer to violence. The difficulty here, as in the celebrated ballad, the "Anniad," is that Brooks risks becoming a period piece,
at some later time when American society has progressed beyond its long
history of injustice. Ideological verse remains ideological; its paradoxes
flatten out too easily. Gwendolyn Brooks is acclaimed for her self-trans-
formations, as nearly all the essays here demonstrate. Whether she has sacrificed part of her gift in an exemplary cause seems to me a legitimate question.

James Dickey

(1923–1997)

I FIRST READ JAMES DICKEY'S EARLY POEM, "THE OTHER," SOME TWENTY
years ago. Having admired his recently published book, *Drowning With
Others*, I went back to his first book, *Into the Stone*, at the recommendation
of a close friend, the poet Alvin Feinman. Though very moved by several
of the earlier poems, I was affected most strongly by the one called "The
Other." It has taken me twenty years to understand why the poem still will
not let me go, and so I begin with it here. I don't think of Dickey as a poet
primarily of otherness, but rather as a heroic celebrator of what Emerson
called "the great and crescive self," indeed of the American self proper,
which demands victory and disdains even great defeats. Dickey, as I read
him, is like what Vico called the Magic Formalists or Blake named the
Giant Forms. He is a throwback to those mythic hypotheses out of which
strong poetry first broke forth, the bards of divination whose heroic vitalism demanded a literal immortality for themselves as poets. But even a
Magic Formalist learns that he is at best a mortal god.

The pain of that learning is the central story of Dickey's poetry, and
I choose to evade that pain here in order to emphasize Dickey's counter-
song of otherness. Since I will take him scarcely into his middle years, I will
be ignoring all of his most ambitious poetry, "the later motion," as he has
called it. Though his work from 1965 to the present clearly is more problematic than the poems I will discuss, its achievement quite possibly is of a
higher order. But it is too soon to prophesy Dickey's final stature, and criticism must discourse on what it loves before it broods upon the limits of the
canonical. What I know and love best, so far, in Dickey's poetry is "the early
motion," and the counter-song of otherness in that motion moves me most.
I have circled back to that poem, "The Other," and turn to it now to locate
an origin of Dickey's quest as a poet.

That origin is guilt, and guilt ostensibly of being a substitute or replacement for a brother dead before one was born. Freud, I think, would have judged such guilt to be a screen memory, and I am Freudian enough to look or surmise elsewhere for the source of guilt in the poems of *Into the Stone*. From the beginning of his poetic career, Dickey was a poet of Sublime longings, and those who court the Sublime are particularly subject to changeling fantasies. The poem he titled "The Other" is manifestly Yeatsian, whether directly or through the mediation of Roethke, but the argument already is Dickey's own, and in all respects it is the meter-making argument, and not the derived diction and metric, that gives this poem its great distinction. Indeed Dickey, an instinctive Emersonian from the start, despite his Southern heritage, literalizes Emerson's trope of a meter-making argument by the extraordinary device of packing the seventy-seven lines of this lyrical reverie into what has always felt to me like a single sentence. How could there be a second sentence in a poem that identifies itself so completely with the changeling's will to be the other, when the other ultimately is the god Apollo?

Somewhere, Dickey identified his triad of literary heroes as the unlikely combination of Keats, Malcolm Lowry, and James Agee, presumably associated because of their early or relatively early deaths, and because of their shared intensity of belief in what could be called the salvation history of the literary art. But Dickey is very much a poet of Sensibility, in the mode that Frye once defined as *the* Age of Sensibility, the mode of Christopher Smart and of William Collins, among other doomed poets whose threshold stance destroyed them upon the verge of High Romanticism. The Keats who moves Dickey most, the Keats of the letters, is the culmination of the major theme of the poets of Sensibility, the theme that, following Collins, I have called the Incarnation of the Poetical Character. Lowry and Agee, though I don't recall Dickey mentioning this, were curiously allied as verse writers by the overwhelming influence that Hart Crane exerted upon both of them. Dickey seems to prefer Crane's letters to his poems, which oddly parallels his preference of Keats's letters. But Keats and Crane, like Lowry and Agee in their verse, represent fully in their poems the Incarnation of the Poetical Character, where the poet, in the guise of a young man, is reborn as the young god of the sun. That is clearly the genre of Dickey's "The Other," but the clarity is shadowed by Dickey's early guilt concerning what the poem accurately names as "my lust of self."

What self can that be except the magic and occult self, ontological rather than empirical, and in Yeatsian or Whitmanian terms, self rather than soul? The guilt that shadows Dickey's marvelous seventy-seven-line utterance is the guilt induced by what Freud came to call the above-I or the over-I (the superego), a rather more daunting though no less fictive entity than Emerson's Oversoul. Emerson had the shrewdest of eyes for anxiety, but Freud's eye, as Wallace Stevens once wrote, was the microscope of potency. The guilt of family betrayal must ensue from the changeling fantasy of the family romance, and for Freud (as for Kenneth Burke), all romance is family romance. But the family romance of the poet *as* poet tends to depart from the domain of the merely biographical family. Dickey's assertion of self as person was the desire to rise from the "strength-haunted body" of a "rack-ribbed child" to the Herculean figure he has been since, a titanic form among contemporary poets. But since poems can attempt the truth only through fictions or tropes, the poem of "The Other" is compelled to treat the child's aspiration as the drive towards becoming Apollo, poetry itself. The youthful Henry James, reviewing *Drum-Taps*, scorned Whitman as an essentially prosaic temperament trying to lift itself by muscular exertion into poetry. The elderly Henry James, weeping over the great *Lilacs* elegy, scorned his own youthful review; but, properly modified, it can give us a critical trope for reading Dickey: an essentially poetic temperament lifting itself by muscular exertion into poetry.

Dickey's most curious characteristic, from "The Other" through *Puella*, is his involuntary but striking dualism, curious because so heroic a vitalist ought not to exemplify (as he does) so Pauline and Cartesian a mind–body split, or even so prevalent a sense of what Stevens termed the dumbfoundering abyss between ourselves and the object. What the poem surprisingly shows for and to Dickey is that his own body becomes his brother, or Apollo, or "the other." If the body is the divine other, then pathos becomes both sublime and grotesque, because the body must change, and the final form of that change is death. "The Other" is almost the first of Dickey's poems, and in some ways he has never surpassed it, not because he has failed to develop, but because it is unsurpassable. The whole of Dickey is in it already, as the whole of Shelley is in *Alastor*, or the whole of Yeats is in *The Wanderings of Oisin*. I repeat that this does not mean that Dickey simply has unfolded; so restless and reckless an experimentalist is outrageously metamorphic. But all his changes quest hopelessly for a disjunctiveness his temperament refuses to allow him. The "holes" that space out the poems of his major phase never represent discursive gaps or even crossings from one kind of figuration to another. Instead, they impressively mark or punctuate the exquisite desperation of the will to live, the lust of self that is not to be railed at, because it does represent what Keats called "a sickness not ignoble": the sickness unto death of heroic poetry.

"The Other," like so much of Dickey's best work, is very clearly a Southern American poem, and yet its Incarnation of the Poetical Character is necessarily universal in its imagery and argument. This is the universal purchased at the high cost of what was to be a permanent guilt, the guilt of a poet who as poet greatly desired *not* to be egocentric, despite the demands of the mythology that found him from the start. Those demands are felt even in the opening movement of "The Other":

> Holding onto myself by the hand,
> I change places into the spirit
> I had as a rack-ribbed child,
> And walk slowly out through my mind
> To the wood, as into a falling fire
> Where I turned from that strength-haunted body
> Half-way to bronze, as I wished to.

Dickey's natural religion always has been Mithraism, the traditional faith of soldiers, and certainly the most masculine and fierce of all Western beliefs. Despite the Persian origins of Mithra, Rome assimilated him to Apollo, and Dickey's major alteration is to make the Incarnation of the Poetical Character into a Mithraic ritual. The "bronze" of this first stanza will be revealed, later in the poem, as both the statue of Apollo and the body of the sacrificial bull slain by Mithra. As the boy Dickey slings up the too-heavy ax-head, he prays

> To another, unlike me, beside me:
> To a brother or king-sized shadow
> Who looked at me, burned, and believed me:
> Who believed I would rise like Apollo
>
> With armor-cast shoulders upon me:
> Whose voice, whistling back through my teeth,
> Counted strokes with the hiss of a serpent.
> Where the sun through the bright wood drove
> Him, mute, and floating strangely, to the ground,
> He led me into his house, and sat
> Upright, with a face I could never imagine,
>
> With a great harp leant on his shoulder,
> And began in deep handfuls to play it.

"Burned" is the crucial trope here, since the brother, as god of the sun, leads only into the heat and light that is the house of the sun. The oracular hiss is Pythian, though the voice truly becomes Dickey's own. What Dickey, *in the poem*, develops most brilliantly is the figure of downward movement, which is introduced in the second stanza as the combined fall of sweat and leaves, and further invoked in the fall of light. Later in the poem, music falls, followed in the final line by the casting down of foliage. All these fallings substitute for the hidden ritual in which the bull's blood falls upon the Mithraic adept, the warrior in the act of becoming Apollo:

> My brother rose beside me from the earth,
>
> With the wing-bone of music on his back
> Trembling strongly with heartfelt gold,
> And ascended like a bird into the tree,
> And music fell in a comb, as I stood
> In a bull's heavy, bronze-bodied shape
> As it mixed with a god's, on the ground,
> And leaned on the helve of the ax.

The "great, dead tree" of the poem's second stanza might be called Dickey's first major fiction of duration, the origin of his quarrel with time. Being Dickey's, it is the liveliest of dead trees, yet it cannot propitiate this poet's poignant longing for a literal immortality:

> Now, owing my arms to the dead
> Tree, and the leaf-loosing, mortal wood,
> Still hearing that music amaze me,
> I walk through the time-stricken forest,
> And wish another body for my life,
> Knowing that none is given
> By the giant, unusable tree
>
> And the leaf-shapen lightning of sun,
> And rail at my lust of self
> With an effort like chopping through root-stocks:
> Yet the light, looming brother but more
> Brightly above me is blazing,
> In that music come down from the branches
> In utter, unseasonable glory,

Telling nothing but how I made
By hand, a creature to keep me dying
Years longer, and coming to sing in the wood
Of what love still might give,
Could I turn wholly mortal in my mind,
My body-building angel give me rest,
This tree cast down its foliage with the years.

"This tree" is at last Dickey himself as fiction of duration, the poet become
his own poem, indeed "made / By hand," and so a house made by hands, a
mortal body. When desire can turn monistic, for Dickey, it can become only
a mortal turn, a trope knowing it is only trope. The other is divine, but only
as Apollo or Mithra was divine, rather than as Jesus or Jehovah. A poem
"about" a body-building child has transformed itself into the Sublime, into
the body-building angel who has never since given Dickey any rest.

Retrospectively, I suppose that the poem "The Other" first moved
me because so few American poems of twenty years ago had anything like
Dickey's remarkable ability to be so humanly direct and yet so trustingly
given to the potential of figurative language. The Dickey of the early
motion seemed to have found his way back, almost effortlessly, to the
secrets of poetry. I remember that the first poem by Dickey that I read was
the title poem of *Drowning With Others*, a title that is itself an unforgettable
trope, worthy of Emily Dickinson's apprehension that an acute consciousness, even when aware of neighbors and the sun, of other selves and outward nature, still died quite alone, except for its own identity, a totemic
single hound. What is Sublime in the self finally is capable only of "drowning with others," but that is only part of what is central in what remains
one of Dickey's most singular and enduring poems.

If I remember aright, Dickey himself doesn't much like this poem,
and thinks it obscure rather than strong. Indeed, I recall his insistence that
he wrote the poem only so as to give status to his book's title. His account
of the poem's referential aspect was strangely literal, but I think this is one
of his poems that sneaked by him, as it were:

There are moments a man turns from us
Whom we have all known until now.
Upgathered, we watch him grow,
Unshipping his shoulder bones

Like human, everyday wings
That he has not ever used,

Releasing his hair from his brain,
A kingfisher's crest, confused

By the God-tilted light of Heaven.
His deep, window-watching smile
Comes closely upon us in waves,
And spreads, and now we are

At last within it, dancing.
Slowly we turn and shine
Upon what is holding us,
As under our feet he soars,

Struck dumb as the angel of Eden,
In wide, eye-opening rings.
Yet the hand on my shoulder fears
To feel my own wingblades spring,

To feel me sink slowly away
In my hair turned loose like a thought
Of a fisherbird dying in flight.
If I opened my arms, I could hear

Every shell in the sea find the word
It has tried to put into my mouth.
Broad flight would become of my dancing,
And I would obsess the whole sea,

But I keep rising and singing
With my last breath. Upon my back,
With his hand on my unborn wing,
A man rests easy as sunlight

Who has kept himself free of the forms
Of the deaf, down-soaring dead,
And me laid out and alive
For nothing at all, in his arms.

I read this as another lyric of poetic incarnation, a rather less willing
assumption of the divine other, perhaps even a defense against the Orphic
predicament, but still a revision of the poem "The Other." Indeed, I

wonder if one way of characterizing Dickey's obsessive strength as a poet is to say that he cannot stop rewriting that essential early poem. For the man who turns from us in the opening line of "Drowning With Others" is the Orphic Dickey, poet and divine other. Like the rich-haired youth of Collins, or Coleridge's youth with flashing eyes and floating hair, or Stevens's figure of the youth as virile poet in "Mrs. Alfred Uruguay," this other Dickey has hair released into "a kingfisher's crest, confused / By the God-tilted light of Heaven." Apollo is reborn again, but as Orphic drowning man, fit version of the poet of Sensibility in America, be he Hart Crane or Roethke or Agee or Dickey. But if the man turning from us in this poem is Dickey in the act of Sublime apotheosis, then whoever is that "I" rather desperately chanting this hieratic spell? Perhaps that is why Dickey as commentator judged this grand lyric too obscure, despite its palpable strength.

Our poet is weird in the true sense, one of the Fates (as Richard Howard, lexicographer among bards, might remind us), and his natural mode is the uncanny. What he has done here may be obscure to his spectral self, but his magic or occult self gathers his spectral self, until even that "I" keeps "rising and singing / With my last breath." And so truly neither self dies, or can die, in this soaring lyric of divination. Perhaps there is a touch, not indeliberate, of Dylan Thomas in the metric here, and even allusive overtones of Thomas at moments in the diction. That resemblance may even be a hidden cause of Dickey's distaste for his poem, but I remark upon it to note the difference between the poets, rather than their shared qualities. On mortality, the warrior Dickey cannot deceive himself, but a poet whose totem seems to be the albatross does not fear death by water. Few lines are as characteristic of Dickey as "And I would obsess the whole sea."

I take it that "drowning with others" is a trope for "winging with others," and that the dominant image here is flight, and not going under. Flight of course is Freud's true trope for repression, and an Orphic sensibility never ceases to forget, involuntarily but on purpose, that its vocation is mortal godhood, or not dying *as a poet*. Drowning with others, then, as a trope, must mean something like dying only as the immortal precursor dies or writing poems that men will not let die. Though its scale is small, this is Dickey's *Lycidas*, even as *The Zodiac* will be his cosmological elegy for the self. The child building up a Mithra-like body is still here in this poem, but he is here more reluctantly, caught up in the moments of discovering that a too-closely-shared immortality becomes mortality again, the stronger the sharing is known.

Dickey, being one of our authentic avatars of the American Sublime, exemplifies its two grand stigmata: not to feel free unless he is alone, and finally to know that what is oldest in him is no part of the Creation. After two poems wrestling with otherness, I need to restore his sense of solitude, his Emersonian self-reliance, and the great poem for this in his early motion is "In the Mountain Tent," which appropriately concludes the book *Drowning With Others*. I remember that Dickey contrasts this with the more famous "The Heaven of Animals," a lovely poem, but not one with the power of this meditation:

> I am hearing the shape of the rain
> Take the shape of the tent and believe it,
> Laying down all around where I lie
> A profound, unspeakable law.
> I obey, and am free-falling slowly
>
> Through the thought-out leaves of the wood
> Into the minds of animals.
> I am there in the shining of water
> Like dark, like light, out of Heaven.
>
> I am there like the dead, or the beast
> Itself, which thinks of a poem—
> Green, plausible, living, and holy—
> And cannot speak, but hears,
> Called forth from the waiting of things,
>
> A vast, proper, reinforced crying
> With the sifted, harmonious pause,
> The sustained intake of all breath
> Before the first word of the Bible.
>
> At midnight water dawns
> Upon the held skulls of the foxes
> And weasels and touseled hares
> On the eastern side of the mountain.
> Their light is the image I make
>
> As I wait as if recently killed,
> Receptive, fragile, half-smiling,
> My brow watermarked with the mark
> On the wing of a moth

And the tent taking shape on my body
Like ill-fitting, Heavenly clothes.
From holes in the ground comes my voice
In the God-silenced tongue of the beasts.
"I shall rise from the dead," I am saying.

Whether a Christian or not, this speaker appears to entertain a belief in the resurrection of the body. Even in this solitude of spirit, the uncanny in Dickey, his *daimon*, enters with the poem's implicit question: Whose body, mine or that of the other? Is it every man who shall rise in the body, or is it not a more Gnostic persuasion that is at work here? The Gnostic lives already in the resurrected body, which is the body of a Primal Man who preceded the Creation. What a Gnostic called the Pleroma, the Fullness, Dickey calls beautifully "the waiting of things." The dead, the animals, and Dickey as the poem's speaker, all hear together the Gnostic Call, a vast crying out of the waiting of things. Without knowing any esoteric Gnosticism, Dickey by poetic intuition arrives at the trope of the Kabbalistic holding in of the divine breath that precedes the rupture of Creation. What Dickey celebrates therefore is "The sustained intake of all breath / Before the first word of the Bible." That word in Hebrew is *Beresit*, and so the vision of this poem is set before the Beginning. At midnight, not at dawn, and so only in the light of a rain image reflected from the beasts, Dickey speaks forth for the beasts, who have been silenced by the Demiurge called God by Genesis. In Dickey's own interpretation, the man experiences both a kinship with the beasts and a fundamental difference, since he alone will rise from the dead. But I think the poet is stronger than the poet-as-interpreter here. To rise from the dead, in this poem's context, is merely to be one's own magical or pneumatic self, a self that precedes the first word of the Bible.

It isn't very startling to see and say that Dickey, as poet, is not a Christian poet, but rather an Emersonian, an American Orphic and Gnostic. This is only to repeat Richard Howard's fine wordplay upon what could be called the Native Strain in our literature. What startles me, a little, is to see and say just how doctrinal, even programmatic, Dickey's early Orphism now seems. The Orphism has persisted, emerging with tumultuous force in the superbly mad female preacher of Dickey's "May Day Sermon," which I recommend we all read directly after each time we read Jonathan Edwards's rather contrary sermon, "Sinners in the Hands of an Angry God." Rhetorically, though, that is a very different Dickey than the poet of *The Early Motion*, whose Orphism perhaps is the more persuasive for being almost overheard, rather than so emphatically heard.

I turn my charting of the early motion to Dickey's next book, *Helmets*, which so far may be his most distinguished single volume, a judgment in which I would neither want nor expect him to concur. "Helmet," as a word, ultimately goes back to an Indo-European root that means both "to cover and conceal," but also "to save," which explains why "helm" and "helmet" are related to those two antithetical primal names, Hell and Valhalla. Dickey's book, of course, knows all this, Dickey being a preternaturally implicit knower, both as a poet and as a warrior—or, combining both modes, as an archer and hunter. Had I time and space, I would want to comment on every poem in *Helmets*, but I will confine myself to its two most ambitious meditations, "Approaching Prayer" and the final "Drinking from a Helmet." Certain thematic and agonistic strains that I have glanced at already can be said not to culminate but to achieve definitive expression in these major poems. I qualify my statement because what is most problematic about Dickey's poetry is that nothing ever is allowed to culminate, not even in *The Zodiac*, or "Falling," or "May Day Sermon." So obsessive a poet generally would not remain also so tentative, but Dickey's is a cunning imagination, metamorphic enough to evade its exegetes.

As a critic himself obsessed with the issue of belatedness, I am particularly impressed by the originality of "Approaching Prayer," which Dickey rightly called "the most complicated and far-fetched poem I've written." I should add that Dickey said that some fifteen years ago, but it is good enough for me that his observation was true up to then. The far-fetcher was the good, rough English term that the Elizabethan rhetorician Puttenham used to translate the ancient trope called metalepsis or transumption, and "Approaching Prayer" is certainly an instance of the kind of poem that I have learned to call transumptive. Such a poem swallows up an ever-early freshness as its own, and spits out all sense of belatedness, as belonging only to others. "Approaching Prayer" is at moments Yeatsian in its stance and diction, but what overwhelmingly matters most in it can only be called "originality." I know no poem remotely like it. If it shares a magic vitalism with Yeats and D.H. Lawrence, its curious kind of wordless, almost undirected prayer has nothing Yeatsian or Lawrentian in its vision. And it is less like Dickey's true precursor, Roethke, than it is like Robert Penn Warren's masterful "Red-Tailed Hawk and Pyre of Youth," which, however, was written long after it and perhaps may even owe something to it.

Originality in poetry, despite Northrop Frye's eloquent assertions, has little to do with the renewal of an archetype. Instead, it has to do with what I would call a struggle against facticity, where "facticity" means being so incarcerated by an author, a tradition, or a mode that neither author nor reader is aware of the incarceration. Dickey calls his poem "Approaching Prayer," but as his revisionist or critic, I will retitle it "Approaching Poetry" or even "Approaching Otherness." I grant that Dickey has said, "In this poem I tried to imagine how a rather prosaic person would prepare himself for the miraculous event which will be the prayer he's going to try to pray," but surely that "rather prosaic person" is a transparent enough defense for the not exactly prosaic Dickey. No one has ever stood in Dickey's presence and felt that he was encountering prose. The poem's speaker is "inside the hair *helmet*" (my emphasis), and this helmet too both conceals and saves. At the poem's visionary center, the boar's voice, speaking through the helmet, gives us the essential trope as he describes his murder by the archer: "*The sound from his fingers, / Like a plucked word, quickly pierces / Me again.*" The bow, then, is poetic language, and each figuration is a wounding arrow. Who then is slaying whom?

Like any strong poet, Dickey puts on the body of his dead father, for him, let us say, the composite precursor Yeats/Roethke. Shall we say that the strong poet, in Dickey's savage version, reverses the fate of Adonis, and slays the boar of facticity? I hear the accent of another reversal, when Dickey writes:

My father's sweater
Swarms over me in the dark.
I see nothing, but for a second

Something goes through me
Like an accident, a negligent glance.

Emerson, in his famous epiphany of transmutation into a Transparent Eyeball, chanted: "I am nothing; I see all; the currents of the Universal Being circulate through me; I am part or particle of God." Dickey's surrogate sees nothing, but for a second is all, since that something going through him, glancingly negligent, accidental, also makes him part or particle of God. Addressing beasts and angels, this not so very prosaic personage speaks both as beast and as angel. But to whom? To part or particle of what is oldest, earliest in him, to the beyond that comes straight down at the point of the acceptable time. But acceptable to whom? The God of the hunt is hardly Yahweh Elohim. Dickey's closing chant salutes the God through the trope of "enough": a violent enough stillness, a brain having enough blood, love enough from the dead father, lift enough from the acuity of slaughter—all enough to slay reason in the name of something being, something that need not be heard, if only "it may have been somehow said."

The apocalyptic Lawrence of the last poems and *The Man Who Died*, and the Yeats of the final phase, celebrated and so would have understood that "enough." As an American Orphic, as pilot and as archer, Dickey is less theoretic, more pragmatic, in having known just that "enough."

If I were writing of the later Dickey, the poet of "The Firebombing," "Slave Quarters," "Falling," and *The Zodiac*, then I would invoke Blake's Proverbs of Hell on the dialectics of knowing enough by knowing more than enough. But I am going to conclude where Dickey himself ends *The Early Motion*, with the gracious approach to otherness that characterizes the nineteen fragments that constitute "Drinking from a Helmet." Dickey remarks that the fragments are set between the battlefield and the graveyard, which I suspect is no inaccurate motto for the entire cosmos of what will prove to be the Whole Motion, when we have it all. Though it is a suite of war poems, "Drinking from a Helmet," even in its title, moves toward meaning both of Dickey's major imaginative obsessions: divination through finding the right cover of otherness, and salvation from the body of this death through finding the magic body of the poet.

A survivor climbs out of his foxhole to wait on line at a green water-truck, picking up another's helmet to serve as a drinking vessel. Behind him, the graves registration people are laying out the graveyard for those still fighting. The literal force of this is almost too strong, and conceals the trope of divination, defined by Vico as the process of evasion by which the poet of Magic Formalism achieves godhood—a kind of mortal godhood, but immortality enough. Drinking from a helmet becomes the magic act of substitution, fully introduced in the luminous intensity of fragment VIII:

> At the middle of water
> Bright circles dawned inward and outward
> Like oak rings surviving the tree
> As its soul, or like
> The concentric gold spirit of time.
> I kept trembling forward through something
> Just born of me.

The "something" is prayer, but again in the peculiar sense adumbrated in the poem "Approaching Prayer." Dickey always has been strongest at *invention* (which Dr. Johnson thought the essence of poetry) and his invention is triumphant throughout the subsequent progression of fragments. We apprehend an almost Blakean audacity of pure vision, as the speaker struggles to raise the dead:

I swayed, as if kissed in the brain.
Above the shelled palm-stumps I saw
How the tops of huge trees might be moved
In a place in my own country
I never had seen in my life.
In the closed dazzle of my mouth
I fought with a word in the water
To call on the dead to strain
Their muscles to get up and go there.
I felt the difference between
Sweat and tears when they rise,
Both trying to melt the brow down.

I think one would have to go back to Whitman's *Drum-Taps* to find an American war poem this nobly wrought. Vision moves from Okinawa to rural America, to the place of the slain other whose helmet has served as the vessel of the water of life:

On even the first day of death
The dead cannot rise up,
But their last thought hovers somewhere
For whoever finds it.
My uninjured face floated strangely
In the rings of a bodiless tree.
Among them, also, a final
Idea lived, waiting
As in Ariel's limbed, growing jail.

Ariel, imprisoned by the witch before Prospero's advent, then becomes the spirit of freedom, but not in this poem, where only to "be no more killed" becomes freedom enough. "Not dying wherever you are" is the new mode of otherness, as vision yields to action:

Enough
Shining, I picked up my carbine and said.
I threw my old helmet down
And put the wet one on.
Warmed water ran over my face.
My last thought changed, and I knew
I inherited one of the dead.

Dickey at last, though only through surrogate or trope, is at once self and other. What was vision becomes domesticated, touchingly American:

> I saw tremendous trees
> That would grow on the sun if they could,
> Towering. I saw a fence
> And two boys facing each other,
> Quietly talking,
> Looking in at the gigantic redwoods,
> The rings in the trunks turning slowly
> To raise up stupendous green.
> They went away, one turning
> The wheels of a blue bicycle,
> The smaller one curled catercornered
> In the handlebar basket.

The dead soldier's last thought is of his older brother, as Dickey's longing always has been for his own older brother, dead before the poet was born. Fragment XVIII, following, is the gentlest pathos in all of Dickey:

> I would survive and go there,
> Stepping off the train in a helmet
> That held a man's last thought,
> Which showed him his older brother
> Showing him trees.
> I would ride through all
> California upon two wheels
> Until I came to the white
> Dirt road where they had been,
> Hoping to meet his blond brother,
> And to walk with him into the wood
> Until we were lost,
> Then take off the helmet
> And tell him where I had stood,
> What poured, what spilled, what swallowed:

That "what" is the magic of substitution, and the final fragment is Whitmanian and unforgettable, being the word of the survivor who suffered and was there:

> And tell him I was the man.

The ritual magic of a soldier's survival has been made one with the Incarnation of the Poetical Character. Of all Dickey's poems, it is the one I am persuaded that Walt Whitman would have admired most. Whitman too would have said with Dickey: "I never have been able to disassociate the poem from the poet, and I hope I never will." What Whitman and Dickey alike show is that "the poet" is both an empirical self, and more problematically a real me or me myself, an ontological self, and yet a divine other. Both poets are hermetic and esoteric while making populist gestures. There the resemblance ends, and to pursue it further would be unfair to Dickey or any contemporary; it would have been unfair even for Stevens or for Hart Crane. The Dickey of the later motion is no Whitmanian; if one wants an American analogue, one would have to imagine Theodore Roethke as an astronaut, which defeats imagination. But I end by citing Whitman because his final gestures are the largest contrast I know to James Dickey's ongoing motions in his life's work. Whitman is up ahead of us somewhere; he is perpetually early, warning us: "Will you speak before I am gone? will you prove already too late?" The burden of belatedness is upon us, but if we hurry, we will catch up to him:

> Failing to fetch me at first keep encouraged,
> Missing me one place search another,
> I stop somewhere waiting for you.

Not Dickey; he cannot stop, yet he has taken up part of the burden for us. Whitman is larger, but then no one is larger, and that largeness is a final comfort, like Stevens's "Large Red Man Reading." Dickey speaks only to and for part of us, but that part is or wants to be the survivor; wants no more dying. Words alone, alas, are not certain good, though the young Yeats, like the young Dickey, wanted them to be. But they can help us to make "a creature to keep me dying / Years longer," as Dickey wrote in the poem of "The Other." I conclude by going full circle, by returning to the poem with the tribute that it could prove to contain the whole motion within it. Dickey cannot "turn wholly mortal in [his] mind," and that touch of "utter, unseasonable glory" will be his legacy.

John Ashbery

(1927–)

IN THE EXQUISITE SQUALORS OF TENNYSON'S *THE HOLY GRAIL*, AS PERCIVAL rides out on his ruinous quest, we can experience the hallucination of believing that the Laureate is overly influenced by *The Waste Land*, for Eliot too became a master at reversing the *apophrades*. Or, in our present moment, the achievement of John Ashbery in his powerful poem *Fragment* (in his volume *The Double Dream of Spring*) is to return us to Stevens, somewhat uneasily to discover that at moments Stevens sounds rather too much like Ashbery, an accomplishment I might not have thought possible.

The strangeness added to beauty by the positive *apophrades* is of that kind whose best expositor was Pater. Perhaps all Romantic style, at its heights, depends upon a successful manifestation of the dead in the garments of the living, as though the dead poets were given a suppler freedom than they had found for themselves. Contrast the Stevens of *Le Monocle de Mon Oncle* with the *Fragment* of John Ashbery, the most legitimate of the sons of Stevens:

> Like a dull scholar, I behold, in love,
> An ancient aspect touching a new mind.
> It comes, it blooms, it bears its fruit and dies.
> This trivial trope reveals a way of truth.
> Our bloom is gone. We are the fruit thereof.
> Two golden gourds distended on our vines,
> Into the autumn weather, splashed with frost,
> Distorted by hale fatness, turned grotesque.
> We hang like warty squashes, streaked and rayed,
> The laughing sky will see the two of us,

Washed into rinds by rotting winter rains.
                    (—*Le Monocle*, VIII)

Like the blood orange we have a single
Vocabulary all heart and all skin and can see
Through the dust of incisions the central perimeter
Our imaginations orbit. Other words,
Old ways are but the trappings and appurtenances
Meant to install change around us like a grotto.
There is nothing laughable
In this. To isolate the kernel of
Our imbalance and at the same time back up carefully
Its tulip head whole, an imagined good.
                    (—*Fragment*, XIII)

An older view of influence would remark that the second of these stanzas "derives" from the first, but an awareness of the revisionary ratio of *apophrades* unveils Ashbery's relative triumph in his involuntary match with the dead. This particular strain, while it matters, is not central to Stevens, but is the greatness of Ashbery whenever, with terrible difficulty, he can win free to it. When I read *Le Monocle de Mon Oncle* now, in isolation from other poems by Stevens, I am compelled to hear Ashbery's voice, for this mode has been captured by him, inescapably and perhaps forever. When I read *Fragment*, I tend not to be aware of Stevens, for his presence has been rendered benign. In early Ashbery, amid the promise and splendors of his first volume, *Some Trees*, the massive dominance of Stevens could not be evaded, though a *clinamen* away from the master had already been evidenced:

The young man places a bird-house
Against the blue sea. He walks away
And it remains. Now other

Men appear, but they live in boxes.
The sea protects them like a wall.
The gods worship a line-drawing

Of a woman, in the shadow of the sea
Which goes on writing. Are there
Collisions, communications on the shore

Or did all secrets vanish when
The woman left? Is the bird mentioned
In the waves' minutes, or did the land advance?
>   (—*Le Livre est sur la Table*, II)

This is the mode of *The Man with the Blue Guitar*, and urgently attempts to swerve away from a vision whose severity it cannot bear:

Slowly the ivy on the stones
Becomes the stones. Women become

The cities, children become the fields
And men in waves become the sea.

It is the chord that falsifies.
The sea returns upon the men,

The fields entrap the children, brick
Is a weed and all the flies are caught,

Wingless and withered, but living alive.
The discord merely magnifies.

Deepe within the belly's dark,
Of time, time grows upon the rock.
>   (—*The Man with the Blue Guitar*, XI)

The early Ashbery poem implies that there are "collisions, communications among us, even in confrontation of the sea, a universe of sense that asserts its power over our minds. But the parent-poem, though it will resolve itself in a similar quasi-comfort, harasses the poet and his readers with the intenser realization that "the discord merely magnifies," when our "collisions, communications" sound out against the greater rhythms of the sea. Where the early Ashbery attempted vainly to soften his poetic father, the mature Ashbery of *Fragment* subverts and even captures the precursor even as he appears to accept him more fully. The ephebe may still not be mentioned in the father's minutes, but his own vision has advanced. Stevens hesitated almost always until his last phase, unable firmly to adhere to or reject the High Romantic insistence that the power of the poet's mind could triumph over the universe of death, or the estranged object-world. It is not every day, he says it his *Adagia*, that the world arranges itself in a poem. His nobly desperate disciple, Ashbery, has dared the dialectic of misprision so as to implore the world daily to arrange itself into a poem:

> But what could I make of this? Glaze
> Of many identical foreclosures wrested from
> The operative hand, like a judgment but still
> The atmosphere of seeing? That two people could
> Collide in this dusk means that the time of
> Shapelessly foraging had come undone: the space was
> Magnificent and dry. On flat evenings
> In the months ahead, she would remember that that
> Anomaly had spoken to her, words like disjointed beaches
> Brown under the advancing signs of the air.

This, the last stanza of *Fragment*, returns Ashbery full circle to his early *Le Livre est sur la Table*. There are "collisions, communications on the shore" but these "collide in this dusk." "Did the land advance?" of the early poem is answered partly negatively, by the brown, disjointed beaches, but partly also by "the advancing signs of the air." Elsewhere in *Fragment*, Ashbery writes: "Thus reasoned the ancestor, and everything / Happened as he had foretold, but in a funny kind of way." The strength of the positive *apophrades* gives this quester the hard wisdom of the proverbial poem he rightly calls *Soonest Mended*, which ends by:

> ... learning to accept
> The charity of the hard moments as they are doled out,
> For this is action, this not being sure, this careless
> Preparing, sowing the seeds crooked in the furrow,
> Making ready to forget, and always coming back
> To the mooring of starting out, that day so long ago.

Here Ashbery has achieved one of the mysteries of poetic style, but only through the individuation of misprision.

II

Another misprision is a haunting lyric of belatedness, Ashbery's recent *As You Came from the Holy Land*, where the parodistic first-line/title repeats the opening of a bitter ballad of lost love attributed to Ralegh, one of whose stanzas lingers throughout Ashbery's gentler poem:

> I have lovde her all my youth,
>   Butt now ould, as you see,
> Love lykes not the fallyng frute
>   From the wythered tree.

"Her" is the personal past in Ashbery's elegy for the self:

> of western New York state
> were the graves all right in their bushings
> was there a note of panic in the late August air
> because the old man had peed in his pants again
> was there turning away from the late afternoon glare
> as though it too could be wished away
> was any of this present
> and how could this be
> the magic solution to what you are in now
> whatever has held you motionless
> like this so long through the dark season
> until now the women come out in navy blue
> and the worms come out of the compost to die
> it is the end of any season
>
> you reading there so accurately
> sitting not wanting to be disturbed
> as you came from that holy land
> what other signs of earth's dependency were upon you
> what fixed sign at the crossroads
> what lethargy in the avenues
> where all is said in a whisper
> what tone of voice among the hedges
> what tone under the apple trees
> the numbered land stretches away
> and your house is built in tomorrow
> but surely not before the examination
> of what is right and will befall
> not before the census
> and the writing down of names
>
> remember you are free to wander away
> as from other times other scenes that were taking place
> the history of someone who came too late

the time is ripe now and the adage
is hatching as the seasons change and tremble
it is finally as though that thing of monstrous interest
were happening in the sky
but the sun is setting and prevents you from seeing it
out of night the token emerges
its leaves like birds alighting all at once under a tree
taken up and shaken again
put down in weak rage
knowing as the brain does it can never come about
not here not yesterday in the past
only in the gap of today filling itself
as emptiness is distributed
in the idea of what time it is
when that time is already past

Ashbery, probably because of his direct descent from Stevens, tends like Stevens to follow rather precisely the crisis-poem paradigm that I have traced in my map of misreading. This model, Wordsworthian-Whitmanian, never restores as much representational meaning as it continually curtails or withdraws, as I have observed earlier. Ashbery's resource has been to make a music of the poignance of withdrawal. So, in this poem, the "end of any season" that concludes the first stanza is deliberately too partial a synecdoche to compensate for the pervasive absences of the ironies throughout the stanza. Ashbery's turnings-against-the-self are wistful and inconclusive, and he rarely allows a psychic reversal any completeness. His origins, in the holy land of western New York state, are presented here and elsewhere in his work with an incurious rigidity that seems to have no particular design on the poet himself, characteristically addressed as "you." The next stanza emphasizes Ashbery's usual metonymic defense of isolation (as opposed to the Stevensian undoing or the Whitmanian regression), by which signs and impulses become detached from one another, with the catalog or census completing itself in the reductive "writing down of names," in which "down" takes on surprising difference and force. The third stanza, one of Ashbery's most radiant, marks the poem's *daemonization*, the American Counter-Sublime in which Ashbery, like Stevens, is so extraordinarily at home. Ashbery's mingled strength and weakness, indeed his deliberate pathos, is that he knowingly begins where Childe Roland ended, "free to wander away" yet always seeing himself as living "the history of someone who came too late" while sensing that "the time is ripe now." Studying his own habitual expression in his prose *Three*

Poems, he had compared himself explicitly to Childe Roland at the Dark Tower. Here also, his Sublime sense that a Stevensian reality is happening in the war of the sky against the mind is necessarily obscured by a sunset akin to Roland's "last red leer."

Ashbery's finest achievement, to date, is his heroic and perpetual self-defeat, which is of a kind appropriate to conclude this book, since such self-defeat pioneers in undoing the mode of transumption that Stevens helped revive. Ashbery's allusiveness is transumptive rather than conspicuous, but he employs it against itself, as though determined to make of his lateness a desperate cheerfulness. In the final stanza of *As You Came from the Holy Land*, the most characteristic of Shelleyan-Stevensian metaphors, the fiction of the leaves, is duly revealed as a failure ("taken up and shaken again / put down in weak rage"); but the metalepsis substituted for it is almost a hyperbole of failure, as presence and the present fall together "in the gap of today filling itself / as emptiness is distributed." The two lines ending the poem would be an outrageous parody of the transumptive mode if their sad dignity were not so intense. Ashbery, too noble and poetically intelligent to subside into a parodist of time's revenges, flickers on "like a great shadow's last embellishment."

III

Ashbery has been misunderstood because of his association with the "New York School" of Kenneth Koch, Frank O'Hara and other comedians of the spirit, but also because of the dissociative phase of his work as represented by much of a peculiar volume, *The Tennis Court Oath*. But the poet of *The Double Dream of Spring* and the prose *Three Poems* is again the Stevensian meditator of the early *Some Trees*. No other American poet has labored quite so intensely to exorcise all the demons of discursiveness, and no contemporary American poet is so impressively at one with himself in expounding a discursive wisdom. Like his master, Stevens, Ashbery is essentially a ruminative poet, turning a few subjects over and over, knowing always that what counts is the mythology of self, blotched out beyond unblotching.

Ashbery's various styles have suggested affinities to composer-theorists like Cage and Cowell, to painters of the school of Kline and Pollock, and "to an assortment of French bards like Roussel, Reverdy and even Michaux. But the best of Ashbery, from the early *Some Trees* on through "A Last World" and "The Skaters" to the wonderful culminations of his great book, *The Double Dream of Spring* and the recent *Three Poems*, shows a clear descent from the major American tradition that began in Emerson. Even as his poetic father is Stevens, Ashbery's largest ancestor is Whitman, and it is the Whitmanian strain in Stevens that found Ashbery. I would guess that Ashbery, like Stevens, turned to French poetry as a deliberate evasion of continuities, a desperate quest for freedom from the burden of poetic influence. The beautiful group called "French Poems" in *The Double Dream of Spring* were written in French and then translated into English, Ashbery notes, "with the idea of avoiding customary word-patterns and associations." This looks at first like the characteristic quarrel with discursiveness that is endemic in modern verse, but a deeper familiarity with the "French Poems" will evoke powerful associations with Stevens at his most central, the seer of "Credences of Summer":

> *And it does seem that all the force of*
> *The cosmic temperature lives in the form of contacts*
> *That no intervention could resolve,*
> *Even that of a creator returned to the desolate*
> *Scene of this first experiment: this microcosm.*

> *... and then it's so natural*
> *That we experience almost no feeling*
> *Except a certain lightness which matches*
> *The recent closed ambiance which is, besides*
> *Full of attentions for us. Thus, lightness and wealth.*

> *But the existence of all these things and especially*
> *The amazing fullness of their number must be*
> *For us a source of unforgettable questions:*
> *Such as: whence does all this come? and again:*
> *Shall I some day be a part of all this fullness?*

The poet of these stanzas is necessarily a man who must have absorbed "Credences of Summer" when he was young, perhaps even as a Harvard undergraduate. Every strong poet's development is a typology of evasions, a complex misprision of his precursor. Ashbery's true precursor is the composite father, Whitman-Stevens, and the whole body to date of Ashbery's work manifests nearly every possible revisionary ratio in regard to so formidable an American ancestry. Though the disjunctiveness of so much of Ashbery suggests his usual critical placement with the boisterousness of Koch or the random poignances of O'Hara, he seems most himself when most ruefully and intensely Transcendental, the almost involuntary celebrator "of that *invisible light* which spatters the silence / Of our everyday festivities." Ashbery is a kind of invalid of American Orphism, perpetually convalescing from the strenuous worship of that dread Orphic trinity of draining gods: Eros, Dionysus, Ananke, who preside over the Native Strain of our poetry.

I propose to track Ashbery back to his origins in another essay, but here I have space only to investigate some poems of his major phase, as it seems developing in his two most recent books. To enter at this point a judgment of current American poets now entering their imaginative maturity, Ashbery and A.R. Ammons are to me the indispensable figures, two already fully achieved artists who are likely to develop into worthy rivals of Frost, Stevens, Pound, Williams, Eliot, Crane, and Warren. Merwin, James Wright, Merrill, perhaps Snyder in the school of Williams and Pound, perhaps James Dickey of a somewhat older generation (if he yet returns to the strength of earlier work) are candidates also. Yet all prophecy is dangerous here; there are recent poems by Howard, Hollander, Kinnell, Pack, Feinman, Hecht, Strand, Rich, Snodgrass, among others, which are as powerful as all but the very best of Ammons, Ashbery, Wright. Other critics and readers would nominate quite different groupings, as we evidently enter a time of singular wealth in contemporary verse.

Ashbery's poetry is haunted by the image of transparence, but this comes to him, from the start, as "a puzzling light," or carried by beings who are "as dirty handmaidens / To some transparent witch." Against Transcendental influx, Ashbery knows the wisdom. of what he calls "learning to accept / The charity of the hard moments as they are doled out," and knows also that: "One can never change the core of things, and light burns you the harder for it." Burned by a visionary flame beyond accommodation (one can contrast Kinnell's too-easy invocations of such fire), Ashbery gently plays with Orphic influx ("Light bounced off the ends / Of the small gray waves to tell / Them in the observatory / About the great drama that was being won."). Between Emerson and Whitman, the seers of this tradition, and Ashbery, Ammons and other legatees, there comes mediating the figure of Stevens:

> *My house has changed a little in the sun.*
> *The fragrance of the magnolias comes close,*
> *False flick, false form, but falseness close to kin.*
>
> *It must be visible or invisible,*
> *Invisible or visible or both;*
> *A seeing and unseeing in the eye.*

These are hardly the accents of transport, yet Stevens does stand precariously, in the renewed light. But even the skepticism is Emerson's own; his greatest single visionary oration is *Experience*, a text upon which Dickinson, Stevens and Ashbery always seem to be writing commentaries:

> Thus inevitably does the universe wear our color, and every object fall successively into the subject itself. The subject exists, the subject enlarges; all things sooner or later fall into place. As I am, so I see; use what language we will, we can never say anything but what we are.... And we cannot say too little of our constitutional necessity of seeing things under private aspects, or saturated with our humors. And yet is the God the native of these bleak rocks.... We must hold hard to this poverty, however scandalous, and by more vigorous self-recoveries, after the sallies of action, possess our axis more firmly....

The Old Transcendentalism in America, like the New, hardly distinguishes itself from a visionary skepticism, and makes no assertions without compensatory qualifications. Still, we tend to remember Emerson for his transparencies, and not the opaquenesses that more frequently haunted him and his immediate disciples. I suspect that this is because of Emerson's *confidence*, no matter where he places his emphases. When Stevens attains to a rare transparence, he generally sees very little more than is customary, but he *feels* a greater peace, and this peace reduces to a confidence in the momentary capability of his own imagination. Transcendentalism, in its American formulation, centers upon Emerson's stance of Self-Reliance, which is primarily a denial of the anxiety of influence. Like Nietzsche, who admired him for it, Emerson refuses to allow us to believe we must be latecomers. In a gnomic quatrain introducing his major essay on self-reliance, Emerson manifested a shamanistic intensity still evident in his descendents:

> *Cast the bantling on the rocks,*
> *Suckle him with the she-wolf's teat,*
> *Wintered with the hawk and fox,*
> *Power and speed be hands and feet.*

This is splendid, but Emerson had no more been such a banding than any of my contemporaries are, unless one wants the delightful absurdity of seeing Wordsworth or Coleridge as a she-wolf. "Do not seek yourself outside yourself" is yet another motto to *Self-Reliance*, and there is one more, from Beaumont and Fletcher, assuring us that the soul of an honest man:

> Commands all light, all influence, all fate
> Nothing to him falls early or coo late.

These are all wonderful idealisms. Whitman, who had been simmering, read *Self-Reliance* and was brought to the boil of the 1855 "Song of Myself." Ashbery, by temperament and choice, always seems to keep simmering, but whether he took impetus from Whitman, Stevens or even the French partisans of poetic Newness, he has worked largely and overtly in this Emersonian spirit. Unfortunately, like Merwin and Merwin's precursor, Pound, Ashbery truly absorbed from the Emerson-Whitman tradition the poet's over-idealizing tendency to lie to himself, against his origins and against experience. American poets since Emerson are all antithetical completions of one another, which means mostly that they develop into grotesque truncations of what they might have been. Where British poets swerve away from their spiritual fathers, ours attempt to rescue their supposedly benighted sires. American bards, like Democritus, deny the swerve, so as to save divination, holding on to the Fate that might make them liberating gods. Epicurus affirmed the swerve, ruining divination, and all poetry since is caught between the two. Emerson, though close to Democritus, wants even divination to be a mode of Self-Reliance. That is, he genuinely shares the Orphic belief that the poet is already divine, and realizes more of this divinity in writing his poems. Lucretian poets like Shelley who find freedom by swerving away from fathers (Wordsworth and Milton, for Shelley) do not believe in divination, and do not worship an Orphic Necessity as the final form of divinity. Orphic poets, particularly American or Emersonian Orphics, worship four gods only: Ananke, Eros, Dionysus and—most of all surely—themselves. They are therefore peculiarly resistant to the idea of poetic influence, for divination—to them—means primarily an apprehension of their own possible sublimity, the gods they are in process of becoming. The gentle Ashbery, despite all his quite genuine and hard-won wisdom, is as much in this tradition as those spheral men, Emerson, Whitman, Thoreau, and that sublime egoist, Stevens, or the American Wordsworth.

The Double Dream of Spring has a limpidly beautiful poem called "Clouds," which begins:

> *All this time he hod only been waiting,*
> *Not even thinking, as many had supposed.*

Now sleep wound down to him as its promise of dazzling peace
And he stood up to assume that imagination.

There were others in the forest as close as he
To caring about the silent outcome, but they had gotten lost
In the shadows of dreams so that the external look
Of the nearby world had become confused with the cobwebs inside.

Sleep here has a Whitmanian-Stevensian cast ("The Sleepers," "The Owl in the Sarcophagus") and the gorgeous solipsism so directly celebrated here has its sources in the same ultimately Emersonian tradition. Though "he," the poet or quest-hero, is distinguished from his fellows as not having yielded to such solipsism, the poem ends in a negative apotheosis:

He shoots forward like a malignant star.
The edges of the journey are ragged.
Only the face of night begins to grow distinct
As the fainter stars call to each other and are lost.

Day re-creates his image like a snapshot:
The family and the guests are there,
The talking over there, only now it will never end.
And so cities are arranged, and oceans traversed,

And farms tilled with especial care.
This year again the corn has grown ripe and tall.
It is a perfect rebuttal of the argument. And Semele
Moves away, puzzled at the brown light above the fields.

The harvest of natural process, too ripe for enigmas, refutes quest, and confirms the natural realism of all solipsists. This poem, urging us away from the Emersonian or Central Self, concludes by yielding to that Self, and to the re-birth of Dionysus, Semele's son. Like his precursor, Stevens, Ashbery fears and evades the Native Strain of American Orphism and again like Stevens he belongs as much to that strain as Hart Crane or John Wheelwright does. In the recent prose *Three Poems*, he ruefully accepts his tradition and his inescapable place in it:

Why, after all, were we not destroyed in the conflagration of
the moment our real and imaginary lives coincided, unless it
was because we never had a separate existence beyond that of

those two static and highly artificial concepts whose fusion was nevertheless the cause of death and destruction not only for ourselves but in the world around us. But perhaps the explanation lies precisely here: what we were witnessing was merely the reverse side of an event of cosmic beatitude for all except us, who were blind to it because it took place inside us. Meanwhile the shape of life has changed definitively for the better for everyone on the outside. They are bathed in the light of this tremendous surprise as in the light of a new sun from which only healing and not corrosive rays emanate; they comment on the miraculous change as people comment on the dazzling beauty of a day in early autumn, forgetting that for the blind man in their midst it is a day like any other, so that its beauty cannot be said to have universal validity but must remain fundamentally in doubt.   (*The Recital*)

The closest (though dialectically opposed) analogue to this passage is the great concluding rhapsody of Emerson's early apocalypse, *Nature*, when the Orphic Poet returns to prophecy:

As when the summer comes from the south the snow-banks melt and the face of the earth becomes green before it, so shall the advancing spirit create its ornaments along its park, and carry with it the beauty it visits and the sons, which enchants it; it shall draw beautiful faces, warm hearts, wise discourse, and heroic acts, around its way, until evil is no more seen. The kingdom of man over nature, which cometh not with observation,—a dominion such as now is beyond his dream of God,— he shall enter without more wonder than the blind man feels who is gradually restored to perfect sight.

Ashbery's apocalyptic transformation of the Self, its elevation to the Over-Soul, is manifest to everyone and everything outside the Self, but not to the blind man of the Self. The Emersonian Self will know the metamorphic redemption of others and things only by knowing first its gradual freedom from blindness as to its own glory. Ashbery's forerunners, the makers of *Song of Myself* and *Notes toward a Supreme Fiction*, were primary Emersonians, involuntary as Stevens was in this identity. Ashbery is that American anomaly, an antithetical Transcendentalist, bearer of an influx of the Newness that he cannot know himself.

IV

I leap ahead, past Frost and Pound, Eliot and Williams, past even Hart Crane, to a contemporary image-of-voice that is another strong tally, however ruefully the strength regards itself. Here is John Ashbery's *The Other Tradition*, the second poem in his 1977 volume, *Houseboat Days*:

They all came, some wore sentiments
Emblazoned on T-shirts, proclaiming the lateness
Of the hour, and indeed the sun slanted its rays
Through branches of Norfolk Island pine as though
Politely clearing its throat, and all ideas settled
In a fuzz of dust under trees when it's drizzling:
The endless games of Scrabble, the boosters,
The celebrated omelette au Cantal, and through it
The roar of time plunging unchecked through the sluices
Of the days, dragging every sexual moment of it
Past the lenses: the end of something.
Only then did you glance up from your book,
Unable to comprehend what had been taking place, or
Say what you had been reading. More chairs
Were brought, and lamps were lit, but it tells
Nothing of how all this proceeded to materialize
Before you and the people waiting outside and in the next
Street, repeating its name over and over, until silence
Moved halfway up the darkened trunks,
And the meeting was called to order.
                                       I still remember
How they found you, after a dream, in your thimble bar,
Studious as a butterfly in a parking for.
The road home was nicer then. Dispersing, each of the
Troubadours had something to say about how charity
Had run its race and won, leaving you the ex-president
Of the event, and how, though many of these present
Had wished something to come of it, if only a distant
Wisp of smoke, yet none was so deceived as to hanker
After that cool non-being of just a few minutes before,
Now that the idea of a forest had clamped itself
Over the minutiae of the scene. You found this
Charming, but turned your face fully toward night,
Speaking into it like a megaphone, not hearing

Or caring, although these still live and are generous
And all ways contained, allowed to come and go
Indefinitely in and out of the stockade
They have so much trouble remembering, when your forgetting
Rescues them at last, as a star absorbs the night.

I am aware that this charming poem urbanely confronts, absorbs and in some sense seeks to overthrow a critical theory, almost a critical climate, that has accorded it a canonical status. Stevens's Whitman pro claims that nothing is final and that no man shall see the end. Ashbery, a Whitman somehow more studiously casual even than Whitman, regards the prophets of belatedness and cheerfully insists that his forgetting or repression will rescue us at last, even as the Whitmanian or Stevensian evening star absorbs the night. But the price paid for this metaleptic reversal of American belatedness into a fresh earliness is the yielding up of Ashbery's tally or image of voice to a deliberate grotesquerie. Sexuality is made totally subservient to time, which is indeed "the end of something," and poetic tradition becomes an ill-organized social meeting of troubadours, leaving the canonical Ashbery as "ex-president / Of the event." As for the image of voice proper, the Whitmanian confrontation of the night now declines into: "You found this / Charming, but turned your face fully toward night, / Speaking into it like a megaphone, not hearing / Or caring." Such a megaphone is an apt image for Paul de Man's deconstructionist view of poetic tradition, which undoes tradition by suggesting that every poem is as much a random and gratuitous event as any human death is.

Ashbery's implicit interpretation of what he wants to call *The Other Tradition* mediates between this vision, of poems as being totally cur off from one another and the antithetical darkness in which poems carry overdetermined relationships and progress towards a final entropy. Voice in our poetry now tallies what Ashbery in his *Syringa*, a major Orphic elegy in *Houseboat Days*, calls "a record of pebbles along the way." Let us grant that the American Sublime is always also an American irony, and then turn back to Emerson and hear the voice that is great within us somehow breaking through again. This is Emerson in his journal for August 1859, on the eve of being burned out, with all his true achievement well behind him; but he gives us the true tally of his soul:

> *Beatitudes of Intellect.*—Am I not, one of these days, to write consecutively of the beatitude of intellect? It is too great for feeble souls, and they are over-excited. The wineglass shakes, and the wine is spilled. What then? The joy which will not let

me sit in my chair, which brings me bolt upright to my feet, and sends me striding around my room, like a tiger in his care, and I cannot have composure and concentration enough even to set down in English words the thought which thrills me—is not that joy a certificate of the elevation? What if I never write a book or a line? for a moment, the eyes of my eves were opened, the affirmative experience remains, and consoles through all suffering.

V

Of the many contemporary heirs of Whitman and of Stevens, John Ashbery seems likeliest to achieve something near to their eminence. Yet their uncertainty as to their audience is far surpassed in the shifting; stances that Ashbery assumes. His mode can vary from the apparently opaque, so disjunctive as to seem beyond interpretation, to a kind of limpid clairvoyance that again brings the Emersonian contraries together. Contemplating Parmigianino's picture in his major long poem, *Self-Portrait in a Convex Mirror*, Ashbery achieves a vision in which art, rather than nature, becomes the imprisoner of the soul:

> The soul has to stay where it is,
> Even though restless, hearing raindrops at the pane,
> The sighing of autumn leaves thrashed by the wind,
> Longing to be free, outside, lust it must stay
> Posing in this place. It must move as little as possible.
> This is what the portrait says.
> But there is in that gaze a combination
> Of tenderness, amusement and regret, so powerful
> In its restraint that one cannot look for long.
> The secret is too plain. The pity of it smarts,
> Makes hot tears spurt: that the soul is not a soul,
> Has no secret, is small, and it fits
> Its hollow perfectly: its room, our moment of attention.

Whitman's Soul, knowing its true hour in wordlessness, is apparently reduced here and now to a moment only of attention. And yet even this tearful realization, supposedly abandoning the soul to a convex mirror, remains a privileged moment, of an Emersonian rather than Paterian kind. Precisely where he seems most wistful and knowingly bewildered by loss, Ashbery remains most dialectical, like his American ancestors.

The simple diction and vulnerable stance barely conceal the presence of the American Transcendental Self, an ontological self that increases even as the empirical self abandons every spiritual assertion. Hence the "amusement" that takes up its stance between "tenderness" and "regret," Whitmanian affections, and hence also the larger hint of a power held in reserve, "so powerful in its restraint that one cannot look for long." An American Orphic, wandering in the Emersonian legacy, can afford to surrender the soul in much the name temper as the ancient Gnostics did. The soul can be given up to the Demiurge, whether of art or nature, because a spark of *pneuma* is more vital than the *psyche*, and fits no hollow whatsoever. Where Whitman and Stevens are at once hermetic and off-hand, so is Ashbery, but his throwaway gestures pay the price of an ever-increasing American sense of belatedness.

W.S. Merwin

(1927-)

> I mean we have yet no man who has leaned entirely on his character,
> and eaten angels' fond; who, trusting to his sentiments, found life made
> of miracles; who, working for universal aims, found himself fed. He
> knew not how; clothed, sheltered, and weaponed, he knew not how,
> and yet it was done by his own hands.
> EMERSON, *The Transcendentalist* (1842)

MY SUBJECT IS A STILL LITTLE-NOTED PHENOMENON, THE REVIVAL OF THE
Native Strain or Emersonian vision, in the poetry of my own generation of American poets, born in the decade 1925–1935. I cannot survey
all these poets here, and will discuss aspects of the work of only three:
W.S. Merwin, A.R. Ammons, and John Ashbery. My choice is affected
by the limitations of personal taste, and I know it could be argued that
the true continuators of the Emersonian strain are to be located elsewhere, not so much in the School of Stevens and Frost as in that of
Williams and Pound. But I am troubled by the equivocal nature (as it
seems to me) of the achievement of Olson, Duncan and their fellows,
down to Ginsberg, Snyder and younger figures. Emersonian poetry is
a diffuse though recognizable tradition: it includes Jeffers as well as
Hart Crane, the Pound of *The Pisan Cantos* together with the Stevens
of "The Auroras of Autumn," middle Roethke just as much as the later
Aiken. The problem of American poetry after Emerson might be
defined as: "Is it possible to be un-Emersonian, rather than, at best,
anti-Emersonian?" Poe is not an Emersonian poet, but then he is also
not a good poet. Perhaps only our Southern poets, down to Tate and
Warren, could be as un-Emersonian as they were anti-Emersonian; the
best of them now (Dickey and Ammons) are wholly Emersonian. Even

in Emerson's own time, irreconcilable poets emerged from his mael-
strom: Dickinson, Thoreau, Whitman, Very, even Tuckerman, whom
Winters judged to be as firm a reaction against Emerson as Hawthorne
and Melville were. American Romanticism is larger than
Emersonianism, but in our time it may no longer be possible to distinguish between the two phenomena. The prophet of a national poetic sensibility in America was the Concord rhapsode, who contains in
the dialectical mysteries of his doctrines and temperament very nearly
everything that has come after.

Let me begin with a representative text, by the indubitably representative poet of my generation, the Protean Merwin. The poem is the wonderful "The Way to the River" from the volume, *The Moving Target*, of
1963. As the poem is about fifty lines, I will summarize rather than quote
it entire. Addressed to the poet's wife, the poem is a kind of middle-of-the-
journey declaration, a creedal hymn reaffirming a covenant of love and a
sense of poetic vocation. Historically (and prophetically) the poem sums
up the dilemma of "the Silent Generation" of young Americans, on the eve
of the astonishing change (or collapse) of sensibility that was to begin at
Berkeley in 1964. After nearly a decade, one sees how brief an episode (or
epicycle) this Time of Troubles was. Merwin, with his curious proleptic
urgency, memorably caught the prelude to that time:

> *The way to the river leads past the names of*
> *Ash the sleeves the wreaths of hinges*
> *Through the song of the bandage vendor*
>
> *I lay your name by my voice*
> *As I go*
> *The way to the river leads past the late*
> *Doors and the games of the children born*
>   *looking backwards*
> *They play that they are broken glass*
> *The numbers wait in the halls and the clouds*
> *Call*
> *From windows*
> *They play that they are old they are putting the*
>   *horizon*
>
> *Into baskets they are escaping they are*
> *Hiding*

I step over the sleepers the fires the calendars
My voice turns to you

This is the "poverty" of Emerson and Stevens: imaginative need. Merwin joins a tradition that includes the E.A. Robinson of "The Man Against the Sky," the Frost of "Directive," the Stevens of "The Auroras of Autumn" as he too follows Emerson in building an altar to the Beautiful Necessity:

To the city of wines I have brought home a
  handful
Of water I walk slowly
In front of me they are building the empty
Ages I see them reflected not for long
Be here I am no longer ashamed of time it is
  too brief its hands
Have no names
I have passed it I know

Oh Necessity you with the face you with
All the faces

This is written on the back of everything

But we
Will read it together

The Merwin of this—still his present phase—began with the central poem, "Lemuel's Blessing," which follows the Smart of "Jubilate Agno" for its form (as do so many recent American poets, including Ginsberg, Strand, Donald Finkel) but which is also an Emersonian manifesto. Addressing a Spirit ("You that know the way") Merwin prayed: "Let the memory of tongues not unnerve me so that I stumble or quake." This hymn to Self-Reliance expanded into the most ambitious poem of *The Moving Target*, a majestic celebration of what Emerson called the Newness, "For Now:" "Goodbye what you learned for me I have to learn anyway / You that forgot your rivers they are gone / Myself I would not know you." In *The Lice*, his next volume (and his best), Merwin defined the gods as "what has failed to become of us," a dark postscript to the Emersonian insistence that the poets are as liberating gods. The poems of *The Lice* are afflicted by light, as in this wholly characteristic brief lyric, the poignant

"How We Are Spared":

> *At midsummer before dawn an orange light*
> > *returns to the mountains*
> *Like a great weight and the small birds cry out*
> *And bear it up*

With his largest volume, *The Carrier of Ladders*, Merwin appears to have completed his metamorphosis into an American visionary poet. The book's most astonishing yet most problematic poems are four ode-like "Psalms," subtitled: "Our Fathers," "The Signals," "The September Vision" and "The Cerements." No recent American poet, not even the Roethke of *The Far Field* or Dickey in his latest work, has attempted so exalted a style:

> *I am the son of hazard but does my prayer*
> > *reach you O star of the uncertain*
> *I am the son of blindness but nothing that we*
> > *have made watches us*
> *I am the son of untruth but I have seen the*
> > *children in Paradise walking in lairs each*
> > *hand in hand with himself*
> *I am the son of the warder but he was buried*
> > *with his keys*
> *I am the son of the light but does it call me*
> > *Samuel or Jonah*
> *I am the son of a wish older than water but I*
> > *needed till now*
> *I am the son of ghosts clutching the world like*
> > *roads but tomorrow I will go a new way*

The form is again that of the "Jubilate Agno," but the most important line in this first "Psalm," and in all of Merwin, is very far from Smart's pious spirit:

> *I am the son of the future but my own father*

As a poet, this latest Merwin hardly approaches that impossible self-begetting; the accent of the Pound-Eliot tradition hovers everywhere in even the most self-consciously bare of these verses. Merwin is more impressive for his terrible need, his lust for discontinuity, than for any actual inventiveness. The poignance of his current phase is the constant attempt at self-reliance, in the conviction that only thus will the poet see. Merwin's true precursors are three honorable, civilized representative poets: Longfellow and MacLeish and Wilbur, none of whom attempted to speak a Word that was his own Word only. In another time, Merwin would have gone on with the cultivation of a more continuous idiom, as he did in his early volumes, and as Longfellow did even in the Age of Emerson. The pressures of the quasi-apocalyptic nineteen sixties have made of Merwin an American Orphic bard despite the sorrow that his poetic temperament is not at home in suffering the Native Strain. No poet legitimately speaks a Word whose burden is that his generation will be the very last. Merwin's litanies of denudation will read very oddly when a fresh generation proclaims nearly the same dilemma, and then yet another generation trumpets finality.

Merwin's predicament (and I hope I read it fairly, as I am not unsympathetic to his work) is that he has no Transcendental vision, and yet feels impelled to prophesy. What is fascinating is that after one hundred and thirty years, the situation of American poetry is precisely as it was when Emerson wrote his loving but ironic essay on his younger contemporaries and followers, *The Transcendentalist*, where they are seen as exposing our poverty but also their own. With that genial desperation (or desperate geniality) that is so endearing (and enraging) a quality in his work, Emerson nevertheless urged his followers out into the wilderness:

> But all these of whom I speak are not proficients; they are novices; they only show the road in which man should travel, when the soul has greater health and prowess. Yet let them feel the dignity of their charge, and deserve a larger power. Their heart is the ark in which the fire is concealed which shall burn in a broader and universal flame. Let them obey the Genius then most when his impulse is wildest; then most when he seems to lead to uninhabitable deserts of thought and life; for the path which the hero travels alone is the highway of health and benefit to mankind. What is the privilege and nobility of our nature but its persistency, through its power to attach itself to what is permanent?

Merwin prays to be sustained during his time in the desert, but his poems hardly persuade us that his Genius or Spirit has led him into "uninhabitable deserts of thought and life." Readers distrustful of *The Carrier of Ladders* either emphasize what they feel is a dominance of style over substance or they complain of spiritual pretentiousness. What I find more problematic is something that Emerson foresaw when he said of his Transcendentalist that "He believes in miracle, in the perpetual openness of the human mind to new influx of light and power; he believes in inspiration, and in ecstasy," and yet went on to observe that such a youth was part of an American literature and spiritual history still "in the optative mood." Merwin's optative mood seems only to concern his impersonal identity as poet-prophet; instead of a belief in an influx of light and power, he offers us what we might contrive to know anyway, even if we had not been chilled with him by his artful mutations:

> *To which I make my way eating the silence of*
> *   animals*
> *Offering snow to the darkness*

> *Today belongs to few and tomorrow to no one*

Emerson's favorite oracular guise was as an Orphic poet. Of the Orphic deities—Eros, Dionysus, and Ananke—Merwin gives us some backward glances at the first, and a constant view of the last, but the Dionysiac has gone out of his poetry. Without the Bacchic turbulence, and haunted by a light that he presents as wholly meaningless, Merwin seems condemned to write a poetry that is as bare of true content as it is so elegantly bare in diction and design. Only the *situation* of the Emersonian Transcendentalist or Orphic Poet survives in Merwin; it is as though for him the native strain were pure strain, to be endured because endurance is value enough, or even because the eloquence of endurance is enough.

Derek Walcott

(1930-)

AFTER READING EACH OF DEREK WALCOTT'S BOOKS AS THEY HAVE APPEARED,
I remain uncertain as to the question of his aesthetic eminence, though few
seem to share my inability to render any verdict, even for myself. Walcott
is an excellent narrator, and is blessed with many verbal gifts. My own bafflement ensues from a concern with poetic voice that centers my own love
for reading and appreciating poetry. Has Derek Walcott developed a voice
altogether his own, the mark of a major poet, or does one hear in him the
composite voice of post-Yeatsian poetry in English?

I want to see if my recent reading of Walcott's long poem, *Tiepolo's
Hound*, will resolve my doubts. The strategy of *Tiepolo's Hound* turns upon
a brilliant doubling of Walcott and the West Indian Impressionist painter
Camille Pissarro, born in 1830, exactly a century before Walcott. In
Pissarro, a Sephardic Jew and so a fellow exile and outsider, Walcott dis-
covers an aesthetic quest he regards as being profoundly akin to his own.

The poem's final section, XXVI, opens with a poignant identity
forged between Pissarro and Walcott:

He enters the window frame. His gaze is yours.

Primed canvas, steaming mirror, this white page
where a drawing emerges. His portrait sighs

from a white fog. Pissarro in old age,
as we stand doubled in each other's eyes.

To endure affliction with no affection gone
seems to have been the settlement in those eyes,

whose lenses catch a glinting winter sun
on mansards and the rigid smoke of chimneys.

This is eloquent and memorable, but do I hear Walcott's voice or an adaptation of the nuanced cadences of Wallace Stevens? Does it matter whose voice it is, when the expression has this much aesthetic dignity? I uneasily recall the poetry of Archibald Macleish, whose eclectic assimilation of Eliot, Pound and others was so wittily satirized by Edmund Wilson in his *The Omelet of A. Macleish*. Here are the closing lines of *Tiepolo's Hound*, which seem to me quite beautiful, but again I hear Wallace Stevens's "hum of thoughts evaded in the mind":

Let this page catch the last light on Becune Point,
lengthen the arched shadows of Charlotte Amalie,

to a prayer's curling smoke, and brass anoint
the branched menorah of a frangipani,

as the lights in the shacks bud orange across the Morne,
and are pillared in the black harbour. Stars fly close

as sparks, and the houses catch with bulb and lampion
to the Virgin, Veronese's and Tiepolo's.

Soon, against the smoky hillsides of Santa Cruz,
dusk will ignite the wicks of the immortelle,

parrots will clatter from the trees with raucous news
of the coming night, and the first star will settle.

Then all the sorrows that lay heavily on us,
the repeated failures, the botched trepidations

will pass like the lights on bridges at village corners
where shadows crouch under pierced constellations

whose name they have never learnt, as the sickle glow
rises over bamboos that repeat the round

of the chartered stars, the Archer, aiming his bow,
the Bear, and the studded collar of Tiepolo's hound.

I cannot deny the distinction of this verse, but the pervasive tonalities of Stevens's kind of impressionism trouble my ear. Walcott, the leading Anglophone poet of the West Indies, is a cultural figure of real importance, and deserves his fame. If I do not find him to be a strong poet, unlike John Ashbery or Seamus Heaney, Geoffrey Hill or James Merrill, Jay Wright or Anne Carson, is that because I set too high a value upon the agonistic element in poetry? My uneasiness may reflect primarily upon myself, and not upon Derek Walcott.

Geoffrey Hill

(1932–)

STRONG POETRY IS ALWAYS DIFFICULT, AND GEOFFREY HILL IS THE STRONGEST British poet now alive, though his reputation in the English-speaking world is somewhat less advanced than that of several of his contemporaries. He should be read and studied for many generations after they have blent together, just as he should survive all but a handful (or fewer) of American poets now active. Such canonic prophecy is founded on the authority of his best work, as I have experienced it in the fifteen years since the publication of *For The Unfallen*, his first book. From his first poem, appropriately "Genesis," on through the *Mercian Hymns*, Hill has been the most Blakean of modern poets. But this is deep or true influence, or Blake's Mental Warfare, rather than the easy transmission of image, idea, diction and metric that superficially is judged to be poetic influence. The merely extrinsic influences on Hill's early verse are mostly American; I can detect the fierce rhetoric of Allen Tate, and the visionary intensities of Richard Eberhart, in some places. Yet the true precursor is always Blake, and the War in Heaven that the strong poet must conduct is fought by Hill against Blake, and against Blake's tradition, and so against Hill himself.

As a war of poetry against poetry, Hill's work testifies to the repressive power of tradition, but also to an immensely individual and deeply moving moral protest against tradition. Like the hero he celebrates in his masterpiece, the *Mercian Hymns*, Hill is a martyrologist. His subject is human pain, the suffering of those who both do and sustain violence, and more exactly the daemonic relationship between cultural tradition and human pain. Confronted by Hill's best poems, a reader is at first tempted to run away, for the intellectual difficulty of the rugged, compressed verse is more than matched by the emotional painfulness and directness of Hill's vision. Hill does not comfort nor console, and offers no dialectic of gain through loss. His subject, like his style, is difficulty; the difficulty of apprehending and accepting moral guilt, and the difficulty of being a poet when the burden of history, including poetic history, makes any prophetic stance inauthentic. In more than twenty years of writing, Hill has given us three very slim volumes, not because his gift is sparse, but because he is too scrupulous to have allowed himself a less organized or less weighted utterance. There are no bad poems in Hill's three books, and so much is demanded of the reader, in concentration and in the dignity of a desperate humanism, that more productive poets are likely to seem too indulgent, by comparison. Hill does not indulge his reader, or himself, and just this remorseless concentration is Hill's assured greatness. The reader who persists will learn to read not only Hill, but other difficult and wholly indispensable poets as well, for only a poet as strong as Hill compels each of us to test his own strength as a reader and so to test and clarify also our own relation to tradition.

Tradition, Freud surmised, was the cultural equivalent of repressed material in the consciousness of the individual. The role of repression in poetry was misunderstood by Freud and has been misunderstood by most of his followers. Freud thought that sublimation was the psychic defense that *worked*, whether in life or in literature, while repression invariably failed, since repression augmented the unconscious. But poetry is figurative language, and in poetry sublimation is accomplished through the self-limiting trope of metaphor, while repression is represented by the expansive trope of hyperbole, with all of its Sublime glories and Grotesque dangers. From the viewpoint of poetry, the "unconscious mind" is an oxymoron, since repressed material in poetry has no place to go but up, onto the heights of what Romanticism called the Imagination. Romantic Imagination, whether in Blake or Coleridge, does not represent a return of the repressed, but is identical with the process of repression itself.

An individual poetic imagination can defend itself against the force of another imagination only by troping, so that a successful defense against poetic tradition always answers repression by an increase in repression. The return of the repressed is only an utopian or apocalyptic dream much indulged in by Marxist speculation, and by assorted contemporary shamans who inspire what is still being termed a counter-culture. Authentic poets show us that Emersonian Compensation is always at work in poetry as in life: nothing is got for nothing. What returns in authentic poetry is never the repressed, but rather the daemonic or uncanny element within repression, which poetic tradition has called by various names, including the Sublime, and the Imagination, both of them hyperbolical figurations for something that has no referential aspect or literal meaning, but that nevertheless guarantees the survival and continuity of poetic tradition. Poets and readers go on questing for one another in order to give a voice to this daemonic impulse that informs and purifies repression. "Purifies" here has no moral or spiritual meaning but refers rather to a process by which the daemonic is reconciled with the writing of poetry.

"Daemonic," in this sense, refers to a realm of power that invades the human world yet seems apart from human origins or human ends. In a very early poem, a visionary lyric in the mode of Eberhart, but like Eberhart reaching back to Blake's "Tyger," Hill laments the inadequacy of poetic language to tell his own experience of daemonic influx:

> I waited for the word that was not given,
>
> Pent up into a region of pure force,
> Made subject to the pressure of the stars;
> I saw the angels lifted like pale straws;
> I could not stand before those winnowing eyes
>
> And fell, until I found the world again.

Hill dislikes his early poems, yet they are not only permanent achievements but also quite essential for understanding all that comes after. "Genesis," for which he has a particular dislike, is superb in itself, a perfect "first" poem, and also a clear intimation of his largest debt to Blake's vision, which is the conviction that the Creation and the Fall were the same event. Another fine early poem, "In Memory of Jane Fraser" (which Hill evidently dislikes most, of all his work), speaks of a single, particular death as uncreating all of nature. For Hill, the natural world is, at best, "a stunned repose," a judgment that allies him to Blake rather than to Wordsworth, Shelley rather than to Keats. Hill's poem on the death of Shelley emphasizes the survival of the animal world, even as Shelley, the Modern Poet proper, or New Perseus, quests aimlessly, "clogged sword, clear, aimless mirror— / With nothing to strike at or blind / in the frothed shallows."

The themes and procedures of both Hill's books of short poems are summed up in what I judge to be his best single poem, the double-sonnet called "Annunciations." Though Hill transcends his own earlier mode in *Mercian Hymns* (as will be seen), "Annunciations" is so important a poem that I will discuss it at some length. A reader who can interpret "Annunciations" can learn to interpret the rest of Hill, and also acquire many insights that will aid in reading any truly difficult poetry of the Post-Romantic tradition. For, in "Annunciations," Hill wrote what later tradition may judge to have been the central shorter poem of his own generation, a poem that is itself a despairing poetics, and a total vision both of natural existence, and of the necessary limitations of what we have learned to call imagination.

An "annunciation" can be any proclamation, but despite Hill's plural title, the reverberation here depends upon the Annunciation proper, the announcement of the Incarnation by the Angel Gabriel in Luke 1:26–38. In some grim sense, Hill's starting-point is the festival (25 March) celebrating Gabriel's announcement. But "the Word" here is not the Logos, nor simply the words of poetry, all poetry, but the idealization of poetry that is so pervasive in Western tradition:

> The Word has been abroad; is back, with a tanned look
> From its subsistence in the stiffening-mire.
> Cleansing has become killing, the reward
> More touchable, overt, clean to the touch.

This Word seems more a tourist than an Eliotic explorer; indeed a hygienic tourist-hunter. Returned, the questers sit together at a literary feast with their scholarly and critical admirers:

> Now, at a distance from the steam of beasts,
> The loathly neckings and fat shook spawn
> (Each specimen-jar fed with delicate spawn)
> The searchers with the curers sit at meat
> And are satisfied.

I do not know how to interpret this except as an attack upon everyone who has to do with poetry: poets, critics, teachers, students, readers. It is as though Yeats, after observing in vision his nymphs and satyrs copulating in the foam, his Innocents re-living their pain and having their wounds opened again, then attended a banquet in honor of his "News for the Delphic Oracle." The poem becomes a "specimen-jar," holding an aesthetic reduction of copulation and bleeding wounds. Is such an attack as Hill's legitimate, since it would apply as much to Homer as to any other poet? Is Hill attacking a false idealization of poetry or the *Ananke* that governs all poetry? The remainder of the first part of "Annunciations" will not answer these questions:

> Such precious things put down
> And the flesh eased through turbulence, the soul

Purples itself; each eye squats full and mild
While all who attend to fiddle or to harp
For betterment, flavour their decent mouths
With gobbets of the sweetest sacrifice.

Primarily this is Hill's uncompromising attack upon himself, for more even than Yeats, or even his contemporary Ted Hughes, he writes a poetry whose subject is violence and pain, thus accepting the danger of easing the flesh through a vision of turbulence. Much of the success with readers, particularly British readers, of the later Yeats and of Hughes is surely based upon feeding the reader's eye with imaginary lust and suffering until that eye "squats full and mild." Hill's attack upon "all who attend to fiddle or to harp / For betterment" is therefore an attack upon the most traditional, Aristotelian defense of poetry, an attack upon the supposed function of catharsis. Poems are "gobbets of the sweetest sacrifice," and readers flavor their mouths decently even as decent Christians swallow the bread of communion. It becomes clear that Hill is attacking, ultimately, neither poetry nor religion, but the inescapable element that always darkens tradition, which is that the living, feeding upon the repressions of the dead, repress further and so become the sustenance of the dead. Hill's "sacrifice" is what Nietzsche and Freud would have termed an Antithetical Primal Word, for it is debatable whether the victims commemorated by the poem, or the readers, are the "sacrifice."

The Antithetical Primal Word of the second part of "Annunciations" is of course "love," and here the majestic bitterness of the Sublime triumphs in and over Hill:

O Love, subject of the mere diurnal grind,
Forever being pledged to be redeemed,
Expose yourself for charity; be assured
The body is but husk and excrement.
Enter these deaths according to the law,
O visited women, possessed sons! Foreign lusts
Infringe our restraints; the changeable
Soldiery have their goings-out and comings-in
Dying in abundance. Choicest beasts
Suffuse the gutters with their colourful blood.
Our God scatters corruption. Priests, martyrs,
Parade to this imperious theme: 'O Love,
You know what pains succeed; be vigilant; strive
To recognize the damned among your friends.'

If I could cite only one stanza by Hill as being wholly representative of him, it would be this, for here is his power, his despair and (in spite of himself) his Word, not in the sense of Logos but in the Hebraic sense of *davhar*, a word that is also an act, a bringing-forward of something previously held back in the self. This Word that rejects being a Word is a knowing misprision or mis-taking of tradition, but even the most revisionary of Words remains a Word, as Hill doubtless knows. Being willing to go on writing poems, however sparsely, is to believe that one possesses a Word of one's own to bring forward. When Hill says, "Our God scatters corruption," he means that the God of lovers (and of poets) is antithetical to Himself, that this God is the ambivalent deity of all Gnostics. I take it that "scatters" does not mean "drives away" but rather "increases" corruption by dispersal, which implies that "corruption" takes something of its root-meaning of "broken-to-pieces." Hill's subject then is the Gnostic or Kabbalistic "Breaking of the Vessels," the Fall that is simultaneously a Creation, as in his first, Blakean, chant-poem "Genesis."

Part II of "Annunciations" is thus more of a proclamation against Love than a prayer to Love. Love, addressed under its aspect of repetition, is urged to more honesty, and to a reductive awareness of the body. Corporeal passion lives and dies according to the old dispensation, or law, but Hill comes to proclaim a new Incarnation, which is only a Gnostic dying into yet more sexual abundance. As an incessant martyrologist, Hill grimly announces the imperious as against the imperial or Shakespearean theme. Love, who knows that pains only succeed or follow one another (but are never successful), is urged at least to distinguish its true martyrs among the panoply of its worshippers, and so recognize accurately its valid theme.

Repeated readings of "Annunciations" should clarify and justify Hill's densely impacted style, with its reliance upon figurations of Hyperbole. Hill's mode is a negative or counter-Sublime, and his characteristic defense against the tradition he beautifully sustains and extends is an almost primal repression:

> Not as we are but as we must appear,
> Contractual ghosts of pity; not as we
> Desire life but as they would have us live,
> Set apart in timeless colloquy:
> So it is required; so we bear witness,
> Despite ourselves, to what is beyond us,
> Each distant sphere of harmony forever
> Poised, unanswerable ...

This is again a Gnostic sublimity. Blake could still insist that pity survived only because we kept on rendering others piteous, but Hill comes later, and for him the intoxication of belatedness is to know that our reality and our desire are both negated by our appearance as legatees. It is tradition that makes us into "contractual ghosts of pity." A Beautiful Necessity represses us, and makes us bear witness to a dead but still powerful transcendence. Hill characterizes one of his sequences as "a florid grim music" or an "ornate and heartless music punctuated by mutterings, blasphemies and cries for help." A baroque pathos seems to be Hill's goal, with the ornateness his tribute to tradition, and the punctuation of pathos his outcry against tradition. Hill's is clearly a poetics of pain, in which all the calamities of history become so many poetic salutes, so many baroque meditations, always trapped in a single repetition of realization. Man is trapped "between the stones and the void," without majesty and without justice except for the errors of rhetoric, the illusions of poetic language. Like his own Sebastian Arrurruz, Hill's task is "to find value/In a bleak skill," the poet's craft of establishing true rather than false "sequences of pain."

"It must give pleasure," Stevens rightly insisted, and any critic responding to Hill should be prepared to say how and why Hill's poetry can give pleasure, and in what sense Hill's reader can defend himself from being only another decent mouth opened wide for the poetry-banquet. How is the reader to evade becoming "the (supposed) Patron" so bitterly invoked in the final poem of Hill's first book? The Gnostic answer, which is always a latecomer's answer, is that the reader must become not a patron but one of those unfallen who gave Hill's first book its title:

> For the unfallen—the firstborn, or wise
> Councillor—prepared vistas extend
> As far as harvest; and idyllic death
> Where fish at dawn ignite the powdery lake.

The final trope here is perhaps too Yeatsian, but the previous trope that gives back priority to the unfallen has a more High Romantic tenor, looking back to Keats' vision of Autumn. Hill cannot celebrate natural completion, but he always finds himself turning again "to flesh and blood and the blood's pain" despite his Gnostic desire to renounce for good "this fierce and unregenerate clay." Of his incessant ambivalence, Hill has made a strong poetry, one that battles tradition on tradition's own terms, and that attempts to make of its conscious belatedness an earliness. The accomplished reader responds to Hill's work as to any really strong poetry, for the reader too needs to put off his own belatedness, which is surely why we go on searching for strong poetry. We cannot live with tradition, and we cannot live without it, and so we turn to the strong poet to see how he acts out this ambivalence for us, and to see also if he can get beyond such ambivalence.

Hill begins to break through his own dialects of tradition in *Mercian Hymns*, the sequence of prose-poems he published on the threshold of turning forty. His hero is Offa, an eighth century Midlands "king," who merges both into a spirit of place and into the poet celebrating him, particularly the poet-as-schoolboy, for *Mercian Hymns* is a kind of *Prelude*-in-little. Yet here the growth of a poet's mind is not stimulated by nature's teachings, but only by history and by dreams. Transcendence, for Hill, returned or re-entered the sublunary world in old tapestries, sculpture, and metal-work, but mostly in historicizing reverie, which is the substance of these hymns. With *Mercian Hymns*, Hill rather triumphantly "makes it new," and though the obsession with tradition is as strong, much of the ambivalence towards tradition is miraculously diminished. Indeed, certain passages in *Mercian Hymns* would approach sentimentality if the poet did not remain characteristically condensed and gnomic, with the familiar spectre of pain hovering uncannily close:

> We have a kitchen-garden riddled with toy-shards, with splin-
> ters of habitation. The children shriek and scavenge, play
> havoc. They incinerate boxes, rags and old tyres. They
> haul a sodden log, hung with soft shields of fungus, and
> launch it upon the flames.

Difficult as Hill was earlier, *Mercian Hymns*, despite the limpidity of its individual sections, is the subtlest and most oblique of his works. It is not only hard to hold together, but there is one question as to what it is "about," though the necessary answer is akin to *The Prelude* again; Hill has at last no subject but his own complex subjectivity, and so the poem is "about" himself, which turns out to be his exchange of gifts with the Muse of History (section X). I suggest that the structure and meaning of *Mercian Hymns* is best approached through its rhetoric, which as before in Hill is largely that of metaleptic reversal or transumption, the dominant trope of Post-Romantic poetry in English. For a full analysis of the trope and its poetic history, I must refer to my book, *A Map of Misreading* and give only a brief account here. Transumption is the trope of a trope, or technically the metonymy of a metonymy. That is, it tends to be a figure that substitutes an aspect of a previous figure for that figure. Imagistically, transumption from Milton through the Romantics to the present tends to present itself in terms of earliness substituting for lateness, and more often than not to be the figure that concludes poems. Translated into psychoanalytic terms, transumption is either the psychic defense of introjection (identification) or of projection (refusal of identity), just as metaphor translates into the defense of sublimation, or hyperbole into that of repression. The advantage of transumption as a concluding trope for belated poems is that it achieves a kind of fresh priority or earliness, but always at the expense of the presentness of the present or living moment. Hill is as transumptive a poet, rhetorically, as Milton or Wordsworth or Wallace Stevens, and so he too is unable to celebrate a present joy.

There is no present time, indeed there is no self-presence in *Mercian Hymns*. Though Hill's own note on the sequence betrays some anxiety about what he calls anachronisms, the genius of his work excludes such anxiety. Nothing can be anachronistic when there is no present:

> King of the perennial holly-groves, the riven sandstone; over-
> lord of the M5: architect of the historic rampart and
> ditch, the citadel at Tamworth, the summer hermitage in
> Holy Cross: guardian of the Welsh Bridge and the Iron
> Bridge: contractor to the desirable new estates: saltmas-
> ter: money changer: commissioner for oaths: martyrolo-
> gist: the friend of Charlemagne.
> 'I liked that,' said Offa, 'sing it again,'

It is not that Offa has returned to merge with the poet, or that Hill has gone back to Offa. Hill and Offa stand together in a figuration that has introjected the past and the future, while projecting the present. Hill's epigraph, from the neglected poet and essayist, C.H. Sisson, analogizes his own conduct as private person and Offa's conduct of government, in all aspects of conduct having to do with "object and justification." Hill's struggle, as person and as poet, is with the repressive power of tradition, with the anxieties of history. Offa is seen by Hill as "the starting-cry of a race," as the master of a Primal Scene of Instruction, an imposition of order that fixates subsequent repression in others, which means to start an inescapable tradition. By reconciling himself with Offa, Hill comes close to accepting the necessary violence of tradition that earlier had induced enormous ambivalences in his poetry.

This acceptance, still somber but no longer grim, produces the dominant tone of *Mercian Hymns*, which is a kind of Wordsworthian "sober coloring" or "still sad music of humanity." But the sequence's vision remains

Blakean rather than Wordsworthian, for the world it pictures is still one in which Creation and Fall cannot be distinguished, and at the end Offa is fallen Adam or every man: "he left behind coins, for his lodging, and traces of red mud." The reader sees that each hymn is like the inscription on one of Offa's hammered coins, and that these coins are literally and figuratively the price of a living tradition, its perpetual balance of Creation and Fall. Hill has succeeded, obliquely, in solving his aesthetic-moral problem as a poet, but the success is as equivocal and momentary as the pun on "succeed" in "Annunciations." Hill now knows better "what pains succeed," and his moving sequence helps his readers to the same knowledge.

No critical introduction to a poet only just past forty in age can hope to prophesy his future development. I have seen no poems written by Hill since *Mercian Hymns*, but would be surprised if he did not return to the tighter mode of For The Unfallen and King Log, though in a finer tone. His achievement to date, as gathered in his volume, seems to me to transcend the more copious work of his contemporary rivals: Hughes, Gunn, Kinsella, Tomlinson, Silkin. Good as they are, they lack poetic strength when compared with Hill. He has the persistence to go on wrestling with the mighty dead—Blake, Wordsworth, Shelley, Yeats—and to make of this ghostly struggle a fresh sublimity. He is indeed a poet of the Sublime, a mode wholly archaic yet always available to us again, provided a survivor of the old line come to us:

> Against the burly air I strode,
> Where the tight ocean heaves its load,
> Crying the miracles of God.

Mark Strand

(1934–)

I HAVE KNOWN MARK STRAND, AS PERSON AND AS POET, FOR MORE THAN half a century. His gift is harbored rather than sparse: that is my interpretation of his major work to date, *Dark Harbor: A Poem* (1993). The poem constitutes a "Proem" and forty-five cantos or sections.

Dark Harbor, like some earlier poems by Strand, is an overt homage to Wallace Stevens. It is as though casting aside anxieties of influences Strand wishes reconcilement with his crucial precursor. The "Proem" sets forth vigorously: "The burning/Will of weather, blowing overhead, would be his muse." But, by Canto IV, we are in the world of Stevens:

> There is a certain triviality in living here,
> A lightness, a comic monotony that one tries
> To undermine with shows of energy, a devotion
>
> To the vagaries of desire, whereas over there
> Is a seriousness, a stiff, inflexible gloom
> That shrouds the disappearing soul, a weight
>
> That shames our lightness. Just look
> Across the river and you will discover
> How unworthy you are as you describe what you see,
>
> Which is bound by what is available.
> On the other side, no one is looking this way.
> They are committed to obstacles,
>
> To the textures and levels of darkness,

To the tedious enactment of duration.
And they labor not for bread or love

But to perpetuate the balance between the past
And the future. They are the future as it
Extends itself, just as we are the past

Coming to terms with itself. Which is why
The napkins are pressed, and the cookies have come
On time, and why the glass of milk, looking so chic

In its whiteness, begs us to sip. None of this happens
Over there. Relief from anything is seen
As timid, a sign of shallowness or worse.

This is the voice of the master, particularly in *An Ordinary Evening in New Haven*. Strand shrewdly outdoes Stevens to the glass of milk, setting aside any more metaphysical concerns. An effort is made, for fifteen cantos, to domesticate Stevens, but the great voice, of Stevens and Strand fused together, returns in Canto XVI:

It is true, as someone has said, that in
A world without heaven all is farewell.
Whether you wave your hand or not,

It is farewell, and if no tears come to your eyes
It is still farewell, and if you pretend not to notice,
Hating what passes, it is still farewell.

Farewell no matter what. And the palms as they lean
Over the green, bright lagoon, and the pelicans
Diving, and the listening bodies of bathers resting,

Are stages in an ultimate stillness, and the movement
Of sand, and of wind, and the secret moves of the body
Are part of the same, a simplicity that turns being

Into an occasion for mourning, or into an occasion
Worth celebrating, for what else does one do,
Feeling the weight of the pelicans' wings,

The density of the palms' shadows, the cells that darken
The backs of bathers? These are beyond the distortions
Of chance, beyond the evasions of music. The end

Is enacted again and again. And we feel it
In the temptations of sleep, in the moon's ripening,
In the wine as it waits in the glass.

It is Stevens who tells us that, without heaven, all farewells are final. What enchants me here are the Strandian variations on farewell. Waves and tears yield to very Stevensian palms, and to the pelicans of Florida, venereal soil. A greater meditation, suitable to Strand and Stevens as seers of the weather, arrives in Canto XXIV:

Now think of the weather and how it is rarely the same
For any two people, how when it is small, precision is needed
To say when it is really an aura or odor or even an air

Of certainty, or how, as the hours go by, it could be thought of
As large because of the number of people it touches.
Its strength is something else: tornados are small

But strong and cloudless summer days seem infinite
But tend to be weak since we don't mind being out in them.
Excuse me, is this the story of another exciting day,

The sort of thing that accompanies preparations for dinner?
Then what say we talk about the inaudible—the shape it assumes,
And what social implications it holds,

Or the somber flourishes of autumn—the bright
Or blighted leaves falling, the clicking of cold branches,
The new color of the sky, its random blue.

Is that final tercet Strand or Stevens? As the sequence strengthens, deliberate echoes of Josh Ashbery, Octavio Paz and Wordsworth are evoked by Strand, until he achieves a grand apotheosis in his final canto:

I am sure you would find it misty here,
With lots of stone cottages badly needing repair.
Groups of souls, wrapped in cloaks, sit in the fields

Or stroll the winding unpaved roads. They are polite,
And oblivious to their bodies, which the wind passes through,
Making a shushing sound. Not long ago,

I stopped to rest in a place where an especially
Thick mist swirled up from the river. Someone,
Who claimed to have known me years before,

Approached, saying there were many poets
Wandering around who wished to be alive again.
They were ready to say the words they had been unable to say—

Words whose absence had been the silence of love,
Of pain, and even of pleasure. Then he joined a small group,
Gathered beside a fire. I believe I recognized

Some of the faces, but as I approached they tucked
Their heads under their wings. I looked away to the hills
Above the river, where the golden lights of sunset

And sunrise are one and the same, and saw something flying
Back and forth, fluttering its wings. Then it stopped in mid-air.
It was an angel, one of the good ones, about to sing.

The aura is Dante's, and we are in a spooky place, paradise of poets or purgatory of poets. If one line above all others in *Dark Harbor* reverberates within me, it is: "They were ready to say the words they had been unable to say—." The accent remains late Stevens, but with a difference is altogether Mark Strand's.

Jay Wright

(1935-)

ONE CENTRAL IMAGE IN JAY WRIGHT'S POETRY IS CREATION-BY-TWINNING, in which a poem becomes a limbo dance, a gateway out of the Middle Passage of the slave trade, a gateway that is also a logbook, and so a poem for passage. The limbo is a West Indian dance performed under a gradually lowered bar, until the dancer is a spider-man, spread-eagling his arms and legs. Interpreters refer the limbo to the terrible Middle Passage, the route of slave ships from Africa to America, during which the slaves were crowded into so little space that they contorted themselves into human spiders. In Jay Wright's art, the limbo is a metaphor for this poet's aesthetic project, a quest for a gateway out of the Middle Passage by making "a log for passage." This logbook offers initiation by twinning, a mode of divine creation in the Dogon mythology of West Africa. There Amma or Yahweh twins himself hermetically as Nommo or Adam, a forerunner for the Black Son of God, who will be the gateway for everyone out of a universal Middle Passage. In his poem, "The Albuquerque Graveyard," Wright had returned to the burial place of early friends and associates:

> I am going back
> to the Black limbo,
> an unwritten history
> of our own tensions.
> The dead lie here
> in a hierarchy of small defeats.
> *Selected Poems* 62]

A somewhat later poem, "The Abstract of Knowledge / The First Test," has an intricate passage adumbrating this image of the limbo, at once

Dante's place outside of Hell, Purgatory, and Heaven, and a dance ironically commemorating bondage:

> If you go from the certainty of oneness
> into solitude and return,
> I must divest you of your double
> and twin you in love's seclusion.
> My instruments toll you into limbo;
>
> [*Selected Poems* 180]

Dogon mythology teaches that every being, indeed every object, has its own language, which is its twin or double, its Nommo or Adam. Western Hermetism has roughly the same teaching, which influenced Symbolist poetry, both in Rimbaud and in Hart Crane. Jakob Boehme's grand phrase for this doubling was "the signature of all things." In many respects, Jay Wright's poetry attempts to read the signatures of all things, a daunting project for any poet, but one peculiarly fraught with hazards for an African-American writer in our America drifting towards Millennium. The extra-literary pressures placed upon the late Ralph Ellison were excruciating, and doubtless had their effect in seeing to it that *Invisible Man* remained a solitary achievement. Ellison once wryly remarked to me that only internal pressures could be fecund; the evidence for his proud truthtelling can be found all about us, in all the clamors of Resentment, emanating as they do from every possible ideology. What Ellison is to the African-American novel, Jay Wright is to black poetry in the United States. It is not accidental that Wright has become the Invisible Man: reclusive, isolated, and ceaselessly meditating in a remote part of Vermont, alone with his wife. What other context does our self-betrayed culture afford him? But I have cried out upon these matters too often, and I am so wearied by Resenters who urge historicizing and politicizing upon me, that for now I will just forget them, and will analyze and appreciate Jay Wright's poetry as it sets him in company of his peers: Rilke, Hölderlin, Hart Crane, Robert Hayden, Paul Celan, and Luis Cernuda, the marvelous Spanish poet of the Sublime who fled Franco and died by his own hand in Mexico. My love for Wright's poetry goes back a quarter-century to *The Homecoming Singer* (1971), and has been heightened with each subsequent volume, culminating with *Boleros* (1991). There has been no book by Wright these last five years, but I will quote and discuss one of his most recent poems. At sixty-one, Wright is one of the handful of major American poets that we have alive among us, but alas he is the least read and studied of them all. Partly this is caused by the authentic cognitive and imaginative difficulties that his work presents, but partly the neglect of his poetry comes from nearly everyone's wrong-headed expectations of an African-American poet. Wright is a protest poet only as Dante was. A visionary poet, whether William Blake or Hart Crane or Jay Wright, has an agenda that an age of politicized criticism cannot apprehend. Wright is a great religious poet, whose spirituality is a syncretic weave of African, American, and European strands. The American component in this weaving is New Mexican and Mexican, the European is Dantesque, the African most often Dogon. We have little capacity for apprehending so complex and original a spiritual vision, which enhances Jay Wright's poetic difficulty for us. Yet I am speaking of a central American poet, one fully comparable to John Ashbery, A.R. Ammons, and only a handful of others now living among us. That so remarkable and capacious a poet is neglected is another, terrible symptom of our current cultural decay.

The American Sublime, however we mock it, remains the crucial mode of our poetry, from Emerson, Whitman and Dickinson through Wallace Stevens and Hart Crane on to James Merrill, Ammons, and Jay Wright. By the Sublime I intend the Longinian sense of being upon the heights, a transcendental and agonistic mode of aesthetic experience, and one that is highly consonant with extraordinary learning. Learned poets are not infrequent, in all the great poetic traditions. Jay Wright legitimately participates in so many strong traditions that inevitably he is an immensely learned poet. The difficulties presented to the reader are different neither in degree nor in kind from those we have to confront in John Milton or in William Blake. I have expressed my critical conviction that only Wright is of Ralph Ellison's eminence among all African-American creators of imaginative literature, up to this present time. But *Invisible Man* is a post-Faulknerian novel, and has much the same relation to *Light in August* or *Absalom, Absalom!* as these books have to Joseph Conrad's principal fictions. Modern poetry, however, is bewilderingly multiform in its relation to anterior poetry, and Wright is syncretic and diverse to an extraordinary degree. If you compare him to an exact contemporary like the admirable Mark Strand, one of your first conclusions will be that Strand has an intense relation to only a few precursors, Wallace Stevens and Elizabeth Bishop in particular. Strand's *Dark Harbor*, a book-length sequence of marvelous eloquence and poignancy, relies upon its intricate evasions of Stevens's influence, at once embraced without ambivalence, yet also warded-off, lest Strand drown in Stevens. Wright seems to me closest to Hart Crane among American poets, but neither Crane nor the Crane-influenced Robert Hayden are as central to Wright's art as Stevens is to Strand's. Sometimes, particularly in *The Double Invention of Komo*, Wright seems as haunted by T.S. Eliot's *Four Quartets* as Crane was by *The Waste Land*. It can be a touch disconcerting to hear Eliot's voice in Wright's St. Augustine:

> This is the dance of the changeless
> and the changing,
> the spirit's intensity
> for the world's endurance.
> Knowledge is motion in twilight,
> a state of falling into sight;
> one by one,
> the spirit's eyes touch and grow.
> *Peregrinus*, the tense spirit
> tenses and returns to its
> own understanding.
> There is always the going forth
> and the returning;
> there is always the act,
> the slow fusion of being.
> All things,
> by the strength of being joined,
> will continue;
> the sin is to turn away;
> ignorance is inattention ...
>
> [*Double Invention* 51]

In his "Afterword" to *The Double Invention of Komo*, Wright comments upon poetic voicing and its relation to ritual:

> In ritual, one does not step back from vision; one follows it. My poem risks ritual's arrogance. It presents a dominant voice, that of the initiate undergoing Komo's rigorous formalities ...
>
> [*Double Invention* 114]

The "dominant voice" of the poem is certainly Wright's own, though it fascinates me as to just why the later Eliot continues to break in, usurping the celebrant of Bambara ritual. I take the Eliotic intrusions, here and elsewhere in Wright, to be a sign that anthropology and poetry do not necessarily dwell together so comfortably as Wright insists they do. It is well worth remarking that Wright is a poet of the Sublime; he is not an anthropologist, a cultural historian, or a revivalist of archaic African religions.

Yes, he is a soothsayer and reads omens, but primarily as a path to writing his own poems. So fiercely fused are his gifts, at their best, that he transforms ritual into poetry, but never poetry into ritual, the prime flaw of Eliot in the *Quartets*. I learn something about African spirituality by reading Wright, and by following up his references to crucial scholarship upon this matter, but after all one can read his sources without reading him. In a review of Wright's *Selected Poems*, a not unsympathetic poet-critic, Robert B. Shaw, called the author of *The Double Invention of Komo* and *Dimensions of History* "a belated High Modernist," and lamented that readers uneducated in the relevant anthropological sources would require commentaries before they could judge the question of value in Wright's work. Yet, like T.S. Eliot and Hart Crane, Jay Wright at his most appealing is an incantatory writer whose initial impact transcends the necessity of commentary. Pindar is an immensely difficult poet, dense with mythological allusiveness, but his passionate pride in his own agonistic poetic prowess eloquently goes beyond his intricate ecstasies of mythic counterpoint. The high song more than sustains its difficulties, and Pindar always asks and answers the triple-question of the Sublime: more than? less than? or equal to? Excellence in the range and reach of the spirit is always the burden of the Sublime—in Pindar, Hölderlin, Shelley, Hart Crane, and very much in the major phase of Jay Wright.

It is one of the central ironies of our poetry that the major African-American poet, one of whose prime tropes being what he calls "the black limbo," should be our crucial composer of the American sublime ode as we approach Millennium. There are a few living poets of Jay Wright's eminence among us—John Ashbery and A.R. Ammons in particular—but their recent work has turned in other directions. If you define the modern Sublime mode with historical precision, then its central characteristic has to be an ambition of transcendence. The American Sublime, though Wallace Stevens nervously mocked it, is nevertheless well defined by the marvelous conclusion of his "The Idea of Order at Key West":

> The maker's rage to order words of the sea,
> Words of the fragrant portals, dimly-starred,
> And of ourselves and of our origins,
> In ghostlier demarcations, keener sounds.

Wright, neither a poet of the sea nor of those Keatsian portals, labors incessantly to order words of ourselves and of our origins in ways that will render the demarcations ghostlier, the sounds keener. Yet his sense of our origins, and his own, is so multiform and complex, that he gives a new and fuller meaning to the descriptive term "African-American." I scarcely can think of another American poet who has so astonishingly adumbrated that particular hyphen.

Wright's poetry is so large and varied, in scope and design, that I will center now, in some detail, upon my personal favorites among all his published work to date, the sequence of five grand odes that conclude his superb volume, *Elaine's Book* (1988; Elaine being the sister of his wife, Lois). These five poems—"The Anatomy of Resonance," "Journey to the Place of Ghosts," "Saltos," "The Power of Reeds," "Desire's Persistence"—are exalted in tone and stance, and attempt to mount the high places of the spirit. They remind us that Wright, like Hölderlin and Hart Crane, is a secular religious poet. Crane rather wistfully called himself a "Pindar of the Machine Age," while Wright should be termed a "Pindar of the Chaotic Age," for that is where we are now, drifting as we do towards a new Theocratic Age. Perhaps most of our current poets who matter—from A.R. Ammons to Jorie Graham—quest for their authentic spiritual ancestors, a search that is essential to the high, Pindaric mode of invocation and celebration. But no other major poet now writing among us carries out this mission with the urgency and intensity of Jay Wright.

The literary context of Wright's sequence of odes is provided by a startlingly effective blend of Hölderlin and Paul Celan, on the one side, and Aztec poetry, on the other. What allies the two visionary modes, in Wright's implicit interpretation, is a kind of despairing transcendence, a triumph of the Negative over the pseudo-spiritualities of much received religious tradition. In a sense, Wright returns to the argument of his long poem, *Dimensions of History*, where Aztec mythology was employed as an intricate instance of mingled creation and destruction in the world-cycles commemorated by the huge pyramid-temples that still survive. But a mythic history of the contending forces of the Aztec versions of Venus and Mars, for all its brazen power, had to be tempered if Wright was to achieve a subtler and more articulated vision than that of *Dimensions of History*. Hölderlin and Celan are played off by Wright against the Aztec splendor, which he knows was in its way as barbaric as the cruel Catholicism of the Spanish invaders who destroyed the Aztec culture. The suicidal intensity of Hölderlin and of Celan retains a personalism that is alien to the Aztec clash of gods and historical cycles, and Jay Wright's heroic insistence upon the individuality of the poet draws much of its authority from the examples of Hölderlin and Celan.

"The Anatomy of Resistance," the first of Wright's cycle of five odes, takes its epigraph from Hölderlin:

And the bird of the night whirs
    Down, so close that you shield your eyes.

Baudelaire wrote of the wing of madness coming so close that it brushed his ear; Hölderlin records a similar immediacy, so that both poets express the terrible cost of imaginative vision. Wright is concerned, not with the cost, but rather with "the anatomy of resonance," the analysis of that close whirring down that makes the poet apotropaically shield his eyes against his own vision. Seven stages mark this resonance, each headed by a crucial word in Hölderlin's sublime, composite metaphor: *The Bird, Night, Whirs, Down, Close, Shield, Eyes.* I rather should say Wright's revision of Hölderlin's trope, since here is the German original, "Die Kürze," written by Hölderlin in 1798:

«Warum bist du so kurz? liebst du, wie vormals, denn
  «Nun nicht mehr den Gesang? fandst du, als Jüngling, doch,
  «In den Tagen der Hoffnung,
    «Wenn du sangest, das Ende nie!»
Wie mein Glück, ist mein Lied.—Willst du im Abenrot
  Froh dich baden? hinweg ists! und die Erd ist kalt,
    Und der Vogel der Nacht schwirrt
    Unbequem vor das Auge dir.
                      [*Selected Verse*, 15–16]

The title is generally translated as "Brevity," and here is the most literal translation that I can give:

"Why are you so brief? Do you love singing less than you did formerly? since, as a young man, in the days of hope, when you sang, there was no end to your singing!"
    As is my fortune, so is my song. Would you bathe happily in the evening redness? It has vanished! And the earth is cold, and the bird of night whirs uncomfortably down towards your eyes.

Unbequem, "uncomfortably," is taken by Wright as "so close that you shield," the eyes being more than uncomfortable with the whirring that threatens to brush them. Hölderlin laments the end of an early poetic joyousness, a primal exuberance that has yielded to a supposedly more limited, or at least less celebratory art. Adroitly, Wright's first movement, *Bird*, has nothing in it of Hölderlin's "theology of existence":

BIRD

There must be an atmosphere,
or an evergreen,
or the green shading into the red-yellow
                              brown of earth, for the eye,
surely,
some choir in which the ornamented arms
might tune themselves
                    to the absolute A of air.
Creatures given to this air
shape their own suspension,
                    a process of weight,
thrust away from the body's substance,
and the depths of a woman's body,
                              of maple and ash,
hold the arc of another substance,
a memory of unrealized absence.
There is a river here,
where the white heron fastens its claws
to the flat blue surface,
as though it stood in a flowing altar
                    to call into the dense grove
of arrested light around the water.
Look and you will see the plume of communion,
a possible intention that arises only here.
It seems that the river has been clay
                              for feather and bone,
for the elastic tissue of the bird's voice.
And the ...
words that begin a theology of existence,
a political history of flight,
an interrupted dream of being definite.
                    [*Elaine's Book* 68–9]

"The absolute A of air" recalls the last of the "Logbook of
Judgments" section in *Dimensions of History*, "Meta-A and the A of
Absolutes" available now in *Selected Poems of Jay Wright*):

I am good when I know the darkness of all light,
and accept the darkness, not as a sign, but as my body.
This is the A of absolutes,

the logbook of judgments,
the good sign.

[*Selected Poems* 176]

This has been Wright's mature poetics, the Dogon insistence that each being (even an object) has its own language which is its own Adam, its Nommo, the Adamic twin or double, frequently antithetical to the being or object. So "the darkness of all light," an emergence from Plato's cave, is also a log for passage, an emergence from the Middle Passage, the black limbo of bondage. *That* is where we are in the first movement of "The Anatomy of Resonance," in the A of absolutes, the absolute A of air, a purged epiphany or moment of vision, an atmosphere tuned for the poetic eye, which then would require no shielding. And so Wright replaces the bird of the night with the Yeatsian (or even Sarah Orne Jewettian) white heron, for whose voice "the river has been clay / for feather and bone," the clay intimating the red clay out of which Adam or Nommo, antithetical double and twin, has been formed. Therefore Wright characterizes his epigraph, *And the bird of the night whirs / Down, so close that you shield your eyes*, as a theology of existence, and even as "a political history of flight," where "political" takes on the shade of "politic," meaning "prudential" and even "artful," as befits a dweller in the city of poetry. And that is why this epiphany is "an interrupted dream of being definite," since the interruption is the whirring of Hölderlin's bird of night, which now distracts Wright from his absolute A of air, his authentic poetic dream of definite being.

Night, the second movement, rewrites the history of darkness, invoking Cuzco, the ancient Incan capital, rebuilt by the conquering Spaniards upon the ruins of the old, streets of the dead. Cuzco here, in "The Anatomy of Resonance," recalls the destroyed cities of *Dimensions of History*, the Mayan capital Labna, and the Aztec capital Tenochtitlán, upon whose remnants Mexico City is built. Wright's "pecked cross" is not Catholic but Aztec, described in a note to *Dimensions of History* as representing the "four points of the compass," and so as an emblem of the wind and the rain, "pecked" because beaked in Aztec bird symbolism. Out of the absence of light, in a poetically reclaimed lost city of the Americas, a radiant voice rises, in an antiphony with the despairing voice of the Old World Hölderlin, visionary of unredeemed loss. Wright, humbly cognizant that he cannot be Pindar or Hölderlin, nevertheless enters the agon that is the Sublime mode by affirming his African and New Mexican heritages, by again asserting his spiritual ancestry in the splendors that the invading Europeans only could ruin. Beautifully modulated, *Night* is a negative epiphany twinning the serenity of *The Bird*.

Taken together, these first two movements define Wright's swerve away from the tradition of the Sublime, in an intricate irony or allegory reliant upon the Dogon mythology of Anima (Yahweh) and the Seventh Nommo (the Christ or Redeemer) that is always central to Wright's mature poetry. *Whirs*, the third movement, attempts instead an antithetical completion of Hölderlin's whirring resonance, by way of the "devastating hum of the jackal's song":

WHIRS

The jackal has learned to sing in the ash,
a severe chanty in praise of the cock and the fish,
of the aureole balm of evening.
When the moment arrives for singing,
palm leaves that are heavy with windlessness
                    vibrate to a star's breath,
and the ear, attuned to all the harmonies of neglect,
lifts the soteriological wisdom of loss
                    from its parish bed.
There is a moment when the boy comes out of the wood,
his feet slippered with a bee sound, his face
turned to the bull roar following his flight.
The boy carries an apple sound in his head,
something to enhance the dissonant eruption
                    of his new morning.
Now, mother night has dressed herself
to dance to the dulcimer of his spring.
Father now to the boy,
she will lock his arms, and twirl him,
and fill his body with the deep
and devastating hum of the jackal's song.
                    [*Elaine's Book* 70]

A mothering night that transforms to fatherhood centers this stately lyric in which sound prevails, from the jackal's singing its severe chanty of what sustains it through the stellar vibration of palms, sounds of bee, bull, and apple, and the dissonance of the boy's own advent. His spring is a dulcimer, and his dance twirls his body into the resonance of the jackal's chanty. Wright gives us here one of the staples of the Sublime ode, the incarnation of the Poetic Character in the poet's younger self, akin to the sensibility of song's abundance that Hölderlin elegizes as his own first phase. Yet brevity is not Wright's burden; his complex ancestry has its saving strand neither in the Old

World nor in the New, but in the indigenous spiritualities of Africa, which is why the *Whirs* movement celebrates "the soteriological wisdom of loss," in opposition to Hölderlin's Sublime grandeur of loss. Soteriology, in Christianity, is the theological doctrine of deliverance by Jesus, a salvation dependent upon a unique biography, both in and out of time. Wright intimates again, here as elsewhere, a different wisdom of loss, the sacrifice of the Nommo figured in the African jackal, a forager who has learned to sing in the ash of his foraging, and whose song is a cyclic repetition. Amma made love to the earth, which first brought forth a jackal, who in turn violated the earth his mother, all evil subsequently proceeding out of that mismatch. Wisdom is in the cycle, and not in the single manifestation of a savior as much out of time as in it, and so not even in the Seventh Nommo.

Down, the fourth movement, returns to another of Wright's geographies, Scotland, where he lived for a year that has been deeply impressed upon all his subsequent poetry, a North Sea vision playing off against Africa, Old and New Mexico, and upper New England. In *Down*, Wright experiences an emptying-out of the poetic self, a defensive movement of the spirit resting from the Sublime:

DOWN

Under the rock, in the hollow,
there are stones the color of cats' eyes.
Old women who have seen these eyes
know that the body should be eiderdown
and bathed with the water of holy wells
and mineral springs, a blue water
with just the hint of hardness
        a slight taste of sulfur.
So the sinistra side of that other body
would drift to the North Sea,
and come down in its emerald armor,
to be welcomed in a Latin wood,
where a crescent moon peeks over
           the empty seawall.
My dunum and dum boots quiver
on the qui vive,
        anxious
to enlist water again
      to unruffle and fix
the mystery of buried stone.

[*Elaine's Book* 70–1]

The supposed Scottish legend here is a variant upon the Celtic myth of Arthur, and "the other body ... in its emerald armor" becomes, in Wright's vision, not the return of a warrior-king but of a poetic vision reconfirmed by the marvelous lyric, *Close*, the next in "The Anatomy of Resonance":

> CLOSE
>
> Time and the deductive season
> teach an intimacy, reason
> enough to set sail under seal,
> a tenaciously secret keel
> of abbeys and cathedrals, found
> in the strictest boroughs, the round
> plot of land dense with unicorns;
> as in a soul's tapestry, horns
> flagellate the air. Now confined
> near an emerald sun, defined
> by my spirit's strictest account,
> I cling to my dole, and dismount.
> I have filled my bowl with the rose
> smoke of ecstasy in a close.

This intricate little Eliotic poem, with its internal and slant rhymes, is itself a miniature of the daemonic Sublime, fusing the Celtic "emerald sun," the warrior-king returned, with the famous unicorn tapestry, Hermetic record of an emblazoned reality unexpectedly regained. Ecstasy, a close only in the sense of an enclosure, leads downwards to the undoing movement, *Shield*:

> SHIELD
>
> Skewed, perhaps,
> the heart's road bends sinister,
> not out of skin and hide,
>   owing nothing
> to the combustible partition
>   crowning
> those trees
>   a doe's leap away.
> Maude had it right—
> John would be closer to love's blossom.
> She had been given nothing,

and had only a desire to see
down the dextrous avenue of self.
Clearly, Maude knew
        who would be impaled,
who would sit on an order's collar,
what weight the father would bear
            against his own kind.
Kindness,
       or call it the valor of salvation,
             roots in a shell,
scaled to catch the rattle of friendship
         and war heat alliance.
We are stretched over the heart's house,
to defend such kindness as remains,
when the sun, strawberry red,
dips itself into the lime green water
        that flows endlessly home.
             [*Elaine's Book* 72]

Maude is Mary Magdalene, John is the Beloved Disciple, and the account of the "impaling" of Christ has a Gnostic flavoring, as Wright again subtly rejects a Western image of salvation not in accord with the Akan doctrine of God, of Amma who would not bear a weight against his own kind, as the Christian God certainly does in the sacrifice of Jesus. Before he turns to *Eyes*, the final movement, Wright gives us a remarkable epigraph from Paul Celan's *Schneebett* (Snowbed): "Augen, weltblind, in Sterbegeklüft ...," rendered here as "Eyes, worldblind, in the lode-break of dying." *Sterbegeklüft* is a tough word, presumably one of Celan's coinages, and perhaps should be translated as "the fissure (or cleft) of dying." Wright wants the fissure to be a break in a vein of ore, as though dying is itself a wealth:

      EYES
Old light, at this depth, knows
the veil of deception, the water valley
through which it leaps and divides.
So here, as the south wind alerts the body
to the season's change, the scarlet poplar
leaf runs, from point through point,
a topsy-turvy body to be fixed
           in a different mirror.

An eye, such as this, may be worldblind
in the lode-break of dying. An eye, such as this,
may be no more than a peacock's tail,
the infant bud in a cutting, or the different
curve of a voice in the earth.
There is a market town in Suffolk,
where the bones and Roman urns and coins
mark a sacred ground with the sound of vision.
Time must tell us everything about sensation
and the way we have come to terms
                              with our failure
to see anything but the blue point of desire
                    that leads us home.
                    [*Elaine's Book* 73]

This is the Return of the Dead, of Hölderlin and of Celan, in Wright's own great ode, and confronts the challenge of answering Hölderlin's despairing vision: "And the bird of the night whirs / Down, so close that you shield your eyes." Wright employs his interpretation of Celan to exalt a rekindled poetic eye, one that transcends: "Old light" and the "veil of deception." To be "worldblind, in the lode-break of dying," whatever it meant to Celan, becomes in Jay Wright a marvelously hopeful image for a fresh poetic beginning. It is a loving critique of the Western Sublime of Hölderlin (and of Celan) that Wright presents, yet a critique nevertheless. The American Sublime, in Wright, becomes identical with the black limbo, the dance that takes slaves out of the Middle Passage.

Remembering a market town in Suffolk, where the sound of vision rose for him from a different curve, or dimension of history in the earth, Wright reaffirms the possibility of his own "The Eye of God, The Soul's First Vision," the opening poem of his epic of poetic incarnation, *Dimensions of History*. There Wright combined Dogon and Aztec symbolism in a riddle of initiation that is very different from the poetic election of Hölderlin's Greco-German Sublime. Implicit in the final movement of "The Anatomy of Resonance" is Wright's African mode of twinning, of election-by-substitution, as here at the start of *Dimensions of History*:

Where did I learn to present myself
to the cut of some other voice,
substitute in a mime
my body breaks to contain?

There is Wright's own intricate balance, poised between "the signs of understanding / that I assert, but cannot reach alone," and the solitary eye of Hölderlin and Celan, agonistic and isolate. Time, which for the African-American Wright, is purely a dimension of history, has to tell us everything about the sensation of confronting the whirring bird of the night, a sensation that for Hölderlin is inviolate and single. The Western Sublime mode, which includes the American Sublime before Ralph Ellison and Jay Wright, is indeed a strenuous way of coming to terms with our tendency to see only "the blue point of desire / that leads us home." With reverence for Hölderlin, Wright dialectically terms that kind of transcendence a failure, one that he has come to seal by bringing us an African-Aztec poetic vision as a saving balance. Such an assertion is audacious, yet "The Anatomy of Resonance" goes a good distance towards sustaining it.

"Desire's Persistence," the last of Wright's five odes, will take us back to that home-seeking, High Romantic "blue point of desire," in another poem as elaborate as "The Anatomy of Resonance." Between come three odes, simpler but no less magnificent, all addressing the poetic vocation. "Journey to the Place of Ghosts" takes another epigraph from Celan, yet is almost entirely African in its setting and emphasis. I pass over it here, except to note that its ritual descent to the dead yields a rekindling of the poetic self, but at the expense of a psychic cost more harrowing than any other I recall in Wright's work. "Saltos," with its title hinting at the need to become a spiritual acrobat, follows and again I must neglect its splendors, though the poignance of being "awakened by a sun I will never see" testifies to Wright's awareness that his Africa is purely a vision, and not an empirical experience. "The Power of Reeds," the fourth ode, retrieves lost connections, in a characteristic Wrightian uncovering of the weave that analogizes ancient Greek, African and Mexican Indian visionary songs and singing. This too, though it is the most powerful of these three middle odes, I set aside while noting that again the African strand is the strongest in the weave. Wright, who is sublimely above the vulgar cultural politics of our academies and our journalists, is far more devoted to African culture and scholarship than are the entire camp of Resenters and cultural nationalists.

"The Anatomy of Resonance," by any rational standards of aesthetic eminence is a great poem, but "Desire's Persistence" seems to me even stronger, and is one of the double handful of Sublime achievements by poets of Jay Wright's own American generation. I return therefore to a rather close reading because Wright, as I reiterate, is a legitimately difficult poet who requires exegesis. I am sufficiently unregenerate so that I regard this as a merit, rather than a flaw, of his poetry. The ultimate archetype of the poet for Wright is Dante. Hart Crane, a difficult poet and a strong rhetorical influence upon the young Jay Wright, was drawn to Dante precisely as Wright is, seeking a paradigm for the poet's relation to his own poetry. In some sense, all of Wright's poetry to date constitutes his *Vita Nuova* and his *canzoni*. Though *Dimensions of History* and *The Double Invention of Komo* are epics in the Pound–Eliot mode, both were composed a little early in Wright's career. His work-in-progress, *Transformations*, consists of extended, meditative lyrics, wisdom literature, rather than the celebratory and lamenting odes of *Elaine's Book* and *Boleros*. Unlike Crane, who suffered a death by water at thirty-two, Wright is at the start of his sixties, and I am moved to prophesy that an African-American Dante may yet be revealed to us.

"Desire's Persistence" is indeed as beautiful as it is difficult. Its title comes from the Aztec, as does the line that Wright quarries for the name of the individual movements: "I lift the red flower of winter into the wind." But before we go to the sequence of *I, Lift, Red, Flower, Winter, Wind*, Wright allows the narrator, Desire, to speak:

> In the region of rain and cloud,
> I live in shade,
> under the moss mat of days bruised
> > purple with desire.
> My dominion is a song in the wide ring of water.
> There, I run to and fro,
> braiding the logical act
> > in the birth of an Ear of Corn,
> polychromatic story I will now tell
> in the weaving, power's form in motion,
> a devotion to the unstressed.
> Once, I wreathed around a king,
> became a fishing-net, a maze,
> > "a deadly wealth of robe."
> Mothers who have heard me sing take heart;
> I always prick them into power.
> > > [*Elaine's Book* 82]

The chanter, Desire, takes on the ambivalent guise of "a fishing-net, a maze / 'a deadly wealth of robe,'" that last presumably an allusion to the shirt of the centaur Nessus that became a fire to consume Heracles. Whether the dangerous desire, "power's form in motion," can be transfigured wholly from a destructive force to a transcending charisma is unclear, even when the chanter, the *I* section, becomes the astral body of resurrection and so an augmented Hamlet, "Dane of Degrees." Yet even the first section ends on the image of fresh life, and this gives a particular aura to "I lift the red flower of winter into the wind." Whatever that meant in its ancient Mexican context, here it carries the burden of vitalization, the blessing of more life, even though the *I* section rocks back and forth between images of rising and descents to the sepulchre:

> Out of the ninth circle,
> a Phoenician boat rocks upward into light
> and the warmth of a name—given to heaven—
> that arises in the ninth realm.
> Earth's realm discloses the Egyptian
> on the point of invention,
>   deprived of life and death,
> heart deep in the soul's hawk,
> a thymos shadow knapping the tombed body.
> Some one or thing is always heaven bound.
> Some flowered log doubles my bones.
> The spirit of Toltec turtledoves escapes.
> A sharp, metaphorical cry sends me
>   into the adorned sepulchre,
> and the thing that decays learns
>   how to speak its name.
>   [*Elaine's Book* 83]

John Hollander has compared Wright to Geoffrey Hill, since they share "a secularized religious power that keeps them questing among the chapels of ruined tropes," though Hollander rightly adds that Hill contends mostly with English poetic history, while Wright's agon gives "a unique relational profundity to the hyphenation itself in 'African-American.'" The dimensions of Wright's personal history, those of an African-American born in Albuquerque and educated in California, have helped him to so uncover the weave of our country's cultural heritages as to make him our only authentic multi-cultural poet of aesthetic eminence, though there are younger poets who follow already on the new roads he has broken. Generally I wince at the term "multi-cultural," because it is a cant term of those who would destroy literary study in the name of what purports to be social justice, but in fact is merely a networking cabal of resentful academic commissars who feel guilty because their teachers (my exhausted self included) once taught them to love poetry for its own sake.

Now I protect myself, because when someone says "multiculturalism" to me, I immediately say: "Ah, yes, you mean the poetry of Jay Wright, at once Hispanic, African, German, Italian, and above all Indic-American and African-American." By then the rabblement have retreated because while they have read Foucault and Lacan, they have read no poems by Jay Wright, fully the peer of John Ashbery and A. R. Ammons and Geoffrey Hill, and so one of the most exalted poets still alive.

My excursus over, I return to "Desire's Persistence," where "the thing that decays learns / how to speak its name." That thing *can* be the resurrected body, returning to an awareness, whether in the ninth Hell or the ninth Heaven of Dante. All of culture, Wright shrewdly implies, shares in a common shamanism, together uttering "a sharp, metaphorical cry," since Wright, like so many heterodox religious poets, locates us in the imaginal world, midway between empiricist reduction and transcendental intensities likely to seem ghostly to many among us. *Lift* concludes with the arcane or astral body and Hamlet's strangely transcendent death, both of which are removed from Wright, yet he himself is curiously removed throughout this movement. His estrangement, more imagined than personal, is enhanced in the brief, reverberating movement called *Red*.

> RED
> The heart, catalectic though it be, does glow,
> responds to every midnight bell within you.
> This is a discourse on reading heat,
> the flushed char of burned moments one sees
> after the sexton's lamp flows
> over the body's dark book.
> There is suspicion
> here that violet
> traces of
> sacrifice
> stand
> bare.
>
> [*Elaine's Book* 84–5]

What syllables does the poet's heart lack? Presumably those that toll the midnight bells of the psyche, intimations of mortality. In the variations of redness—the glowing of the heart, the reading of heat, flushed char, burned moments, flowering lamplight, the violet traces of sacrifice—this masterly, brief lyric reads the body's dark book by the illumination of the majestic Aztec trope: *I lift the red flower of winter into the wind*. We come to see that winter's red flower is an image of resurrection-through-sacrifice, another evidence of the persistence of desire, a persistence at the center of the next movement *Flower*:

FLOWER

This marble dust recalls that sunset
with the best burgundy, and the way,
after the charm of it, the peacocks
escaped their cages on the green.
I would now embellish the flame
that ornaments you,
even as it once in that moment

                                      did.

I carry you blossomed,
cream and salt of a high crown.
You *must* flare,
        stream forth,
blister and scale me,
even as you structure the enveloping kiss,
           sporophore of our highest loss.
                  [*Elaine's Book* 85]

The flame, now of sexual passion, flaming forth, is an extension of the Aztec flower's redness of resurrection. But between comes the *Winter* movement of our decline, an intimation of mortality that prompts one of Jay Wright's triumph in the Sublime mode:

WINTER

Under the evergreens,
the grouse have gone under the snow.
Women who follow their fall flight
tell us that, if you listen, you can hear
their dove's voices ridge the air,
a singing that follows us to a bourne
           released from its heat sleep.
We have come to an imagined line,
            celestial,
that binds us to the burr of a sheltered thing
and rings us with a fire that will not dance,
        in a horn that will not sound.
We have learned, like these birds,

to publish our decline,
when over knotted apples and straw-crisp leaves,
the slanted sun welcomes us once again
to the arrested music in the earth's divided embrace.

[*Elaine's Book* 85–6]

This intricate music, eloquently arrested and divided, conveys a
northern New England ambiance, the poet's most persistent context in
these mature years of his solitude. What matters most about this Winter
chant is its astonishingly achieved high style, its hushed yet piercingly
pitched voice altogether Wright's own. The birds' singing yields to the
now soundless, stationary image of desire's flame, a desire paradoxically
kept constant by its temporal awareness both of cyclic renewal and of cyclic
decline. Since the organizing Aztec metaphor relates to sacrifice and its
transformations, we ought not to be startled that the concluding *Wind*
movement shifts shamanistically to a woman's identity, desire speaking
with a radically altered voice:

WIND
Through winter,
harmattan blacks the air.
My body fat with oil,
I become another star at noon,
when the vatic insistence
of the dog star's breath clings to me.
Though I am a woman,
I turn south,
toward the fire,
and hear the spirits in the bush.
But this is my conceit:
water will come from the west,
and I will have my trance,

be reborn,

perhaps in a Mediterranean air,
the Rhone delta's contention
with the eastern side of rain.
In all these disguises,
I follow the aroma of power.
So I am charged in my own field,
to give birth to the solar wind,
particles spiraling around the line

                                    of my body,
            moving toward the disruption,
            the moment when the oil of my star at noon
                                            is a new dawn.
                                        [*Elaine's Book* 86–7]

Giving birth to the solar wind renews the Aztec sense of desire's persistence, but this shamaness is an African woman, since the harmattan is a dust-laden wind on the Atlantic coast of Africa. Turned towards the flames, she enters her spirit-trance and is reborn, perhaps where the Rhone comes down to the Mediterranean, in a Latin culture. With his reincarnation assigned to her, the poet accepts immolation, joining the finished Tolteca singers, whose work was subsumed by the Aztecs:

                3

            I shall go away, I shall disappear,
            I shall be stretched on a bed of yellow roses
            and the old women will cry for me.
            So the Toltecas wrote: their books are finished,
            but your heart has become perfect.
                                        [*Elaine's Book* 87]

The Toltec bed of yellow roses goes back to the powerful dramatic monologue, "Zapata and the Egúngún Mask," which comes earlier in *Elaine's Book*. There Zapata cries out:

            When there is no more flesh for the thorn,
            how can I nurture this yellow rose of love between us?
                                        [*Elaine's Book* 23]

The yellow rose yields to the Aztec red flower of winter, and Wright's book is finished even as those of the Toltecas are concluded. Yet, addressing himself, he can assert a Sublime consultation: "But your heart has become perfect." Perfect returns to its origin in *perfectus*, complete or finished, fashioned as a carpenter of the spirit might have fashioned it "in the region of rain and cloud."

The step beyond the namings of the Sublime odes in *Elaine's Book* was taken by Wright in his next volume, *Boleros* (1988). Boleros are, in the first place, stately Spanish dances marked by sharp turns, punctuated by foot-stamping, and most dramatically by sudden gestured pauses, when the dancer holds one arm arched over the head. Jay Wright's *Boleros* are intricately interlaced odes, lyrics, and meditations, most of them paced with a deliberate slowness, and many with their own sharp punctuations, positioned and poised archings. Some of the poems are among Wright's finest, and almost all contain astonishing touches of grace and grandeur. Of the forty separate pieces, the central work is the fifth, a three-part ode celebrating and lamenting names and naming, in an American tradition strongest in its founders—Emerson, Whitman, Dickinson—and in their great inheritor, Wallace Stevens. Jay Wright, both more Spanish (by way of New Mexico), and more African in his culture, handles naming and unnaming very differently than did Stevens and his precursors. Take as representative Emersonian unnaming the penultimate section of "The Man With the Blue Guitar":

> Throw away the lights, the definitions,
> And say of what you see in the dark
>
> That it is this or that it is that,
> But do not use the rotted names.

The fifth *Bolero* opens with the rather categorical line: "all names are invocations, or curses," and proceeds to the namelessness of a particular child who never came forth. It is not clear whether the poet laments his own unborn child, or a generic one of

> those who were impeached for unspeakable desire,
> even as they lay in mothers' cave hollow wombs,
> speechless, eyeless, days away from the lyrics of light
> and a naming.
>   [*Boleros* 9]

A lyrical second movement of the poem returns to the images of loss and of the child:

> These are memory's accoutrements, reason to have searched
> a flowered place with a name that fits,
> where love's every echo is a child's loss.
>   [*Boleros* 10]

Presumably the name that fits invokes the flowered place, and the child's loss is part of the curse of namelessness. Yet the poem's wonderful concluding movement refuses names, whether as invocations or as curses:

All names are false.
The soothsaying leaves call winter a paradox—
a northern traveler on a southern wind.
The ice on a weather-broken barn recalls May poppies.
I would have you recall the exhilaration
of reading broken sonnets, on cinnamon—
scented nights, in a tiled room,
while the charity doctors disputed their loves
                    on the cobblestones below.
I enter again the bells and traces of desire,
call and recall, the pacing of love stalking us.
What is love's form when the body fails,
or fails to appear? What is love's habitation
but a fable of boundaries, lovers passing
athwart all limits toward a crux ansata?
I have carried your name on velvet,
knowing you are free, having never suffered the
heartache of patience that love and naming
that this our divided world requires.
                    [*Boleros* 10–11]

    This returns to the Sublime arena of the great ode, "Desire's Persistence," for the "bells and traces" surely include that poem. A superb meditation that is part of the work-in-progress, *Transformations*, resumes the quest for desire's persistence, under the highly appropriate title, "The Cradle Logic of Autumn":

En mi país el otoño nace de una flor seca, de algunos pájaros ...
o del vaho penetrante de ciertos ríos de la llanura.
                  Molinari, *"Oda a una larga tristeza"*
Each instant comes with a price, the blue-edged bill
on the draft of a bird almost incarnadine,
the shanked ochre of an inn that sits as still
as the beavertail cactus it guards (the fine
rose of that flower gone as bronze as sand),
the river's chalky white insistence as it
moves past the gray afternoon toward sunset.
Autumn feels the chill of a late summer lit
only by goldenrod and a misplaced strand
of blackberries; deplores all such sleight-of-hand;
turns sullen, selfish, envious, full of regret.

Someone more adept would mute its voice. The spill
of its truncated experience would shine
less bravely and, out of the dust and dunghill
of this existence (call it hope, in decline),
as here the blue light of autumn falls, command
what is left of exhilaration and fit
this season's unfolding to the alphabet
of turn and counterturn, all that implicit
arc of a heart searching for a place to stand.
Yet even that diminished voice can withstand
the currying of its spirit. Here lies——not yet.

If, and only if, the leafless rose he sees,
or thinks he sees, flowered a moment ago,
this endangered heart flows with the river that flees
the plain, and listens with eye raised to the slow
revelation of cloud, hoping to approve
himself, or to admonish the rose for slight
transgressions of the past, this the ecstatic
ethos, a logic that seems set to reprove
his facility with unsettling delight.
Autumn might be only desire, a Twelfth-night
gone awry, a gift almost too emphatic.

At sixty, the poet rehearses the season's cradle logic, this sense that what begins anew each autumn, in a blue light, is the prospect of a "diminished voice." What to make of a diminished thing, the Frostian project, suits only Wright's Vermont landscape, but not the persistence of the Sublime in his spirit. He counts the price, instant by instant, tallying what Emerson would have called his cost of confirmation. It is high enough to make him cast out his mythologies; this meditation is remarkably direct and poignant. Or perhaps the mythologies—Dogon, Bambara, Aztec, Romantic Sublime—are held just barely in abeyance in this latest Jay Wright, who beholds no celestial birds, such as Toltec turtledoves, but rather "a bird almost incarnadine." As Wright well knows, you hardly can use the word "incarnadine" without evoking Macbeth's "this my hand will rather / The multitudinous seas incarnadine." Deftly allusive as this is, we are cautioned by it to see that the poet struggles to keep desire's persistence from becoming mere ambition's survival, lest he follow Shakespeare's most imaginative villain and fall "into the sear, the yellow leaf." Autumn's cradle logic finally (and very subtly) is repudiated, since what persists in it is not the desire that will lift the red flower of winter into the wind. *That* desire, more truly Jay Wright's, retains an element of sacrifice, rather than the emphatic persistence of "a Twelfth-night / gone awry."

When Ralph Ellison's *Invisible Man*, nameless and yet at last all-knowing, concluded by going down and living underground, he asserted that he spoke for us, whoever we were. I can trace Ellison's spirit in Jay Wright's poetry, partly because, on a higher frequency, I find that Wright speaks for me. West African religion seems to me the likeliest point-of-origin of our American gnosis, our sense that there is a little man or woman inside the big man or woman. That little being is the true self, the Gnostic spark or *pneuma* that has access to the Seventh Nommo, the black Christ. Twinning or doubling, as we have seen (by glimpses only) is Wright's preferred mode of troping, his downward path to wisdom. Without the power of Wright's metaphors, he could not aid us in our struggle against the jackal who mates with the earth, and who brings forth from the earth the bad verse and worst prose of the counter-culture. Multiculturalism, in our literary journalism and in our ruined literary education, is the ideology that says: our bad writers are no worse than your bad writers. [...] Without standards—aesthetic, cognitive, and imaginative—we will all perish, indeed are perishing already. In one of his better moments, T.S. Eliot spoke of the spirit as "unappeasable and peregrine." I can locate few such spirits among us now: I have to wait for them to locate me. Jay Wright's poetry first found me a quarter century ago, and has not abandoned me since.

Seamus Heaney

(1939–)

AT THIRTY-NINE, WALLACE STEVENS WROTE "LE MONOCLE DE MON Oncle"; at about the same age Yeats wrote "Adam's Curse." Texts of the fortieth year form a remarkable grouping; I can think immediately of Browning's "Childe Roland" and Poe's "Eureka," and I invite every reader to add more (Whitman's "Out of the Cradle" and "As I Ebb'd" suddenly come to mind, but there are many others). I would not say that the Northern Irish poet Seamus Heaney, at forty, has printed any single poem necessarily as fine as "Adam's Curse," but the lyric called "The Harvest Bow" in *Field Work* may yet seem that strong, against all of time's revenges. There are other poems in *Field Work* worthy of comparison to the Yeats of *In the Seven Woods* (1904), and it begins to seem not farfetched to wonder how remarkable a poet Heaney may yet become, if he can continue the steady growth of an art as deliberate, as restrained, and yet as authoritative and universal as the poems of *Field Work*—his fifth and much his best volume in the thirteen years since his first book, *Death of a Naturalist* (1966).

That book, praised for its countryman's veracity and vividness of soilsense, reads in retrospect as a kind of dark hymn of poetic incarnation, a sombre record of the transgression of having been a Clare-like changeling. Heaney's first poems hold implicit his central trope, *the vowel of earth*, and move in a cycle between the guilt of having forsaken spade for pen, and the redemption of poetic work: "I rhyme. To see myself, to set the darkness echoing." *Door into the Dark* (1969) seems now, as it did to me a decade ago, mostly a repetition, albeit in a finer tone, and I remember putting the book aside with the sad reflection that Heaney was fixated in a rugged but minimalist lyrical art. I was mistaken and should have read more carefully the book's last poem, "Bogland," where Heaney began to open both to the Irish, and to his own abyss. Reading backwards from *Field Work* (and the two other, intervening books) I am taught now by the poet how he passed from description to a visionary negation:

> Our pioneers keep striking
> Inwards and downwards,
>
> Every layer they strip
> Seems camped on before.
> The bogholes might be Atlantic seepage.
> The wet centre is bottomless.

Such a center indeed could not hold, and Heaney was poised upon the verge of becoming a poet of the Northern Irish Troubles, a role he now wisely seeks to evade, but in a morally rich sense of "evade," as I will try to show later. *Wintering Out* (1972) seems stronger than it did seven years ago, when it began to change my mind about Heaney's importance. It is a book about nearing the journey's center, and takes as its concern the poet's severe questioning of his own language, the English at once his own and not his own, since Heaney is of the Catholic Irish of Derry. Few books of poems brood so hard upon names, or touch so overtly upon particular words as words. No single poem stands out, even upon rereading, for this is the last volume of Heaney's careful apprenticeship as he works towards his deferred glory. *North* (1975) begins that glory, a vital achievement by any standards, perhaps a touch dimmed for American critics by the accident of its appearance so close to Geoffrey Hill's *Somewhere Is Such a Kingdom*, which gathered together in America Hill's first three volumes. But the power of *North* is that four years of reading have enhanced it, while *Field Work* seems to me the only recent British book of poems worthy of sustained comparison to the magnificence of Hill's *Tenebrae*, published in 1978.

Heaney's first three books sparred gently with local and contemporary precursors; the alert reader could find the colors and flavors of Kavanagh and Montague, of Ted Hughes and R.S. Thomas. Like the deliberate touches of the late Robert Lowell in *Field Work*, these are all "screen-memories," of interest only as tactical blinds. What emerges in *North*, and stands clear in *Field Work*, is the precursor proper, the middle Yeats, with whom the agon of the strong Irish poet must be fought, as much by Heaney in his maturity as it is by Kinsella, with the agon itself guaranteeing why Heaney and Kinsella are likely to become more memorable than Kavanagh and Clarke, among the Irish poets following Yeats.

I hear behind the poems of *North* the middle Yeats of *The Green Helmet* and of *Responsibilities*, a hearing reinforced by *Field Work*. This is the

Yeats of a vision counting still its human cost, and so not yet abandoned to daemonic presences and intensities:

I passed through the eye of the quern,

Grist to an ancient mill,
And in my mind's eye saw
A world-tree of balanced stones,
Querns piled like vertebrae,
The marrow crushed to grounds.

That is Heaney's "Belderg" from *North*, but I do not think Yeats would have disowned it. The enduring poems in *North* include the majestic title-piece, as well as "Funeral Rites," "Kinship," "Whatever You Say Say Nothing," and, best of all, the sequence of poetic incarnation with the Yeatsian title, "Singing School." The poem "North" gave and still gives Heaney his poetics, as a mythic voice proclaims what must be this new poet's relation to the Irish past:

It said, 'Lie down
in the word-hoard, burrow
the coil and gleam
of your furrowed brain.

Compose in darkness.
Expect aurora borealis
in the long foray
but no cascade of light.

Keep your eye clear
as the bleb of the icicle,
trust the feel of what nubbed treasure
your hands have known.'

The reader of *Field Work* comes to realize that Heaney's eye is as clear, through discipline, as the air bubble in an icicle, as clear, say, as the American eye of the late Elizabeth Bishop. "Funeral Rites" inaugurates what seems doomed to be Heaney's central mode, whether he finally chooses Dublin or Belfast. "Kinship," a more difficult sequence, salutes the bog country as the "outback of my mind" and then flows into a grander trope:

This is the vowel of earth
dreaming its root
in flowers and snow,

mutation of weathers
and seasons,
a windfall composing the floor it rots into.
I grew out of all this

like a weeping willow
inclined to
the appetites of gravity.

Such inevitability of utterance would be more than enough if it were merely personal; it would suffice. Its grandeur is augmented in the last section of "Kinship" when Heaney acquires the authentic authority of becoming the voice of his people:

Come back to this
'island of the ocean'
where nothing will suffice.
Read the inhumed faces

of casualty and victim;
report us fairly,
how we slaughter
for the common good

and shave the heads
of the notorious,
how the goddess swallows
our love and terror.

The problem for Heaney as a poet henceforward is how not to drown in this blood-dimmed tide. His great precedent is the Yeats of "Meditations in Time of Civil War" and "Nineteen Hundred and Nineteen," and it cannot be said in *North* that this precedent is met, even in "Whatever You Say Say Nothing," where the exuberance of the language achieves a genuine phantasmagoria. But "Singing School," with its queerly appropriate mix of Wordsworth and Yeats, does even better, ending poem and book with a finely rueful self-accepting portrait of the poet, still waiting for the word that is his alone:

I am neither internee nor informer;
An inner émigré, grown long-haired
And thoughtful; a wood-kerne

Escaped from the massacre,
Taking protective colouring
From bole and bark, feeling
Every wind that blows;

Who, blowing up these sparks
For their meagre heat, have missed
The once-in-a-lifetime portent,
The comet's pulsing rose.

That is true eloquence, but fortunately not the whole truth, as *Field Work* richly shows. Heaney is the poet of the vowel of earth and not of any portentous comet. In *Field Work*, he has gone south, away from the Belfast violence, heeding the admonition that Emerson addressed to himself in the bad year 1846, when the American slaveholders made war against Mexico:

Though loath to grieve
The evil time's sole patriot,
I cannot leave
My honied thought
For the priest's cant,
Or statesman's rant.

If I refuse
My study for their politique,
Which at the best is trick,
The angry Muse
Puts confusion in my brain.

Like Emerson, Heaney has learned that he has imprisoned thoughts of his own which only he can set free. No poem in *Field Work* is without its clear distinction, but I exercise here the critic's privilege of discussing those poems that move me most: "Casualty," "The Badgers," "The Singer's House," the lovely sequence of ten "Glanmore Sonnets," "The Harvest Bow" (Heaney's masterpiece so far), and the beautiful elegy "In Memoriam Francis Ledwidge," for the Irish poet killed on the Western Front in 1917. All of these lyrics and meditations practice a rich negation, an art of excluded meanings, vowels of earth almost lost between guttural consonants of history. Heaney's Irish sibyl warns him that "The ground we kept our ear to for so long / Is flayed or calloused." The muted elegy "Casualty," which cunningly blends the modes of Yeats's "The Fisherman" and "Easter 1916," concludes in a funeral march giving us the sea's version of Heaney's vowel of earth:

> They move in equal pace
> With the habitual
> Slow consolation
> of a dawdling engine,
> The line lifted, hand
> Over fist, cold sunshine
> On the water, the land
> Banked under fog: that morning
> I was taken in his boat,
> The screw purling, turning
> Indolent fathoms white,
> I tasted freedom with him.
> To get out early, haul
> Steadily off the bottom,
> Dispraise the catch, and smile
> As you find a rhythm
> Working you, slow mile by mile,
> Into your proper haunt
> Somewhere, well out, beyond ...

Even as the slain fisherman's transcendence fuses with Heaney's catch of a poem to send the poet also "beyond," so Heaney has revised Yeats's ambition by having written an elegy as passionate as the perpetual night of the Troubles. Even stronger is "The Badgers," an oblique poem of deepest self-questioning, in which the elegiac strain is evaded and all simple meanings are thwarted. Sensing "some soft returning," whether of the murdered dead or of the badgers, Heaney places upon his reader the burden of difficult interpretation:

> Visitations are taken for signs.
> At a second house I listened
> for duntings under the laurels
> and heard intimations whispered
> about being vaguely honoured.

The first line of this passage does not reach back to Lancelot Andrewes through Eliot's "Gerontion" but rather itself boldly revises John 4:48, "Except ye see signs and wonders, ye will not believe" and perhaps even Matthew 12:38–39. "An evil and adulterous generation seeketh after a sign." The duntings are at once the dull sounds of badgers and, more crucially, the Wordsworthian "low breathings" of *The Prelude* 1,323. Though an external haunting, testifying to the laurels of poetic election "vaguely honoured," they are also Heaney's hard-drawn breaths, in this text and out of it, in a murderous Northern Ireland. Heaney, once so ruggedly simplistic in his only apparent stance, has entered upon the agonistic way of a stronger poetry, necessarily denser, more allusive, and persuasively difficult.

I read this entrance as the triumph of "The Singer's House," a poem I will forebear quoting entire, though I badly want to, and give only the superb three stanzas of the conclusion, where Heaney laments the loss of every thing in his land that should be "crystal," and discovers an inevitable image for his audacious and determined art that would reverse lament and loss:

> People here used to believe
> that drowned souls lived in the seals.
> At spring tides they might change shape.
> They loved music and swam in for a singer
>
> who might stand at the end of summer
> in the mouth of a whitewashed turf-shed,
> his shoulder to the jamb, his song
> a rowboat far out in evening.
>
> When I came here first you were always singing,
> a hint of the clip of the pick
> in your winnowing climb and attack.
> Raise it again, man. We still believe what we hear.

The verve of that final line is a tonic even for an American reader like myself, cut off from everything local that inspires and appalls Heaney. Closer to ordinary evenings in New Haven are the universal concerns that rise out of the local in the distinguished "Glanmore Sonnets" that open, again, with Heaney's central trope: "Vowels ploughed into other: opened ground." Confronting an image of the good life as field work, with art redeemed from violence and so "a paradigm" of new-ploughed earth,

Heaney finds even in the first sonnet that his ghosts come striding back. Against the ghosts he seeks to set his own story as a poet who could heed Moneta's admonition to Keats, or Nietzsche's to all of us: "Think of the earth."

> Then I landed in the hedge-school of Glanmore
> And from the backs of ditches hoped to raise
> A voice caught back off slug-horn and slow chanter
> That might continue, hold, dispel, appease:
> Vowels ploughed into other, opened ground,
> Each verse returning like the plough turned round.

Yet the ninth sonnet is driven to ask with true desperation: "What is my apology for poetry?" and the superb tenth sonnet ends the sequence overtly echoing Wyatt's most passionate moment, while more darkly and repressively alluding to the Yeatsian insight of the perpetual virginity of the soul: "the lovely and painful / Covenants of flesh; our separateness." More hopeful, but with a qualified hope, is the perfect lyric "The Harvest Bow," which I quote in its entirety:

> As you plaited the harvest bow
> You implicated the mellowed silence in you
> In wheat that does not rust
> But brightens as it tightens twist by twist
> Into a knowable corona,
> A throwaway love-knot of straw.
>
> Hands that aged round ashplants and cane sticks
> And lapped the spurs on a lifetime of game cocks
> Harked to their gift and worked with fine intent
> Until your fingers moved somnambulant:
> I tell and finger it like braille,
> Gleaning the unsaid off the palpable,
>
> And if I spy into its golden loops
> I see us walk between the railway slopes
> Into an evening of long grass and midges,
> Blue smoke straight up, old beds and ploughs in hedges,
> An auction notice on an outhouse wall—
> You with a harvest bow in your lapel,

Me with the fishing rod, already homesick
For the big lift of these evenings, as your stick
Whacking the tips off weeds and bushes
Beats out of time, and beats, but flushes
Nothing: that original townland
Still tongue-tied in the straw tied by your hand.

The end of art is peace
Could be the motto of this frail device
That I have pinned up on our deal dresser
Like a drawn snare
Slipped lately by the spirit of the corn
Yet burnished by its passage, and still warm.

Heaney could not have found a more wistful, Clare-like emblem than the love knot of straw for this precariously beautiful poem, or a sadder, gentler motto than: "*The end of art is peace.*" Certainly the oversong of the poem, its stance as love-lyric, seems to sing against Yeats's Paterian ringers in the tower, who have appointed for the hymeneal of the soul a passing bell. But the end of married love may be peace; the end of art is agonistic, against time's "it was," and so against anterior art.

The hands which plait the harvest bow are masculine and hardened, but delicate in the office of marriage, which brings in harvest. Implicated in the making is the knowable corona of mellowed silence, not the unreliable knowledge of poetry; and Heaney as poet must both love and stand back and away from this wisdom, paternal and maternal. The fingers which follow a human tradition can move as if moving in sleep—"asleep in its own life," as Stevens said of the child. But Heaney must "tell and finger it like braille," for that is the poet's field of work: "Gleaning the unsaid off the palpable," the slender pickings after the granary is full.

Though his vision, *through her emblem*, in the third stanza approximates a true peace, it breaks into something both richer and more forlorn in what comes after. The young Yeats sang of "The Happy Townland," where "Boughs have their fruit and blossom / At all times of the year" and "all that are killed in battle / Awaken to life again." Heaney, leaving youth, hears in recollections of innocent venery a music that "Beats out of time, and beats, but flushes / Nothing." There is nothing for it to start up since the happy or original townland belongs only to those "still tongue-tied" in the frail device of the harvest bow. Heaney's genius is never surer than in his all-but-undoing of this emblem in his final trope, where the love knot becomes a drawn snare recently evaded by the corn-king, an evasion that itself both burnishes and animates the knowable corona of achieved marriage. Obliquely but firmly, the struggle of poetry displaces the lover's stance, and the undersong finds a triumph in the poem's closure.

I verge upon saying that Heaney approaches the cunning stance of the strong poet, evasion for which I cite not its American theorists and bards, from Emerson through Whitman and Dickinson to Frost and Stevens but the central British master of the mode:

> Know ye not then the Riddling of the Bards?
> Confusion, and illusion, and relation,
> Elusion, and occasion, and evasion?

That is Tennyson's Seer, not Emerson's Merlin, and must become Heaney's poetic, if like Yeats he is to transcend the vowel of earth. It will be a painful transition for a poet whose heart is with the visionary naturalism of Wordsworth and Keats and Clare (and Kavanagh, Montague, R. S. Thomas) rather than with a vision fighting free of earth. But there are signs in *Field Work* that the transition is under way. Heaney ends the book with a grim rendition of Dante's Ugolino, too relevant to the Irish moment, and with his not altogether successful title poem which invokes the Gnostic doubloon of Melville's Ahab. I end here by reading in the noble quatrains of Heaney's "In Memoriam Francis Ledwidge" a powerful evasion of a fate that this poet will never accept as his own:

> In you, our dead enigma, all the strains
> Criss-cross in useless equilibrium
> And as the wind tunes through this vigilant bronze
> I hear again the sure confusing drum

> You followed from Boyne water to the Balkans
> But miss the twilit note your flute should sound.
> You were not keyed or pitched like these true-blue ones
> Though all of you consort now underground.

Not my way to go, as Heaney tells us, for he is keyed and pitched unlike any other significant poet now at work in the language, anywhere. The strains cross-cross in him in so useful an equilibrium that all critics and lovers of poetry must wish him every cunning for survival. To this critic, on the other side of the Atlantic, Heaney is joined now with Geoffrey Hill as a poet so severe and urgent that he compels the same attention as his strongest American contemporaries, and indeed as only the very strongest among them.

Anne Carson

(1950-)

THE CANADIAN POET ANNE CARSON IS SO ORIGINAL AND AUTHENTIC IN her works that I can think of only two other poets of her eminence now alive and writing in English: John Ashbery and Geoffrey Hill, and they are a full generation older.

A classical scholar by profession, Carson is a learned poet, but always with a difference. She is like no one else alive. Emily Brontë and Emily Dickinson are her authentic precursors. Carson is a poet of the Sublime, in the sense that she revives in her "Essay with Rhapsody," *FOAM*. Longinus, the true origin of literary criticism, is her quarry, because his Sublime consists of quotations, "lustres," as Plutarch and Emerson called them. These come at us like volcanic eruptions, and clearly Carson is fond of active volcanoes, as Longinus must have been:

> Look this is the real Homer who storms like a wind alongside
> the fighting
> men, none other than Homer who "rages as when spearshaking
> Ares or
> ruinous fire in the mountains rages, in folds of deep forest, and
> foam is
> around his mouth."
> —Longinus, *On the Sublime* 9.11; Homer, *Iliad* 15.605-7

Carson's genius is to spot that foam and elucidate it:

> Foam is the sign of an artist who has sunk his hands into his
> own story,
> and also of a critic storming and raging in folds of his own deep theory.

Carson's first book was *Eros the Bittersweet: An Essay* (1986), a meditation upon a trope of Sappho (all of whose fragments Carson has now translated). In the dance of Sappho's mind: "Desire moves. Eros is a verb." Invoking Plato's *Phaedrus, Eros the Bittersweet* breaks off (it cannot end, or come to rest) with a luminously resigned paragraph:

> From the testimony of lovers like Sokrates or Sappho we can construct what it would be like to live in a city of no desire. Both the philosopher and the poet find themselves describing Eros in images of wings and metaphors of flying, for desire is a movement that carries yearning hearts from over here to over there, launching the mind on a story. In the city without desire such flights are unimaginable. Wings are kept clipped. The known and the unknown learn to align themselves one behind the other so that, provided you are positioned at the proper angle, they seem to be one and the same. If there *were* a visible difference, you might find it hard to say so, for the useful verb *mnaomai* will have come to mean "a fact is a fact." To reach for something else than the facts will carry you beyond this city and perhaps, as for Sokrates, beyond this world. It is a high-risk proposition, as Sokrates saw quite clearly, to reach for the difference between known and unknown. He thought the risk worthwhile, because he was in love with wooing itself. And who is not?

The wisdom of Socrates was not to think that he knew what he did not know. I suppose that the use of literature for life is reaching wisdom, not to reach wisdom, which cannot be done. Carson is a wisdom writer of genius, rather than a Socratic wise woman. She is an artist who has sunk her hands into her own story, and she has a Homeric effect upon a critic (at least this one), causing me to storm and rage in my own deep theory of influence. Her strong reading of Emily Brontë and of Emily Dickinson is implicit in much of her poetry, and sometimes emerges with fierce explicitness.

Carson's first book after *Eros the Bittersweet* was *Short Talks* (1992), available now as Part II of *Plainwater* (1995). The scariest of these thirty-two prose poems is "On Walking Backwards":

> My mother forbad us to walk backwards. That is how the dead walk,
> she would say. Where did she get this idea? Perhaps from
> a bad

> translation. The dead, after all, do not walk backwards
> but they do
>   walk behind us. They have no lungs and cannot call out
> but would
>   love for us to turn around. They are victims of love, many
> of them.

With my own number of beloved recently dead, I have taken to turning around as I walk. Carson, more even than Geoffrey Hill, makes me
uneasy. Her "Introduction" to *Short Talks* serves as prelude to everything
she has written since:

> Early one morning words were missing. Before that, words were
> not. Facts were, faces were. In a good story, Aristotle tells us, ever
> thing that happens is pushed by something else. Three old
> women were bending in the fields. What use is it to question us?
> they said. Well it shortly became clear that they knew everything
> there is to know about the snowy fields and the blue-green shoots
> and the plant called "audacity," which poets mistake for violets. I
> began to copy out everything that was said. The marks construct
> an instant of nature gradually, without the boredom of a story. I
> emphasize this. I will do anything to avoid boredom. It is the
> task of a lifetime. You can never know enough, never work
> enough, never use the infinitives and participles oddly enough,
> never impede the movement harshly enough, never leave the
> mind quickly enough.

This is the task of her lifetime, and since I am two decades older than
Carson, one of my likely regrets when I depart is that I will not have
absorbed her lifetime's work. I pass on here to what seem her first published verse poems, *The Life of Towns*, a sequence of thirty-six brief meditations, with overtones of Emily Dickinson, who receives the elliptical
tribute of "Emily Town":

> Riches in a little room.
> Is a phrase that haunts.
> Her since the mineral of you.
> Left.
> Snow or a library.
> Or a band of angels.
> With a message is.

Not what.
It meant to.
Her.

Dickinson favored no punctuation except dashes—Carson gives us ten periods for ten very short lines. Christopher Marlowe's "infinite riches in a little room" (*The Jew of Malta*) is echoed ironically by Touchstone's allusion to the murder of Marlowe in *As You Like It*: "it strikes a man more dead than a great reckoning in a little room." This becomes the room in her father's house in Amherst where Dickinson wrote her poems and letters. Where is Carson in this poem, or is this not her town, but then, none of the towns in the sequence is hers.

Carson's own story of the self is first told (more or less) in the long narrative essay, *The Anthropology of Water*, that concludes *Plainwater*, where she identifies herself as the only one of the fifty Danaides who did not slay her bridegroom, and thus drowned instead in the deep water:

Water is something you cannot hold. Like men. I have tried.
Father,
brother, lover, true friends, hungry ghosts and God, one by one
all took
themselves out of my hands.

The Anthropology of Water is eloquently memorable, but I prefer *The Glass Essay*, the narrative poem that leads off *Glass, Irony, and God* (1995), where Carson's greatness as a poet first fully emerges. Emily Brontë is Carson's daemon, as Heathcliff was Catherine Earnshaw's. Visiting her mother, who lives alone on a Brontë-like moor in the north of Canada, Carson confronts her main fear: "I feel I am turning into Emily Brontë,/ my lonely life around me like a moor."

The story of loss—of a man called Law—is perhaps the same as in *The Beauty of the Husband* (2001), but there the recital is harsh and direct, while here we are in an atmosphere of glass, where context would be shattered were the poet to express fury. Instead she meditates upon morning visions she calls Nudes: "naked glimpses of my soul." The central vision is the final night with Law, "a night that centred Heaven and Hell,/ As Emily would say." Law is no Heathcliff, only another cad, to the reader, but Carson effectively presents herself as a living wound of love, her own "pain devil," as Heathcliff was Emily Brontë's. The poet-novelist of *Wuthering Heights* and a handful of magnificent lyrics addressed a transcendental Thou in a few poems that seem to me Gnostic hymns to the

Alien God, who is a stranger in this cosmos. All but identified with Emily Brontë, Anne Carson disengages from this relation to a Thou:

> Very hard to read, the messages that pass
> between Thou and Emily.
> In this poem she reverses their roles,
> speaking not *as* the victim but *to* the victim.
> It is chilling to watch Thou move upon thou,
> who lies alone in the dark waiting to be mastered.
>
> It is a shock to realize that this low, slow collusion
> of master and victim within one voice
> is a rationale
>
> for the most awful loneliness of the poet's hour.
> She has reversed the roles of thou and Thou
> not as a display of power
>
> but to force out of herself some pity
> for this soul trapped in glass,
> which is her true creation.
>
> Those nights lying alone
> are not discontinuous with this cold hectic dawn.
> It is who I am.

Mutually trapped in glass, the two poets again fuse. After a series of harrowing Nudes, *The Glass Essay* attains its majestic closure:

> I saw a high hill and on it a form shaped against hard air.
>
> It could have been just a pole with some old cloth attached,
> but as I came closer
> I saw it was a human body
>
> trying to stand against winds so terrible that the flesh was
> blowing off
>   the bones.
> And there was no pain.
> The wind

was cleansing the bones.
They stood forth silver and necessary.
It was not my body, not a woman's body, it was the body of us
all.
It walked out of the light.

Overwhelming in context, this remains extraordinary even on its own. There is no consolation in this cleansing, yet there is also no pain. Since this is a vision, and not a privileged moment, we cannot speak of a secular epiphany. Nor can one find the spirit of Emily Brontë in this: it is Anne Carson transcending—momentarily—her own suffering, because erotic loss is universal, male and female. For this visionary moment, melancholia recedes, and we are given an exemplary figure for what Sigmund Freud brilliantly termed "the work of mourning."

The epilogue to *The Glass Essay* is a sequence of eighteen poems called *The Truth About God*. Two of them are astonishing: "Deflect" and "God's Name," both founded upon the early Kabbalah of Isaac the Blind. What is deflected is the light that emanated from the Adam Kadmon, the God-Man:

From the lights of his forehead were formed all the names of
the world.
From the lights of his ears, nose and throat
came a function no one has ever defined.

From the lights of his eyes—but wait—
Isaac waits.
In theory

the lights of the eye should have issued from Adam's navel.
But within the lights themselves occurred
an intake of breath

and they changed their path.
And they were separated.
And they were caught in the head.

And from these separated lights came
that which pains you
on its errands (here my friend began to weep) through the
world.

For be assured it is not only you who mourn.
Isaac lashed his tail.
Every rank of world

was caused to descend
(at least one rank)
by the terrible pressure of the light.

Nothing remained in place.
Nothing was not captured except
among the shards and roots and matter

some lights
from Adam's eyes
nourished there somehow.

The intake of breath is the *zimzum*, God's withdrawal to permit creation, but the lights separate, and the *kelim* or vessels shatter into "shards and roots and matter." Carson adds her own lively touches; Isaac the Blind becomes a dragon of the Deep, lashing his tail and roaring, witnessing the catastrophe creation. "God's Name" also shows Carson as her own Kabbalist:

The name is not a noun.
It is an adverb.
Like the little black notebooks that Beethoven carried

in his coatpocket
for the use of those who wished to converse with him,
the God adverb

is a one-way street that goes everywhere you are.
No use telling you what it is.
Just chew it and rub it on.

Carson will not tell us that adverb but I suspect it is "endlessly," while the verb that goes with it is "suffers." "Book of Isaiah," which follows later in *Glass, Irony, and God* may be Carson's most disjunctive narrative, and the strongest so far. Guy Davenport accurately notes that Carson captures prophetic narrative with a peculiar felicity:

It was a blue winter evening, the cold bit like a wire.

Isaiah laid his forehead on the ground.

God arrived.

Why do the righteous suffer? said Isaiah.

Bellings of cold washed down the Branch.

Notice whenever God addresses Isaiah in a feminine singular
verb
   something dazzling is
about to happen.

Isaiah what do you know about women? asked God.

Down Isaiah's nostrils bounced woman words:

Blush. Stink. Wife. Fig. Sorceress—

God nodded.

Isaiah go home and get some sleep, said God.

Isaiah went home, slept, woke again.

Isaiah felt sensation below the neck, it was a silk and bitter sensation.

Isaiah looked down.

It was milk forcing the nipples open.

Isaiah was more than whole.

I am not with you I am *in* you, said the muffled white voice of
God.

Isaiah sank to a kneeling position.

New pain! said Isaiah.

New contract! said God.

Carson's comic Sublime evades bitterness, whether in Hebraic context or in the classical convolutions of her extraordinary "novel in verse," *Autobiography of Red* (1998), too long and intricate for me to describe here. A remarkable outburst of Carsonian fecundity gave us *Men in the Off Hours* (2000) and *The Beauty of the Husband* (2001), from which I will draw a few texts for consideration, only to suggest the expanding contours of her achievement. But I cite, as her *intended* aesthetic, the opening paragraph of her "Note on Method" that preludes *Economy of the Unlost* (1999), her study of verbal economy in Simonides and Paul Celan:

> There is too much self in my writing. Do you know the term Lukács uses to describe aesthetic structure? *Eine fensterlose Monade.* I do not want to be a windowless monad—my training and trainers opposed subjectivitystrongly, I have struggled since the beginning to drive my thought out intothe landscape of science and fact where other people converse logicallyand exchange judgments—but I go blind out there. So writing involves some dashing back and forth between that darkening landscape wherefacticity is strewn and a windowless room cleared of everything I do not know. It is the clearing that takes time. It is the clearing that is a mystery.

I do not know what to do with this. Could one imagine Emily Brontë or Emily Dickinson or Gertrude Stein saying: There is too much self in my writing? Lukács, a Marxist, deplored too much self, since the single person is a myth, according to Marx. Why read Carson rather than a thousand other poets now writing, except that she sensibly goes blind in the absurd realm of "objectivity"? That mode or landscape is easy, vulgar, and therefore disgusting: authentic subjectivity is difficult, sublime, and inspiring. In any case, Carson's genius is to write on the self, not fashionably off it.

There is so much superb poetry available by reading *Men In the Off Hours*, that all I can do here is discuss the poem that most moves me, "Father's Old Blue Cardigan," the elegy for the loss of love to Alzheimer's disease:

Now it hangs on the back of the kitchen chair
where I always sit, as it did
on the back of the kitchen chair where he always sat.

I put it on whenever I come in,
as he did, stamping
the snow from his boots.

I put it on and sit in the dark.
He would not have done this.
Coldness comes paring down from the moonbone in the sky.

His laws were a secret.
But I remember the moment at which I knew
he was going mad inside his laws.

He was standing at the turn of the driveway when I arrived.
He had on the blue cardigan with the buttons done up all the
way to the top.
Not only because it was a hot July afternoon

but the look on his face—
as a small child who has been dressed by some aunt early in the
morning
for a long trip

on cold trains and windy platforms
will sit very straight at the edge of his seat
while the shadows like long fingers

over the haystacks that sweep past
keep shocking him
because he is riding backwards.

If that *is* pathos, the control is so firm that I cannot locate the point
where logos takes over. I reread Carson's poem and suddenly remember
the day I encountered an old friend and Yale colleague sitting on the pave-
ment in front of the Graduate School, shoe in one hand and the other hand
counting his toes, over and over. A month before, we had encountered
each other at the same spot, and enjoyed an intense discussion of American
religion, about which he knew everything. The look on his face, as he

counted over his toes, was the small child's expression so precisely caught by Carson's train-ride metaphor.

The Beauty of the Husband, dancing its twenty-nine death-tangos, has the remorseless drive of Freud taking us beyond the pleasure-principle. It would be grisly to select a favorite tango, but I cannot get no. XXII "Homo Ludens," out of my head, though I would like to. The nameless husband, after a three-year separation, takes his wife to Athens, supposedly for reconciliation. At night, in the hotel room, they dispute as ever concerning his serial infidelities, and suddenly his nose begins to bleed:

> Then blood runs down over his upper lip, lower lip, chin.
> To his throat.
> Appears on the whiteness of his shirt.
>
> Dyes a mother-of-pearl button for good.
> Blacker than a mulberry.
> Don't think his heart had burst. He was no Tristan
> (though he would love to point out that in the common version
> Tristan is not false, it is the sail that kills)
> yet neither of them had a handkerchief
> and that is how she ends up staining her robe with his blood,
> his head in her lap and his virtue coursing through her
>
> as if they were one flesh.
> Husband and wife may erase a boundary.
> Creating a white page.
>
> But now the blood seems to be the only thing in the room.
>
> If only one's whole life could consist in certain moments.
> There is no possibility of coming back from such a moment
> to simple hatred,
> black ink.

Cold-heartedly, I might observe that I know no other moment like this, in literature, but that praise seems pointless in confronting Carson's eloquent immediacy. Our lives, even in retrospect, do not consist in certain moments, secular epiphanies that come back to us, glories or humiliations. That is part of the dark wisdom of a long poem that beings: "A wound gives off its own light" and ends with the former husband fictively saying: "Watch me fold this page now so you think it is you."

Yet I don't want to end this brief appreciation of Anne Carson with that voice, but with her own. She is a highly active volcano, and fascinates a critic who has been a Longinian all his long life. Somewhere in *Plainwater* she writes: "Language is what eases the pain of living with other people, language is what makes the wounds come open again." Not language, not at all language, I want to murmur, but only language's rare masters—like Emily Brontë, Emily Dickinson, Anne Carson.

Further Reading

Abrams, M.H. *The Mirror and the Lamp: Romantic Theory and the Critical Tradition*. New York: Oxford University Press, 1953.

Attridge, Derek. *Poetic Rhythm: An Introduction*. New York: Cambridge University Press, 1995.

Bloom, Harold. *the Best Poems of the English Language: From Chaucer Through Frost*. New York: HarperCollins, 2004.

————. *Figures of Capable Imagination*. New York: Seabury Press, 1976.

————. *Poetry and Repression*. New Haven: Yale University Press, 1976.

————. *A Map of Misreading*. New York: Oxford University Press, 1975.

————. *Kabbalah and Criticism*. New York: Continuum, 1975.

————. *The Anxiety of Influence*. New York: Oxford University Press, 1973.

Brooks, Cleanth. *The Well Wrought Urn: Studies in the Structure of Poetry*. New York: Harcourt Brace, 1956.

Brooks, Cleanth, and Robert Penn Warren. *Understanding Poetry* 3rd ed. New York: Holt, Rinehart and Winston, 1960.

Courthope, W.J. *History of English Poetry*. London: Macmillan, 1895–1910.

Eliot, T.S. *The Use of Poetry and the Use of Criticism: Studies in the Relation of Criticism to Poetry in England*. London: Faber and Faber, 1970.

Frye, Northrop. *The Anatomy of Criticism: Four Essays*. Princeton: Princeton University Press, 1957.

Fussell, Paul. *Poetic Meter & Poetic Form* (rev. ed.). New York: Random House, 1979.

Harmon, William, ed. *Classic Writings on Poetry*. New York: Columbia University Press, 2003.

Heaney, Seamus. *The Redress of Poetry: Oxford Lectures*. London: Faber and Faber, 1995.

Hirsch, Edward. *How to Read a Poem: And Fall in Love with Poetry*. New York: Harcourt Brace & Co., 1999.

Hollander, John. *Rhyme's Reason: A Guide to English Verse*, 3rd ed. New Haven: Yale University Press, 2001.

Johnson, Samuel. *Lives of the Poets: A Selection*, J.P. Hardy, ed. Oxford: Clarendon Press, 1971.

Knight, George Wilson. *The Starlit Dome: Studies in the Poetry of Vision.* New York: Oxford University Press, 1971.

Magill, Frank N., ed. *Critical Survey of Poetry: English Language Series.* Pasadena: Salem Press, 1992.

Paglia, Camille. *Break, Blow, Burn: Camille Paglia Reads Forty-three of the World's Best Poems.* New York: Pantheon, 2005.

Parini, Jay, ed. *The Columbia History of American Poetry.* New York: Columbia University Press, 1993.

Parisi, Joseph and Stephen Young, ed. *Dear Editor: A History of Poetry in Letters.* New York: W.W. Norton, 2002.

Paschen, Elise, and Rebekah Presson Mosby, ed. *Poetry Speaks: Hear Great Poets Read Their Work from Tennyson to Plath.* Naperville: Sourcebooks MediaFusion, 2001

Paz, Octavio. *The Bow and the Lyre: The Poem, Poetic Revelation, Poetry and History.* Austin: University of Texas Press, 1987.

Pearce, Roy Harvey. *The Continuity of American Poetry.* Princeton: Princeton University Press, 1961.

Perkins, David. *A History of Modern Poetry: Modernism and After.* Cambridge, Mass.: Belknap Press of Harvard University Press, 1976–1987.

Preminger, Alex, Terry V.F. Brogan, and Frank J. Warnke, ed. *The New Princeton Encyclopedia of Poetry and Poetics.* Princeton: Princeton University Press, 3rd edition, 1993.

Raffel, Burton. *How to Read a Poem.* New York: Plume Books, 1994.

Schmidt, Michael. *The First Poets: Lives of the Ancient Greek Poets.* New York: Knopf, 2005.

———. *Lives of the Poets.* New York: Vintage, 2000.

Spiller, Michael R.G. *The Development of the Sonnet: An Introduction.* New York: Routledge, 1992.

Turco, Lewis. *The Book of Forms: A Handbook of Poetics* 3rd ed. Hanover, NH: University Press of New England, 2000.

Turner, Mark, and George Lakoff. *More than Cool Reason: A Field Guide to Poetic Metaphor.* Chicago: University of Chicago Press, 1989.

Vendler, Helen. *Poems, Poets, Poetry: An Introduction and Anthology* 2nd ed. New York: Bedford/St. Martin's, 2002.

———. *The Given and the Made: Strategies of Poetic Redefinition.* Cambridge, Mass.: Harvard University Press, 1996.

———. *Soul Says: On Recent Poetry.* Cambridge, Mass.: Belknap Press of Harvard University Press, 1996.

————. *The Music of What Happens: Poems, Poets, Critics.* Cambridge, Mass.: Harvard University Press, 1989.

Welsh, Andrew. *Roots of Lyric: Primitive Poetry and Modern Poetics.* Princeton: Princeton University Press, 1978.

Index

About the Author

HAROLD BLOOM is Sterling Professor of the Humanities at Yale University. He is the author of over 20 books, including *Shelley's Mythmaking* (1959), *The Visionary Company* (1961), *Blake's Apocalypse* (1963), *Yeats* (1970), *A Map of Misreading* (1975), *Kabbalah and Criticism* (1975), *Agon: Toward a Theory of Revisionism* (1982), *The American Religion* (1992), *The Western Canon* (1994), and *Omens of Millennium: The Gnosis of Angels, Dreams, and Resurrection* (1996). *The Anxiety of Influence* (1973) sets forth Professor Bloom's provocative theory of the literary relationships between the great writers and their predecessors. His most recent books include *Shakespeare: The Invention of the Human* (1998), a 1998 National Book Award finalist, *How to Read and Why* (2000), *Genius: A Mosaic of One Hundred Exemplary Creative Minds* (2002), *Hamlet: Poem Unlimited* (2003), and *Where Shall Wisdom be Found* (2004). In 1999, Professor Bloom received the prestigious American Academy of Arts and Letters Gold Medal for Criticism, and in 2002 he received the Catalonia International Prize.